Sociolinguistic Variation in Seventeenth-Century France

This book provides the first systematic study of sociolinguistic variation in seventeenth-century France. Drawing on a range of case studies, Wendy Ayres-Bennett makes available new data about linguistic variation in this period, showing the wealth and variety of language usage at a time that is considered to be the most 'standardizing' in the history of French. Variation is analysed in terms of the speaker's 'pre-verbal constitution' – such as gender, age and socio-economic status – or by the medium, register or genre used. As well as examining linguistic variation itself, the book also considers the fundamental methodological issues that are central to all socio-historical linguistic accounts, and more importantly, addresses the question of what the appropriate sources are for linguists taking a socio-historical approach. In each chapter, the case studies present a range of phonological, morphological, syntactic and lexical issues, which pose different methodological questions for sociolinguists and historical linguists alike.

WENDY AYRES-BENNETT is Reader in French Philology and Linguistics at the University of Cambridge. Her most recent publications include *Problems and Perspectives: Studies in the Modern French Language* (with Janice Carruthers, 2000), *A History of the French Language through Texts* (1996), and *Les Remarques de l'Académie Française sur le Quinte-Curce de Vaugelas 1719–1720* (with Philippe Caron, 1996), which won the French Academy's Prix d'Académie.

Sociolinguistic Variation in Seventeenth-Century France

Methodology and Case Studies

Wendy Ayres-Bennett
University of Cambridge

CAMBRIDGE
UNIVERSITY PRESS

PUBLISHED BY THE PRESS SYNDICATE OF THE UNIVERSITY OF CAMBRIDGE
The Pitt Building, Trumpington Street, Cambridge, United Kingdom

CAMBRIDGE UNIVERSITY PRESS
The Edinburgh Building, Cambridge, CB2 2RU, UK
40 West 20th Street, New York, NY 10011–4211, USA
477 Williamstown Road, Port Melbourne, VIC 3207, Australia
Ruiz de Alarcón 13, 28014 Madrid, Spain
Dock House, The Waterfront, Cape Town 8001, South Africa

http://www.cambridge.org

First published 2004

Printed in the United Kingdom at the University Press, Cambridge

Typeface Times 10/12 pt.   *System* LATEX 2$_\varepsilon$ [TB]

A catalogue record for this book is available from the British Library

Library of Congress Cataloguing in Publication data
Ayres-Bennett, Wendy.
Sociolinguistic variation in seventeenth-century France / Wendy Ayres-Bennett.
     p.   cm.
Includes bibliographical references and index.
ISBN 0-521-82088-X
1. French language – Variation.   2. French language – 17th century – History.
3. Sociolinguistics.   I. Title: Sociolinguistic variation in xvIIth century France.
II. Title: Sociolinguistic variation in 17th century France.   III. Title.

PC2074.7.A98   2004
306.44'0944'09032 – dc22   2004045193

ISBN 0 521 82088 X hardback

Contents

Contents vii

Preface

This study is the first systematic examination of sociolinguistic variation in seventeenth-century France. A primary aim is to enrich our knowledge of the wealth and variety of usages of seventeenth-century French by making available new data about linguistic variation in a period usually considered the most 'standardizing' and 'purist' of all periods in the history of French. It will be argued that a distorted image of seventeenth-century French emerges if only certain types of literary texts are consulted in conjunction with the work of grammarians and lexicographers. According to this rather narrow approach, our period witnessed the radical marginalization and elimination of variation and the standardization of French; this is symbolized above all in the foundation of the French Academy and the reign of good usage. It is, however, clearly fallacious to assume homogeneity of usage, whatever the nature of the speaker, register, location or context, for any period in the history of French. It is hoped that the study of non-standard usages in the seventeenth century will in turn have repercussions for the appreciation of literary texts, both in highlighting their specificity and in helping to sharpen notions of different genres. Through an understanding of the linguistic status of the variants selected by authors we may better understand the effects they are trying to achieve.

A second main aim of this study is to consider fundamental methodological issues which are central to all socio-historical linguistic accounts. First, and perhaps most importantly, we will need to address the question of what the appropriate sources are for the linguist favouring a socio-historical approach. Whereas sociolinguistic studies of contemporary French can construct a carefully balanced corpus based on a representative sample of different types of informants, historians of the language are obliged to use those written documents which have survived. This study will consider, for example, which texts best reflect non-standard and spoken usages, and will argue that it is necessary to try and seek convergence of evidence from a range of different sources. Secondly, we will need to explore how 'non-standard' forms are to be interpreted. Since we often lack precise details about the writer or speaker, or about the sociocultural and linguistic context of a given text, it can be difficult to evaluate variants. What texts, for example, best represent *français populaire* and to what extent is it possible to differentiate this from *français familier* or *français vulgaire*, or, for that matter, from features which are associated with spoken language generally? Also important is the avoidance of anachronistic judgments about a feature identified in a seventeenth-century text: a feature will not necessarily have the same value in the language system of the past as it has today.

Thirdly, I shall examine the relationship between variation and change. Change in progress is reflected in variation (although of course not all variation represents change in progress). Studies of past variation allow us to look for continuities and discontinuities, how innovations enter the norm and how variants are lost. Without studies of variation in earlier periods there is a danger of making false or exaggerated claims about, for example, the innovatory nature of modern spoken French, and of wrongly identifying certain contemporary features as presaging future developments in the language. Features which are said to be twentieth-century innovations may be found in earlier texts if a wider range of sources is consulted.

A number of parameters of variation have been selected for analysis. These are determined either by aspects of what may be thought of as the speaker's 'preverbal constitution' – here the gender, socio-economic status (SES) and age of the speaker – or by the medium, register or genre used. Where appropriate, the relationship between the different types of variation is explored. For instance, in Chapter 3 I shall discuss the extent to which differences of social class correlate with differences of register, while in Chapter 5, in considering variation according to the age of the speaker, I shall examine the relationship between variation and change. I decided not to treat regional variation systematically – partly since this is worthy of a monograph in its own right and partly because it is the area which has traditionally received most attention from historians of the French language. In each chapter a number of case studies have been selected, often based on information provided by the metalinguistic texts. In choosing these topics, I have tried to include phonological, morphological, syntactic and lexical questions, since each of these poses different methodological issues.

Acknowledgments

I am grateful for the support of a number of institutions and individuals in the writing of this book. These include the Department of French, Cambridge University, the AHRB, the Staff of the Rare Books Room, Cambridge University Library, and the Editors at CUP. Special thanks are due to Sophie Marnette and to Janice Carruthers, both of whom read and commented on the complete manuscript. This book would never have been completed without the help and encouragement of my husband, Andrew. It is dedicated to him, and to my two sons, Matthew and Luke.

Abbreviations

A: *Le Dictionnaire de l'Académie Françoise,* first edition, 2 vols., Paris: La Veuve J. B. Coignard and J. B. Coignard, 1694.

C: R. Cotgrave, *A Dictionarie of the French and English Tongues,* London: A. Islip, 1611.

F: A. Furetière, *Dictionaire universel, Contenant generalement tous les mots françois tant vieux que modernes, & les Termes de toutes les sciences et des arts* [. . .], 3 vols., The Hague/Rotterdam: A. and R. Leers, 1690.

N: J. Nicot, *Thresor de la langue francoyse, tant ancienne que moderne* [. . .], Paris: D. Douceur, 1606.

O: A. Oudin, *Curiositez françoises, pour supplement aux Dictionnaires. Ou Recueil de plusieurs belles proprietez, auec vne infinité de Prouerbes & Quolibets, pour l'explication de toutes sortes de Liures,* Paris: A. de Sommaville, 1640.

R: P. Richelet, *Dictionnaire françois, contenant les mots et les choses, plusieurs remarques nouvelles sur la langue françoise* [. . .], Geneva: J. H. Widerhold, 1680.

1 Introduction: Methodological issues

1.1 Introduction

Whilst there has been a number of socio-historical linguistic studies of English there is relatively little which is comparable for French. Indeed French scholars have been comparatively slow to embrace sociolinguistics in general, perhaps for two main reasons. On the one hand, we may point to the strength of the normative tradition in France which has perpetuated the stance that anything outside *le bon usage* is not worthy of serious study.[1] On the other hand, there has long been in France a preoccupation with one kind of variation, namely dialectology and the production of linguistic atlases.[2] This is not to say that there have not been studies of variation, including accounts of past periods of linguistic history; we need only think of Brunot's monumental history of the French language (1905–53), which displays a keen interest in, for example, usage of different genres and registers. Nevertheless, the treatment of variation has often been anecdotal and unsystematic, and has not been informed by the insights of modern sociolinguistic methodology.

The growth of interest in sociolinguistic variation in relation to contemporary French is associated, particularly from the 1970s on, with the work of non-French scholars, notably German (e.g. Söll 1985 [first edition 1974]; Hausmann 1975, Müller 1985) and subsequently British, Canadian and American linguists (e.g. Ashby 1981, 1991; Coveney 1996; Poplack 1989, 1992). In more recent times work on variation, and particularly on the spoken language, has gained in importance in France, especially with the work of members of the Groupe Aixois de Recherche en Syntaxe (GARS, now DELIC), and of scholars such as Gadet, who in 1997 edited a special number of the periodical *Langue Française* devoted to syntactic variation. Early impetus for investigating non-standard usages in the past came from the growth in studies of the characteristics of modern spoken French which led to an attempt, notably by German Romanists

---

[1] Note, for example, the normative implications of the title of an early study of non-standard usage, first published in 1929, Frei's *La Grammaire des fautes* (Frei 1982).

[2] One of the earliest studies of seventeenth-century variation by Veÿ (1911) typically focuses on regional variation.

in the late 1970s and early 1980s, to determine whether these features were recent innovations or had a long historical tradition (see Chapter 2).

1.1.1   The development of socio-historical linguistics

Especially important to the development of socio-historical approaches to language have been the theoretical discussions of Suzanne Romaine which aim to cross-fertilize historical linguistics with sociolinguistics.[3] Romaine makes a major contribution towards the elaboration of a methodology for this discipline in her 1982 book *Socio-historical Linguistics: Its Status and Methodology*, which attempts to reconstruct a past state of English within its social context. She admits that the assumption of the homogeneity of language has been necessary in order to provide systematic accounts of language states on which sociolinguistics can build. Since, however, the contemporary language is demonstrably not homogeneous, she hypothesizes that language of the past showed the same variation. It is an essential principle of historical sociolinguistics that the linguistic forces which operate today are not unlike those of the past, that is, there is no reason for assuming that language did not vary in the same patterned way in the past as it does today. Moreover, while sociolinguistics has largely been elaborated to describe variation in speech, one can hypothesize that written language as evidenced in texts also varies in a patterned way.

For Romaine (1988: 1453) the main goal of socio-historical linguistics is 'to investigate and provide an account of the forms and uses in which variation may manifest itself in a given speech community over time, and of how particular functions, uses and kinds of variation develop within particular languages, speech communities, social groups, networks and individuals'. From a methodological perspective there are two separate, albeit related, aims: 'to develop a set of procedures for the reconstruction of language in its social context, and to use the findings of sociolinguistics as controls on the process of reconstruction and as a means of informing theories of change'. In other words, the findings of sociolinguistics may be used to help reconstruct past language states or explain how language changes. Romaine notes that Labov explicitly recognizes the second aim in his use of the findings of synchronic sociolinguistics to explain language change, but is not concerned – as we will centrally be in this book – with the reconstruction of language of the past in its social context. Labov (1994), for example, looks at current variation and its correlation with social structure and patterns of human interaction and notably at sound change in progress, and considers how this may be applied to the historical record ('the use of the present to explain the past') as a way of elaborating general principles of linguistic change. Milroy (1992: 5) similarly argues that our understanding

---

[3] Regrettably French scholars have on the whole made relatively little reference to her work.

of linguistic change can be greatly enhanced by observing recurrent patterns of spoken language as it is used around us in day-to-day contexts by live speakers, and aims to use this evidence in constructing a social model for the interpretation of language change. In his account more attention is given to the social side than in the Labovian account, which tends to be mainly system-orientated.

As regards the reconstruction of language in its social context, this may occur on at least two levels: at the macro-level there is the reconstruction of language in relation to society, and at the micro-level there is the reconstruction of linguistic form in relation to social meaning context. Romaine (1982) is perhaps the best example of an attempt to apply variationist theory to a problem of historical syntax; she argues forcefully that the historical data should be considered in their own right, regardless of the extent to which they reflect or are removed from the production of native speakers (1982: 122). Data may be provided by patterns of variation in speech and writing in contemporary societies and written texts of all kinds from earlier periods, including reports from historians and grammarians. One of the major methodological questions is how to extract social information from these and other sources.

Despite the relative neglect in France of the important body of sociolinguistic work written in English, whether synchronic or diachronic, scholars have nevertheless begun gradually to be interested in socio-historical studies of French. Research into past variation has been nurtured by members of the Groupe d'Études en Histoire de la Langue Française (GEHLF), who have worked, for example, on 'non-conventional' French (GEHLF 1992) and on syntactic variation in seventeenth-century travel accounts. Within GARS, André Valli has produced some historical studies of syntactic variation. Equally, the concern with historical sociolinguistics has gradually been reflected in the type of histories of the French language being written. A number of British scholars have recently produced histories of the French language which attempt to introduce a socio-historical dimension (Lodge 1993, Ayres-Bennett 1996a, Posner 1997), and Lodge has published on the history of the urban dialect of Paris (Lodge 1998).

Whilst Labov and Milroy have concerned themselves primarily with using the findings of sociolinguistics to inform theories of change, in this work we will concentrate particularly on reconstructing different varieties of seventeenth-century French. It will become evident that a number of aspects of Labovian quantitative approaches to sociolinguistics are highly problematic if we try to apply them to studies of past variation.[4]

1.1.2   *The scope of this book*

At first sight it might seem perverse to try and reconstruct variation in seventeenth-century French, since this period is generally characterized as one

---

[4] On Labovian methodology, see, for example, Labov 1972a, Hudson 1980: 143–90.

of rigid codification and standardization, concerned with the establishment of the norms of written French, and thus of the elimination of variation. In fact, while promoting good usage, the authors of grammars and observations and remarks on the French language frequently characterize or criticize 'non-standard' usages – what people actually say although according to the norm being advanced they should not – and from such comments we may begin to reconstruct some of the different varieties. Paradoxically, then, in such a climate of standardization there is hypersensitivity towards small degrees of variation, thus making the seventeenth century a surprisingly rich source of information for socio-historical investigation. If sixteenth-century grammarians such as Meigret, Ramus and Estienne already associate certain usages with specified groups in society, they are as yet relatively tolerant of variation. For instance, Meigret (1550: 93) accepts both *je laisserai* and *je lairrai* as future forms of the verb 'to leave'. Once variation becomes increasingly stigmatized in the seventeenth century, the number of comments on non-standard usages multiplies, especially in the work of the *remarqueurs*, that is, authors of volumes of *remarques* or observations on the French language.[5]

There is much evidence to suggest that the *remarqueurs* were aware of socio-linguistic variation and the importance of selecting the correct word or expression according to the nature of the interlocutors and the context of speaking or writing. Here are two typical examples:

Et en effet, la pluspart des mots sont bons ou mauvais selon le lieu où ils sont placez; selon les personnes qui les disent, & selon celles à qui on les dit. Par exemple: *atrabile*, qui seroit un tres-mauvais mot dans la conversation des Dames & des Cavaliers, est un tres-bon mot dans un traité de Medecine, où il s'agit du tempérament des hommes. (Ménage 1676: 339)

Les termes y sont marquez chacun selon leur caractere propre, & plusieurs y sont appellez bas & populaires, sans qu'on prétende pour cela les condamner: Car tous les mots ont leur place, souvent il est à propos de se servir d'expressions communes, selon la nature du sujet; quelquefois mesmes elles donnent de la force aux choses.

D'ailleurs nostre Langue abonde en toutes sortes de façons de parler, elle en a pour le stile médiocre & pour le sublime, pour le sérieux & pour le burlesque; il faut tâcher d'en faire le discernement: & c'est en quoy consiste presque toute la science des paroles. (Andry de Boisregard 1689: Preface)

As we shall see, different authors of observations adopt different attitudes towards variation and give priority to different types of variation according to their own interests and purposes (see also Ayres-Bennett 2003). However, from their discussions a number of key parameters emerge which will be the main focus of our study: the relationship between written and spoken French; variation according to socio-economic status or social class; variation according

---

[5] For a description of the genre, see, for example, Ayres-Bennett 1987, 1991, 2002.

to register, style, or genre;[6] variation according to the sex of the speaker; variation according to the age of the speaker; the relationship between variation and change. One major preoccupation of at least some of the *remarqueurs*, notably Ménage, is regional variation, excluded from the present study for the reasons outlined in the Preface.[7] It was also decided not to treat some of the more minor types of variation discussed during the century, such as usage according to the technical or specialized field,[8] differences of usage between poetry and prose, or between concrete and figurative contexts.

1.2   Collecting data

Sociolinguistic methodology requires a number of stages in preparation for the collection, processing and interpretation of the data, including the selection of the appropriate speakers, circumstances and linguistic variables (cf. Hudson 1980: 144). There are a number of obvious problems with trying to apply a Labovian-style quantitative model, based on the selection of representative informants and the composition of a balanced corpus, to the study of a past language state. Inevitably the socio-historical linguist is obliged to adopt methodologies which would be deemed unacceptable for a sociolinguistic analysis of contemporary French. In this section we will discuss problems associated with identifying appropriate textual sources. In addition we will consider the difficulties of deciding upon the variables and particularly of treating syntactic issues in a socio-historical perspective.

1.2.1   *The question of sources and defining a corpus*

One of the major preoccupations throughout this study will be the question of sources: what documents can be used as sources of the non-standard in

---

[6] There is much variation in the way the terms *register, style* and *genre* are applied (for discussion in two different perspectives, see Lyons 1977, chapter 14 and Biber 1995: 8–9). Here *register* is used to refer to socio-situational variation, characterized by the degree of formality or informality of the speech or writing; the degree of formality will depend on factors such as the relationship between the interlocutors and the nature of the setting. *Style* is used to refer to a characteristic way of using language, especially with regard to literary language, while *genre* denotes a category of texts which are similar in form, style or subject matter.

[7] While dialects were still spoken by the majority, French was spoken in most of the towns in the north of France. In the south, French was known, but was a second language. Racine, for example, speaks of the difficulty of understanding and being understood by the locals once he got as far as Lyon (Brunot 1905–53: V, 48). During the century new territories, including successive areas of Alsace (1648–81), Artois and Roussillon (1659), Flanders (1668), and Franche-Comté (1679), were added to the kingdom, thereby expanding the linguistic diversity. This was, however, a period of increasingly autocratic and centralized government, culminating in the personal reign of Louis XIV (1661–1715). The French language came to be an instrument of social conformity. The socially upwardly mobile and provincials wanting to integrate themselves at the court turned to works such as Vaugelas's *Remarques* to learn 'good usage'.

[8] For a study of the argot of the criminal fraternity 1455–1850, see Sainéan 1907.

seventeenth-century France? This, according to Labov, is the fundamental methodological problem at the heart of historical sociolinguistics (Romaine 1982: 122). Labov laments the fact that historical linguists have no control over their data, that it is a matter of accident which texts survive, so that 'the great art of the historical linguist is to make the best of this bad data'. Milroy (1992: 45–7) is so concerned about what he considers to be the inherent limitations of historical enquiry – the problem of using written texts and the impoverished nature of the data which survive from past periods – that he argues that the best way in which to observe, in a detailed way, the contexts in which linguistic change takes place is to focus rather on present-day data. Romaine, however, argues that the study of historical sociolinguistics is not fruitless. In her view historical data are only 'bad' if an invidious comparison is made with data from authentic spoken language; instead historical data should be considered as valid in their own right (Romaine 1988: 1454).

It is, of course, not only a question of the quality of the data; data may be entirely absent. The problem is naturally most acute when we come to consider the question of sources of spoken French, since inevitably we are obliged to rely on written texts which at best can only be an imperfect reflection of the spoken language of the past (see Chapter 2). We are, in addition, forced to compromise on another of our principles as historians of French, namely that when carrying out a diachronic study one should always seek to compare texts of similar genres or discourse types, since in looking at the history of spoken French comparison is made between data gleaned from contemporary recordings and written textual sources. Other studies have shown, however, that providing one is aware of all the potential problems and does not attempt to make inflated claims about the nature of spoken language of the past, attempts to look at the history of spoken French can be productive. For example, Fleischman (e.g. Fleischman 1990), analysing tense usage in medieval texts intended for oral performance, has shown convincingly that the apparently bewildering mixture of present and past tenses which is so characteristic of certain medieval texts is equally a feature of contemporary spoken narratives.

The problems associated with the use of written texts are not restricted to examining the history of spoken French; written texts are also problematic as sources of variation and change. In the case of phonological change, for example, the recording of the new variant in writing may represent a rather late stage in the change, once it has been accepted into the writing system, rather than innovation.

The necessity of relying on those written texts which through chance have survived to this day poses questions as to how reliable and representative these sources are. Some of these problems are evident in Romaine's selection of texts (1982: 114) for her study of variation in relative clauses in Middle Scots texts between 1530 and 1550 with a view to establishing differences between genres according to whether they are more or less representative of familiar usage of the period. Surprisingly, there is no discussion of the rationale behind her choice of corpus, which comprises just seven texts. Of these seven texts three are chosen to illustrate official and legal prose; there is one example of literary narrative prose, one example of epistolary prose, one example representing both courtly or serious verse and moralizing religious verse, and one example of comic verse. In short, we are offered no explanation as to why these texts were selected, or of the extent to which they may be viewed as typical or representative of their genre.

The general problems we have discussed so far are compounded by the fact that there is a relative paucity of documents illustrating informal, 'substandard' or semi-literate usages dating from the seventeenth century compared with later periods (cf. Martineau and Mougeon 2003). For the eighteenth century we can point, for example, to the journal of Ménétra (Roche 1982, Seguin 1985), the memoirs of Valentin Jamerey-Duval (Jamerey-Duval 1981) or of Pierre Prion (Le Roy Ladurie and Ranum 1985), the writings of 'inexperienced' or 'clumsy' writers at the time of the Revolution (Branca-Rosoff 1989, Branca-Rosoff and Schneider 1994), or plays such as Marivaux's *Télémaque travesti* (Valli 1984). This is, however, compensated for to some extent by the wealth of metalinguistic texts (see below).

In each chapter we shall consider the potential sources and discuss the problems associated with them. In view of the difficulties with textual sources, I thought it unwise to rely exclusively on one type of source; rather convergence of evidence from different types of source was sought. This means that wherever possible, confirmation of the status of a variant is sought through comparing evidence from different sources and looking for indication of convergence. For example, in Chapter 3 I consider the extent to which the dictionary style label 'burlesque' coincides with usage in actual burlesque texts. In this way it is hoped to minimize some of the difficulties with the data. This is not to say that there are not potential dangers with such an approach. First and foremost there is the risk of circularity, that is deciding that a certain usage must be appropriate for a certain genre, style, register, sex or age, perhaps on the basis of modern usage, and then considering that the dictionary which uses this label must be the most faithful. Equally, convergence between sources may suggest the emergence of a stereotype which may be exploited, for example, for comic purposes (see below pp. 30–31).

Throughout this work the comments made in metalinguistic texts are set beside usage in other kinds of texts. These metalinguistic observations frequently constitute the starting point of our discussion by indicating the linguistic variables appropriate for analysis. The metalinguistic texts exploited comprise a range of documents including volumes of observations and *remarques* on the

French language, dictionaries, formal grammars, and linguistic commentaries, notably on grammatical texts.

Perhaps the most interesting and useful amongst these as sources of variation are the volumes of observations and remarks on the French language, since they offer a plethora of information about contemporary non-standard usages in their criticism of *mauvais usage* (see Ayres-Bennett 2003). The founder of the genre, Vaugelas (1647), characterizes himself as a simple observer of usage, and presents his comments in a series of randomly ordered, generally short, remarks about individual points of doubtful usage. While subsequent *remarqueurs* adapt the format to their own needs (an alphabetical presentation is adopted, for example, by Alemand (1688) and Andry de Boisregard (1689, 1693)), they continue to focus on areas of uncertainty – or variation – in contemporary usage.[9] Thirteen volumes of observations were selected for our main corpus; these are listed in the Appendix (I:A).

The three major monolingual dictionaries of the last two decades of the century constitute a second important source of variation (Richelet 1680, Furetière 1690, Académie Française 1694).[10] To these were added data from the dictionaries of Nicot (1606), Cotgrave (1611) and Oudin (1640) as appropriate (Appendix, I:B). *Marques d'usage* in dictionaries (rendered henceforth as 'style labels') have received considerable attention over the past fifteen years (Bray 1986, Glatigny 1990a, 1998). In assessing the judgments made about a lexical item, the policy of the particular lexicographer and his attitude towards variation must be borne in mind; for example, Furetière's dictionary (1690) has a much more encyclopaedic quality than those of Richelet or the Academy. Moreover, different lexicographers place different emphases on different parameters; thus while Furetière's concern is primarily with the social class of the speaker employing a particular word or expression, Richelet is more interested in questions of register and genre (see Chapter 3).

Formal grammars, especially those intended for foreigners, tend on the whole to adopt a more normative approach, and therefore to contain less information about non-standard usages. Nevertheless, in particular the grammars of Maupas (1618) and Oudin (1632), and to a lesser extent, Irson (1662), constitute important sources of data (Appendix, I:C).

---

[9] So great was the authority of *remarqueurs* such as Vaugelas, Ménage and Bouhours that their observations tended to be copied and incorporated into the works of their successors, who did not necessarily observe contemporary usage themselves. I have therefore excluded from my primary corpus compilations of observations; D'Aisy's two volumes (1685a, 1685b), for example, principally comprise a summary of the observations of these three *remarqueurs* on French grammar and style.

[10] The dictionaries of Nicot, Cotgrave, Richelet, Furetière and the Academy were searched electronically using the CD-ROM, *Dictionnaires du XVIIe et XVIIIe siècles* produced by Champion (1998). Oudin (1640) was consulted on the CD-ROM, *L'Atelier historique de la langue française* produced by Redon (2001).

We also make reference to linguistic commentaries, particularly here the commentaries on the observations and remarks (Streicher 1936).[11] These are especially valuable in tracking changes of usage since the original comment was made (Appendix, I:D).

Other types of metalinguistic text are exploited in the different chapters as appropriate. For example, I shall discuss the important contribution of conversation manuals in Chapter 2. Also consulted are works on French pronunciation, works on spelling (especially those which consider spelling reforms), works on versification, and a number of other miscellaneous works which discuss questions of style or usage (see Appendix II).

In each chapter the data from metalinguistic texts are complemented by information from other sources. These may be literary texts, and the database known as FRANTEXT has been particularly valuable for researching usage in these.[12] A wide range of non-literary texts has also been exploited, including journals, popular pamphlets, informal correspondence and translations. In each case the advantages and disadvantages of the particular source are discussed.

1.2.2 Deciding upon the variables

A major difficulty with researching variation in the past is selecting the variables for analysis. Once again the problems associated with conducting sociolinguistic studies of contemporary French are intensified when we research the past. The present study is limited to the reconstruction of a number of key features for each parameter of variation which serve as case studies; the intention is not to attempt a reconstruction of every detail of every variety of seventeenth-century French, since this would take us far beyond the scope of the present volume.

Two main strategies have been adopted here for selecting which linguistic features will be studied. On the one hand I examined the metalinguistic texts to identify areas of variation, and this was particularly helpful where a topic

[11] An example of a commentary on a literary text is Ménage's observations on Malherbe's poetry, published in editions of the poems from 1666 onwards (Malherbe 1666). Some of the comments are concerned with what is appropriate for poetry, but others make more general comments about variation. See also Ayres-Bennett and Caron (1996) on the Academy's commentary on Vaugelas's translation of Quintus Curtius Rufus' life of Alexander.

[12] Base textuelle FRANTEXT, CNRS-ATILF (http://atilf.inalf.fr/frantext.htm). Full details of the size of the corpus and bibliographical details of the texts may be found on the website. It is important to remember that texts are continually being added to this database and that the statistics cited from it in this book relate to its contents in the period during which the present research was conducted. Account must also be taken of the edition selected for inclusion in the database, which may date from the seventeenth century or be a more recent or modern one. In addition, generally only one edition of each text is included, making the corpus unsuitable for tracking changes through different editions. In exploiting FRANTEXT, I had to take account of possible variant spellings (e.g. savoir/sçavoir; vrai/vray). When searching for occurrences of particular verbs, '&c' placed before the infinitive of the verb allowed the search for all conjugated forms of the verb (providing it was a verb form recognized by the program); similarly '&m' permitted the identification of all the declined forms of nouns and adjectives.

was discussed in a number of different metalinguistic texts. On the other hand, especially in the case of features of spoken French I wanted to consider whether certain features which are said to typify contemporary spoken French were also characteristic of our period. This is not without potential problems, not least since there is a lack of agreement as to what the defining characteristics of modern spoken French are (see Chapter 2). Finally, I have included in the case studies a range of different kinds of features including phonological, morphological and syntactic questions; syntactic variation poses particular problems which will be discussed in the next section.

1.2.3   Syntactic variation in a socio-historical perspective

There has been considerable debate as to whether Labovian sociolinguistic methodology, elaborated for phonology, can successfully be applied to syntactic research (Sankoff 1973, Lavandera 1978, Romaine 1981, 1982, 1984). For Labov, social and stylistic variation presupposes that you can say the same thing in different ways (that is, that variants have the same referential meaning but are different in their social or stylistic significance; Labov adopts a truth-definitional point of view). The concept of the linguistic variable has been successfully applied to phonological variation because of the arbitrariness of the linguistic sign; thus the meaning of the word *père* is unchanged whether the 'r' is pronounced as a uvular fricative or a rolled trill. In the case of syntax the problem of determining identity of meaning for all variants of the variable is much more acute. Gadet (1997b: 11) suggests that this necessitates a looser interpretation of functional equivalence, namely 'dire des choses proches à propos d'un même référent'.

Romaine (1981: 15–17) draws a distinction between on the one hand morpho-syntactic variables of the type of negation in Montreal French, or deletion of the complementizer *que*, which may be conditioned linguistically by both phonological and grammatical features and which are conditioned by social and stylistic factors, and on the other hand what she terms 'pure' syntactic variables, such as the agentless passive, which she hypothesises may be conditioned not by social and stylistic factors, but simply by syntactic factors. In other words, the variation between active and passive is conditioned only by surface structure constraints, and does not convey any social or stylistic information. Similar doubts about the social significance of syntactic variation are raised by Cheshire (1996: 2) and Gadet (1997b: 9).[13]

---

[13] Working within a different framework Berrendonner, Le Guern and Puech (1983: 20) also contend that not all variants correlate with social factors; indeed, variation may not connote anything in particular. They argue that if social correlations alone are sought, other explanations may be overlooked, and they themselves place emphasis on 'des considérations intra-systématiques'. In their view, 'une langue est une polyhiérarchie de sous-systèmes, et certains de ces sous-systèmes offrent aux locuteurs des *choix* entre diverses variantes'.

A further difference between morpho-syntactic variation and what Romaine terms 'pure syntactic' variation, in her view, is that in the former case we are dealing with the presence or absence of a term, whereas in the latter there is alternation with a whole construction or arrangement of items. This means that it may be possible to identify examples of 'complementary distribution' for morpho-syntactic variation. Romaine cites the example of Sankoff and Thibault (1977), who look at variation between *avoir* and *être* as the auxiliary verb in the conjugation of compound tenses in the French of Montreal. For Romaine this does not constitute an example of syntactic variation because it does not account for how, if at all, some speakers mark the aspectual distinction drawn by other speakers. Moreover, in her view this instance does not require a radical change to the Labovian concept of linguistic variable because the question is formulated in terms of presence or absence of the variants. The key question is therefore whether there is any semantic distinction in the variation (e.g. +complete/−complete).

The problematic nature of this question is highlighted by the fact that there has been considerable controversy as to whether pairs such as *j'ai resté/je suis resté* have the same sense. Whereas the Montreal linguists argue that they do, and that the difference between them is 'basically class-determined', the Aix linguists maintain on the contrary that the auxiliaries represent 'deux visées différentes' (Blanche-Benveniste 1997: 20). The same issues have been raised, for instance, about the choice between the French simple and compound future (*je ferai/ je vais faire*). The difficulties of establishing equivalence are magnified once we consider past variation, since we have no direct access to native speakers' intuitions about semantic equivalence.

This work includes discussion of questions of simple presence versus absence of a form (e.g. *ne* of negation); of substitution of one form for another (e.g. *quand je le suis, quand je la suis*); and of constructions which involve the rearrangement of elements (e.g. inversion versus non-inversion in interrogative sentences). Questions of semantic equivalence will be raised where appropriate and I shall return to the methodological issues posed by my analysis in the conclusion.

1.3   Interpreting the data

1.3.1   *Processing the data: the question of statistics*

In sociolinguistic studies of the contemporary language, analysis of the data and attempts to establish links between linguistic variables and speaker variables usually require quantitative methods which may involve sophisticated statistical techniques (Milroy 1992: 80). Quantitative methodology implies that there will be a reasonably high frequency of individual variants (Schneider 2002), although even with studies of contemporary French, this may be difficult for rare forms (see Carruthers 1999). Moreover, there are problems of sampling; when you take into account the different social variables, the individual cells may each comprise only four or five informants.

As regards historical studies, the random survival of certain kinds of texts, and the often small number of occurrences of a variable make any attempts at statistical analysis highly problematic or indeed impossible. Romaine (1982), by concentrating on one common feature, identifies approximately 6300 relative clauses from seven different texts, and uses statistics to try and show the extent to which differences between the various texts are significant. For some of the features I have selected the number of occurrences across all text types is so small that even percentages are unreliable. As Schneider (2002: 89) notes, even if it is not possible to analyse quantitatively how often a variable occurs, 'it still makes sense to ask if it occurs at all, which variants are found, and, possibly, who its users are'. That is, there may be two levels of analysis – which are still valuable – below the level of quantification: a token-based approach which simply lists which forms are found, and a slightly broader strategy which examines in addition the social characteristics of the users of these forms.

1.3.2   Separating the different parameters of variation and the problem of metalanguage

Studies of variation in contemporary French generally seek to separate out the different parameters of variation. Coseriu (1970: 32), for example, distinguishes the *diatopisch*, that is geographical or regional variation; the *diastratisch*, that is variation according to the different sociocultural layers or groups in society and which is largely determined by what has been termed the 'pre-verbal' constitution of the speaker (age, sex, profession, education, etc.); and the *diaphasisch*, that is variation according to the communicative situation linked to the context and the nature of the speakers and embracing differences of register, style and genre. To these types we might add differences of medium, that is, between the written and spoken codes.

Blanche-Benveniste and her team at GARS have been fiercely critical of the equation of spoken French with *français populaire*, low-register usage which is often considered impoverished, substandard or incorrect (Blanche-Benveniste and Jeanjean 1987: 11–14); spoken language may equally be formal or carefully constructed as in the case of a speech or lecture. Branca-Rosoff and Schneider (1994) are at pains to point out that the writings of the semi-literate which they analyse are not spoken French, yet at the same time they consider them in relation to five sociolinguistic markers which are features often associated with modern spoken French: use of *on* rather than *nous*; extension of the use of the compound future; decline of negative *ne*; the use of *ça*; and the use of the *passé composé* rather than the *passé simple*. While they conclude that these texts do not constitute a faithful representation of speech, they nevertheless argue that they 's'appuie[nt] sur du parlé' (1994: 81). Another idea commonly expressed is that it is in spoken French that innovation occurs, and therefore language change is located there; this has led to a prolonged debate in Germany as to whether spoken French is innovative or conservative (see Chapter 2).

When we consider textual evidence, the separation of different parameters of variation is naturally artificial since, as seventeenth-century writers were aware, each time one speaks a number of different considerations intervene:

Il n'est rien de plus important au commerce de la vie, que de parler juste dans la conversation, & pour cela il faut observer que la justesse dont nous parlons, doit être reglée par les matieres dont on parle, par les personnes à qui l'on parle, par ceux devant qui l'on parle, par le tems & le lieu où l'on parle [. . .] (Renaud 1697: 145)

One of the greatest challenges for a historian trying to analyse variation in a past language state is to know what status to attribute to a particular variant. Our reliance on written sources also means that we cannot systematically change the social variables and then establish correlations (cf. Schlieben-Lange 1983: 38). Indeed we do not necessarily know what the social value is for the variables within the speech community.

A few examples will serve to illustrate the difficulty of apportioning seventeenth-century sources to our different parameters of variation. For instance, comments about conversation and examples of conversational usage might equally well be discussed in the chapters on spoken French or on women's language, just as some of the examples of informal and uneducated dialogue might equally underpin a discussion of spoken or low-register usage. In practice, therefore, the decision to assign priority to one parameter of variation over another – and therefore to discuss it in one chapter rather than another – may sometimes be somewhat arbitrary and based on intuition. A telling example is the case of the *Journal d'Héroard*, written by the Dauphin's personal physician, which will be discussed in Chapter 2 (see Gougenheim 1931, Ernst 1985, Prüssmann-Zemper 1986, De Gorog 1990).

The problems of distinguishing the different parameters of variation are compounded in the seventeenth century by the attitude of certain *remarqueurs* and even some lexicographers towards the non-standard. Since the emphasis is firmly on describing good usage, 'bad' usage is defined by what is excluded from this, without necessarily focusing on the reason for the exclusion. Discussions of variation therefore tend to make little attempt to separate out different types of variation, and the variants are not discussed objectively. For instance, the Statutes of the French Academy (1634) portray everyday speech in a negative light, since the body aims to 'nettoyer la langue des ordures qu'elle avoit contractées [. . .] dans la bouche du peuple' (Pellisson and d'Olivet 1858: I, 23). The challenge of knowing what status to attribute to a particular variant

is increased for the historian of seventeenth-century French by terminological difficulties posed by the metalinguistic texts. Many of the *remarqueurs* in
particular, anxious not to appear overly scholarly or pedantic and thereby to
deter their intended *mondain* audience, deliberately avoid technical terminology and cultivate a lack of attention to such questions. For instance, Vaugelas
aims to minimize the use of specialized vocabulary and favours instead general
labels such as *bon*, *commode*, *meilleur*, *elegant*, and *necessaire*.[14] The terms are
not explicitly ordered into any scale of values, and their meaning is typically
context-dependent according to the combinations in which they occur, thus
throwing the burden of evaluation heavily on the reader if s/he is to gain more
than a vague impression of Vaugelas's judgments. Even where grammatical terminology is employed there is a deliberate inattention to precision; for instance,
Vaugelas refers to *nous* as a noun and then adds in parentheses 'que j'appelle
nom, quoy qu'il soit pronom, parce que cela n'importe' (1647: 177). The difficulties of interpreting the metalanguage used in the corpus of observations and
dictionaries will be alluded to constantly throughout this study.

1.3.3   Avoiding anachronistic judgments

A major risk in interpreting evidence is that of making overhasty or anachronistic judgments about the significance of a linguistic feature once it has been
located in a seventeenth-century text. This problem has been labelled 'concep-
tual inertia', which may involve applying the linguistic concepts and grammatical categories of a modern language in a simplistic way to the data of a past
state, or the failure to recognize a category or distinction in a past state of the
language because it is no longer operative in the modern language. Fleischman
(1996) cites the example of Old French 'si' which she considers a 'same subject'
marker, to be interpreted within the context of Old French as a 'verb second'
(V2) language; traditionally this 'si' has variously been considered an adverb,
a conjunction or a hybrid of the two categories.

It is also important not to assume that, just because the same linguistic form
is attested in a past language state, it has the same value within that system as it
does within the modern language. As Posner notes (1994: 77), any attempt to
reconstruct spoken varieties must be embedded in a picture of social intercourse;
the features must be situated within the contemporary system and in relation to
the contemporary norm. An example of this problem is the case of *on*, which
will be discussed in Chapter 2.

Finally, it is crucial to avoid the risk of considering something new in the
contemporary language on the basis of inadequate evidence for past usage. The
non-occurrence of a feature in earlier texts (e.g. the loss of negative *ne* or the use

---

[14] On the use of *françois*, *n'est pas françois*, see Ayres-Bennett 1996b.

of intonation alone to mark interrogation) does not necessarily mean that this was not a feature of that period; it may be because we are looking at the wrong kind of texts, or because the different conventions of the period exclude the non-standard or the spoken or the informal from the texts which survive.

1.4 The value of studying variation in seventeenth-century French

Given the fundamental difficulties associated with trying to investigate variation for past language states, it is worth considering why linguists continue to pursue this line of enquiry. Study of past variation is an essential component in the search for a better understanding of the relationship between variation and change, enabling us to consider continuities and discontinuities, how variants enter the norm and how variants are lost. Only when we have detailed sociolinguistic studies of seventeenth-century French and of attitudes towards the variants – however imperfect these may be – will we be in a position to try and identify some of the causes of innovation and change. A number of linguists, including Marchello-Nizia (1995) and Posner (1994), have suggested that loss of variants is vital in the understanding of language change. Posner (1994: 79, 80) summarizes this position as follows:

In my terms, while social norms continue to tolerate the variation, 'change' has not taken place, even though the social weighting of the variants may vary. Change, in this perspective, would result from a shift in social attitudes, including the rejection of previously tolerated norms [. . .] If perceptions about acceptable norms are altered, however, restructuring may manifest itself more patently, as obsolete forms fall out of use. This is possibly what happened in seventeenth-century France.

Secondly, study of past variation can prevent us making exaggerated claims about innovations and the status of variants in modern French. This is perhaps most obvious in the case of the status of features of modern spoken French (see Chapter 2). For historians of the French language there is a tension between the knowledge that we inevitably can state nothing with absolute certainty about spoken usage of the past and, on the other hand, the desire to counter false claims about the innovatory nature of modern spoken French. Without diachronic studies there is a real danger of incorrectly identifying certain modern features as presaging future change in the language, following Harris's (1978) model according to which it is non-standard usages which are driving change – or, to put it succinctly, that the faults of today will become tomorrow's standard usage.

Thirdly, in a time when the study of literature and that of linguistics are often viewed as incompatible or rival pursuits, it is worth emphasizing that the study of non-standard usages in the seventeenth century should have important repercussions for our appreciation of the literary texts of arguably one of the most significant periods of French literature, from which many of the great texts of the canon date. The setting of literary usage within a broader context of usages allows us better to appreciate a writer's purpose, and the effects he or she is attempting to achieve. This is of particular interest in a genre like burlesque, where the literary effects are in part at least achieved by a conscious mixing of registers.

1.5   The structure of this book

For each type of variation I shall consider the treatment of the question in the metalinguistic texts, and discuss terminological issues. The strengths and weaknesses of the possible textual and other sources for each case will be enumerated and reasons adduced for the selection of sources made. I shall then concentrate on a number of case studies in order to focus the discussion. Thus, for example, my study of social and stylistic variation will consider lexical usage, pronunciation issues and 'constructions louches', while the chapter on age, variation and change will include treatment of questions of word order, verb morphology and pronunciation. My investigation of women's language in Chapter 4 will offer the opportunity to explore in depth the position of women in seventeenth-century French society, and the ways in which their linguistic usage is shaped by or reflects the sociocultural context. In addition, I shall consider attitudes towards women's language and whether the general characteristics attributed to the usage of women or the *Précieuses* can be associated with specific linguistic features.

2   Spoken and written French

2.1   Introduction

The difference between spoken and written French of past ages is the most difficult parameter of variation to investigate, not least since there are no direct sources of speech available to us. Even if we look at direct discourse in written texts, which may be assumed to approximate to spoken language, we do not have straightforward access to speech.[1] A major consideration here will therefore be to examine the extent to which it is possible to find *reflections* of spoken French in textual and other sources, and to evaluate their reliability.

In this chapter and the following one we will also be constantly forced to consider to what degree it is possible to separate differences of medium (spoken versus written French) from other types of variation, and in particular from differences of register. As we have already noted (section 1.3.2), all too often a simple equation is made between spoken and informal usages on the one hand, and written and formal usages on the other. In some cases 'spoken French' is even equated with 'faulty French' and a narrow range of features is discussed such as negation, the 'incorrect' choice of auxiliary, or the extension of the use of *que* (Blanche-Benveniste 1995: 26). Bayley's (1980) study of pulpit oratory and Zoberman's (1998) account of 'ceremonial' language, such as set-piece speeches, are just two indications of the range of spoken usages in the seventeenth century. The dangers associated with trying falsely to compartmentalize spoken French are articulated convincingly by Blanche-Benveniste and Jeanjean (1987: 11):

---

[1] Cf. Seguin's comment (1985: 437) in his article on Ménétra's journal: 'Faut-il croire que l'on atteint ici le vrai, l'oral, l'anecdotique, l'enregistrement de la parole de l'homme du peuple de la fin du XVIIIe siècle? Ce n'est pas le cas, et c'est – heureusement – impossible: même s'il nous tombait du ciel des paroles dégelées des années 1760–1780, elles seraient ou peu nombreuses et non représentatives, ou d'une multiplicité sociovariante telle que l'infini des situations, des lieux, des temps, des jeux psychologiques interhumains nous découragerait. Immanquablement, nous projetterions sur ces "faits" nos propres réflexes, nous referions de faux systèmes, et la langue nous échapperait.'

Assimiler *le parlé* au *populaire*, c'est le retrancher du français légitime;[2] y voir la source
des innovations et des conservatismes, c'est le retrancher dans le temps; opposer le parlé
à l'écrit, c'est lui assigner une place bien à part; l'accabler d'étiquettes et de 'niveaux',
c'est vouloir le cantonner dans certaines activités de langage et l'exclure des autres.

As Gadet notes (1996), the dichotomy between written and spoken French is an
abstraction away from a continuum of usages, but one which it is nevertheless
vital to include in descriptions of French. Orality may indeed be thought of
as more important in the seventeenth century than today, given the relatively
low literacy rates of the period. For example, Muchembled (1990: 140) notes
that 86% of women and 71% of men were incapable around 1686–1690 of
signing a marriage register (although there are large regional differences and
discrepancies between urban and rural communities; for example as many as
75% of Parisians may have been literate under Louis XIV).

Fresh impetus was given to the investigation of the spoken French of the past
in the late 1970s and 1980s by the work of a number of German Romanists.[3]
New research into the characteristics of twentieth-century spoken French provoked a debate as to whether the features identified as such were relatively
new innovations, typical of that century, or whether they had long characterized spoken varieties.[4] The latter position, adopted by the anti-evolutionists,
depended on the assertion that the impression of innovation is illusory and
entirely due to lack of documentary evidence for spoken French of the past.
This inevitably provoked attempts to find ever earlier textual attestations of features considered characteristic of contemporary spoken French (e.g. Hunnius
1975; Hausmann 1979; Steinmeyer 1979; Chervel 1983; Ernst 1985). As a result
of this research a number of scholars have adopted a medial position: contemporary French is said to comprise both features which have long been part of the
spoken language and relatively recent innovations (see, for example, Hausmann
1992).

This, of course, presupposed that there was agreement as to which features typify contemporary spoken French or what the relevant sociolinguistic
markers are. In fact it is striking that there is considerable variation from one
researcher to another as to what precisely the defining characteristics of spoken
French are. Blanche-Benveniste and Jeanjean (1987: 31–2), for example, offer

---

[2] In Vaugelas's famous definition of *le bon usage* (1647) the spoken usage of the 'healthiest' part
of the court is included and thereby legitimized (see section 2.3).

[3] For an early attempt to describe seventeenth-century informal speech, see Ramm (1902).

[4] The debate is well summarized by Schweickard (1983) and Hausmann (1992). Guiraud (1958:
110) already seemed to favour an evolutionist's position, in his argument that the differences
between different varieties of French are much greater today than they were in the seventeenth
century: 'Un autre problème est posé par la spécialisation toujours croissante des fonctions du
langage. Dans le passé, la langue de Corneille ne diffère pas notablement, style mis à part, de
celle de Descartes; et par ailleurs, il ne semble pas que leur langue parlée, toujours style mis à
part, s'écartât considérablement de leur usage écrit.'

a consolidated list of fifteen characteristics often attributed to spoken French, nine of which are generally thought to be in decline and therefore conservative ('de recul') – decline in usage of the relative pronouns *dont* and *lequel*; decline of negative *ne*; decline in inversion, including in interrogation; decline of *être* as an auxiliary; decline of the simple future and of the subjunctive; simplification of verb morphology; simplification of noun morphology; [i] for 'il'; 'arb' for 'arbre' – and six to which are assigned the more positive labels 'avancé' or 'de progrès', that is, innovations presaging future standard usage – advance of *que* as a 'passe-partout' relative pronoun; use of *qu'est-ce que* for *ce que*; redundancy (e.g. *mon frère il l'a dit*);[5] use of the periphrastic future; of *ça*; and of *on* for *nous*.[6] Koch and Oesterreicher (1990: 150–65) on the other hand list fourteen morpho-syntactic features which are said to characterize modern spoken French. It is remarkable that the two lists have only eight items in common. Koch and Oesterreicher maintain that very few of these are cases of archaisms or conservative features (omission of the impersonal unstressed subject pronoun, placing the direct object in initial position). A second group comprises early innovations dating at least from before 1600, which are not however to be considered 'conservative' traits (use of *ça*, [i] for *il*, *qu'* for *qui*, non-use of negative *ne*, use of topicalization structures). However, the largest group is those which they term 'Innovation jüngeren Datums', by which they mean from the seventeenth century; these include non-agreement of the past participle with a preceding direct object; replacement of the *passé simple* by the *passé composé*; use of the compound future in place of the simple future; loss of the imperfect subjunctive; loss of use of negative *ne* alone; decline of inversion in interrogation; obligatory use of unstressed subject clitic pronouns; and perhaps also the reduction of *tu*, the use of constructions such as *du bon vin* (instead of *de bon vin*) and of *on* for *nous*.

Perhaps because of these difficulties, Hausmann (1992) selects a very short list of syntactic features for his study of the extent to which modern spoken French may be said to be conservative or innovatory: segmentation or dislocation; non-use of *ne* in negative sentences; the absence of the *passé simple*; non-use of inversion in interrogative structures; the use of *on* as an equivalent of the first person plural subject pronoun *nous*. In this chapter I have similarly selected a restricted number of case studies since my intention is not primarily to consider the history of features said to typify modern spoken French. Where this is the principal aim, it would seem more fruitful to try and compose a

---

[5] Blasco-Couturier (1990) looks at the case of constructions characterized by reduplication in the seventeenth and eighteenth centuries.

[6] They note that there has been much less interest in those features which are not considered 'faults', such as the choice between 'en' and 'dans', the left dislocation of the object, the use of pseudo-clefts and the designation of numbers.

maximally long consolidated list of possible traits, and to attempt to trace the history and significance of each of them.

Even if the same feature is identified in the French spoken in the seventeenth century, care needs to be taken to determine whether the item has the same value within that linguistic system as it has today. Thus Marchello-Nizia (1998) argues that although there are superficial similarities between the structure of dislocated structures in Old and Modern French, their pragmatic values are different; in Old French, when word order patterns are not yet syntactically fixed, left dislocation is particularly used to highlight the rheme, whereas in Middle and Modern French these structures are employed rather to emphasize the theme.[7] Similar issues are raised in my discussion of the use of *on* for *nous* (see section 2.5.2).

2.2   Terminological difficulties

A major difficulty with investigating spoken French is the problem of identifying and interpreting the terminology used in the metalinguistic texts to refer to this medium. The labels which we might expect to find today, notably 'oral' and 'parlé', are not used by seventeenth-century writers in this way. Nor can we rely on the use of the verb *dire* on its own to indicate spoken usage; for example, in many of the *remarques* it is used indiscriminately in conjunction with both *parler* and *écrire*. Part of the difficulty stems from the rather cultivated lack of attention on the part of some *remarqueurs* to precision of terminology, since this might smack of pedantry. The following is a typical example from Ménage (1675: 19), where the use of *dire* – and indeed here also of *parlé* – is not intended to refer to spoken language:

S'il faut dire *Missel*, ou *Messel* [. . .]
Il faut dire *Missel*, comme l'a dit M. de Balzac dans son Discours de la Langue de l'Eglise & du Latin de la Messe. C'est comme tous nos Escrivains modernes ont tousjours parlé; à la reserve du savant M. l'Abbé Voisin, qui dans sa Traduction du Missel s'est avisé de dire *Messel*, acause qu'on dit *Messe* [. . .]

In some cases it is obvious that a contrast is being established between written and spoken usages. For example, Vaugelas uses pairs such as 'en parlant' / 'en escriuant', 'se disent'/ 'les bons Autheurs ne l'escriuent', 'ne s'escrit jamais'/ 'quoy qu'il se die'. In other cases the context makes it clear that this is how an observation is to be understood; for example, 'le stile' in the following example is clearly intended to refer to written language: 'Certes en parlant on

---

[7] The distinction between theme and rheme is similar to that between topic and comment: the theme expresses little or no extra meaning, whereas the rheme conveys the larger amount of extra meaning in addition to what has already been communicated.

ne l'obserue point [a new syntactic rule], mais le stile veut estre plus exact' (1647: 80).[8]

More problematic are the terms *discours familier* and *conversation*. In some instances these are clearly used to refer to spoken usages, as in the following examples:

C'est un grand rompement de teste. Cela ne se dit que dans la conversation, & on ne l'écrit point. (Bouhours 1675: 216)

Comporter [. . .] Ces façons de parler sont assez vieilles: mais elles sont de la Cour; & les personnes qui ont le plus de politesse s'en servent dans le discours familier. Je ne voy pas que cela soit en usage dans les livres. (Bouhours 1675: 266)

Difficulties arise from the fact that neither of these expressions is used solely to refer to spoken usage in contrast to written language. Both *discours familier* and *conversation* may be employed to refer either to spoken language in general or to informal speech alone. For example, discussing the superlatives *habilissime, grandissime, bellissime* and *rarissime* Bouhours notes:

Ces superlatifs se disent dans le discours familier, & les gens de la Cour en usent souvent [. . .] Tout cela ne s'écrit point, & ne se dit point en public; & il n'y a gueres d'apparence que ces superlatifs, qui sont contre le génie de nostre Langue, entrent jamais dans les livres; c'est bien assez pour eux d'estre soufferts dans la conversation. (Bouhours 1675: 296–7)

Similarly, he asserts that the expression 'ce fut une étrange scene' is used at court but has not moved beyond 'discours familier'; he continues, '& un Escrivain, ou un Orateur n'oseroit gueres s'en servir sans faire paroistre de l'affectation. Ce sont de ces mots qui se disent en conversation seulement, & qui s'écrivent tout au plus dans une Lettre' (Bouhours 1693: 193), thereby associating spoken conversational usage with the written usage of letters. The polysemy of *discours* is attested in seventeenth-century dictionaries. The Academy's definition of the word is typical in this respect:

Discours. Propos, assemblage de paroles pour expliquer ce que l'on pense [. . .]
Il signifie aussi, Entretien. *Par maniere de discours, en discours familier.*
Il se prend pour ce que l'on recite, ou que l'on escrit sur differents sujets. *Il a fait un beau discours sur ce sujet, un discours relevé, premedité.*

---

[8] While the dictionary definitions of 'style' indicate written usage as its primary reference, the possibility of it referring to spoken language is not excluded. For example, Furetière defines the term as follows: 'Stile, signifie principalement la façon particuliere d'expliquer ses pensées, ou d'escrire, qui est differente, selon les Auteurs, & les matieres', but he notes that 'le stile mediocre ou familier' is used in conversation. Richelet's entry is also somewhat ambiguous: '*Stile*. Ce mot se dit en parlant de *discours*. C'est la maniere dont chacun s'exprime. C'est pourquoi il y a autant de stiles que de personnes qui écrivent [. . .]'.

A similar blurring of the distinction between spoken and written usages occurs with the term 'conversation', since many of the models of good conversation, notably those by Madeleine de Scudéry, Méré and Bouhours, appeared in printed form.[9] As Denis notes (1997: 26): '[conversation] englobe au XVIIe siècle non seulement une pratique sociale réelle, mais aussi un certain type de production littéraire, alors en vogue'. These published conversations are mostly carefully crafted and suggest a conscious selection of the elements to be included; they do not include, for example, the hesitations, repetitions or false starts which are so characteristic of spontaneous conversation. Denis concludes (1997: 28) that 'le dialogue littéraire est une réécriture, un remodelage du dialogue réel'. Fumaroli (1992: 14) likewise describes conversation as a 'genre *littéraire* oral' (my emphasis), which requires the mastery of inventive and linguistic skills and of the appropriate accompanying gestures, while still giving the impression of spontaneity and improvisation (see section 4.3).[10] A range of works concerned with conversation was published during the century; alongside the comments of grammarians and rhetoricians, and the model conversations by literary authors, there were a number of courtesy manuals and other works on conversational skills (e.g. Bary (1662), Vaumorière (1688); Callières (1693), Bellegarde (1698, 1700); see Strosetzki (1978)). Different views were expressed as to which style is appropriate for conversation; thus while Leven de Templery considers a simple style should be employed, Renaud favours instead use of his middle level of style.

As in the case of *discours familier* discussed above, there is also a close relationship between conversation and letter-writing in seventeenth-century France (see also section 4.3.2). This is evident from the way Mme de Sévigné describes her letters to her daughter: 'Ce sont des conversations que vos lettres; je vous parle et vous me répondez' (1680, cited from FRANTEXT). Once again, we should not, however, think of these letters being in any sense a literal transcription of a conversation.[11]

---

[9] See also Furetière definition of 'conversation': 'Entretien familier qu'on a avec ses amis dans les visites, dans les promenades [. . .] Conversation, se dit dans le même sens des assemblées de plusieurs personnes sçavantes & polies. Les *conversations* des Sçavants instruisent beaucoup: celles des Dames polissent la jeunesse. Mademoiselle de Scuderi, le Chevalier de Meré, ont fait imprimer de belles *conversations*.'

[10] Madeleine de Scudéry comments in her conversation entitled 'De parler trop ou trop peu et comment il faut parler': 'Car comme ordinairement les livres ne parlent pas comme les gens parlent en conversation, il ne faut pas non plus parler en conversation, comme les livres' (Denis 1998: 95).

[11] Letters were also the subject of a number of works, including those which furnished model letters such as La Serre's *Secrétaire de la Cour, ou la Manière d'écrire selon le temps* (1623), which ran to some forty editions in the course of the century. The century witnessed a wide range of different styles of letter, including Balzac's formal letters alongside the more informal letters of Mme de Sévigné to her daughter.

A final term to consider is *entretien*. This has a wide range of meanings of course, but can be used as a synonym for conversation (cf. Furetière's (1690) definition, 'Entretien, se dit aussi de la conversation. Ces deux Messieurs ont eu ensemble un long *entretien* sur vostre chapitre [. . .]').[12] Bouhours's *Entretiens*, published in 1671, illustrate that this term may also be used to denote carefully crafted conversations (Bouhours 1962).

What use is made of the different potential labels to refer to spoken usages by the major dictionaries of the century? It is striking that if we search the electronic versions of Nicot (1606) and Cotgrave (1611) for use of the terms *discours*, *discours familier*, *entretien*, *entretien familier*, *conversation*, *en parlant* and *en e(s)crivant*, in no case is reference made to usage specific to spoken language in contrast to written usage, suggesting a lack of interest in differences of usage according to medium in these two works.[13] In the dictionaries of Richelet (1680, henceforth R), Furetière (1690, F) and the Academy (1694, A) the term *discours* alone is also not used in this way, but rather the expression *discours familier* (the expression occurs in total twice in R, twelve times in F and on 36 occasions in A). In one of Richelet's comments there appears to be a contrast with written usage (+ *Oratoire*: 'Congrégation des *Péres de l'Oratoire*. Le mot d'*oratoire* en ce sens ne se dit guere seul que dans le discours familier, car en écrivant on dira toujours la congrégation des Prêtres de l'oratoire [. . .]'), whilst in the other, which discusses the expression *Gentilhomme à simple tonsure*, marked with both a cross and an asterisk (see section 3.2.2), usage is further limited to contexts where the expression is used 'par raillerie'. In Furetière's case, no explicit contrast is made with written usage, and indeed on one occasion (*oratoire*) a distinction is made between *discours familier* and *style oratoire*. The verb (*se*) *dire* co-occurs with it on seven occasions, *figurément* twice, and *en raillerie* once. Furetière also favours the expression *discours ordinaire*, but this expression often seems to refer to a non-technical usage. Usage in A of the label *discours familier*, which occurs frequently in the expression '(que) dans le discours familier', is equally ambiguous as to whether medium as well as register is being referred to; on one occasion (*épleuré, ée, éploré, ée*) a contrast is made with *style soustenu*. None of the three major monolingual dictionaries employs *entretien* on its own to refer to spoken usages; however, in this case, the expression *entretien familier* also does not appear relevant (occurring only once in R in the definition of *conversation*, four times in F and five times in A), since on no occasion is a specific contrast made between written and spoken usage.

---

[12] Beugnot (1971) notes that works featuring the terms *discours* and *harangues* were particularly common in 1610–20, while the fashion for dialogues and *entretiens* peaked in 1680–90.

[13] *Dictionnaires des XVIe et XVIIe siècles*, Champion Electronique, 1998.

Turning now to the use of *conversation*, in the thirty-six relevant usages in R,[14] only very rarely does *conversation* appear on its own. In the majority of occurrences, usage in conversation is coupled either with an indication of register (*stile familier, stile bas*), of style (*stile simple, burlesque*), or of tone, and notably with *en riant, en plaisant, en raillant* etc.; for example:

+ Tripotage [. . .] ne peut entrer que dans la conversation en plaisant & dans le stile le plus bas.
+ Bâailleur [*Rems sur le dict*] [. . .] est fort bas & il ne se dit qu'en riant dans la conversation.

On only one occasion is there a specific contrast made with written usage (*Raconteur*, see below). In F only six of the fifty occurrences of the term *conversation* are cases where the lexicographer signals a usage particular to that medium; on two occasions the expression *conversation ordinaire* is employed, but there is never a specific contrast with written usage. Of the twenty-three relevant occurrences of *conversation* in A, nearly half are in the expression *conversation familiere* and very frequently conversation is cited as the only possible place that a word or expression may be used (e.g. *Radoterie*: 'Il n'a guere d'usage que dans la conversation'; *Sermoner*: 'Il n'a guere d'usage que dans la conversation familiere').

Finally, it is occasionally possible to glean some evidence of the difference between written and spoken usage in the three monolingual dictionaries by searching for the expression *en e(s)crivant*.[15] On seven occasions in R a specific contrast is made between the two media; for example:

Christofle [. . .] En parlant familiérement on dit *Chrestofle*, & en écrivant ou prêchant, on se sert de Christofle.

Raconteur. [. . .] Il pourroit passer en rïant & dans la conversation, mais on croit qu'en écrivant il auroit de la peine a échaper.

Elsewhere, Richelet notes that usage of a word or expression is permitted in both media:

On. Se met en un sens nouveau pour la prémiere personne *je*; car pour dire *je songerai à vos interêts*, je dirai fort bien en écrivant, ou parlant familierement, *on songera à vos interêts, on aura soin de vous*.

In F *en e(s)crivant* is never used to make a contrast with spoken usage, whilst in A it is used thus on only one occasion (*Index*).

---

[14] Some of the references are to Méré's *Conversations*, for example.
[15] The expression *en parlant* cannot be searched for in the same way, since it is very frequently used as a simple means of saying 'when referring to'.

2.3   The relationship between written and spoken French

Whilst grammarians such as Maupas (1618), Oudin (1632) and Irson (1662) make no explicit references to the difference between spoken and written usages of French, the *remarqueurs* are interested in variation according to medium. The relationship between spoken and written French is discussed on a number of occasions in Vaugelas's *Remarques* (1647). The question is raised from the outset in his definition of good usage as 'la façon de parler de la plus saine partie de la Cour, *conformément* à la façon d'escrire de la plus saine partie des Auteurs du temps' (Preface II, 3; my emphasis). The idea that written and spoken usage should mirror each other is repeated on a number of occasions (e.g. 1647: 395, *482–*483, 519); indeed, Vaugelas claims that the worst error which can be committed when writing is not to write as one speaks, and therefore the different registers of speech should match the corresponding written registers (509–11). Speech is said to take priority over writing since it precedes it: 'puis que celle qui est escrite n'est que son image, comme l'autre est l'image de la pensée'; the work of authors is like a seal or verification of spoken usage, and may be invoked in cases of doubtful usage (Preface II, 5; IV, 3).[16] However, alongside this model which identifies written and spoken usage, there is a different conception of the relationship between the two media, which seems to suggest that spoken language is more flexible and spontaneous, for example in creating neologisms (1647: 569, 446, cf. Preface II, 5), and that greater demands are placed on written language. For example, discussing the use of what he terms 'certaines particules' (e.g. *l'on* rather than *on*), Vaugelas comments that they are not really used in speech, 'mais que le stile qui est beaucoup plus seuere demande pour vne plus grande perfection'; their usage can therefore only be acquired by reading good authors (Preface VI). In his treatment of solecisms he notes that mistakes are made in the conjugation of verbs when speaking, which he has never seen written (e.g. *i'alla* for *i'allay*, *il allit* for *il alla*). In practice, then, a number of observations are devoted to noting differences between written and spoken French; for example:

Nu-pieds. Ce mot se dit ordinairement en parlant, mais jamais les bons Autheurs ne l'escriuent [. . .] (1647: 66)

S'il faut dire, Si c'estoit moy qui eusse fait cela, ou *si c'estoit moy qui eust fait cela.* [. . .] Mais comme *auous* ne s'escrit jamais; quoy qu'il se die, aussi il se pourroit faire que l'on diroit *eust,* en parlant, mais qu'il faudroit tousjours escrire *eusse,* & *eusses,* aux deux personnes. Et c'est le plus seur d'en vser ainsi, puis que mesmes ceux qui approuuent *eust,* ne desapprouuent pas l'autre [. . .] (1647: 89)

---

[16] Note, however, that in the case of *pluriel* Vaugelas (1647: 470) argues in favour of this spelling against the established spelling *plurier,* even though the pronunciation does not allow one to determine whether there should be an 'r' or an 'l' at the end.

Il n'y a rien de tel, il n'y a rien tel. Tous deux sont bons, & il semble qu'en parlant on dit plustost *il n'y a rien tel*, que l'autre, mais qu'en escriuant, on dit plustost *il n'y a rien de tel*. Pour moy je voudrois tousjours escrire ainsi. (1647: 323)

In addition, rather than seeing a correspondence between the registers of speech and writing, there is a suggestion that Vaugelas identifies speech with the lowest registers of writing:

Y, auec les pronoms. [. . .] on dit, *enuoyez-y moy*, & non pas, *enuoyez-m'y, portez-y moy*, & non, *portez-m'y*, mais oüy bien, *enuoyez-nous y, enuoyez-l'y, portez-nous-y, portez l'y*. Cela se dit en parlant, mais ie ne voudrois pas l'escrire, que dans vn stile fort bas. (1647: 95)

Ce dit-il, ce dit-on. On dit tous les jours l'vn & l'autre en parlant, mais on ne le doit point dire en escriuant, que dans le stile bas. (1647: 308)

Dupleix points out some of the inconsistencies in Vaugelas's thinking and challenges a number of his principles. He argues that the view that writing should reflect speech may be countered in two ways: first, greater care should be taken over writing, and secondly, French spelling does not consistently represent pronunciation (1651: 118). Moreover, he questions Vaugelas's insistence on the priority of the spoken word, noting that sometimes things are written before they are spoken, notably by preachers, lawyers and doctors (1651: 28). He makes very few comments himself about differences in usage between the two media.[17]

Bouhours's (1675, 1693) comments on differences according to media at times undermine a simple distinction between written and spoken usages. In some cases this is because informal written styles such as letters and notes are aligned with spoken usages (e.g. *opera* (1675: 165–6), *intrigue* (1693: 232)); in others it is because more formal or serious spoken contexts are said to behave like written French (1675: 296, 324). A typical example is his observation on *rendre graces, rendre des actions de grace* (1675: 324–5); the former is said to be 'plus de la conversation & du stile mediocre', whereas the latter is deemed more appropriate for written language, 'sur tout dans le stile sublime'. Again the formulation of this observation 'En écrivant, nous *disons* [. . .]' (my emphasis) suggests that care must be taken in interpreting the terminology. Bouhours believes that many new words and expressions originate in speech, from which

---

[17] Similarly, Buffet (1668: 70) simply repeats Vaugelas's comment on *il n'y a rien tel, il n'y a rien de tel*. Bérain (1675) implies that written and spoken usage should closely match each other, in that many of his observations are entitled 'S'il faut dire & écrire [. . .]' When he points out errors which occur in speech and which are to be avoided (the use of *alle* or *a* as the feminine singular subject pronoun or *ils* as the feminine plural subject pronoun), he adds that they must also be avoided in writing (1675: 29–30). In addition he favours changing spelling to reflect pronunciation, most notably in those cases where 'oi' is pronounced [ɛ] (see Chapter 3). Neither Alemand (1688) nor Tallemant (1698) are greatly concerned with differences between spoken and written French.

they may spread into more general usage (1675: 298–9; 1693: 393). This is challenged by Ménage (1676: 372), who maintains that most words are created in writing and remain there before 'descending' to conversational usage. Both Ménage and Andry de Boisregard use the expression 'discours familier' on some twenty occasions, but it is very rarely explicitly contrasted with written usage. Like Bouhours, Andry at times associates conversational usage with the usage deemed appropriate for letters (1689: 172, 366–7).

The difference between written and spoken usage is clearly an important parameter for some of the *remarqueurs*, notably Vaugelas and Bouhours (see Ayres-Bennett 2003). It also features in the three principal monolingual dictionaries of the period (although not in Nicot and Cotgrave, see above), albeit much less prominently than other types of variation. Moreover, as was clear in the last section (2.2), whilst the lexicographers devote some attention to specifying which words and expressions are appropriate to this medium, the labels used to refer to spoken language are often ambiguous or coupled with other style labels. Bray (1990: 47) notes that for the letter 'P', only five entries in R relate to differences of medium, compared to 617 which relate to professional or social activities, seventy-eight which are said to be typical of certain contexts, registers or styles ('burlesque', 'stile simple & comique', etc.), and thirty-two which are associated with a particular social class. This is confirmed by my own analysis of the letters A and B which together constitute about one-tenth of the total dictionary; here there are only three clear examples of spoken usage being indicated. While sometimes a simple contrast is made between written and spoken usage (e.g. *passereau*: 'ce mot s'écrit, mais il ne se dit guere en parlant'), at other times questions of medium once more intersect with questions of register or genre:

Pourceau: Ce mot signifie, *porc*, *cochon*; mail il ne se dit guere en parlant familierement & sérieusement, & en sa place on dit ordinairement *porc* ou *cochon*, mais en écrivant on se sert du mot de *pourceau*. On emploie aussi ce mot de *pourceau* quand on parle familierement & qu'on rit, ou qu'on injurie.

+Bretauder: Ce mot se dit quelquefois en riant, mais il ne s'écrit pas, & tout au plus il ne peut entrer que dans le comique, ou le bas burlesque.

Rey (1990: 17) suggests that the axis of spoken versus written usage is very rarely exploited in F; it is, as we have seen, also employed relatively little in A.

2.4   Sources of spoken French

The attempt to identify sources of spoken French brings with it the potential danger of circularity; it is tempting to try to list in advance features which are typical of seventeenth-century spoken French and then to consider those texts which display these features as the best reflections of oral usage. As

the starting point for this discussion I shall take Ernst's (1980) proposed list
of sources of seventeenth-century spoken French (cf. Ayres-Bennett 2000).
One of the six principal types of source noted by Ernst is metalinguistic texts,
which I discussed above (section 2.3) and in Chapter 1 (section 1.2.1). Note
that his list does not attempt to include works such as pronunciation treatises or discussions of orthographic reform which may be searched for data on
seventeenth-century pronunciation;[18] perhaps paradoxically, it has proved easier to reconstruct non-standard pronunciations than morpho-syntactic features
(see, for example, Thurot 1881–83; Rosset 1911, 1972; Tolmer 1938; Cohen
1946, 1954; Martinet 1974; Straka 1985; Ayres-Bennett 1990; Dagenais 1991;
Lodge 1996).

Ernst's list highlights the difficulties of separating out different parameters
of variation, and of deciding whether to place emphasis on the spoken nature
of the source, on its register, or on the characteristics of the speaker. These
problems are evident in the first source listed by Ernst – historical transcriptions
of authentic speech – since the key example here is the journal of Héroard,
which records in quasi-phonetic script the speech of the Dauphin, the future
Louis XIII, between 1605 and 1610 when the child was aged between three
and nine years old (Ernst 1985). This is an isolated, if not unique, document,
which makes it at once more precious and more difficult to interpret. Should a
non-standard feature of the Dauphin's speech be considered typical of spoken
French of the day, of a particular informal register, of high-class usage, of the
usage of a young child or as idiolectal (see Chapter 5; cf. Ayres-Bennett 1994)?
Héroard's general lack of concern with transcribing accurately the speech of
the adults surrounding the young prince makes it at times difficult to adjudicate
between these different hypotheses (but see section 2.5.4).

Ernst's second source is model dialogues in didactic texts. Radtke (1994)
has made the most comprehensive study of this material to date; he analysed a
corpus of twenty-two seventeenth-century conversation manuals or collections
of model dialogues intended for foreigners wanting to learn French, using a
historical pragmatic approach. These dialogues are often bi- or multi-lingual.
According to Radtke, model dialogues offer the best reflection of spoken usage

---

[18] Other possible sources include works such as Marin Mersenne's *Harmonie universelle (1636)*
(Lesure 1963), which, particularly in Book 6 Part IV of the *Traitez des consonances, des disso-
nances, des genres, des modes, & de la composition*, discusses questions of French pronunciation. Salazar (1999) notes that interest in the human voice ('la voix' as opposed to 'oralité' or
'parole') or vocal expression manifested itself in a number of ways in the seventeenth century,
including in early work on acoustics, in works on the art of pronouncing and the appropriate use
of volume, tone and pitch, whether in formal state discourse or in sermons, and in discussions
of the relationship between song and speaking (see also Salazar 1995). Song texts and opera
libretti might also be fruitfully pursued as sources of spoken French, although the songs made
popular by Gaultier Garguille, for example (Fournier 1858), were traditional anonymous verses
which contain much repetition, and are therefore not useful as sources of spontaneous discourse.

since they aim to teach spoken French, use natural conversational situations (e.g. eating and drinking, travel, shopping), and are relatively numerous, allowing comparison between the different texts. In his view they are particularly valuable in shedding light on pragmatic features, and on the speakers' attitude towards what they are saying.[19] For example, they contain numerous instances of *Gliederungssignale*, that is, words and expressions which help structure the discourse. Typical are the following exclamations and interjections used by La Faye (1608): 'hai quoy!'; 'Eh bien Monsieur!'; 'Morbleu si ne galoppe pas bien'; 'Ho, ho, bellement!' In addition, there are often reformulations or rewordings of the same idea; for instance in La Faye's third dialogue (1608) we find 'En mon logis mesme, la ou ie demeure, ou ie fay ma demeurance'. His fifth dialogue contains a number of proverbs and proverbial expressions, all of which add to the impression of informality. The extended use of French in specific contexts also allows the examination of morpho-syntactic features; for example, Evang (1984) considers the use of the *passé simple* and the *passé composé* in eight volumes of seventeenth-century dialogues.

These dialogues are, however, not entirely unproblematic as sources of spoken French, as Radtke himself admits (even if he tends to ignore the difficulties in his analysis of their macro- and micro-structures). First, the conversations are not spontaneous but are planned or elaborated in advance, and indeed are often idealized. Their authenticity is compromised by the fact they are transcribed using the conventions of written language; speakers are made to utter complete sentences[20] and there are very few pauses, false starts or hesitations which we know to be characteristic of unplanned speech. No information is available on intonation or other prosodic features. At times the dialogues appear conventionalized or even ritualized, especially in their openings, or in the formulae used in greetings etc. While the reformulations may be useful, the inclusion of alternatives for didactic purposes detracts from the naturalness of the conversation. Other difficulties include the fact that the majority of the speakers are young, aristocratic and male, and are placed in stereotypical situations such as the arrival at an inn.[21] There are also questions as to the currency of some of the material, both because there are occasionally whole scenes which are virtually identical in different dialogues (for example between La Faye (1608) and Wodroephe (1623)), suggesting a common written source rather than personal

---

[19] This subject will not be further discussed here since it is admirably covered by Radtke. Radtke (1994: 343) makes the interesting suggestion – which merits further exploration – that there is less continuity of usage between the seventeenth and twentieth centuries with respect to pragmatic usage than regarding the phonology or morphology of the French of the two periods.

[20] Radtke (1994: 110), rather controversially, seems to suggest that this use of complete sentences is not just due to the fact that we have written records of spoken language; rather he notes a reduction in this usage between 1580 and 1750.

[21] Oudin's dialogues (1650) include a slightly greater range of characters including a mule-driver, a woman inn-keeper and pages.

observation, and because some of them go through many reprints or new editions. Finally the authors of these dialogues are often foreigners who do not themselves have a complete command of French; it is striking that 'sic' is used repeatedly by Radtke in his quotations. Moreover, we know relatively little about the authors of these dialogues or the circumstances in which they were composed.

Ernst's third source is (fictitious) direct speech in plays. A number of linguists have commented on difficulties with this source. Romaine (1988: 1462) notes that, while quoted or indirect speech in texts may appropriate to speech to some extent, it is not speech, and the conventions of the genre need to be taken into account. Similarly, Schlieben-Lange (1983: 38) cites Henne, who comments that any dramatist who writes dialogue is in a sense an analyst of spoken language: the language has already been interpreted and adapted to fit literary conventions. Dramatists often work with stereotypes which have to be easily recognizable on stage.

Historians of seventeenth-century French have particularly focused on Molière's representation of the linguistic usage of different strata of society: Dauzat (1927: 37) and Steinmeyer (1979: 23–4), for example, have both underlined the significance of this evidence of variation. This view is neatly summarised by Lodge (1991: 485):

The sensitivity of Molière's observations of a range of varieties of seventeenth-century French makes him a valuable source for the linguistic historian interested in the development of spoken norms [. . .] in that period.

One of the advantages of Molière's characterization of non-standard speech is that this is achieved not just by phonological and lexical means, as is so often the case with literary texts, but also by the inclusion of morpho-syntactic traits.[22] The best-known example of this is perhaps the portrayal of peasant speech in *Dom Juan* (see, for instance, Lodge 1991). Despite this, a number of scholars including Ernst, Stéfanini and myself have expressed reservations about considering dialogue which has been constructed with a view to making people laugh as evidence of authentic spoken language of the period. The ability to transform and intensify linguistic reality to create humorous caricatures is surely part of Molière's comic genius (see also section 4.5.2). These caricatures may be created either through exaggeration or by using features which are no longer current. For instance, Fleischman (1996: 403) notes how the clause-initial particle *si*, which seems to have been virtually extinct by the fifteenth century, is employed by Molière as a quaint archaism to characterize uneducated

---

[22] Studies of later texts such as Caylus's *théâtre poissard* (Hausmann 1980) and Marivaux's *Le Télémaque travesti* (Valli 1984) support the view that the linguistic characterization is achieved through the selection of lexical and phonological features, and that morpho-syntactic features are rare or even absent.

or dialect speech. Moreover the same linguistic stereotypes are passed from text to text. Stéfanini (1994: 195) comments how the portrayal of peasant speech becomes more and more conventionalized from Cyrano to Molière to generate easy laughter, and he concludes 'la littérature française classique ignore ainsi la quasi totalité de la nation, ses langues et ses dialectes'. For example, comparison of the speech of Molière's peasants Pierrot and Charlotte in Act 2 Scene 1 of *Dom Juan* with that of the peasant Gareau in Cyrano de Bergerac's *Le Pédant joué* or indeed with the representation of peasant speech in the *Agréables Conférences* (see below) points clearly to increasing stylization over the period. Conversely, linguistic features may be absent from theatre because they are not yet stereotyped; for instance, it may be that the omission of negative *ne* is attested in Héroard, but not in the theatre of the period, because it is not yet overtly stigmatized (cf. Martineau and Mougeon 2003: 126).

It is important to be clear about the nature of our reservations here, since convergence between sources of different types will generally be viewed in a positive light. Why is the convergence between Molière, Cyrano and the anonymous author of the *Agréables Conférences* not equally evidence of the authenticity of the representation?[23] As we have already noted, a number of features used to characterize peasant speech in these texts are considered archaic by the writers of the metalinguistic texts. For example, the substitution of [z] for [r] (as in *Pazis* for *Paris*) was well established in the sixteenth century and probably archaic by the time Molière was writing, suggesting that the features were chosen as being so strongly non-standard that there was no doubt in the audience's mind that the speech was intended to be ridiculous. Paradoxically, then, the selection of these features by writers of comic texts may occasionally be taken as evidence to suggest that they were no longer in current usage. In addition, Garapon (1957: 225) has noted that the range of morpho-syntactic features used by Molière is similarly restricted and highly marked: 'il multiplie les "j'avons" et les "je disons" qui ont toujours suffi à donner l'allusion du patois aux Français ne sachant que le français'.

Discussion of the portrayal of peasant speech in comedies brings us back to the difficulties of separating questions of medium from differences of register. Another related potential source of low-register usage is the *comédies burlesques* which will be discussed in Chapter 3.

The fourth source listed by Ernst (1980) is direct speech in other genres, and particularly in narrative texts. Many of the same difficulties arise with the so-called *romans réalistes* of Scarron, Sorel and Furetière, which we will discuss in Chapter 3. Scarron's *Roman comique*, for instance, may contain some low-register terms to lend an air of authenticity to the dialogue, but the syntax

---

[23] There is also, of course, a difference between convergence *within* one type of source and convergence between the different types of sources we are considering.

tends towards the clarity promoted by the *remarqueurs*, and familiar language is juxtaposed with elevated style. While then, in theory, such dialogue may be exploited as a source of informal speech, in practice the harvest, notably in terms of morpho-syntactic features, is very meagre. Other forms of satire and burlesque, which tend not to be very different in this respect, will also be discussed in Chapter 3.[24]

Finally under this category, there are the literary representations of conversations (see, for example, Goldsmith 1988, Strosetzki 1978). We will return to Madeleine de Scudéry's conversations in Chapter 4, but we have already noted the artificial and literary nature of many published conversations. Denis (1997: 28) argues that there are significant differences between what she terms 'dialogues littéraires' and 'conversations authentiques' with respect to both the treatment of prosodic features and the representation of the linguistic content. While Madeleine de Scudéry clearly aims to include some features of orality such as rewordings, other typical features such as slips of the tongue, long pauses and mumblings are absent, once more suggesting stylization.

Ernst's final source of spoken French is not a textual source, but rather comparative reconstruction, similar to the technique employed to reconstruct Vulgar Latin. This is at once the most difficult, and also potentially the most fruitful and most exciting source. The aim is to look at the French spoken overseas or the creoles formed on the basis of spoken French taken abroad by colonizers in the seventeenth century. If common features can be identified in these varieties, notably if they occur in areas which are geographically scattered, it may be possible to hypothesize that these features were present in the common source, namely seventeenth-century spoken French (cf. Chaudenson 1973, 1994; Valdman 1979). The seventeenth century is a particularly fertile area for such investigation since French was taken to three principal areas which are geographically widely separated: North America, notably Acadia and Quebec; Central America, notably Caribbean islands such as Guadeloupe, Martinique, Dominica and Saint Lucia; and the Indian Ocean islands of Réunion and Madagascar.

Ernst (1980) provides the following exemplification of his methodology (cf. Chaudenson 1973). To convey the notion of committing suicide in Mauritian or Réunion Creole, the expression [tjesōkor] ('tuer son corps') is used. Significantly, a similar expression is used in the creole of Martinique, namely *tuéco*. In Old French *mes cors*, *ses cors*, etc. ('my body', 'his body') could be employed

---

[24] Maigne (1992) argues that Tallemant des Réaux's *Historiettes* (c. 1657) provides many examples of spoken language, especially provincial usage, since these purport to contain citations of speech. Here again what we tend to find is the citation of odd words and utterances, particularly *bons mots*, rather than a sustained attempt to transcribe spoken French. Typically the syntax is much more standardized: note, for example, the presence of *ne* in negative clauses, the use of inversion in questions, the occurrence of the imperfect subjunctive, and *cela* alongside *ça*.

in the place of certain personal pronouns, but according to Brunot (1905–53: II, 414), this usage disappeared in the sixteenth century. Since, however, these expressions occur in creoles which are from very different parts of the world, it might be legitimate to hypothesize that this expression still existed in the spoken usage which constituted the common source for these creoles.[25] A different example is cited by Chaudenson (1973) who considers the use of [mun], [mõd] or [mɔn] in Indian Ocean and Caribbean creoles, and in Canadian French, in the expression *grand monde* to refer to an individual, as well as to people in general. Once again the evidence suggests that 'monde' could be used in this way in seventeenth-century spoken French (cf. Stein 1987: 64). In this case the comparative data are confirmed by Furetière's entry on 'Monde: se dit aussi d'une seule personne', but this is not always the case; indeed data may be available only from creoles.[26]

While this seems an interesting line of enquiry, it raises fundamental questions about which variety of French was the source of the French or creole spoken in the various colonies, and how the varieties of French or creoles of the colonies were created and subsequently developed. There has been extensive debate as to the origins of Canadian French, for example, given the provenance of the early colonizers from different regions of northern France and early reports of the 'quality' and relative linguistic uniformity of the French spoken by the colonists (see especially Mougeon and Beniak 1994: 1–55).[27] In simple terms, some scholars, such as Dulong and Barbaud, believe that many of the colonizers were patois speakers, a significant proportion of whom knew no French.[28] If this is the case, we need to enquire when, why and how these speakers abandoned their dialect. On the other hand, scholars such as Poirier, Chaudenson and Valdman maintain that the vast majority of colonizers spoke French before they left France, even if they were also patois speakers. According to this account, those who left for Canada were not typical of their class (many of the early settlers were craftsmen, city dwellers, and relatively more educated than the general population), and spoke a kind of *koine*, variously thought of as being similar to *français populaire* (as Chaudenson seems to suggest), mixing Ile-de-France and Picard features (Wittmann's view), as a mesolect[29] (which

---

[25] Chaudenson (1994: 176–8) cites a similar case, the formation of the future tense.

[26] Chaudenson, Mougeon and Beniak (1993: 41) give the example of *en haut (de)* and *en bas (de)* which are used as alternatives to *sur/sus/dessus* and *sous/(en) dessous (de)* in varieties of the French of North America (the Acadian French of Louisiana and creoles).

[27] For instance, Brunot cites Bacqueville de la Potherie (1698) on the French of Quebec: 'On parle ici parfaitement bien, sans mauvais accent. Quoiqu'il y ait un mélange de presque toutes les provinces de France, on ne saurait distinguer le parler d'aucune dans les canadiennes' (Mougeon and Beniak 1994: 133).

[28] Fewer than 7000 Frenchmen went to Canada in the seventeenth century and about half of these emigrated in the decade 1663–73 (Asselin and McLaughlin 1981).

[29] The term 'acrolect' refers to the prestige or standard variety (or lect), 'basolect' to the variety most remote from this prestige variety, and 'mesolects' to intermediate varieties.

Hull calls *français maritime*), or as a kind of regional French (favoured by Wolf and by Morin). If this second broad hypothesis is correct – and the balance of opinion seems to favour this line – then the common spoken source or *koine* will be of interest to us. It is nevertheless important to check that superficial similarities are not the result of independent developments or innovations rather than a common origin. In this respect early records of Canadian French, such as the account book of the Quebec miller Pierre Simon, called Delorme (1662–1711), are particularly valuable (Juneau and Poirier 1973), as is the corpus of texts currently being collected for the project 'Microvariation linguistique et épistolarité en Nouvelle-France' under the direction of France Martineau.[30]

Even more fundamental questions have been raised about the creation of creoles, which continues to be a subject of intense debate. There is far from general agreement with Chaudenson's position that these developed from the popular spoken language of the colonizers. Many consider creolization to be a special case of catastrophic change and radical restructuring which is the result of contact between typologically different languages, and the product of the use of a pidgin as a simplified transactional language. Some indeed have argued that they involve the relexification of an original Portuguese trading pidgin. Other hypotheses include the view that creoles are 'mixed languages' created from European and African languages, or that they are basically African languages with European lexical items inserted into their essentially African sentence structures. Problems then arise about which African language could have provided the syntactic structures – difficulties which are heightened by the fact that it is difficult to establish parallels between creole and African features.

If we adopt the view that creoles do develop from pidgins, we are still left with differing opinions as to how this might have happened. One controversial proposal has been Bickerton's bioprogram hypothesis (e.g. Bickerton 1981, 1984). According to this view, children, faced with degenerate language input, rely on their innate grammar to create rules for a new language. The grammar of the new language will then draw on universal features of the innate grammar, but will derive its lexicon from the data that the child hears. All creoles therefore share the same basic grammatical features since they have all been created by the same process.

---

[30] See http://www.uottawa.ca/academic/arts/lettres/nf/index.htm. It is striking, however, that there are very few letters for the entire period 1666–1749, and none at all for the seventeenth century. In his study of the pronunciation of Canadian French as represented in historical archives, Juneau (1972) analysed about 1000 legal documents, inventories, account books, letters etc. dating from the seventeenth to the nineteenth centuries. The majority of these documents are formulaic and therefore of little use as sources for the topics we have selected. Another interesting document which is rather late for our study is Marie Morin's *Histoire simple et veritable* (Legendre 1979), which she wrote over a period of twenty-eight years commencing in 1697.

All this means that we must be wary of evidence derived from creoles alone; once again it will be more convincing if there is seen to be convergence between different types of evidence. That said, Chaudenson (1994) notes that great care must be taken when comparing what he terms 'français marginaux' such as the French of North America – which are still essentially French varieties – with creoles, which are autonomous systems. Even when a common feature has been identified, a decision has to be made whether this is a historically datable and locatable trait, a regional feature, or a permanent tendency of popular French.

All the sources we have considered for spoken French are at once potentially very valuable and inherently problematic. Before I outline which sources I intend to employ in this chapter, it is worth briefly considering other possible textual sources not included by Ernst. One possibility is legal documents, including depositions, verbatim reports of court evidence such as in defamation cases, or inquisitorial material from witchcraft interrogations. Davis's (1988) study of sixteenth-century *lettres de rémission* sounds a warning note about the way these narratives were composed. While the narratives purport to contain direct citations of speech, they have narrative, and indeed 'fictional', qualities since the events leading up to the crime are structured into a coherent account. A *notaire du roi* and his clerks would begin by agreeing a draft with the defendant or his representative and then a final version would be written on parchment; these legal scribes would probably have been responsible for much of the wording, including the opening and closing formulae. As Davis notes, the narrative may even have been related in the local dialect but committed to paper in a standardized French. Muchembled (1991) makes the same point in his discussion of witchcraft trials: here too the legal clerk simplified or modified the oral account given by the illiterate suspect. All this suggests that these documents are flawed as sources of spontaneous spoken usage. My own research in departmental archives uncovered much legal jargon, but very few apparently verbatim comments. A work such as *Les Proces civil, et criminel* (Le Brun de la Rochette 1618) contains a section on 'les Injures', which includes their definition and types, but no examples. While legal archives seem potentially to be a fruitful source of material, to quote Chaudenson (1994: 174), 'la recherche de telles attestations s'apparente à celle de l'or'.

Similar problems are associated with investigating *canards*, occasional publications which report *faits divers*. While they are often narrated in the first person and report testimonies of the events recorded, they also clearly mix fact with fiction and employ rhetorical devices (see Seguin 1964, Arnould 1995). Likewise, the *cahiers de doléances* of the Third Estate were a synthesis made by the bailiff of the registers of the parish deputies who themselves came from a wide range of professions, including labourers (see, for example, Durand 1966). Finally, we might mention the genre known as *ana*, the name given to the posthumous collections of casual remarks and anecdotes of literary figures

Category	Reality of speech event	Speaker–writer identity	Temporal distance speech-record	Characteristic text type
1. Recorded	Real, unique	Different	Immediate	Interview transcripts, trial records
2. Recalled	Real, unique	Different	Later	Ex-slave narratives
3. Imagined	Hypothetic, unique	Identical	Immediate	Letters, diaries
4. Observed	Usually real, unique	Different	Later	Commentaries
5. Invented	Hypothetic, unspecified	Not applicable	Unspecified	Literary dialect

Figure 2.1

such as Ménage, which, in Wild's eyes, represent 'la transcription du discours oral' (Wild 2001: 21). However, she quickly modifies this statement; while they clearly derive from an oral source, Wild notes that a degree of 'transposition' is necessary, since oral style cannot faithfully be represented in writing:

Pour conserver à son texte les qualités du discours oral, les saillies, l'esprit, la drôlerie, il lui faut chercher à produire des effets précis avec des moyens stylistiques qui ne sont pas ceux de l'énonciation originale [. . .] Toute une stratégie d'écriture est en jeu.

Thus the *Ménagiana* (Ménage 1693) does not transcribe Ménage's speech word for word, but rather aims to convey in writing the tone of Ménage's comments.

This list is not intended to be exhaustive: we have already mentioned the records of more formal rhetorical discourse such as pulpit oratory and the ceremonial language of the French Academy (see also Radtke's list of sources, 1994: 21–2). Moreover, it is often difficult to decide where best to discuss a particular source. Should dialogues in popular patois, for instance, be considered primarily for their oral qualities or as representations of low-register and low-class usage?

Schneider (2002) outlines five possible categories of written texts which may be used as a basis for variationist studies and which he places on a continuum of increasing distance between the original speech event and its written record. The characteristics of each may be summarized as in Figure 2.1. The boundaries between these categories are fuzzy, as Schneider himself admits, and not all of the categories are equally relevant when we come to consider the seventeenth-century textual evidence. As regards the first two categories, which are closest to the actual speech event, Héroard's record of the Dauphin's speech is likely to be partly Recalled – that is, not taken down on the spot but noted later from memory, possibly supported by notes – and partly Recorded. Similarly the model dialogues are largely Imagined, since they record hypothetical, unique speech events, but are not immediate and the speaker(s) and writer are not identical. Our metalinguistic texts provide commentary on spoken usages (Observed), but they are not necessarily a comment on a real, unique event.

In this chapter I decided to focus – in conjunction with evidence from the metalinguistic texts and comparative evidence from French spoken overseas and creoles – on those texts which seem most clearly to represent spontaneous speech, such as the journal of the young Dauphin and, albeit to a lesser extent, the model dialogues.[31] These are also compared with usage in certain types of theatre, bearing in mind the importance of caricature in such works (Invented). Those texts which seem to me to have more 'written' qualities, such as popular literary texts, 'private texts' including journals, memoirs, autobiographies, *livres de raison* and travel accounts, will be discussed in the next chapter.[32] Particularly difficult to categorize are the Mazarinades, including the *Agréables Conférences*, since, as we shall see in the next chapter, these embrace a range of documents, including dialogues, letters, low-register pamphlets and burlesque verse. Finally, various types of works on conversation (see above), including literary conversations, and theoretical and didactic works will be reviewed in Chapter 4 when we consider women's conversation. Here too we will return to the question of letters. Whilst Bar (1981), like Schneider, sees letters as a possible source of spoken usages, it should be remembered that they are never intended to represent speech or be spoken.

2.5   Case studies

2.5.1   Introduction

In assessing possible sources and determining which traits appear to typify seventeenth-century spoken French, it is important to bear in mind that the 'reconstruction' of spoken French is particularly difficult since very often writers attempt to convey the 'spoken' quality of a text through a marked choice of phonetic and lexical features, and pay much less attention to variation in syntax. An additional problem concerns the way speech is almost always 'tidied up' when committed to paper, and the lack of the kind of transcription now typically employed by the researchers in Aix-en-Provence (see, for instance, Blanche-Benveniste and Jeanjean 1987).

---

[31] The dialogues analysed here are from Erondell (1969 [1605]), La Faye (1608) and Duez (1669). Since Duez 1669 comprises four dialogues, the same number was selected from the other two texts: dialogues 1, 4, 8 and 12 from Erondell, and the first four dialogues of La Faye.

[32] Schneider places private letters by semi-literate authors and other autobiographical records, such as diaries by semi-skilled writers, in his third category (Imagined), but he notes that this is often a disappointing source with the language appearing very standardized. Diaries are relatively untypical of semi-literate authors and there is also the difficulty of eliminating regional variation, which is very marked for our period (see Chapter 3 for further discussion).

Unsurprisingly, the largest number of remarks and observations which discuss differences between spoken and written French are concerned with the appropriate usage of particular words and expressions. There are over twenty of these, including discussion of the usage of *mais que* (Vaugelas 1647: 162), *opera* (Bouhours 1675: 165) and *scene* (Bouhours 1693: 193). In the domain of morphology, there are few comments regarding differences between spoken and written usages. Vaugelas (1647: 572) discusses the conjugation of the forms of the *passé simple* (see section 2.5.3); Bouhours (1675: 296) treats the status of synthetic superlative adjectives such as *grandissime, rarissime*, etc.; and Bérain (1675: 29–30) notes the usage in speech of *a, alle* and *ils* as feminine plural pronoun forms. Many of the observations devoted to differences in syntactic usage according to the medium examine very specific questions rather than addressing general issues; for example, Vaugelas comments on the use of *il n'y a rien (de) tel* (1647: 323), *ce dit-il, ce dit-on* (1647: 308), and *ce pour afin* (1647: 532). Of more general import we may note the discussion of questions of agreement (*si c'etoit moy qui eusse / eust fait cela* (Vaugelas 1647: 88), *c'est eux / ce sont eux* (Tallemant 1698: 137–8)); and of government (*verbes regissans deux cas, mis auec vn seul* (Vaugelas 1647: 79–80)). Here, as elsewhere, it is difficult to classify observations discretely as discussions of medium or of register. For example, the observation entitled *Tant & de si belles actions* (Vaugelas 1647: 348), which we will discuss in the next chapter along with other 'asymmetrical' constructions, notes that this type of construction is more acceptable in speech than in writing, while also characterizing it as 'vieux' and 'rude'.

In the sections below we will discuss a range of morphological and syntactic topics from different sources which have been identified as being of potential interest. First, there are those topics raised by the *remarqueurs*, such as the use in the same construction of a third person direct and indirect object pronoun, or the conjugation of the forms of the *passé simple*. Secondly, there are features which are said to be typical of contemporary spoken French – such as the use of *on* for *nous*, and the non-use of inversion in interrogative sentences[33] – the history of which we wished to examine with a view to determining whether these are recent innovations in modern spoken French or rather cases of long-standing differences in written and spoken usage. Thirdly, there is the case of features which are typical of creoles or non-metropolitan varieties; here the intention is to test whether there is evidence for their usage in the French spoken in France at the time of the colonization (verb periphrases).

---

[33] For a discussion of another example of this type, the non-use of *ne* in negative sentences, see Ayres-Bennett (1994).

2.5.2   Pronoun usage

In this section we will explore two questions. First we will consider very briefly the omission of the direct object personal pronoun when an indirect personal pronoun, and especially *lui* or *leur*, is used; second, we will examine whether there is evidence to suggest that *on* could already be used in place of *nous* in seventeenth-century spoken French.

The case of the omission of the third person direct object pronoun when there is also an indirect object pronoun, and especially *lui* or *leur*, is interesting since the authors of the metalinguistic texts confirm that, just as today, considerations of brevity, spontaneity and euphony dictate that different usages occur in speech and in writing. While Maupas and Oudin had recommended the omission of the accusative pronoun (Fournier 1998: 76), Vaugelas already criticizes its omission as a fault, typical, for example, of Amyot's usage. Although his examples are clearly written ones, there is a suggestion that this usage is particularly common in speech: 'parce que ce n'est qu'auec *luy* et *leur* qu'ils parlent ainsi, comme j'ay dit, à cause de la cacophonie des deux *l, l*' (Vaugelas 1647: 33). This point is developed by Tallemant (1698: 33), who maintains that the direct object pronoun is always omitted in conversation; on the other hand, its use in writing is obligatory, although he suggests that it may be better to avoid the construction completely. Commenting on Vaugelas's observation, the Academy (Streicher 1936: 63) observes that omission of the direct object pronoun is incorrect and that 'la promptitude de la prononciation est cause qu'on supprime quelquefois ce pronom'.

There are no examples of such omissions in our model dialogues – perhaps precisely because of their lack of spontaneity – but the Dauphin frequently omits *le* when *li* ('lui') is used (Ernst 1985: 68); for example:

12.1.1605: ce sera doun pou soupé allé li dire, je l'en pie ('aller le lui dire')

3.1.1606:   Me de Montglat le menace de le dire au Roy. *he non maman ga ne li dite pa, je le diray pu* ('ne le lui dites pas')

5.12.1607: ho non jl li a di mais jl a menti ('il le lui a dit').

Whilst the number of omissions of the direct object pronoun with the indirect object pronoun decreases from written texts after the intervention of the *remarqueurs*, Fournier (1998: 76–7) cites examples from Balzac, François de Sales, Molière, Mme de Sévigné and La Bruyère. A representative case is this example from Molière's *Georges Dandin*: 'Moi? et comment lui aurois-je dit?'

The discussion of the history of *on* for *nous* is typical of the debate about the age of certain features of contemporary spoken French: on the one hand some linguists, such as Doppagne and Grafström, see it as a change in progress (Grafström, writing in 1969, comments that usage of *on* for *nous* expanded rapidly in the period 1900–60), while others, including Blanche-Benveniste, view it as a case of stable variation (Coveney 2000: 448). Differing opinions about its value and status in contemporary French are articulated: some argue that the widespread use of *on* for *nous* is characteristic of working-class and informal French; conversely, Blanche-Benveniste denies that use of *nous* is associated with any particular social or regional identity.

Much of the debate concerning the history of the use of *on* revolves around the question of its interpretation and the extent to which it is possible or appropriate to separate those contexts in which *on* is employed as a stylistically marked substitute for the first, second or third person pronoun, without special privilege for the first person plural, from those cases where *on* is being employed as an informal alternative for *nous*.[34] On the one hand, anti-evolutionists such as Hunnius (1981) argue that *on* for *nous* is not a recent innovation and point to examples, from the twelfth-century *Roman d'Alixandre* onwards, which seem to illustrate this usage. One of the most frequently cited examples is taken from the fourteenth-century *Miracles de Nostre Dame* (e.g. Moignet 1965, Bonnard 1975, Hunnius 1981) where the first person plural reference is unambiguous: 'La ou on le visitera / Moy et vous, chacune sepmaine'. On the other hand, the evolutionists assert that in earlier periods *on* was used not only in place of *nous*, but also as a substitute for other persons of the verb. Moignet (1965: 132) records that there are examples of *on* for *je* as early as Old French, for *ils* from the late thirteenth century and *nous* from the fourteenth century onward; use for the second person occurs somewhat later.[35] In other words, as Marchello-Nizia (1979: 176) notes, commenting on the example from the *Miracles de Nostre Dame*, *on* for *nous* does not have privileged status in Middle French; rather the pronoun has, to use Moignet's (1965: 132) term, 'un caractère omnipersonnel', so that there are equally examples of *on* as equivalent to *je* or *ils* (although not yet *tu*).[36] It is argued that the usage of *on* as a substitute for other pronouns in earlier periods was a marked, stylistic one, and that it therefore does not have the same value as the quasi-mechanical usage typified in contemporary French by an example like 'nous, on se marie' (e.g. Nyrop 1916a, 1916b, Schalk 1957, Grafström 1969, Söll 1969, Muller 1970). For Grafström (1969: 285–6), for example, this earlier usage is motivated by a desire for self-effacement or assimilation to the collectivity. According to Moignet (1965: 155–6), this made it particularly favoured by seventeenth-century polite society:

---

[34] In fact, the question is more complex than this, and there has been debate about the number and nature of the values of *on*; see Viollet 1988: 67.

[35] Moignet (1965: 132) observes that there are also regional differences: in the east one finds agreement of *on* with a first person plural verb (*on aurions tort*), whereas in the west (Normandy), *nous* is used with a third person singular verb (*comment l'en devise cerf que nous a veu*).

[36] Boutet (1988: 59) maintains that 'on omnipersonnel' became fashionable and valued in the seventeenth century.

On était à la mode dans la bonne société du XVIIe siècle; il permettait, par une sorte de litote, de rester dans le vague tout en laissant entendre le précis, et cette aptitude devait lui valoir la faveur d'une société pour laquelle une expression trop nette était réputée brutale et de mauvais goût. Il importe en effet de souligner que, dans ces effets de sens, *on* ne perd rien de sa valeur spécifique et que c'est le seul discours qui l'oriente vers la suggestion de telle ou telle personne déterminée.

According to the evolutionists' account, the modern usage – the substitution of *on* for *nous* – dates from the nineteenth century, and spread during that century (Grevisse 1993: 1101). This is when we first find it exemplified in literary representations of working-class and colloquial speech (Hausmann 1979: 438), the earliest example being in the informal speech of Deslauriers in Flaubert's *L'Éducation sentimentale* (1869). Grafström (1969: 276–8) suggests that its use further generalized between 1900 and 1960, moving into *français parlé familier*, perhaps under the combined influence of *français parlé populaire* and dialect and regional usages.

Clearly the differences in analysis are, in part at least, due to the difficulty of interpreting particular examples, even in context. Another factor which gives *on* (as in *on va*) a different place in the linguistic system of the past is the existence of the form *je* + *-ons* (*j'allons*, etc.) as a first person plural form in the speech of the lower classes alongside the form *nous allons*, typical of the speech of the bourgeoisie and cultivated classes. There are several examples of the *je* + *-ons* form, for instance, in the peasant speech in Molière's *Dom Juan* (Act 2 scene 1):

Enfin donc j'estions sur le bord de la mar, moi et le gros Lucas, et je nous amusions à batifoler avec des mottes de tarre que je nous jesquions à la teste.

je l'ai tant sarmonné, que je nous sommes boutés dans une barque, et pis j'avons tant fait cahin caha, que je les avons tirés de gliau, et pis je les avons menés cheux nous auprès du feu, et pis ils se sant dépouillés tous nus pour se sécher, et pis il y en est venu encore deux de la mesme bande, qui s'equiant sauvés tout seul, et pis Mathurine est arrivée là, à qui l'en a fait les doux yeux.

This usage is still found in Acadian French today (Hull 1979, Chaudenson 1992), as well as in certain regions such as Berry and Jersey (Chaudenson, Mougeon and Beniak 1993: 90). Hausmann (1992: 359) therefore maintains that the type *on va* was probably only marginally used before the second half of the nineteenth century in the speech of the lower classes and hardly at all in that of the upper classes.

Let us now consider the evidence for the seventeenth century. As regards the metalinguistic texts, Cotgrave's (1611) discussion of *on* is inconclusive; while he glosses 'on le voit par experience' as both 'men see it, [and] we see it, by experience', his general definition does not make any reference to the definite use of *on* as equivalent to *nous*: 'Such a particle as our One, or something more generall, and the signe of a Verbe Impersonall, or impersonally used'. Both Richelet and Bouhours (1962: 53) in his *Entretiens* make reference to a new familiar usage of *on*, but the examples make it clear that *on* is equivalent here to a first person singular, not a first person plural pronoun. Moreover, Bouhours specifically notes that this usage may occur in a familiar register in both speech and writing; the comment is repeated by Richelet (see above). Andry de Boisregard (1693: 212–14) adds that *on* is used to refer to oneself out of politeness or modesty.

What evidence is there from the Dauphin's speech? Prüssmann-Zemper (1986: 106–9) notes that *on* is frequently used in Héroard, but that it mostly occurs in constructions expressing a command or a wish: *qu'on appote mon vere* ['verre'] (7.5.1606); *qu'on li pote vn ban* ['banc'] (27.1.1607). There appear to be few, if any, clear examples of *on* being used for *nous* in the modern sense. One convincing example does not appear in the main text (and is therefore not in Ernst's edition), but is in the notes for 1607: 'Moucheu de Veneul vené icy, on va joué! / et le faict mettre aupres de luy' (9.7.1607). As Prüssmann-Zemper observes, the use of the periphrastic future adds to the example's authenticity. Ernst (1985: 69) cites the example, 'Pourquoy n'y a ton pa logé' (9.9.1606) as the sole instance of the construction, and notes that there are also cases of *on* being used for other persons (including the royal 'we'), suggesting that there was not at the time a special preference for *on* in place of *nous*.

As always with the Dauphin's speech, there is difficulty in interpreting the data. Prüssmann-Zemper maintains that *on* for *nous* was not unknown in seventeenth-century spoken French, but that the fact that there is only one convincing example is problematic. Should it be considered a feature of a child's speech (according to Söll (1985: 137) use of *on* for *nous* in contemporary French is particularly common in children's speech), is there some dialect influence or was it a frequent feature of court usage? Prüssmann-Zemper adds that the use of *nous* is relatively rare (Hausmann (1992: 360) notes seventy-five occurrences of *nous* compared to some 300 occurrences of *on*), and that the number of occurrences of *nous* declines as the child gets older. She suggests this is perhaps because his status as a prince did not lend itself naturally to the use of 'inclusive' *nous*, since there were no others of the same status; where *nous* is employed this is at times as a *nous de majesté*. While Hausmann (1992) is convinced that the lack of examples of *on* for *nous* shows that the construction was not current in the seventeenth century, Prüssmann-Zemper asserts that the lack of examples may be due to the peculiar situation of the Dauphin and therefore does not prove that the construction was marginal.[37]

---

[37] There appear to be few, if any, examples of the construction in popular texts and pamphlets of the century; Greive (1984: 69) cites only one convincing example from the journal of the Lille worker Chavatte (see Chapter 3), a text which is not analysed here because of its region.

Our corpus of model dialogues, on the other hand, contains numerous occurrences of the subject pronoun *nous* with a first person plural verb (twenty-eight in Erondell (1969 [1605]), nine in La Faye (1608), 113 in Duez (1669)). The following is a typical example from La Faye's third dialogue: 'Pierr. Maintenant que sommes en chemin, ou irons nous? Isa. Là ou le destin nous voudra guider'. Indeed this pronoun occurs more than twice as often as the pronoun *on* in all of our dialogues. Moreover, virtually all the examples of *on* are clear cases of an indefinite usage. Only very rarely do we find examples where the interpretation is potentially ambiguous. For example, in La Faye's fifth dialogue (which is not part of our main corpus) we find the following example:

AN. Soyez le tresbien venu: toute la compagnie vous remercie, de ce qu'avez daigné nous visiter: Mais! Que veut dire que l'on vous voit si rarement? (unpaginated)

Similarly, Duez (1669: 393) includes the following dialogue, although the *on* is clearly glossed as *man* in the parallel German text:

Ie ne sçay autre chose, que ce que nous avons dans les nouvelles ordinaires.
N'a-on rien d'Allemagne?

Part of the difficulty here is that it is not clear whether the second utterance is intended to follow on from the first, or whether it is considered to be an alternative to it. Finally, there is also an example which suggests that *on* is used for the second person pronoun in Erondell's first dialogue:

Il est trop haut, abbaissez le vallet de miroir, deffaites ma coifeure de nuict: que n'appelle-on le page pour chauffez les frotoirs, faittes l'appeler [given in the English parallel text as 'Why doe you not call the Page to warme the rubbers?']

Turning now to usage in drama, the most detailed study of this question to date is by Schapira (1995: 559), who has found numerous examples of *on* being used in place of other persons of the verb in Corneille, Racine, Molière, Mme de Sévigné, Bossuet, La Bruyère, La Fontaine, Fénelon, Regnard and others.[38] She cites examples from Racine's *Britannicus* of *on* for *je, tu, il, vous* and *ils*. A typical example of *on* for *nous* is the following from Racine's *La Thébaïde ou les Frères ennemis* (1664): 'Qu'ils entrent. Cette approche excite mon courroux. / Qu'on hait un ennemi quand il est près de nous!' (Act 4 scene 2). However, Schapira observes (1995: 561) that the use of *on* 'omnipersonnel' is especially favoured in comedy and that this genre deliberately exploits the ambiguity of the pronoun. Moignet (1965: 155) similarly reports that there are examples in Molière of *on* being used for all three persons singular and for the first and third persons plural.

---

[38] Hunnius (1981: 80) also cites an example from d'Aubigné's *Tragiques*: 'Ils [nos anciens] appelloyent brigand ce qu'on dit entre nous / Homme qui s'accommode, et ce nom est plus doux'. No mention is made of the use of *on* by Haase (1898).

Schapira (1995: 557) considers the use of *on* for other persons as 'hautement littéraire', and as having a marked stylistic value. In her view there is a range of stylistic values associated with the construction, depending on the context (1995: 560), which are loosely united in the desire to cultivate vagueness and ambiguity; a significant instance is *Tartuffe* in which Molière deliberately plays on the polysemy of *on*. In order to reveal Tartuffe's duplicity, Elvire exploits the ambiguity of *on*: she pretends to address Tartuffe using the pronoun *on*; in fact she is addressing Orgon, designated by the same *on*, about the impossible situation she is in, referring to herself sometimes by *je*, sometimes by *on*. It has been argued that *on* was favoured particularly by women at this period 'dans la langue parlée de la galanterie, par affection de décence', as in the following example spoken by Célimène in Molière's *Le Misanthrope*, in which *on* is used instead of the first person singular pronoun: 'Allez, vous êtes fou, dans vos transports jaloux / Et ne méritez pas l'amour qu'on a pour vous.' This is clearly the usage motivated by politeness or modesty alluded to by Andry de Boisregard, but Schapira (1995: 560) asserts that this is not exclusive to the speech of women or to a 'contexte galant'. Where *on* is used to refer to other persons of the verb, the appropriate agreement is made (cf. Fournier 1998: 47); for example, Magdelon uses *on* for *je* in *Les Précieuses ridicules*, scene 9, which requires the feminine agreement for *instruite*: 'Mais pour moi, ce que je considère tout particulièrement, c'est que, par le moyen de ces visites spirituelles, on [je] est instruite de cent choses qu'il faut savoir de nécessité.'

So far the textual evidence from the seventeenth century to support the use of *on* for *nous* in a way similar to modern spoken French has been sparse and far from conclusive. Whilst there are occasional instances of *on* being used for the first person plural, there are equally examples for other persons of the verb, and if anything, use for the first person singular appears to attract more comment. The evidence of usage in non-metropolitan French, taken as a basis for comparative reconstruction, is also somewhat ambiguous. For instance, in Quebec and in the French of Louisiana, *on* is used systematically for the first person plural (Hull 1994, Chaudenson 1989). On the other hand, in the creoles of Réunion, Martinique, Mauritius, Seychelles, Haiti, Saint Lucia and French Guiana, the first person plural pronoun is *nou* (it is also used for the second person plural in Haitian Creole; see Chaudenson 1992), and it is rare that, as in Louisiana creole, both *nous* and *on* occur.

Different possible interpretations have been offered for the systematic usage of *on* for *nous* in Quebec. A first possibility, which cannot be discounted, is that the usage of *on* developed independently in Quebec, and probably earlier than in France itself. Hull (1994: 186, 195) argues that while the acrolect usage was *nous venons*, the mesolect usage *je venons* – which has been retained in the New Brunswick Acadian dialect – was potentially ambiguous for speakers outside its area of usage (first person singular or plural?). *On parle*, used in

Quebec and Louisiana, in his view probably evolved in the Parisian mesolect later, but certainly not as late as the nineteenth century, given its presence in the New World. A second position is that the usage was attested in seventeenth-century France, but that it was regional. Grafström (1969), for instance, notes that it is recorded in the centre and west of France in the *Atlas Linguistique de la France*, as well as in Switzerland and Belgium. Mougeon and Beniak (1994: 34–5) therefore hypothesize that forms of the type *nous autres on veut* replaced the type *je voulons* early in the history of Quebec French, since they were typical of the popular French spoken in central France in the seventeenth century. This explanation is refuted by linguists such as Bonnard (1975: 2633) and Grafström himself (1969: 279); they claim that the widespread usage of *on* for *nous* in the spoken French of Canada suggests that this usage must have been generalized in France by the time Quebec was colonized.

There is clearly evidence that *on* for *nous* was possible in the seventeenth century. The key question is how generalized its usage in spoken French was, how much this usage already took precedence over the usage of *on* to refer to other persons, and the extent to which it had lost its marked stylistic value. The rare examples in the Dauphin's usage indicate that *on* for *nous* could be employed in spontaneous conversation without any marked stylistic value, and that, at the very least, the seeds of the future development were present at this period – a development which may have already happened in the language of the settlers in Quebec or have occurred as a natural independent development there. As in the case of negation (Ayres-Bennett 1994), the paucity of evidence does not allow us to conclude firmly in favour of the evolutionists or anti-evolutionists.

2.5.3   Verb morphology and usage

A large number of topics could be included under this section. For instance, Vaugelas (1647: 572) lists various solecisms of conjugation which are peculiar to speech, including the incorrect formation of the *passé simple* and imperfect subjunctive:[39] 'car combien y en a-il, qui y pechent en parlant, mettant des *i*, pour des *a*, & des *a* pour des *i*, comme on fait en plusieurs endroits du preterit simple, quand on dit par exemple *i'alla*, pour *i'allay*, *il allit*, pour *il alla*, & en vne autre temps *nous alliβions*, pour *nous allaβions*?' These forms are well

---

[39] Another topic which has been of considerable interest is that of the status of the *passé simple* in speech at this period (cf. Fournier 1998: 399, Evang 1984). It is noticeable, for example, that while the *passé simple* is much rarer in the Dauphin's speech than the *passé composé* (33 vs. 903 examples; see Prüssmann-Zemper 1986, Koch 1988), it is attested in a range of texts, including theatre (and even in the speech of Molière's peasants), correspondence, reported speech, the *Agréables Conférences* etc. Fournier (1998: 399) suggests that the tense was probably already less used in spoken French in the second half of the seventeenth century since it is in obvious decline in the following century.

attested in Héroard's record of the Dauphin's speech: *je le laissi* (26.10. 1605), *je me coupi* (15.12.1607); *j'attendé que vous m'appotissié* [*m'apportassiés*] *a boire* (25.7.1606), etc. (Ernst 1985), and there are also rare examples in Molière (e.g. Lucas in *Le Médecin malgré lui*, Act 1, scene 5: 'Un petit enfant de douze ans se laissit choir du haut d'un clocher'), although, not unsurprisingly, they do not feature in our corpus of model dialogues.[40]

Of particular interest is the usage and status of various verbal periphrases in seventeenth-century French, since a number of these are the source of Tense–Mood–Aspect markers in Americo-Caribbean and Indian Ocean creoles alike (see below) and are also used with greater frequency in North American French varieties which were formed from the French spoken at this period. These include the use of *aller* + infinitive to express the future, of *être pour* + infinitive,[41] and of *être à* + infinitive and *être après* (*à/de*) + infinitive to express durative aspect. I intend to focus here particularly on the status of the last construction, not least since the evidence from non-metropolitan French and French creoles is fascinating and has generated debate as to the status of the construction in seventeenth-century spoken French.

What is the status and usage of other verbal periphrases? The use of *aller* and *s'en aller* + infinitive to express the future is well attested in our seventeenth-century texts.[42] Prüssmann-Zemper (1986: 148–50) notes that *s'en aller* began to decline in usage in the eighteenth century and that already in the previous century it was particularly associated with the first person singular; this perhaps explains why there is a predominance of periphrastic futures with *s'en aller* in Héroard (79 vs 13 with *aller*), although these represent only a very small proportion of the total number of future verb forms. Both forms are attested in the dialogues, again with a notable preference for the use of *s'en aller* with the first person singular: '& luy dites que vostre Maistre & moy allons faire une promenade' (Duez 1669: 447), 'ie m'en vay coucher' (Duez 1669: 466); 'Ie m'en vay cercher de l'apast' (Erondell 1969 [1605]: dialogue 12).[43] Here, the high frequency of use of the periphrasis with the first person pronoun apparently goes hand in hand with its usage in conversation. Fydal, on the other hand, cites

---

[40] Note that there are also examples in Boursault's *Les Fables d'Esope*; for example, 'quand je l'alli prier d'un peu mieux en agir, / Il me disi des mots, qui me firent rougir' (cited from FRANTEXT).

[41] Vaugelas (1647: 342) criticizes the construction, which he considers equivalent, according to context, to *pouvoir*, *oser* or *courir fortune de*. In many creoles, *pou* is used to mark futurity, with the sense of 'sur le point de'.

[42] Note that *vas*, *vais* and *m'as* (from *m'en vas*) are all used as the first person singular form of *aller* in the compound future in Quebec. *Vas* is socially unmarked, *vais* is considered bourgeois or *recherché*, and *m'as* is associated with popular and familiar registers (see Mougeon 1996).

[43] Another indication of the informal and conversational usage of the dialogues is afforded by Duez's use of the *passé surcomposé*: 'Il est sorty des aussi tost que nous avons eu disné' (1669: 458).

fifty-three future examples with *je vais* and fifteen with *je m'en vais* in seven comedies by Molière (Prüssmann-Zemper 1986: 148).

Gougenheim (1971: 378–9) associates the origin of many of the verbal periphrases created between the fourteenth and sixteenth centuries with what he terms 'un jaillissement de langage populaire expressif et coloré'. He argues that one of the reasons why the seventeenth- and eighteenth-century grammarians are so critical of them, and indeed largely succeed in removing them from literary usage, is because they focus more on the written than on the spoken language. However, the forms could survive in French creoles, 'qui, dépourvus de toute norme grammaticale, ont exagéré certaines tendances expressives de la langue'.[44]

The history of *être après* (*à* / *de*) + infinitive is perhaps typical of this trajectory. According to Gougenheim (1971: 56), the earliest examples of *être après à* + infinitive to express duration date from the second half of the sixteenth century. The metalinguistic texts of the period generally agree that the construction is unsuitable for 'le beau style', although they vary in the way they characterize it. Vaugelas (1647: 332–3), citing examples by Malherbe, is typical in his criticism of the periphrasis: 'Ce mot [sc. après] deuant vn infinitif pour denoter vne action presente & continuë, est François, mais bas, il n'en faut jamais vser dans le beau stile.' Dupleix (1651: 146) for once is even more severe in his criticism of the construction, although he accepts *être après* followed by a noun. Andry de Boisregard (1689: 52–3) suggests that usage of *être après* + infinitive is current, but Corneille and the Academy support Vaugelas's condemnation of *être après à* / *de* + infinitive, the Academy considering that 'toutes les phrases que M. de Vaugelas rapporte [. . .] ont quelque chose de dur, dont l'oreille a peine à s'accommoder' (Streicher 1936: 561). For Macé the construction is 'de stile bas', whereas for Alcide de Saint-Maurice it is characteristic of the usage 'du menu peuple' (Gougenheim 1971: 58). The dictionaries are, however, less censorious: F accepts *être après à* + infinitive, and – in spite of the criticism in the observations on Vaugelas's *Remarques* – it is also cited without comment in A.

The Dauphin makes no use at all of the construction, nor are there any examples in the corpus of model dialogues. In F R A N T E X T the construction is

---

[44] By contrast, another construction used in the seventeenth century to express durative or continuative aspect, *aller* + V-*ant* (*aller* + *gérondif*), seems to be increasingly associated as the century progresses with poetic usage and contexts where there is actual movement. While, for example, Maupas (1618: 155ᵛ) still deems this usage elegant, and it is attested in La Faye's (1608) dialogues (e.g. 'Voila de la monoye tien, va courrât'; 'que vas tu badinant, qu'as tu à faire?'), Oudin (1632) considers it dated, while Vaugelas (1647) argues that it is only acceptable if there is visible movement, as in *elle va disant ses prières* or *la rivière va serpentant*. Ménage sets the same restrictions on the usage of the construction, although not for poetry, while Corneille suggests that its usage is declining even in poetry (Streicher 1936: 378–81). For a discussion of the demise of the progressive construction comprised of *aller*, *être* or *venir* + V-*ant* as an example of degrammaticalization, see Schøsler (forthcoming).

relatively rare (thirteen occurrences). The best attested of the different variants is *être après à* + infinitive (eight examples, dating from 1630 to 1687); there are two examples each of *être après pour* + infinitive (1627, 1644) and *être après* + infinitive (1637, 1694), and a single example of *être après de* + infinitive (1639). Of the thirteen examples, four occur in correspondence (e.g. Mme de Sévigné: 'J'ai été après dîner chez Mme D'Arpajon; j'y ai vu cent Beuvron, qui vous révèrent'), and three in drama, including one from Molière's *Les Fourberies de Scapin* ('Je suis après à m'équiper, et le besoin que j'ai de quelque argent me fait consentir, malgré moi, à ce qu'on me propose'), perhaps confirming the association with spoken and informal usages. Gougenheim (1971: 56) similarly notes that there are examples of *être après à* in prose texts which are informal in character, and includes a number of examples from correspondence.[45]

The main source of evidence to suggest the currency of the construction in seventeenth-century spoken French is therefore that derived from comparative reconstruction. The conjugation of the verb system of French creoles – whether Indian Ocean or (Americo-)Caribbean – rather than relying on inflections, is essentially derived from verbal periphrases indicating aspect; from these are formed Tense–Mood–Aspect (TMA) particles which are used in agglutinative structures (see, for example, Chaudenson 1992; Hazaël-Massieux 1999). To cite Chaudenson (1973: 363):

> Les grammairiens des XVIIe et XVIIIe siècles ont lutté pour les éliminer [les périphrases verbales] de la langue; il est néanmoins sûr que, hors de France, dans les conditions socio-culturelles et linguistiques particulières qui ont vu naître ces créoles, ces tours sans doute très courants dans la langue des colons ont donné naissance à un système nouveau, radicalement différent du système français quoique manifestement issu de lui.

The particle *ap((r)é)/pé*, derived from *être après (à)* + infinitive, used in both geographical zones as a progressive or continuative marker, is one such particle which has the advantage of allowing invariability of the verb stem.[46] According to Chaudenson (1979: 80) it occurs in the creoles spoken in Réunion, Haiti and Louisiana, all first colonized in the seventeenth century, as well as in the creoles of Mauritius, Rodrigues Island and the Seychelles. For example, Valdman (1988: 16) cites the following examples from Haitian creole:

M'kenbe: 'I get/got along'   M'**ap** kenbe: 'I'm getting along'
Li rive lavil: 'S/he arrived in town'   L'**ap** rive lavil: 's/he is arriving in town'

The following examples from Hazaël-Massieux (1996: 293–5) show how the particles may be combined:

---

[45] His only examples of *être après de* are by Malherbe.
[46] Others include *alon/anou* (*allons* + INF; *à nous de* + INF); *fine/fini* (*avoir fini de* + INF); and *fèk* (*ne faire que* + INF).

Haiti	*Réunion* (basilect)	*Mauritius*
l ap manjé	mwen l apré manzé	mo pé manzé
'il est en train de manger/il mangera'	'je suis en train de manger'	'je suis en train de manger'
l t ap manjé	mwen té apré manzé	mo ti pé manzé
'il mangeait'	'j'étais en train de manger'	'j'étais en train de manger'
l ava p manjé	m sra apré manzé	mo va/pu pé manzé
'il sera en train de manger'	'je serai en train de manger'	'je serai en train de manger' (indef/def)

Moreover, use of these constructions derived from periphrastic structures is not limited to creoles; they are also attested in the French of North America at a higher frequency than in France. The French of Missouri, the French of Louisiana and the Acadian French of Louisiana all make widespread use of the periphrasis *être après* to mark progressive aspect (Chaudenson, Mougeon and Beniak 1993: 83, 87). For instance, Chaudenson (1989: 100) cites the following examples: *J'sus après planter* (Acadian); *L'était après tord' des nouèyers* (French of Missouri). Chaudenson, Mougeon and Beniak (1993: 95) comment on the widespread attestation of *être après*, *être à*, *être pour*, *finir de* + INF in the French of North America, but the relative paucity of examples of verbal periphrases (with the exception of *aller* + INF) in their corpus of seventeenth- and eighteenth-century popular texts which they use as, albeit imperfect, sources of the spoken French of the time. They suggest that the scarcity of examples is the result of the fact that these texts are much more faithful in recording phonetic and lexical traits than morpho-syntactic features. They conclude:

> Il en résulte que, pour le domaine morphosyntaxique, ces textes anciens en français réputé populaire ne nous fournissent sans doute pas les preuves attendues et que c'est, dans ce domaine surtout, la comparaison des français d'Amérique et des créoles qui peut nous éclairer sur l'état ancien du français parlé.

The question remains whether these usages were widespread or regional in seventeenth-century French. Gougenheim (1971: 60), for instance, suggests that usage in Canada may derive from regional uses of the construction.[47] Valdman (1979: 195) convincingly argues, however, that the widespread attestation in geographically and chronologically separated varieties militates against the

---

[47] He also notes its use in the Midi, in Franco-Provençal, and in the Loire valley and surrounding areas.

survival of localized regional features. Hazaël-Massieux (1996: 78) also notes
that missionaries signalled early on the tendency in Caribbean creoles for words
to be invariable and for particles to be used to mark tense and aspect. In a letter
dated 1682, the Jesuit Jean Mongin writes about Guadeloupe in the following
terms:

> Les nègres ont appris en peu de temps *un certain jargon français* que les missionnaires
> savent et avec lequel ils les instruisent, qui est par l'infinitif du verbe, sans jamais le
> conjuguer, en y ajoutant quelques mots qui font connaître le temps et la personne de qui
> l'on parle. (Hazaël-Massieux 1996: 101)

In my view the widespread attestation of *être après* (*à*) + infinitive in both Indian
Ocean and Caribbean creoles and the French of North America, together with
the range of comments and criticisms of the construction in metalinguistic texts
right up to the end of the century, suggest that the periphrasis was common in
seventeenth-century speech. While its absence from Héroard and the dialogues
is disappointing, the few attestations in FRANTEXT – which is, after all a
corpus of written texts – particularly in correspondence and drama seem to
confirm this conclusion.

2.5.4   *Interrogation*

In this section we will consider the extent to which alternatives to inversion
to mark interrogation – and notably the use of intonation and *est-ce que* –
appear to be employed in seventeenth-century spoken French, since non-use of
inversion is frequently cited as one of the characteristic features of contemporary spoken usage. Non-use of inversion in interrogatives occurs, according to
Fournier (1998: 125), only in very specific contexts in texts, but she claims 'on
peut imaginer que l'usage oral et familier connaissait les schémas du français
moderne'. Do our sources suggest that this was indeed the case?

The writers of observations and remarks are relatively silent on this question.
Vaugelas (1647: *457–*458), criticizing certain uses of *c'est que*, comments
that opinion is much more divided as to the acceptability of *est-ce que* in constructions such as *quand est-ce qu'il viendra?*, but that he considers it 'fort
bonne'. Thomas Corneille agrees that the construction is extremely common,
but prefers to use an inverted structure; the Academy asserts that the construction
with *est-ce que* is very familiar and is hardly ever used in written language
(Streicher 1936: 822). Duez's (1669: 232) choice of examples in his grammar also seems to suggest that *est-ce que* is frequent in partial interrogation,
especially with the common people.

There is much less comment on the use of intonation alone to mark interrogation. Prüssmann-Zemper (1986: 115–16) wonders whether Oudin's comment in
the second edition of his grammar (1640: 198) to the effect that 'nostre vulgaire'

says 'Monsieur N. n'est pas party?' suggests that the construction was more widespread than previously thought. She also notes examples from Raillet's *Triumphus linguae gallicae* (1664) of total interrogatives marked by intonation alone (as signalled by a question mark). The metalinguistic texts therefore seem to point to an association between *est-ce que* and partial interrogation, and intonation and total interrogation.[48]

Turning now to the evidence provided by Héroard's record of the Dauphin's speech, there is a high overall frequency of partial interrogatives (493 occurrences), particularly in the child's early years. Of these, 397 use inversion (80.5%), and sixty are to be discounted since they include the interrogative subject *qui* (Prüssmann-Zemper 1986: 118). This leaves thirty-four partial interrogatives (6.9%) which use *est-ce que* (of which twenty-four are formed with *que*, four with *pourquoy*, and two with *où*), and only two (0.4%) where there is non-inversion (*pouquoy le jui ont mis dieu a la croi* (15.2.1605); *pouquoy papa fai cela* (14.8.1605)). As regards total interrogation, there is an even greater predominance of questions marked by inversion, since here there are no examples at all of the use of *est-ce que* and only twenty-eight of non-inversion (5.7%). As Ernst notes, non-inversion therefore plays a marginal role (for a comparison with modern French data, see below), although it is equally striking that Héroard does not consider it necessary to gloss them. The following are typical examples of the Dauphin's non-use of inversion:

Vou n'avé pu la fievre maman doundoun? (26.3.1605) (note that two lines earlier we find *avié vou la fievre dan la teste?*)

C'e pa t'hermite qui vin au palemail (20.10.1605)

J [ils] son atheure [à cette heure] au por de Nully? (20.1.1606)

Mais jl est en paradi? (12.1.1608)

Papa e pa encore venu? (22.3.1608).

Prüssmann-Zemper (1986: 118–19) notes that the examples of non-inversion seem to fall into groups and sometimes have a different function from questions formed by inversion. A first group – typified by a sub-group in which all examples contain *donc* – are those where the interrogative form is used, not to ask a true question, but rather to get confirmation of its content from the addressee. For example:

---

[48] The higher incidence of *est-ce que* with partial interrogation is probably explained at least in part by the history of the construction, since it was first used with this type of question, and is only later attested with total interrogatives (Price 1971: 267). It is noticeable that in our texts there are also very many examples of questions which do not include a finite verb (e.g. *quelles bonnes nouvelles? mais où le trouver? et comment donc?* (Duez 1669)). In my analysis I have focused on those cases where there is a finite verb present.

D. *d'ou vené vou?* I[ndret] M^r je viens de la foire St Denys. D. *de la foire, c'e don pa de la foire du cu* (11.10.1605)

M^{le} de Vendelet luy dict que maman estoit accouchée. D. *a ton oui le canon? V. non M^r. D. c'e don une file* [fille] . . . (11.2.1606)

A second group are those questions where the Dauphin expresses surprise or indignation; these are frequently accompanied by an interjection of the type *comment, quoi* or *allons*:

Quoi vou me vené faché atheure que j'ay eté a confesse. (8.4.1605)

A six heures estant assis a table, Madame luy dict, Monsieur ostés vos gants. D. *comment vou pale ainsi a moy?* (24.2.1607)

These then may be thought of as echo questions, either seeking confirmation or registering indignation or surprise at what has just been said. For Koch (1988) this suggests that the construction was marked at this period; consequently he considers the unmarked or neutral value of the construction to be an innovation in modern spoken French. An isolated comment in Du Val's grammar (1604: 132) seems to support the idea that non-inverted questions are marked semantically:

L'Interrogant dont nous vsons est vne marque qui esleue nostre voix en feinte pour signification que nous interrogeons autruy ou nous-mesmes par les paroles que nous proferons, qui autrement sans ceste marque pourroient auoir vn sens contraire, Exemple: *Ie le diray? Ie le feray?* qui auec nostre Interrogant sont negatifs, au lieu que sans iceluy ils seroiët affirmatives. Ceste marque donc faict qu'ils signifient, *N'estimés-pas que ie diuulgue vostre conseil*, ou, *que ie face vne chose que i'ay juré de ne point faire.* Comme qui respondroit simplement, *le ne le diray pas; Ie ne le feray pas.*

However, there are also examples of non-inversion which seem to be straight questions seeking information:

D. *jl é en pison le comte d'Auvegne.* H. oui M^r est Il en prison! (12.6.1605)

D. *son frere eti saint?* H. non M^r. D. *mais jl est en paradi?* H. ouj M^r (12.1.1608).

As always with the Dauphin's speech it is essential to bear in mind whether this non-inversion could be seen as a feature of a child's speech. Whilst the Dauphin's age may be a contributory factor, is it interesting that, as well as in other texts of the period, there are examples of non-inverted total interrogatives and partial interrogative using *est-ce que* in the speech of the adults around the young prince, which is not often the case for other non-standard features:

Ce sera donc dans mon registre? (Héroard, 17.11.1605)

M^r vous gastés tout cela? (M. de Ventelet, 11.5.1606)

Quoy vous ne me dictes mot, vous ne m'embrassés pas quand je m'en vais (Henri IV, 7.12.1608)

M^r laquelle est ce que vous aimés le mieux (Mme de Montglat, 6.10.1605)

Sire qu'est ce que les princes haient le plus? (M. Le Fèvre, 3.9.1610).

Furthermore, Prüssmann-Zemper suggests (1986: 122) that Héroard himself may have been conscious of the different usages appropriate for speech and writing, since he 'corrects' his own usage in one example, where he changes a question formed by intonation alone into an inverted structure by the addition of a pronoun:

Le pince[s] le decaussé [deschaussoient]/ il? (20.10.1605)

A similar pattern of usage – namely a tendency to use *est-ce que* as a minor alternative to inversion with partial interrogation and intonation instead of inversion for total interrogation – emerges from our corpus of model dialogues. Of the 271 examples of partial interrogatives in our three volumes of dialogues, 253 (93.4%) are formed by inversion, sixteen (5.9%) with *est-ce que*, and only two (0.7%) by intonation. Erondell (1969 [1605]) is somewhat atypical in that there are no examples in his text of *est-ce que*; conversely, the association of *est-ce que* with partial interrogation is clearest in Duez (1669) where there are 156 examples of inversion, twelve examples of *est-ce que*, and no examples of intonation. As regards total interrogation, of the 278 examples, there are 266 (95.6%) of inversion, and twelve (4.3%) of non-inversion; there are no examples at all of *est-ce que*.[49] Again Erondell (1969 [1605]) differs from the other texts in using inversion exclusively, perhaps from a desire to focus on the more difficult structure. As regards the function of the questions in our corpus which do not use inversion, the partial interrogatives with *est-ce que* appear to be simple questions asking for information. In the case of the total interrogatives without inversion, the majority of examples again seem to be cases where the speaker is seeking confirmation of something, and which may either include *donc*, or use a tag:

C'est une chambre de lovage cecy, non pas? (La Faye 1608, dialogue 1 [unpaginated])

Vous aviez donc fait collation deuant que de venir icy? (La Faye 1608, dialogue 4)

Il couppe tout ce qu'il void, non pas? (Duez 1669: 424)

La purée de Septembre vous est fort contraire; n'est-ce pas? (Duez 1669: 427)

Par ainsi donc vous y estes tout resolu? (Duez 1669: 478)

Our third source of textual evidence is the direct speech of literary texts, especially that furnished by contemporary theatre. Finke (1983) conducted a

---

[49] A similar pattern is identified by Evang in her analysis of La Faye's usage (1608). She cites the following examples from the fifth dialogue: 'Turq. Ie le feray: Vous le cognoissez peut estre? Rob. Il y a long temps. Tur. Paraventure vous avez estudié ensemble? Ro. Ouy? nous avons esté compagnons deschole, & compagnõs de table.' She notes (1984: 163) that Wodroephe, in adapting this passage, substitutes inversion for one of these examples. However, in his first book of dialogues he includes two examples of questions indicated by intonation alone and five examples of questions introduced by *est-ce que*.

major survey of the form and function of 2322 examples of total interrogatives in seventeenth- and eighteenth-century French theatre. Her statistics again
point to very sparing usage of *est-ce que* for total interrogatives, but a significantly larger percentage of questions marked by intonation alone. Averaging
usage in her corpus of seventeenth-century comedies, we find that about three
quarters of the total interrogatives use inversion (73.4%), and about a quarter (26%) non-inversion, while less than one per cent are formed with *est-ce
que*. Significantly, use of inversion is more frequent in tragedies, which are
presumably further removed from everyday speech (for the two centuries, the
percentages are: inversion 82%, intonation 17.7%, *est-ce que* 0.3%), but less
frequent in Molière's comedies (inversion 68%, intonation 29%, *est-ce que* 3%).
She also finds (1983: 79ff.) different tendencies in the way the forms are used
by Molière: interjections like *quoi* or *comment* tend to co-occur more frequently
with questions formed by non-inversion (twenty-five examples with questions
formed by intonation versus four inverted questions); conversely, expressions
like *dis-moi, dites-moi* or direct forms of address co-occur more frequently with
inverted questions (sixty-one examples with inverted questions versus twelve
examples with non-inverted questions). She concludes (1983: 85, 128–31) that
in Molière's comedies questions formed by intonation tend to have low infor-
mational content, to link back anaphorically to the previous context, and to
express surprise, indignation or astonishment. Prüssmann-Zemper (1986: 120)
cites examples from Molière's *Le Médecin malgré lui* where, as in the case of
the Dauphin's usage, non-inverted forms are clearly echo questions:

Et tu prétends ivrogne, que les choses aillent toujours de même?
C'est donc le médecin des paroquets?
Il n'est pas vrai qu'ous sayez médecin?
Je gagnerai ce que je voudrai?

To these we may add examples from other texts of the period. A good source
of questions is the 'Recueil general des Rencontres, Questions, Demandes et
autres Oeuvres tabariniques, avec leurs responses', by Tabarin, the Parisian
author of popular farce, first published in 1622 (Aventin 1858).[50] The statistics
of interrogative usage in Tabarin mirror closely that of contemporary texts (see
Table 2.1, p. 56).[51]

Finally, usage in FRANTEXT of interrogatives formed with *est-ce que* was
analysed to see whether any patterns emerged. The first thing to note is that,

---

[50] I have analysed the first part here.
[51] Greive (1984) also points to examples of non-inverted questions in the *Agréables Conférences*.
In the first 110 pages of the *Ménagiana* there is one example of a total interrogative formed
with *est-ce que* ('Est-ce que vous vous estes égarez? (Ménage 1693: 15)), and one example of
a question formed by intonation ('M. Ménage, qui est si savant dit qu'il n'en connoît point; &
toy tu prétens en connoître?' (Ménage 1693: 102–3)).

although questions formed with *est-ce que* are in a minority, there are some 1220 examples of the interrogative *est-ce que* in the corpus for the century as a whole.[52] Of these, the vast majority are examples of *qu'est-ce que* (775 occurrences; 64%), perhaps suggesting that this was well established as a semi-fixed expression. Of other interrogative words, the ones which most commonly occur with *est-ce que* are *comment* (fifty-four examples), *pourquoi* (forty-nine examples), *où* (forty-one examples), and *combien* (twenty-four examples).[53] If we add the examples with interrogative words to the examples of *qu'est-ce que* we account for 974, or 79.8% of our examples, once more confirming the strong association of *est-ce que* with partial interrogation.

Of the total interrogatives formed with *est-ce que*, 131 occur with a personal pronoun subject. It is perhaps worth noting – while bearing in mind that much depends on the overall frequency of each pronoun in the discourse – that there is a particular preference for *vous* (thirty-nine examples), *il* (twenty-eight examples) and *je* (twenty-one examples), and that conversely examples with *ils* (six examples), *elle* (five examples), and *elles* (two examples) are relatively rare. Other patterns of usage are clearly discernible. First, of the 131 examples of total interrogatives with a pronominal subject, only nineteen (14.5%) occur in texts published before 1650, whilst 112 (85.5%) occur in the second half of the century. Second, over a third of the 131 examples (forty-seven tokens, 35.9%) occur in plays by Molière, while another seventeen (13%) feature in letters by Mme de Sévigné. These two authors together therefore account for nearly half of the examples (48.9%). If we further analyse these examples according to the genre in which they occur, parallel results emerge. Sixty-one examples (46.6%) occur in theatre, while another twenty-three (17.6%) occur in letters, suggesting an association with spoken and informal usages. However, there is a second important group of examples which feature in religious and philosophical treatises by authors such as Bernier, Pascal, Nicole and Abbadie, where they are used for rhetorical effect. In the following examples, the person asking the questions formed with *est-ce que* is clearly not asking for information, but posing what we might think of as 'loaded' questions, that is, ones which clearly expect a certain response:

Il est vray que cela pourroit causer quelque diversité dans les saisons, dans le chaud, dans le froid, et consequemment dans les generations, et les corruptions ordinaires: mais est-ce que ce n'est pas aussi là le train ordinaire de la nature? Est-ce que nous voyons jamais deux années semblables, soit à l'egard de la chaleur, soit à l'egard de la generation des grains, des fruits, et de tant d'animaux, ou d'insectes differens? (Bernier, *Abrégé de la philosophie de Gassendi*, 1684)

---

[52] In each case the figures include the elided form *est-ce qu'*, etc.
[53] Similarly in Duez (1669: 232) the largest number of examples of partial interrogation with *est-ce que* include *que* (ten examples), followed by *combien*.

On prétend que cette parenthese est d'un homme qui rapporte des choses qui sont fort anciennes. Mais sur quel fondment le prétend-on? Est-ce qu'on ne pouvoit pas garder le lit d'Og du tems de Moïse? Est-ce que Moïse ne peut pas faire souvenir les israëlites de la défaite de ce roi, en leur disant que son lit est à Rabbath? Ou est-ce que le lit de ce roi ne pouvoit pas avoir été transporté à Rabbath? (Abbadie, *Traité de la vérité de la religion chrétienne*, 1684)[54]

The evidence from non-metropolitan French is much less significant in this case than in the previous one. We should note, however, that non-inversion for interrogatives is usual in the French creoles, for example, *To fin manzé?* (Chaudenson 1992: 166). In the case of total interrogation, *èské* (or *èski* in the Indian Ocean) can also be added: *Eski ou kontan?* (Martinique, Valdman 1978: 254).

To summarize: in the case of total interrogation, non-inversion – where the question is marked by intonation alone – is attested in virtually all our seventeenth-century texts as an alternative structure, whereas examples with *est-ce que* are much rarer. If we divide our sources into two chronological periods (Tables 2.1, 2.2) we find not only that our first examples of total interrogation with *est-ce que* are in the second half of the century but also that there is an increase in the use of non-inverted structures in the same period. If

Table 2.1 *Total interrogation, texts dating from the first quarter of the century*

	INVERSION	*Est-ce que*	INTONATION
Erondell 1605 (1969)	100% (54)	0	0
La Faye 1608	95.7% (45)	0	4.3% (2*)
Prüssmann-Zemper 1605–1611	94.3% (465)	0	5.7% (28)
Tabarin 1622	92.1% (70)	0	7.9% (6)
TOTALS	94.6% (634)	0	5.4% (36)
TOTALS excluding Erondell	**94.2% (580)**	**0**	**5.8% (36)**

* One elliptical example not included

Table 2.2 *Total interrogation, texts dating from the second half of the seventeenth century*

	INVERSION	*Est-ce que*	INTONATION
Duez 1669	94.4% (167)	0	5.6% (10)*
Finke: Molière	68%	3%	29%
Average percentages	**81.2%**	**1.5%**	**17.3%**

* Two elliptical examples not included

[54] The citations are from FRANTEXT. Here, and for all citations from FRANTEXT, full bibliographical details of the texts may be found on the database.

we exclude Erondell from our calculation (since he is unusual in only using inverted questions), we can see that non-inverted questions account for only 5.8% of usage in the first quarter of the century, but for 17.3% in the second half of the century. These raw figures are, however, misleading, since Duez's (1669) percentages are very similar to those for the earlier period, and it is the data from Molière which are markedly different. Moreover, if we average Finke's figures for all the seventeenth-century comedies she analyses, the percentages here (inversion 73.4%; *est-ce que* 0.6%; intonation 26%) are much closer to Molière's. This suggests that type of text is an important factor.

As a point of comparison, it may be interesting to consider statistics derived from twentieth-century surveys of usage (Table 2.3, taken from Coveney 1996). The first thing to emphasize is the fact that, with the exception of Terry's survey of plays, we are considering different types of data in that our seventeenth-century texts are written texts which are thought to reflect spoken usage to some extent and most of our twentieth-century statistics are derived from studies of oral usage. It is highly likely that questions formed using intonation will feature more prominently in a corpus of actual spoken usage, and we must therefore be wary of any simplistic comparisons. Nevertheless, the very large difference in the relative proportions of the different constructions in the two periods is remarkable. Inversion occurs in only 11.2% of possible constructions in Terry's survey and only reaches 20% in the most formal middle-class usage; conversely, intonation is used in 85.5% of cases in Terry's survey, the lowest percentage being 41%. As regards *est-ce que*, it is interesting that the figures for Terry's survey of twentieth-century plays are not dissimilar to those for Molière's theatre.

The second important fact to stress as regards our seventeenth-century data is that where non-inverted structures are selected, they often have a particular semantic value, whether this is seeking confirmation, or expressing surprise or indignation. This perhaps suggests that the inverted and non-inverted

Table 2.3 *Total interrogation in twentieth-century surveys*

	Type of discourse	INVERSION	*Est-ce que*	INTONATION
Pohl 1965	Middle-class	8.9%	8.9%	82.2%
Pohl 1965	Working-class	4.6%	4.6%	90.7%
Behnstedt 1973	Formal middle-class	20%	39%	41%
Behnstedt 1973	Colloquial middle-class		10%	90%
Behnstedt 1973	Working-class		5%	95%
Ashby 1977	Middle-class	9.2%	10.8%	80%
Söll 1982	Nine-year-olds	1.3%	7.7%	90.9%
Terry 1970	Plays	11.2%	3.2%	85.5%
Coveney 1996	Informal	0%	20.6%	79.4%

Table 2.4 *Partial interrogation in the first quarter of the seventeenth century*

	INVERSION	*Est-ce que*	INTONATION
Erondell 1969 [1605]	98% (50)	0	2% (1)
La Faye 1608	90.4% (47)	7.7% (4)	1.9% (1)
Prüssmann-Zemper 1605–11	91.7% (397)	7.9% (34)	0.5% (2)
Tabarin 1622	91.1% (72)	6.3% (5)	2.5% (2)
TOTALS	92% (566)	7% (43)	1% (6)
TOTALS excluding Erondell	**91.5% (516)**	**7.6% (43)**	**0.9% (5)**

Table 2.5 *Partial interrogation in Duez (1669)*

	INVERSION	*Est-ce que*	INTONATION
Duez 1669	92.9% (156)	7.1% (12)	0

constructions were not simple variables in this period, but that the latter was a marked structure. We should, however, be wary of coming to oversimplistic conclusions, given the difficulties of gaining direct access to seventeenth-century speech. The most we can say is that non-inversion was already a possible alternative, but one which, according to our evidence, was more restricted in usage and possibly more specialized in function. We cannot, however, conclude that the modern usage is a recent innovation, since absence of clear evidence does not mean that the construction was not more widely used than our sources have indicated.

Turning now to partial interrogation, we find a similar predominance of inverted structures. Examples where questions are formed by intonation and the interrogative word are extremely rare in all our sources. The main alternative to inversion here, then, is clearly *est-ce que*, which accounts for between 7 and 8% of the examples (Tables 2.4, 2.5).

It is much more difficult to make a simple comparison with studies of twentieth-century French in the case of partial interrogation because of the greater range of possibilities available. However, if we extract the relevant data from Coveney's results (1996: 118) we find that in his survey of spoken usage inversion (with a pronominal or nominal structure) accounts for only 9.1% of his examples, *est-ce que* for 48.4%, and non-inversion (whether the question word is in initial position or after the subject and verb) for 39.4%. Here – again bearing in mind the different nature of our data which probably reduces the likelihood of non-inversion – the different frequencies of the occurrence of *est-ce que* are obvious. The evidence as regards the semantic function of the interrogatives formed with *est-ce que* is less clear, since alongside 'marked' examples such as the echo or 'loaded' questions, there are also examples of questions requesting information.

Finally, Fournier (1998: 122) considers interrogation marked by the particle *ti*, the status of which in Modern French is controversial (see Désirat and Hordé 1976: 152–3). In her view, the only evidence of *ti* in this period occurs in the expression *voilà-t-il pas* where *ti* is used in conjunction with *ne voilà pas*. There are only five examples of *(ne) voilà-t-il pas* in FRANTEXT, three of which occur in Molière plays; for example, in *Tartuffe* we find 'Voilà-t-il pas Monsieur qui ricane déjà'. The very limited usage and restricted context suggest that this should probably not be considered a productive device in our period.

2.6   Conclusion

The case studies we have considered here all bear witness to the difficulty of finding appropriate sources for spoken language, and the problems of interpreting the metalinguistic texts and their style labels. Only in the case of interrogation – and perhaps of *on* for *nous* with respect to the absence of convincing evidence – is there some degree of consensus between the different types of sources. The difficulty of finding reliable textual evidence is nowhere more evident than in our discussion of *être après (à)* + infinitive, since all the comparative evidence seems to point towards widespread usage of the construction in the seventeenth century, but the textual evidence is relatively slight (no examples in Héroard, or in the dialogues, very few examples in FRANTEXT). It has also been clear that, except in the discussion of interrogation, quantitative analysis is meaningless, since the number of attestations of each feature is so low.[55] We have also demonstrated the need to consider carefully the function and meaning of forms, since they may well not have had the same value in the seventeenth century as today; obvious cases of this are the use of *on* in place of a personal pronoun and non-inverted total interrogatives. In addition *qu'est-ce que* seems to be particularly favoured as a semi-fixed expression. On the other hand it is striking that Héroard never feels the need to gloss the meaning of interrogatives without inversion or with *est-ce que*.

It is important to underline that absence of evidence does not necessarily mean that the feature was not widely used in speech. For instance, we have

---

[55] Since the number of occurrences is generally so low – for example, only eight occurrences of *être après à* and five examples of *(ne) voilà-t-il pas* in the whole corpus – even normalized figures per 10,000 words of texts would not be helpful. Where numbers of occurrences and percentages are given, they are included only to suggest the relative frequency of features and general trends.

suggested, in the case of *on* for *nous*, that the paucity of examples of this in the Dauphin's usage may in part at least be due to the nature of the speaker and context. Here it seems likely that *on* for *nous* could be used as in modern French, but that it was perhaps no more common than, say, the use of *on* for *je* as an expression of modesty, which is the usage most commented on in the metalinguistic texts.

3 Social and stylistic variation

3.1   Introduction

In this chapter I intend to examine, on the one hand, evidence for variation in the French language in the seventeenth century according to the socio-economic status (SES) or social class of the speaker, and, on the other hand, that relating to register, *niveau de langue*, style or genre. In addition, we will consider the extent to which these two different parameters of variation are separated or are separable, both in seventeenth-century discussions of variation and in our textual sources. Labov has argued that linguistic facts which pattern significantly along the social class continuum will exhibit parallel behaviour along a stylistic continuum, so that if a feature is found to be more common in the lower than in the upper classes, it will also be more common in less formal than in more formal styles for all speakers (Romaine 1982: 123).[1]

In seventeenth-century France an equation is made between the ability to speak well and good social breeding. This emerges most obviously in Vaugelas's definition of good usage as 'la façon de parler de la plus saine partie de la Cour, conformément à la façon d'escrire de la plus saine partie des Autheurs du temps' (Vaugelas 1647: Preface II, 3). It is equally evident in Sorel's characterization (1664: 2) of the way people are judged in seventeenth-century French society:

> On prend aujourd'huy pour des Hommes de basse condition & de peu d'esprit, ceux qui parlent mal François; au moins on les tient pour des Provinciaux qui n'ont jamais veu la Cour & le grand Monde, ou pour des gens mal instruits.

This explains the proliferation of courtesy books and manuals advising people how to speak correctly in the period, since to speak badly was to run the risk of ridicule. Avoiding ridicule was especially important in a period of social mobility when the purchasing of new offices allowed *roturiers* to enter the ranks of the nobility; in order, however, also to become socially integrated they needed to acquire the good manners and especially the good usage of their new social rank. The link between social class and lower register usage is equally

---

[1] Conversely, there are clearly markers that are stylistically but not socially diagnostic within a speech community (see Romaine 1988: 1454–5).

made at the other end of the social scale: for example, F defines a *mot bas* as a word 'qui ne se dit que par le peuple'. There is also the occasional indication that class differences sometimes made communication difficult. Brunot (1905–53: IV, 74) recounts an anecdote which hints at the gap between the linguistic usage of Louis XIV and that of his people: when a mother whose son had been killed by the works at Versailles shouted insults at the king, he is said not to have understood and to have been obliged to enquire whether the insults were being addressed to him.

In discussing social and stylistic variation in seventeenth-century France, at least two other considerations come into play. The educational level of the speaker is inevitably related to his or her social class. In addition, as we shall see, the identification of the best speakers with the *honnêtes gens* of the king's court leads to a dichotomy being established between the usage of the court and of the town.

3.2   Seventeenth-century models of social and stylistic variation

3.2.1   Modelling variation

The categorization and modelling of register variation in seventeenth-century French is highly problematic for a number of reasons. First, as we have already seen, there is a tendency to conflate differences of register with the difference between written and spoken forms of language, that is, to equate high register with written usage and informal registers with spoken language. Second, there is the perennial problem of categorizing what is essentially a continuum into discrete categories.

A third difficulty relates to the question whether it is possible to define certain registers independently of considerations of social class. This is perhaps most obvious in the case of *français populaire*. Modern-day definitions of this register vary in the extent to which it is seen to be limited to a particular social class. For example, *Le Nouveau Petit Robert* (Rey-Debove and Rey 1993: xxviii) explains its usage of 'pop' in the following terms:

qualifie un mot ou un sens courant dans la langue parlée des milieux populaires (souvent argot ancien répandu), qui ne s'emploierait pas dans un milieu social élevé.

Guiraud (1965: 6) continues to identify *français populaire* with the usage of the people, but also suggests that a large proportion of the population uses it:

Notre *français populaire* n'est ni une langue technique, ni un argot, dans la mesure où il est commun à une vaste partie de la population et non à un métier particulier ou à un cénacle fermé. (Guiraud 1965: 8)

Perhaps the clearest example of this difficulty is Müller's attempt (1985: 239) to define *français populaire*, in which he refers in turn to the education of the speaker, the degree of spontaneity of usage, and the conventions of spoken French. Having denied its association with a particular social group or class, he suggests it is more linked with the middle and lower classes:

Dans la réalité contemporaine, le français populaire est un **registre inférieur à la norme, pratiqué par la grande masse des Français 1. qui n'ont généralement pas suivi d'études supérieures** et/ou 2. qui **utilisent la langue spontanément**, sans contrôle, pour la seule communication instantanée; et/ou 3. qui, éventuellement, ne connaissent **pas d'autres normes linguistiques** que celles qui organisent l'état actuel de ce registre et semblent être les règles d'usage de la langue parlée quotidienne. On ne peut donc pas cantonner le français populaire dans tel groupe ou telle classe de la société. S'il fallait cependant l'insérer dans une stratification sociale, il faudrait le centrer dans les **couches moyennes ou inférieures** qui constituent la **grande majorité** de la communauté linguistique [emphasis in original].

It is important not to project these twentieth-century definitions on to seventeenth-century discussions, but rather to consider the extent to which seventeenth-century metalinguistic texts identify *français populaire* with the 'langue du peuple' (see below).[2]

Many of the difficulties we have so far discussed are magnified when we come to consider seventeenth-century discussions of differences of register, genre and style. While, as Gemmingen-Obstfelder notes (cited by Glatigny 1990b: 7), style labels, or 'marques d'usage' in metalinguistic texts, are a rich source of information which counterbalance the monolithic purist tradition, they are frequently very difficult to interpret. As we shall see, one of the most problematic terms is *bas*, since it appears to be used to characterize both the speaker and the type of utterance, to relate ambiguously to the social and to the rhetorical. In addition, there is a tendency at times for terms to be considered low register or vulgar because they refer to something which is deemed vulgar (Collinot and Mazière, cited by Glatigny 1990b: 8). Moreover, different models of variation apparently underpin the different volumes of observations, grammars and dictionaries, making it difficult to compare them.

A final difficulty concerns the interpretation of the social structures of seventeenth-century France and the labels used to refer to the different classes. While French society was divided into three principal estates, the clergy, the nobility and the third estate, within each of these estates there were further divisions and hierarchies. This is particularly true of the third estate, which included writers, lawyers, financiers, businessmen and merchants – all of whom might be termed 'bourgeois' if they lived in one of the privileged towns – alongside

---

[2] Note that Vaugelas (1647: Preface II, 2) explicitly rejects the notion that the usage of the majority constitutes good usage; rather it is the usage of the elite.

workmen, artisans, craftsmen, mercenaries, beggars and vagrants (Mousnier 1969).

Carrier (1989: 390) stresses the need for careful interpretation of the terms *peuple* and *bourgeoisie* in the seventeenth century. Both terms may be used by contemporaries with a broad, ill-defined focus; for example, *peuple* for someone like La Rochefoucauld was defined in relation to his own social situation and included almost everyone outside his own social grouping.[3] Similarly, *bons bourgeois* could at times include judicial office holders, or be restricted to refer more narrowly to rich merchants. The polysemy of the term *bourgeois* is clear from the definitions provided by A: it may be used to refer to an inhabitant of a town, to a member of the third estate, to someone who is not part of the court milieu ('Cela sent bien son bourgeois'), or it may be used by workers to refer to the person for whom they work, whether that person is a member of the court or of the town.

3.2.2   Style labels: dictionaries

The style labels in dictionaries have been the subject of considerable analysis.[4] The three principal monolingual dictionaries – R, F and A – each reflect in their choice of style labels a different emphasis in their perception of variation. R uses a combination of symbols and textual comments. Bray (1990: 44) notes, for example, that for the letter P, 39% of the entries include some sort of comment,[5] while 21% have a symbol alone. The symbols used are defined as follows:

* montre que le mot ou la phrase sont au figuré
+ veut dire que le mot ou la façon de parler n'ont proprement leur usage que dans le stile simple, dans le comique, le burlesque, ou le satirique
*+ cela signifie que le mot ou la façon de parler se prennent figurément, mais qu'ils n'ont cours que dans le stile le plus simple, comme dans les vaudevilles, les rondeaux, les épigrammes, & les ouvrages comiques.

These symbols, together with the descriptors used in the definitions, suggest that Richelet's primary emphasis is on genre and style, rather than on differences according to the register or class of the speaker. This is borne out in the descriptive terms used (see Table 3.1, p. 67), where *burlesque* features much more prominently than *familier* or *populaire*. It is also significant that the term

---

[3] 'Populace' on the other hand clearly refers to the 'petit peuple'.
[4] See, for example, Wooldridge (1977), Glatigny (1990a) and Lindemann (1997–8).
[5] He includes in this analysis not only comments on the type of text or social group which uses the term under discussion, but also such factors as whether the term is a neologism, an archaism or a foreign borrowing.

bas occurs primarily in correlation with *burlesque*. As in all the dictionaries, there is relatively little explicit indication of higher register usage. As regards the class of the speaker, occasional reference is made to the usage of *le petit peuple* (*de Paris*).

There is clearly a different emphasis in F, which in general has a more open and encyclopaedic quality than the other two works. Whilst *burlesque* remains a significant category, there is a striking increase in the use of *populaire*, especially in the collocation *terme populaire*. *Populaire* in F seems primarily to characterize the speaker: although *populaire* is used in a linguistic context, the adjective is defined as 'qui concerne le peuple'; this suggests that here more weight is placed on the social, with register (*familier*) of less import. However, there is only a very occasional reference to the usage of *bourgeois* speakers (the expression *le bourgeois dit* occurs only twice in the dictionary, under *halle* and *repas*).[6] In his definition of *bas*, F introduces both a stylistic usage ('stile bas qui est rampant, sans figure') and a social one ('un mot bas qui ne se dit que par le peuple'), thereby emphasizing the interplay between rhetorical considerations and sociolinguistic ones. Even more marked is the rise of *proverbialement*. The ambiguity of this term in the seventeenth century has been noted: it may be used to refer not only to proverbial or fixed expressions, but also, in Furetière's words, to 'les façons de parler triviales et communes qui sont en la bouche de toutes sortes de personnes'. R, moreover, establishes a link with lower-class usage in one of his examples, noting 'il n'y a guere que le peuple qui parle proverbe'.

There has been considerable debate about the extent to which A admits non-standard usages or restricts itself to recording the language of the *honnête homme*. The uncertainty reflects the contradictory statements which are expressed in the Preface to the dictionary. On the one hand, a strongly purist position is suggested by the following:

Quant aux termes d'emportement ou qui blessent la Pudeur, on ne les a point admis dans le Dictionnaire, parce que les honnestes gens évitent de les employer dans leurs discours.

This restrictive attitude is apparently confirmed by the fact that the Academy chose to publish separately a two-volume *Dictionnaire des arts et des sciences*, edited by Thomas Corneille (1694).[7] Here we find not only words from

---

[6] We have already noted the polysemy of the term *bourgeois* in this period. According to F, it can be used to refer to the inhabitants of a town, to refer to members of the third estate, or, in contrast to a courtier, to refer to 'un homme peu galant, peu spirituel, qui vit & raisonne à la maniere du bas peuple'.

[7] Note, however, that in the 1694 edition of the dictionary published by Veuve Coignard and Jean Baptiste Coignard these two volumes are labelled as Volumes 3 and 4 of the Academy's lexicographical work.

specialized domains such as falconry, architecture, heraldry, arithmetic and chemistry, but also words considered 'old' which therefore fall outside *le bon usage*. However, there are two other statements in the Preface, which are much less often quoted, but which suggest a more open approach:

On a eu soin aussi de marquer ceux qui commencent à vieillir, & ceux qui ne sont pas du bel usage, & que l'on a qualifiez de bas ou de style familier selon qu'on l'a jugé à propos.

Les Proverbes ont esté regardez dans toutes les Langues comme des Maximes de Morale qui renferment ordinairement quelque instruction; Mais il y en a qui se sont avilis dans la bouche du menu Peuple, & qui ne peuvent plus avoir d'employ que dans le style familier. Cependant comme ils font une partie considerable de la Langue, on a pris soin de les recueillir, aussi bien que les façons de parler Proverbiales, dont on a marqué les significations & les differens employs.

This more tolerant attitude towards variation is in evidence in many of the definitions: as Table 3.1 indicates, there is a high occurrence of *bas* (especially *il est bas*) and of *familier* where the usage of a particular term is specified. A's definition of *familier* suggests an informal usage which is appropriate for conversation and letters. In the dictionary the collocation *conversation familiere* occurs eleven times and it is common also in the *remarqueurs*:

On appelle, Discours familier, style familier, Un discours, un style naturel & aisé tel que celuy dont on se sert ordinairement dans la conversation entre honnestes gens, & dans les lettres qu'on escrit à ses amis. Et on dit, qu'Vn terme est familier. pour dire qu'Il n'est pas assez respectueux eu esgard aux personnes à qui, ou devant qui on parle. Les termes d'affection & d'amitié sont des termes familiers à l'égard des personnes qui sont au dessus de nous.

According to the definition of *populaire*, this has a social significance for the Academy ('qui est du peuple, qui appartient au peuple').

Particularly useful for investigating lower register usage is Oudin's *Curiositez françoises, pour supplement aux Dictionnaires. Ou Recueil de plusieurs belles proprietez, auec vne infinité de Prouerbes & Quolibets, pour l'explication de toutes sortes de Liures* (1640). In the *Advertissement* Oudin explains 'pour ce qui est des estoiles et du mot vulg. il faut entendre que ce ne sont pas des phrases dont on se doive servir qu'en raillant'. Oudin includes many expressions which are not recorded in other dictionaries, including those labelled *vulg.* or *vulgairement*. The following is a typical entry: '*Foüailler*, i. "fesser. [vulg.] faire l'acte charnel."'; this sense is not given by R, F or A. A social dimension is included in the very many references to *le vulgaire* in expressions such as *le vulgaire dit, le vulgaire se sert de, mot du vulgaire*, etc.

Table 3.1 *Style labels in Richelet, Furetière and the Academy dictionary**

		R (1680)	F (1690)	A (1694)
BURLESQUE		[333]	[68]	[26]
	Dans le burlesque	86	9	10
	En burlesque	9	17	4
	Bas & burlesque†	58	2	0
	Vieux & burlesque	21	2	0
	Burlesque &/ou satirique	7	0	0
	Burlesque & comique	3	0	0
	Terme burlesque	3	13	1
	Stile/style burlesque	8	2	4
	Burlesquement	3	31	3
FAMILIER		8[/16]	[42]	[140]
	Stile/style familier	5	3	87
	Discours familier	2	12	36
	Terme familier	0	1	1
POPULAIRE	Populaire	0[/6]	[204]	[59]
				+3 *pop.*
	Populairement	0[/1]	[50]	[62]
	Terme populaire	0	107	3
	Stile/style populaire	0	0	0
	Façon de parler populaire	0	0	6
VULGAIRE	Vulgaire	[19]	[43]	[15]
	Terme vulgaire	0	0	0
	Stile/style vulgaire	0	0	0
	Vulgairement	4[/5]	24	20
	Le vulgaire dit	0	2	2
BAS	Bas	[525]	[889]	[673]
	Bassement	1	38	139
	Bas & burlesque	58	2	0
	Il est bas	11	29	287
	Bas & vieux	9	2	7
	Bas & comique	2	0	0
	Bas & de mépris	2	0	0
	Le stile/style bas	4	2	0
	Terme bas	1	12	10
	Façon de parler basse	5	1	3
MEDIOCRE	Stile/style mediocre	0	2	2
SUBLIME		[17]	[26]	[32]
	Stile/style sublime	7	5	8
	Genre sublime	0	3	3
LE PETIT PEUPLE	Le petit peuple	14[/22]	2[/4]	1[/3]
	Le petit peuple de Paris	7	0	0
PROVERBIALEMENT		1	[1848]	[65] +1106
		(definition)		(*prov[erb.]*)
	Dit proverbialement	0	1743	55
	On dit proverbialement	0	1276	55

* These figures are generally derived from the CD-ROM *Dictionnaires des XVIe et XVIIe siècles* (see Chapter 1, note 8); in the case of the abbreviated forms, however, the figures are derived from the CD-ROM *Les Dictionnaires de l'Académie française (1687–1798)* (Paris: Champion Electronique, 2000), since it is impossible to search on abbreviations on the other database. There are slight differences in the text of A in these two sources. The figures in the square brackets give the global use of the term, regardless of sense or context.
† In each case the reverse ordering of the terms is included; e.g. the figures for *bas & burlesque* also includes the occurrences of *burlesque & bas.*

3.2.3   Style labels: observations

Much less attention has been paid to the use of style labels by the *remarqueurs*, but there is equally a range of models of variation among the *remarqueurs*, and indeed sometimes within the work of one *remarqueur*. This is perhaps most obvious in the case of Vaugelas (1647). This partly derives from the fact that at times Vaugelas seeks merely to distinguish good and bad usage and is relatively unconcerned about the reason why a certain usage is unacceptable. For example, discussing the use of *possible* in the sense of 'perhaps', he concludes:

> Les vns l'accusent d'estre bas, les autres d'estre vieux. Tant y a que pour vne raison, ou pour l'autre, ceux qui veulent escrire poliment, ne feront pas mal de s'en abstenir. (Vaugelas 1647: 149)

However, there also appear to be two different models of usage underpinning the work.

In the first model, a simple distinction is established between *le bon usage* and *le mauvais usage*, the latter being found in burlesque, comedy and satire. Furthermore, *le bon usage* is equated with *le bel usage*, which is said to exclude anything considered 'bas' or 'de la lie du peuple':

> Au reste, quand je parle du *bon Vsage*, j'entens parler außi du *bel Vsage*, ne mettant point de difference en cecy entre le bon & le beau; car ces Remarques ne sont pas comme vn Dictionnaire qui reçoit toutes sortes de mots, pourueu qu'ils soient François, encore qu'ils ne soient pas du bel Vsage, & qu'au contraire ils soient bas & de la lie du peuple. (Vaugelas 1647: Preface VII, 1)

This model may be represented in the following way:

$\Big\langle$
Le bon usage = *le bel usage*

Le mauvais usage = *bas, de la lie du peuple*
        associated with comedy, burlesque, satire

In a second model, however, the relativity of good usage and the importance of choosing the right word according to the genre, register, style and context are emphasized. For example, Vaugelas characterizes the expression *comme ainsi soit* as follows: 'J'auoüe que dans vne lettre il seroit exorbitant; mais qui ne sçait qu'il y a des paroles & des termes pour toutes sortes de stiles?' (1647: *470).[8] In this scheme there are three levels *within* good usage, *le bas, le mediocre* and *le sublime*; in other words, terms deemed *bas* or *familier* may constitute good usage:

---

[8] Another difference discussed by writers of observations is that between poetry and prose, but we will not include it here.

mais il y a bien de la difference entre vn langage soustenu, & vn langage composé de mots & de phrases du bon Vsage, qui comme nous auons dit, peut estre bas & familier, & du bon Vsage tout ensemble. (Vaugelas 1647: Preface VII, 3)

Here, then, *le bon usage* and *le bel usage* are differentiated, as is evident in Vaugelas's comment on the expression *pour l'heure*: 'Cette façon de parler pour dire *pour lors*, est bonne, mais basse, & ne doit pas estre employé dans le beau stile, où il faut dire *pour lors*' (Vaugelas 1647: 192). This provides us with a different schema:

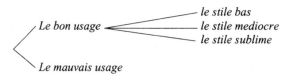

Table 3.2 (p. 71) indicates that description of variation according to the speaker's SES is less frequent in collections of observations, and Vaugelas is typical in this respect. This may partly be because Vaugelas equates the usage of the people with bad usage ('Selon nous, le peuple n'est le maistre que du mauuais Vsage', Preface VIII, 3) and he is not concerned with recording the crude faults typical of provincial speakers or of 'la lie du peuple de Paris' (Preface XIV, 3). On the whole, the usage of 'le peuple', 'la lie du peuple' or 'le peuple de Paris' is censured, and may be considered outdated (1647: 466, 512); indeed Vaugelas is critical of Malherbe's advice to adopt the linguistic habits of lockpickers (thieves) and fishwives.[9]

A number of *remarqueurs* refer specifically to the usage of 'le peuple de Paris'. Vaugelas also makes reference to the difference between the usage of the royal court and that of the town of Paris on a number of occasions (see Wolf 1984). While he includes, in his definition of the court, people from the town who have associations with the court and who thereby 'participent à sa politesse' (Preface II, 3), he establishes as a principle that the usage of the court is always to be preferred to that of the town (1647: *482). This principle is generally followed; for example, he is critical of the Parisian usage of *solliciter* (57) and of the two-syllable pronunciation of *aoust*, which he explicitly identifies with

---

[9] These occupations are repeatedly used to refer to the lowest social groups. As Brunot (1891: 223–42) points out, Malherbe's comment has to be interpreted with care in view of his general condemnation of *expressions 'plébées'*. It is likely that, rather than inviting people to follow this low-class usage, Malherbe intended to distance himself from the ideals of the Pléiade and learned poetry. His intention may also have been to suggest that an author's use of language should be so clear that it could be understood even by common people.

'le peuple de Paris' (322). Nevertheless, he sometimes allows both court and town usages (366), or suggests the advantages of the form favoured by the town (*Je vais, ie va*, 27). As Wolf (1984: 358, 364) notes, this makes it difficult to assess both what exactly is being referred to when he talks of 'la ville' and the position Paris has in his observations.

Neither Dupleix (1651) nor Buffet (1668) has much to say about social or stylistic variation. Dupleix makes an explicit link between low-register usage and education: on two occasions he refers to 'le vulgaire ignorant' (380–1, 386) and in his discussion of *recouvert* for *recouvré* he comments 'Si *recouvert* pour *recouvré* se dit à la Cour, c'est entre ceux qui n'ont point de lettres, & qui l'ont ainsi appris des artisans de Paris' (1651: 530–1). Buffet refers critically to the usage of 'le petit peuple' on five occasions and to that of the bourgeoisie once. Bérain (1675) and Tallemant (1698) likewise make few comments relating to variation of this kind. Bouhours places his emphasis very firmly on differences of register, although occasionally he makes an explicit link between this and SES: '*Né natif.* Cette façon de parler est de ces locutions basses qui ne sortent point de leur bassesse, & il n'y a que le petit peuple qui dise, *un tel est né natif de Paris*. Les honnestes gens disent, *un tel est né à Paris*, ou *est natif de Paris*' (1675: 133). Like many of the *remarqueurs*, Bouhours (1693: 147–8) makes it clear that low-register terms may not be used in serious texts and are only acceptable if used humorously or in *discours familier*. Alemand often chooses to formulate his comments in terms of the style with which a particular usage is associated, employing such expressions as 'un stile pompeux & magnifique' (contrasted with 'le discours ordinaire & familier', 1688: 63–4), 'un stile sublime' (119), 'le stile le plus haut' / 'le stile le plus bas' (403–4) and 'le stile historique' (481). While he has relatively little to say about social variation, he refers explicitly to the usage of the 'bourgeois des Villes' (281), which differs from that of the court.

Of all the *remarqueurs* Ménage and Andry de Boisregard are the most pre-occupied with social and stylistic variation. Ménage includes twenty comments on the usage of 'le petit peuple de Paris', 'le peuple de Paris', 'les Badeaux de Paris' and, more rarely, of simply 'le peuple'. In another observation (1675: 537) he is critical of what he terms 'locutions plébées', an expression repeat-edly used by Malherbe (see note 9). It is particularly noteworthy that many of these comments concern unacceptable pronunciations. He very rarely employs the term *bas*, preferring instead *familier*, especially in the expression *discours familier*. Andry refers not only to the usage of 'le petit peuple', 'le peuple' and 'le peuple de Paris', but also to 'le menu peuple', 'la populace' and 'le vulgaire'. Interestingly Andry uses both register labels such as *familier* and *bas* and a whole range of labels to refer to different types of styles including 'stile simple & familier', 'stile plaisant', 'stile dogmatique', 'stile burlesque', 'stile oratoire', 'stile sublime' and 'stile mediocre'.

Table 3.2 Social and stylistic variation in observations on the French language

	Vaugelas 1647	Dupleix 1651	Buffet 1668	Bouhours 1674, 1675, 1693	Ménage 1675, 1676	Bérain 1675	Alemand 1688	Andry de Boisregard 1689, 1693	Tallemant 1698	TOTALS
REGISTER										
Words	12	0	2	16	17	2	10	50	0	109
Expressions	12	2	5	14	8	2	3	22	3	71
Pronunciation	1	0	0	1	4	0	3	0	0	9
Morphology	1	0	0	1	1	0	1	1	1	6
Syntax	4	1	0	1	3	1	3	3	1	17
General	3	1	0	0	1	0	0	4	0	9
TOTAL	33	4	7	33	34	5	20	80	5	221
SES										
Words	3	0	3	1	5	0	3	7	0	22
Expressions	2	0	2	4	2	0	0	6	0	16
Pronunciation	1	1	0	0	18	0	0	4	0	24
Morphology	1	2	1	0	1	0	0	1	0	6
Syntax	0	0	0	0	3	0	0	2	0	5
General	3	0	0	0	0	0	0	1	0	4
TOTAL	10	3	6	5	29	0	3	21	0	77

Table 3.2 (p. 71) presents the number of observations devoted to social and stylistic variation by the *remarqueurs* and indicates which topics are most discussed in relation to these parameters of variation. It is clear that variation is more often expressed in terms of the register or *niveaux de langue* than in terms of the characteristics of the speaker; indeed there are almost three times as many comments on the appropriate choice of register as there are on the SES or education of the speaker. The emphasis on register is particularly evident in the work of Vaugelas, Bouhours, Alemand and Andry de Boisregard, and Ménage is unusual in the number of observations he devotes to SES. As regards register, it is clear that lexical issues dominate: over 80% of the comments are to do with the appropriate style or *niveau de langue* for a particular word or expression. Lexical issues also constitute nearly half of the comments relating to the speaker's class or education. Here, however, questions of pronunciation also feature prominently, notably in Ménage's two volumes of observations.

3.2.4   Style labels in other metalinguistic texts

Neither Maupas (1618) nor Oudin (1632) is concerned in his grammar with differences of usage according to register, genre or style. Occasionally a usage is associated with 'le grossier populaire', 'le (bas) populas' or 'le vulgaire', often in order to criticize it: 'Ie trouve niaise, la fantasie d'aucuns, qui affectent une lasche prononciation du bas populas, d'obmettre & supprimer du tout, toutes les *r*, finales' (Maupas 1618: 11r). Irson (1662), on the other hand, has a section entitled 'Du stile' in which he defines and exemplifies the three principal types of style: *le simple, le mediocre* and *le sublime*. He emphasizes the need to use the appropriate register for the subject matter: 'Ce n'est pas vn moindre defaut d'abaisser les grands sujets par des termes vils & rampans, que d'éleuer les petits par des expressions pompeuses & éclatantes, l'vn & l'autre repugne visiblement à la nature des choses, dont la conformité fait toute la beauté' (Irson 1662: 285). Bouhours in his *Entretiens* praises the French language for its richness in terms appropriate for different contexts and styles; French has terms 'pour le discours familier, & pour l'eloquence; pour le stile mediocre, & pour le stile sublime; pour le serieux, & pour le burlesque; pour la chicane mesme, & pour les affaires' (1962: 47).

Two other works deserve mention. Renaud in his *Maniere de parler la langue françoise selon ses differens styles* (1697) defines and exemplifies different styles. There are a number of interesting features of his elaboration of the well-established division between *le style sublime, le style mediocre* and *le style bas* (1697: 122–3).[10] First, he asserts that 'Style Mediocre ou familier'

---

[10] Having made this distinction, he elaborates on a whole range of other styles including *style historique, style oratoire, style poétique, style délicat, style agréable, style badin & frivole*.

is used in conversation, thereby introducing considerations of medium into his definition. While the examples he cites are the published conversations of Mlle de Scudéry, Le Chevalier de Méré and Bouhours, he later suggests that it is appropriate in a wide range of oral contexts: 'pour la Ruelle & pour le Cabinet; pour les Entretiens familiers & pour les negociations [. . .] il peut même tenir une place honorable dans les Assemblées savantes, que l'on appelle neanmoins plutôt du nom de Conferences & d'Academies, que de celui de Conversation' (1697: 149). Second, he suggest that 'Style Bas ou populaire', which is used in comedy and burlesque, is not very different from the 'Jargon de la populace, où il n'y a souvent ni guéres d'esprit, ni guéres de raison' (1697: 123). It comprises 'pensées grossieres' and 'locutions de la lie du peuple'; 'peuple' for him signifies 'une foule de petites gens par opposition à ceux qui sont nobles, riches & éclairés'. There is therefore a clear link for him between low-register style and low social class: the people use 'un langage bas & trivial' and favour 'les Turlupinades, les Quolibets & les Rebus' (1697: 152–3).

The title of Callières's (1693) work indicates its interest to us as one of the rare sources of bourgeois linguistic features: *Du bon, et du mauvais usage, dans les manieres de s'exprimer. Des façons de parler bourgeoises. Et en quoy elles sont differentes de celles de la Cour* [. . .]. For example, a number of words and expressions used by the son of a bourgeois from Paris are discussed critically (1693: 15ff.). Unlike many of his contemporaries, Callières (1693: 189–90) makes a clear distinction between words and the things to which they refer:

Les mots bas, répondit le Commandeur, sont ceux qui expriment bassement des choses qui ne sont pas basses par elles mêmes, au lieu qu'il y a des choses basses qui s'expliquent par des mots qui n'ont rien de bas.

Like Renaud, he establishes a clear link between the use of 'expressions basses & populaires', the people, and a lack of education (1693: 239–40). However, the bourgeois are also said to be negligent and crude in their use of language since they may equally employ these low-register expressions (1693: 12–13). Callières nevertheless acknowledges that there are differences between the usages of 'la petite bourgeoisie' and 'le peuple' (1693: 185–6). Even rich Parisian bourgeois, who necessarily have contact with the court, use different expressions from those at court, such as 'je vous prie de venir manger de ma souppe' (1693: 35–6), although there are equally people in the town and provinces who can speak just as well as the best courtiers (1693: 64).

3.3   Case studies

3.3.1   Textual sources

Given the predominance of comments in the metalinguistic texts about usages below the norm, the case studies in this chapter focus on 'substandard' registers and 'popular' usages. As regards register, I decided to concentrate on usages labelled *bas*, and to a lesser extent those deemed *populaire* or *vulgaire*, since these terms are less problematic than *familier*, an adjective which is often used in the expression *conversation familière* to denote spoken usages (see section 2.2).[11] With respect to SES, our case studies look principally at those labels associated with *le peuple*, *le menu peuple* or *la lie de peuple*, and in particular those of the Parisian people. This will lead us to explore further the opposition made between *Cour* and *Ville*, and also to examine examples of Parisian *patois*. Since low-register usages are often said to be only permissible in comedy, satire and *burlesque*, we also intend to explore the extent to which words and expressions labelled *burlesque* by the *remarqueurs* occur particularly in this or other comic genres.[12]

There are a number of major problems in identifying and analysing sources of low-register and popular language. First, as we have already noted, it is often difficult to disentangle whether a given feature is predominantly associated with low-register usage, low-class usage, or indeed, with spoken usage. Thus, a dialogue written in the popular patois of Paris might be thought to display both spoken and low-register usage, and it is a somewhat arbitrary decision to assign it to one category or the other. Secondly, lower-class speakers tended to be less literate; consequently, it seems likely that most of the so-called 'popular' texts of the period were composed artificially by authors who wanted, often for comic effect, to present lower-class or lower-register usages. It is possible therefore that there will be at least an element of caricature or stereotyping in the presentation of the non-standard. Related to this is the problem that some of the possible sources of popular words and expressions are not written in a consistently low register, but deliberately juxtapose the popular and the learned to achieve comic effects. Moreover, the artificial nature of the texts and the rather superficial presentation of their popular character means that this is often conveyed lexically and phonetically, whereas the syntax tends to remain more standardized.

Previous commentators have similarly emphasized the difficulty of trying to link a particular register or style with textual examples in the seventeenth century. For example, Bar (1957: 221), in an article entitled 'Style burlesque et langage populaire', notes the problems with trying to equate *langue populaire* with specific literary texts, arguing that there is no single defining text of the register. His provisional definition of *langue populaire* is therefore very broad: 'tout ce qui est étranger, par les formes, la syntaxe ou le vocabulaire à la langue

---

[11] Argot, the jargon of the criminal fraternity, is also excluded from the discussion; for details of this, see, for example, Sainéan 1907.

[12] In Labovian models style is defined quantitatively, that is, in terms of the relative frequency of features or style markers. The paucity of examples for many of our features makes the use of statistics difficult or impossible here.

des "honnêtes gens" comme à celle des "doctes"' (1957: 222). He offers as suggestions of writers who are closest to popular usage Scarron, Saint-Amant, d'Assoucy (Dassoucy, or Dassouci) and Brébeuf, and notes that *langue populaire* may be found in prose texts such as Cyrano de Bergerac's *Le Pedant joué*, but is more usual in verse, typically parodical in nature, such as the rhymed Mazarinades. In his view it may be found in the theatre of Scarron, Cyrano and Thomas Corneille amongst others, as well as in travel accounts, political pamphlets and rhymed gazettes. Lathuillère (1984) argues that examples of *langue populaire* may be found in texts written in Parisian patois (see below (d) for details) such as the Mazarinades, and especially the *Agréables Conférences*, in farces and in certain 'realistic' novels by authors such as Sorel, Scarron and Furetière. He also mentions the *Caquets de l'accouchée*, *Oeuvres de Tabarin*, and *Chansons de Gaultier-Garguille*. In the following sections we intend to consider the extent to which these different texts may be used as sources of low-register and popular usages.

(a)   Burlesque texts

For Vaugelas and many seventeenth-century commentators on the French language words and expressions considered non-standard, and especially those labelled *bas*, are generally not acceptable, either in written texts or in spoken French where they might make the speaker appear ridiculous. However, they are tolerated in burlesque, and other related comic forms such as satire. The burlesque genre was fashionable for a relatively short period, peaking between 1643 and 1653. It was associated above all with Paul Scarron (1610–60), who published a series of burlesque texts, notably the *Recueil de quelques vers burlesques* (1643), *Le Typhon* (1644) and *Le Virgile travesti* (1648–51). Amongst other burlesque authors we may cite Brébeuf, Saint-Amant, Perrault and d'Assoucy. It is common to find a noble subject (such as the Aeneid) presented in a low setting using low-register language.[13]

Burlesque language was not restricted to poetry: it could also be found in comedies such as Scarron's *Le Jodelet* (performed 1643), *L'Héritier ridicule* (performed 1649; burlesque language is particularly used to characterize the lackey Filipin, alias Dom Pedro), *Les Trois Dorothées* (performed 1645) and *Don Japhet d'Arménie* (performed 1651–2). As we shall see, burlesque verse lent itself to the popular satire of the Mazarinades. Burlesque texts also found a wider audience through the *Bibliothèque bleue*, so called because of the blue sugar paper wrappers of these small, cheap books which were sold throughout France by pedlars (*colporteurs*). The books, produced in vast numbers and

---

[13] For example, Scarron (1988: 80) in *Le Virgile travesti*: 'Un gouffre à la fin l'absorba / Ou, pour mieux dire, la goba'; the final verb *gober* is a popular term, only used in a comic context. A similar composite use of language, mixing *mots nobles* and *mots bas*, is found in Jacques Jacques's *Le faut mourir* (Costa 1998).

priced very cheaply, were aimed at those who did not traditionally buy books. Some of them were read aloud at village gatherings, which brought the texts to a wider public given the low levels of literacy amongst their intended audience (see Bollème 1971).

Bar (1960) provides a key study of the linguistic features of burlesque texts and it is not my intention to duplicate his work here. The humour of burlesque writings was derived in no small part through the use of a composite language: burlesque writers consciously and artificially mixed registers, and did not attempt to sustain a consistent tone. Guez de Balzac is typical in his criticism of burlesque for its use of archaisms, low-register language and mismatch between the register and subject matter. D'Assoucy affirms that neither he nor Scarron reproduce faithfully popular French, but rather view it as a source on which to draw: 'ni Scarron ni moi n'avons jamais parlé ce langage, et, si par hazard nous l'avons quelquefois employé, ce n'a pas été par ignorance, mais par jugement, par choix et de propos délibéré' (Bertrand 1997: 153).[14]

Scarron's description of burlesque authors in his poem *A M. d'Aumalle* (Bar 1960: xxxii) suggests that these texts may be a fruitful source of low-register French of the period:

> Ils ont pour discours ordinaires,
> Des termes bas et populaires,
> Des proverbes mal appliquez,
> Des quolibets mal expliquez,
> Des mots tournez en ridicule
> Que leur sot esprit accumule
> Sans jugement et sans raison [. . .]

Features of the genre do indeed include low-register terms, and especially *mots bas*, *mots déshonnêtes* and *mots réalistes* (see Bar 1960, Richardson 1930); there are also traits which are thought to typify low-class usage such as proverbs, archaisms (especially words which have disappeared from good usage but are still used by the people), neologisms (not yet established in good usage), and patois words. However, these popular features are juxtaposed with learned features such as Latinisms and other words of foreign origin, with technical and other pedantic terms. In short, from a lexical point of view the language is extremely composite. Rhetorical devices such as accumulation, periphrases and word play are also consciously exploited.

In general the morphology and syntax of these texts are much more standardized. Morphological features include the elision of *si*, and the use of the

---

[14] Bertrand (1997: 154) suggests that d'Assoucy's usage in *Les Aventures* differs from that of some of the other burlesque writers in that he makes rather sparing use of argot and popular forms drawn from Les Halles.

archaic forms *cil, icelle(s), cettui-ci, cettui-là*. Burlesque syntax equally combines archaic usages – such as the non-use of articles before nouns, subjunctives used in main clauses without an introductory *que*, and the omission of *pas*, *point* from negative structures – with features of popular syntax such as the pleonastic use of subject pronouns and the omission of the impersonal pronoun *il* (cf. Richardson 1930, Bar 1960). The syntax is also typified by asymmetrical coordination, elliptical structures, *constructions louches* and inversion (see below).

All this leads Bar (1960: 388–94) to conclude that burlesque is not a popular, but rather an artificial, genre. He counsels caution when using burlesque texts as sources of popular language:

Pour l'historien de la langue, il y a là, non pas un témoignage direct sur le parler de telle ou telle classe sociale, mais, en ce qui concerne le vocabulaire, un ensemble de matériaux aussi copieux que mêlé [. . .] le fait d'avoir été employés par les burlesques a pu avilir encore certains termes familiers, et inciter les puristes à les éliminer avec une particulière sévérité. (Bar 1960: 393)

Given these difficulties, I decided to look first at the extent to which those words and expressions considered *bas* or low class by the metalinguistic texts occur particularly in burlesque works in FRANTEXT (section 3.3.2), and secondly – bearing in mind the potential danger of circularity – at the correlation between usage in these texts and words and expressions designated as *burlesque*. A number of burlesque writers are included in FRANTEXT, as Table 3.3 shows.

(b)   *Other literary texts*
Lathuillère (1984) argued that certain 'realist' novels, such as Sorel's *Francion* (1623–33) and *Le Berger extravagant* (1627–8), Scarron's *Roman comique* (1651–7) and Furetière's *Roman bourgeois* (1666), may also be used as sources of popular French. (Of these only *Le Berger extravagant* is currently in FRANTEXT.) Bar (1960: 383) notes that these novels have some vocabulary in common with burlesque texts, particularly as regards low-register and colourful terms. He points out, however, that care must be taken in interpreting the term 'realist' in relation to seventeenth-century novels. The intention of these works is not to given an exact and detailed picture of 'real life'; rather they are comic or satirical works (see also Bar 1959). As we noted in Chapter 2, while the dialogue in these texts may contain some informal lexical features, the syntax tends to be much more standardized. For example, the characterization of bourgeois speech in Furetière's *Roman bourgeois* is achieved not by syntactic means, but by the insertion of the occasional lexical item, such as Javotte's use of the proverbial expression *ferrer la mule*. However, even more significant are the general qualities of the dialogue; it is the literal nature of Javotte's language, its lack of sophistication and almost childish quality, which are the principal

Table 3.3 *Burlesque texts in* FRANTEXT

AUTHOR	Texts in FRANTEXT
Assoucy, Charles d'	• *Le Jugement de Paris en vers burlesques* (1648; verse) • *Les Amours d'Apollon et de Daphné* (1650; theatre, verse) • *L'Ovide en belle humeur* (1650; verse) • *Poësies et lettres* (1653; verse) • *Le Ravissement de Proserpine* (1653; verse)
Brébeuf, Georges de	• Translation (5 vols.) of Lucan's *Pharsalia* (1654–5; verse) • *Lucain travesti* (1656; verse) • *Entretiens solitaires* (1660; verse)
Perrault, Charles	No burlesque texts, only the *Contes de fées* (1697)
Saint-Amant, Marc-Antoine de Gérard (or Girard) sieur de	No texts
Scarron, Paul	• *Le Jodelet* (1645; theatre, verse) • *L'Héritier ridicule* (1650; theatre, verse) • *Don Japhet d'Arménie* (1653; theatre, verse) • *Le Gardien de soy-mesme* (1655: theatre, verse; also the verse dedication)

devices exploited to portray his bourgeois speech habits (Furetière [1955]: 9–10). A similar example is furnished by Sorel's *Histoire comique de Francion* (Roy 1924–31; see also Béchade 1981, Fournier 2001). In the *Advertissement d'importance aux lecteurs* (1626; Roy 1924–31, I: xi–xxiii) Sorel claims: 'dans mon livre on peut trouver la langue Françoise toute entiere, et [. . .] je n'ay point oublié les mots dont use le vulgaire'; however, he equally claims that, 'ceux qui me cognoissent sçavent bien que ne suis pas si ignorant que de pecher contre les loix de la Grammaire'. If we then consider the episodes which present ordinary people or peasants (e.g. in Book 6, Roy 1924–31, II: 181–3), we find their language typified by a relatively small number of phonological features (e.g. *chappiau, darnier, couraine*) and lexical features (e.g. *par la verti gué, regardure*) and one or two morphological traits (e.g. *ou* for *vous*, perfects in *–i*). In short, these texts are of relatively little use in the investigation of specific morpho-syntactic features.

The same caveats apply to the use of comic theatre – whether by Cyrano de Bergerac, Thomas Corneille or Molière – as a source of linguistic data (see below); excess and caricature play a large role in the use of language. A recurring difficulty is the fact that the characterization is largely achieved through lexical and phonetic means; on the whole, the morphology and syntax are standardized. This is evident, for example, in an otherwise interesting text, *Les Caquets de l'accouchée* (Fournier 1855). This anonymous work[15] was first published in instalments in 1622, and then appeared a year later in one volume. The text presents the conversations of a gathering of women from different social classes around the bedside of a new mother. While it includes a number of low-register usages as noted by Oudin (1640) such as *cahin, caha* (Oudin: 'vulgaire, i. "avec peine, et par secousses."') and *faire le papelart* (Oudin: 'un *papelard*, i. "un hypocrite."'), the syntax follows the standard norms for the period.[16]

In our analysis of the extent to which terms identified as being low-register or popular are used in FRANTEXT we will examine the extent to which they cluster in certain literary texts. It is hoped that this will allow us better to evaluate the relative value of different types of texts as sources of social and stylistic variation.

(c)   'Private texts': Livres de raison, *journals and memoirs*
Memoirs, journals and *livres de raison* may all be seen as 'private texts' (Foisil 1986: 331), and as such are possible sources of more informal usages. A *livre de raison*, to cite Furetière, is a book in which 'un bon mesnager, ou un Marchand escrit tout ce qu'il reçoit & despense, pour se rendre compte & raison à luy-même de toutes ses affaires'. While these, by definition, are private documents, not intended for circulation or publication, clearly not all journals or memoirs fall into this category. Some of the best-known memoirs of the period are written by the high-ranking and famous, and chronicle their deeds for the benefit of others within the context of contemporary events, including military campaigns and political deeds.[17]

Gerhard Ernst and Barbara Wolf are currently undertaking a major research project to publish and analyse a series of twelve texts of a private nature dating from the seventeenth and eighteenth centuries, that is personal journals, autobiographies, memoirs and *livres de raison*; to date four texts have been published on two CD-ROMs (Ernst and Wolf 2001–2).[18] As well as being texts of a private nature, for which the holograph is available, the texts are selected

---

[15] The first three conversations, which Fournier considers to be the most original part, are by the same hand. The remaining conversations are by other hands.

[16] Note that there are no examples of *faire le papelard* in FRANTEXT, and only one of *cahin caha*, which occurs in the peasant speech in Molière's *Dom Juan* (see below).

[17] Another possible source of a similar type suggested by Bar (1981) is travel accounts; many of these, however, pose the same problems. For example, Robert Challe, author of a *Journal d'un Voyage fait aux Indes Orientales 1690–91* (Deloffre and Menemencioglou 1979), despite his bourgeois origins, was well educated and became a lawyer and subsequently *Ecrivain du roi*.

[18] In the study to accompany these editions they intend to refer to a thirteenth text, the Journal of Louis Simon (1809–20), which has been edited by Anne Fillon (1996). Ernst (1999: 91) notes that while the low social origin of the writer and the private nature of the texts tends to make them 'nähesprachlich', the fact that they are written, not spoken, gives them distance.

because they are by people of modest social standing (but see below), and by what Ernst (1999: 92) terms 'semicolti', for whom writing is not their occupation. Of these twelve texts, four (by Reveillard, Girard, Montjean and Ménétra) were excluded since they were chronologically too late for this study. Another seven were discounted since they are regional in origin, all emanating from places more than 150 kilometres from Paris, including Anjou, Brittany and Allier.[19] This leaves one Parisian *livre de raison*.

Livres de raison initially appear to be a promising source of informal writing, but they pose a number of difficulties. First, many of the texts are written by those, such as lawyers or doctors,[20] whose profession required sustained education. Equally, they may be composed by the upper middle classes or nobles; thus the Parisian *livre de raison* edited by Ernst is by Anne-Marguerite le Mercier, a member of a noble Huguenot family of intellectuals. Second, the majority of surviving texts come from the regions and especially the Midi, and have to be excluded here since these 'private' texts often display strong regional features.[21] Third, the entries are typically brief and rather formulaic, recounting births, marriages and deaths or providing inventories of household goods and expenditures. As a result they provide little or no information about non-standard syntax.

(d)   Texts in Parisian patois

The peasant speech of the Ile-de-France is occasionally reflected in texts apparently written entirely or partially in Parisian patois. The most notable examples of works entirely in the Parisian patois are Mazarinades, and especially those entitled the *Agréables Conférences*, which we will discuss in the next section (3.3.1e). Nisard (1980 [1876]: 215–32) lists alongside these works Berthaud's (or Berthod's) *La Ville de Paris, en vers burlesques, dernière édition,*

---

[19] One of the most interesting examples is the autobiography of Chavatte, a sayette or sagathy weaver from Lille (Lottin 1979).

[20] Note that one of Ernst and Wolf's texts, the journal of Guillaume Durand, is by a surgeon from Poligny. The same comment applies to some of the diaries and memoirs. For instance, at first glance, a work entitled *Memoires. Enfance et éducation d'un paysan au XVIIIe siècle* appears a promising source of low-class usage until you discover that the 'peasant' of the title is Valentin Jamerey-Duval, who was indeed born into a modest rural family but who subsequently became librarian of the Duc de Lorraine and was awarded the title of professor at the Académie de Luneville. A similar case is Jacques Flournoy's *Journal* written between 1675 and 1693. Flournoy was of bourgeois origin and became a historian, numismatist and epigraphist (Fatio 1994).

[21] Amongst those held in the British Library there are texts from the Lot-et-Garonne, Rodez and Agen. I also consulted a large number of *livres de raison* in the Archives Départementales de la Haute-Vienne in Limoges. The use of French in them tends to be formulaic and rather conservative; sentences are at times long and unstructured, and there is much individual variation in spelling. Although their authors had a range of occupations and professions, unsurprisingly there is no document from a peasant family, who would presumably have transmitted family history orally.

augmentée de nouveau de La Foire Saint-Germain, par le sieur Scarron (Paris, 1665). His second list of works written essentially in standardized language but which have a number of words, expressions or passages in the Parisian patois is more problematic. Nisard lists over forty items for the seventeenth century, including a number of Mazarinades in burlesque verse; many of these, such as the *Caquets de l'accouchée*, provide little or no evidence of the patois, but are rather sources of familiar language, and of proverbs, archaisms and other popular and colourful terms.[22]

A number of commentators, including Lathuillère (1984) and Lodge (1991), have pointed to literary representations of the Parisian patois, most notably the peasants in Cyrano de Bergerac's *Le Pédant joué* (*PJ* II, 3);[23] the language of the nurse Jacqueline and her husband Lucas in Molière's *Le Médecin malgré lui* (*MML* I, 4, 5; II, 1–4; III, 3, 4); the language of the peasants Pierrot and Charlotte in Molière's *Dom Juan* (*DJ* II, 1–3; see Lodge 1991); and of those in Brécourt's *La Nopce de Village* (*NV* 1666 [1681]). There has been much debate about the authenticity of these literary portrayals of low-class speech. On the one hand it is striking that many of the features recorded by the metalinguistic texts and also used in the Mazarinades also occur in these texts. As a result Lathuillère (1984) concludes that there is little difference between the language of the fishwives of Les Halles and the peasant patois of the area beginning at the gates of Paris in places such as Vaugirard and Saint-Ouen. Lodge (1991: 497) agrees that the lower class in Paris appears to have spoken a dialect related to those of the surrounding country region.[24]

On the other hand it is essential to remember that these are stylized presentations of peasants, caricatures in which the linguistic traits are particularly emphasized for the sake of comedy. A number of stereotypical features, which would be instantly recognized by the theatre-going public, are consistently employed to characterize peasant patois, some of which were undoubtedly going out of use by the time they were used in these comic texts. Thus we find the recurrence of similar morphological features such as *je pensons, j'avons pris* (*MML*) / *j'étions* (*DJ*) / *je somme, j'en connoisson* (*NV*); *les médecins y avont tous pardu leur latin* (*MML*) / *ils l'avont r'habillé* (*DJ*); phonetic features such as the reduction or syncopation of unstressed vowels as in *vlà* (*MML*) / *vlà* (*DJ*) / *vela* (*NV*), the use of 'ar' for 'er' as in *charcher* (*MML*) / *renvarsés, tarre* (*DJ*) / *parmission* (*NV*), and incorrect liaisons such as *quand tu z'en aurois quatre,*

---

[22] See also Jacob (1859), which includes texts by Berthod, Colletet, Scarron and Boileau-Despréaux. It should be noted that it is the subject matter rather than the style which unifies this collection.

[23] Note also Cyrano de Bergerac, *Mazarinades. Préface de René Briand*. Paris: Editions de l'Opale, 1981.

[24] Wittmann (1995: 290) asserts that the *français populaire* spoken in Paris was a sort of inter-dialectal koine, created because of Paris's status as a 'ville-refuge'.

on za biau (*NV*). Lexical features include the use of exclamations and swear words which involve the deformation of words such as *parguenne, morguenne* (*MML*) / *parguienne, morguienne* (*DJ*) / *marguene* (*NV*); *une guéble de commission* (*MML*) / *guiable* (*NV*); and the inclusion of popular terms such as *cahin caha* or *ébobi* (*DJ*). These features combine to create the illusion of a peasant speaker of patois. One of the difficulties with these texts is that once again – presumably because of the necessity of making the speech comprehensible to a non-patois-speaking audience – the syntax is much more regular. Brécourt is unusual in his inclusion of a number of non-standard constructions such as this interrogative: 'Veux-tu sçavoir pourquoy que je suis en colere?' (1681: 3); he also uses archaic structures, such as *ne . . . goutte* in negative clauses.

Jacob's (1859) edition of a number of burlesque and satirical texts relating to Paris includes the anonymous *Cris de Paris*. This is a seventeenth-century version of a collection of verse and prose texts which was first published around 1500. These texts which present the cries of Parisian street sellers are, like many of the texts we have already discussed, a representation by the educated of the spoken language of the people, and are not an example of spontaneous popular culture produced by the lower classes themselves (Milliot 1995: 148–9). Milliot points out, moreover, that the text tends to change little after the end of the sixteenth century and that the presentation of the different social types becomes stereotyped (1995: 351). This example of the cry of the *crocheteur* is typical:

Je crie: *Coterets, bourées, buches!*
Aucune fois: *Fagots, ou falourdes!*
Quand vois que point on ne me huche,
Je dis: *Achetez femmes lourdes!* (Jacob 1859: 300)

(e)   Mazarinades

Many of the problems we have discussed in relation to other possible sources of low-register and popular speech are also associated with the source on which I propose to concentrate in this chapter, the Mazarinades. These are pamphlets in verse or prose which were produced during the Fronde, mostly directed against Mazarin, Anne of Austria and the financiers. According to Carrier (1982: I, i) more than 5000 such pamphlets were published between 13 May 1648 and 31 July 1653; most of them appeared anonymously, although there are also some by writers such as Patru, Sarasin and Cyrano de Bergerac. The authorship of the best known of the Mazarinades, the *Agréables Conférences*, has been the subject of debate; Deloffre (1961: 20) favours L. Richer, a burlesque writer, perhaps a clerk of the court or prosecutor. This again points to the artificiality of the texts.

One of the reasons I have decided to focus on the Mazarinades is because they fall into a number of different types, and reflect some of the different usages, which were discussed above. They also have the advantage of having been produced within a short chronological span, thereby excluding change as a possible complicating factor: all the texts examined here date from the period 1649–51.

The four main types which I intend to examine are dialogues between members of the lower class, pamphlets written in a *style bas* (especially those in the form of letters), burlesque verse and texts written in the Parisian patois. As before, care must be taken in interpreting these labels. For example, the popular pieces, written in what Carrier (1989: 396) calls the 'style du Pont-Neuf et de la Samaritaine', may couple with features of popular style (proverbs, archaisms, low-register terms, neologisms, etc.) learned references and citations in Latin, suggesting a rather higher level of education on both the part of the author and the intended audience. One of the pamphleteers makes this point explicitly: '& quoy que mon style soit de tres-bas pris, neantmoins ie vous diray ce petit passage d'Horace' (*La Lettre d'vn secretaire de S. Innocent [. . .]*, p. 8). While the Mazarinade entitled *Les Contens et mescontens sur le suiet du temps* introduces a number of lower-class speakers, the text closes with a quotation from Cicero in Latin; similarly the Parisian in *La Sottise des deux partis* cites Aristotle in Latin. A related question, raised by H.-J. Martin, is whether the Mazarinades were intended for a popular readership. It is likely that many were rather aimed at notables, although one pamphleteer does suggest that some of the prose patois pieces were read by a lower-class audience: 'Ie te le donne en vers [. . .] ne le presentant qu'aux personnes de qualité, sçachant bien que la populace ne s'arrête qu'en la lecture de son ancien patois, les pensées Poëtiques surpassant par trop la bassesse de son Esprit' (Carrier 1989: 397). This is probably also true of some of the dialogues which present speakers of the lower classes, since these seem to reflect not only the language of these classes but also their mentality. The Mazarinades probably also reached a wider audience since many of them were reprinted in the *Bibliothèque bleue*, and sold by pedlars in vast numbers; the *Agréables Conférences*, for example, became one of its classics (Deloffre 1961: 11). The association of popular literature with the lower classes is not straightforward and must be approached with care. Mandrou has argued, for instance, that the *Bibliothèque bleue* was produced to keep the people subservient and not produced by it, although there is a positive side in that it created new reading habits (Muchembled 1990: 143).

The ten texts to be analysed in detail may be broadly classified into the following four types:[25]

---

[25] Where possible, Mazarinades with a readily accessible printed version were selected for analysis. Collections of original pamphlets were consulted in the Cambridge University Library (Ggg.

1. Dialogues between representatives of the lower classes:
   a. *Dialogue de Jodelet et de Lorviatan Sur les affaires de ce temps* (1649) [Carrier 1982, I: number 14]. Jodelet, a comic actor of Molière's troop, created characters bearing his name, which became synonymous with a buffoon or comic fool.
   b. *Les Contens et mescontens sur le suiet du temps* (1649) [Carrier 1982, II: number 44]: a number of different voices are heard including those of a fishwife, a butcher and a seller of second-hand clothes.[26]
   c. *La Sottise des deux partis. Dialogue du Parisien et du Mazariniste* (1649) [Ggg. 22(6)]
2. *Style bas*:
   d. *La Lettre d'vn secretaire de S. Innocent a Iules Mazarin* (1649) [Ggg. 34(64)]
   e. *Lettre de Guillaume Sans-Peur, Aux Trouppes de Mazarin* (1649) [Ggg. 34(75)]
3. Burlesque:
   f. *Agreable recit de ce qui s'est passé aux dernieres barricades de Paris. Faites le 26. Aoust 1648. Descrites en vers Burlesques* (3rd edition 1649) [Carrier 1982, II: number 46]. (Carrier argues that this text, by the 'Baron de Verderonne, gentilhomme ordinaire de Monsieur', is notable for the way it illustrates the power of the people and for its picturesque language.)
4. Paris patois:[27]
   Prose
   g. *Agréables Conférences de deux paysans de Saint-Ouen et de Montmorency sur les affaires du temps* (1649–51) [Deloffre 1961]:[28] considered by Rosset (1911: 5) to be an 'artifice littéraire', the work of an educated person who has transcribed the patois for comic effect. Seguin (1999: 294) is of the same opinion, describing it as a caricature. Deloffre (1961), however, views it as the most complete record of the French spoken in the Ile-de-France in the seventeenth century.

19–37, F164.c.4.2–3), and in the Taylor Institution Library, Oxford (Vet Fr IB. 192–197, 221). Other interesting texts, such as the *Nouveaux complimens de la place Maubert, des halles, cimetière S.-Jean, Marché-Neuf, et autres places publiques* (1644), in which there is a clear difference in the portrayal of the speech of the bourgeois woman and the fishwife, may be found in Fournier (1855–63).

[26] The speech of the different characters is framed by a first-person narrative.

[27] Since we have excluded regional variation from our analysis, the focus here is on texts from the Ile-de-France, but there are also Mazarinades representing the patois of Orleans, Normandy and Picardy. Typical groups of speakers are portrayed as using this language, including merchants and tradespeople from Les Halles, especially fishwives. The texts may be in verse or prose.

[28] Quotations are taken from the 1961 edition. A new edition, with a revised bibliography, appeared in 1999 (Geneva: Slatkine reprints).

Verse

h. *La Gazette des Halles touchant les affaires du temps. Premiere nouvelle* (1649) [Ggg. 31(94)]

i. *La Gazette de la Place Maubert ou Suitte de la Gazette des Halles. Touchant les affaires du temps. Seconde nouvelle* (1649) [Ggg. 31(95)]

j. *Suitte de la Gazette de la Place Maubert par l'Autheur de la Gazette des Halles; touchant les affaires du temps* (1649) [Ggg. 31(96)]

3.3.2   Vocabulary

In this section I intend first to look at the degree of convergence between the comments of the metalinguistic texts and the textual evidence of FRANTEXT, with a view to evaluating the reliability of the data afforded by the *remarqueurs* and lexicographers about social and stylistic variation. Secondly, I shall consider the question from the opposite standpoint by analysing some of the popular lexical features employed in my corpus of Mazarinades.

Three types of observations were selected for discussion: those where the usage is considered *bas, burlesque* or typical of the people; in each case ten representative examples were chosen. It should be noted that these different parameters of variation are not always clearly kept apart by the *remarqueurs*. In some cases a clear link is established between low-register usage and the lower classes; for instance, *né natif* is described by Bouhours (1675: 133) as a 'locution basse' which would only be employed by 'le petit peuple'. In each case the *remarqueur*'s comment on the word or expression is compared with the views expressed in six dictionaries (Nicot (N), Cotgrave (C), Oudin (O), Richelet (R), Furetière (F), Academy (A)); these comments are then set beside seventeenth-century usage of the term as evidenced by FRANTEXT (Tables 3.4–3.6).

As regards terms considered *bas* (Table 3.4), in the majority of cases there is a clear correlation between the metalinguistic comments and usage in FRANTEXT, in that examples of the words and expressions tend to occur predominantly in either comedies, satires and burlesque texts, genres identified as low-register or in letters; only in the case of *à l'aveugle* is there a significant discrepancy between the observation and dictionaries on the one hand and textual usage on the other. Perhaps the clearest example of the observations reflecting usage is *des mieux*, but it is also true for *cheoir, corner* and *goguenard*. In the case of *mal-gracieux* and *né natif* – the latter presumably disliked because it was considered tautological – the paucity of examples likewise suggests that these terms were not considered suitable for the kind of texts included in FRANTEXT. In the case of *pour l'heure, vitupere* and *entaché* it is less clear how far the *remarqueur* reflected current usage or helped to shape subsequent usage. In each of these cases the majority of examples occur up to the time

Table 3.4 *Terms considered* bas

Word/expression	Comment by *remarqueur*	Comments in the dictionaries	Usage in FRANTEXT
1. Des mieux	Vaugelas (1647: 123): 'Il n'y rien de si commun, que cette façon de parler, *il danse des mieux, il chante des mieux*, pour dire *il danse fort bien, il chante parfaitement bien*; mais elle est tres-basse, & nullement du langage de la Cour'; Dupleix (1651: 231) disagrees.	Not commented on by any of the dictionaries; F uses the expression once in one of his definitions.	There are twenty-seven examples of this usage dating from 1623 to 1696. However, the type of texts in which they occur is significant. Of the ten texts which pre-date Vaugelas's comment, six are by Sorel, two come from P. Corneille's comedies, one is by Scarron, and one is from Du Lorens, *Satires*. Among the remaining examples, there are four by Molière, one by Scarron and three from P. Corneille's comedies.
2. Pour l'heure (= pour lors)	Vaugelas (1647: 192): 'est bonne, mais basse, & ne doit pas estre employée dans le beau stile, où il faut dire *pour lors*'.	Not commented on by any of the dictionaries.	Of the thirty-six examples dating from 1601–82, twenty-nine pre-date 1647; of the remaining seven, two come from M. de Pure's *Prétieuse*, two from P. Corneille's comedies and there is one example each by Molière, La Fontaine and Mme de Sévigné.
3. Vitupere	Vaugelas (1647: 412–13): 'Ce mot n'est gueres bon [. . .] Ie n'en voudrois vser qu'en raillerie, & dans le stile bas.'	Cited by N, C without comment. F, A consider it archaic; R considers it archaic and adds '& ne peut servir tout au plus dans des sujets de railleries & dans le plus bas style'.	Usage in FRANTEXT apparently confirms the metalinguistic comments that by the middle of the century it was becoming dated and therefore reserved for lower-register or comic contexts. There are twenty-three examples up to 1646; of the five remaining examples four are by d'Assoucy (1648–53) and one is by Brébeuf (1656).
4. Mal-gracieux	Vaugelas (1647: 526): 'il est bas, & ie ne le voudrois pas escrire dans le stile noble'.	Not in N, C, O. Given without comment by F and A. R cites Vaugelas in his entry.	Only two examples. One, by the valet La Flèche in Molière's *L'Avare* (1669), supports the metalinguistic comments; the other is from Benserade's translation of Ovid's *Metamorphoses* (1676).

5. Entaché	Vaugelas (1647: 542): 'Ce mot est dans la bouche presque de tout le monde [. . .] mais il est extrêmement bas.'	Given without comment by N, C and F. R assigns it a '+' and follows Vaugelas in considering it low register. A comments that the participle is the only form commonly used.	Eleven examples (1610–60), including three satirical texts.
6. Né natif	Bouhours (1675: 133): 'Cette façon de parler est de ces locutions basses qui ne sortent point de leur bassesse, & il n'y a que le petit peuple qui dise, un tel est né natif de Paris.'	Not commented on by any of the dictionaries.	One example only, by Pasquier (1613).
7. A l'aveugle	Bouhours (1675: 228): 'C'est une locution basse & populaire, dont les personnes polies ne se servent point.'	The expression is not noted in any of the dictionaries.	Bouhours's comments are not supported by FRANTEXT: twenty-five examples 1623–91 including examples by Coëffeteau, Bossuet and Arnauld d'Andilly.
8. Ch(e)oir*	Alemand (1688: 365): 'ce verbe avec ses deux ou trois temps n'est usité au propre que dans le discours familier ou dans le stile le plus bas'.	Included by N, C, F and A. Not in R.	Sixty-six examples (1602–60). It is significant that all the examples pre-date Alemand's comments and that eleven of the last thirteen of these examples are by Brébeuf and Cyrano de Bergerac.
9. Corner	Andry de Boisregard (1689: 137): 'L'usage ne reçoit ce mot qu'en cette manière de parler, les oreilles luy cornent. Ce terme est bas & populaire, il est venu de ce que le bruit qu'on entend alors, est semblable à celuy d'un cors.'	O: 'Corner, qui se dit de la chair, i. "sentir mauvais, estre puante ou corrumpuë", vulg. Les oreilles me cornent, i. "on parle de moy en quelque lieu", vulg.'. R assigns both senses '*+'; C and F give both without comment on register; A gives only the second usage, as a figurative one.	No examples of Oudin's first sense; eight examples of Oudin's second usage (1628–81), including two by Molière, two in the correspondence of Mme de Sévigné and two in the correspondence of Bussy-Rabutin.
10. Goguenard	Andry de Boisregard (1689: 242): 'ne se dit que dans le stile bas & familier'.	Not discussed in N, C or O. F and A include it without comment on its usage, but R assigns it '+'.	Six examples (1661–96), including three from Molière's comedies and two from Bussy-Rabutin's letters.

* Alemand (1688: 366) prefers the spelling *choir*, adding that he considers it pointless to discuss whether the verb should be spelt *choir* or *cheoir*.

Table 3.5 *Words and expressions labelled* burlesque *by the* remarqueurs

Word/expression	Comment by remarqueur	Comments in the dictionaries	Usage in FRANTEXT
1. N'en pouvoir mais	Vaugelas (1647: 142): 'Cette façon de parler est ordinaire à la Cour, mais elle est bien basse pour s'en seruir en escriuant, si ce n'est en Satyre, en Comedie, ou en Epigramme, qui sont les trois genres d'escrire les plus bas, & encore faut-il que ce soit dans le Burlesque'; Andry de Boisregard (1689: 290): 'n'est plus d'usage, que dans le stile goguenard & burlesque'; Ménage (1675: 122–3) disagrees.	The expression is not discussed in N, C, O or F. R assigns it a '+'. A includes the expression, but comments that it is little used in the infinitive; the example 'je ne puis mais de cela' is cited without comment about its usage.	There are no examples of this construction in the infinitive. The expression ne pouvoir mais de + noun occurs ten times, but all the examples date from the 1610s. The expression n'en pouvoir mais occurs eighteen times, with eleven of the examples dating from 1610–31. Of the remaining examples, one is by Cyrano (1655), one by M. de Pure (1656), one by Molière (1663) and two by La Fontaine (1668).
2. Seriosité	Vaugelas (1647: 254): 'Ce mot jusqu'icy ne s'est dit qu'en raillerie'; only for comedy, satire and burlesque epigrams.	Only in F and R: R comments that it is not established.	There are only two examples, both by Guez de Balzac (1654).
3. Gent	Ménage (1675: 61): [Gens] 'Mais aujourd'hui il n'est plus guère en usage qu'au plurier, si ce n'est en vers burlesques.'	In C and O without comment. R considers it rather old and thinks it is better in burlesque, citing an example from Scarron. F claims it used to be used in poetry, while A states it is still used, but only in poetry.	Of the ninety-three occurrences of gent, seventy-five date from 1601 to 1653; of the remaining eighteen, seventeen are by La Fontaine.
4. Accoustrement	Andry de Boisregard (1689: 20): only in burlesque or 'Stile bas'.	Not as a headword in N, O, R. In C without comment. F comments 'il ne se dit que parmy le peuple', while A considers it 'vieux'.	Usage in FRANTEXT confirms that it had fallen out of good usage by Andry's day; seventeen of the eighteen examples date from 1601–36, and the last example is by Voiture (1654).
5. Alambiquer	Andry de Boisregard (1689: 43): 'Ce mot n'est d'usage qu'au figuré burlesque, alambiquer son esprit, mais on ne dira pas alambiquer des herbes, pour distiller des herbes.'	Not in N, O or F. C gives the sense 'to extract, distil' and s'alambiquer 'to consume [. . .], weare away'. R cites only s'alambiquer to which he assigns '+' and illustrates with an example from Scarron; A lists only the figurative sense approved of by Andry.	Usage in FRANTEXT seems to confirm Andry's position. Of the twenty examples, twelve date from 1603–40. The remaining occurrences generally occur with esprit, cerveau or tête and include examples by Du Lorens, Cyrano de Bergerac, Brébeuf and Molière.

6. D'avanture / par avanture	Andry de Boisregard (1689: 74): 'ne se disent plus que dans le style badin, & burlesque'; Buffet (1668: 73) considers *par avanture* to be archaic and therefore used only by 'le petit peuple'.	There are dozens of examples of *d'avanture** used adverbially, but all the examples date from before 1669; over half of them are of *si d'avanture*. There are fewer examples of *par avanture* (forty-two). Thirty-eight are from before 1669; of the remaining four, two seem to reflect Andry's comment, since they occur in comedies by Molière and P. Corneille.
	D'avanture (or *d'aventure*) is not cited in N, C or O. F and A include it without comment on its usage (F has the expression *si d'avanture*), but R considers that it is archaic. The comments on *par avanture* (or *par aventure*) mirror those for *d'avanture* exactly.	
7. Chanceux	Andry de Boisregard (1689: 116): 'Chanceux, heureux. C'est une maniere de parler familiere, qui n'entre point dans le discours un peu relevé, elle est bonne dans le burlesque.'	Only four examples, two by Molière (1669, 1673), one by La Fontaine and one by Mme de Sévigné.
	O: 'chanceux "s'entend en deux façons, heureux, et mal heureux," vulg.'. N and C cite it without comment. R assigns it '+' and gives only the positive meaning. F gives both senses, but A only the positive one; both cite the expression 'un homme bien chanceux'.	
8. Chenu	Andry de Boisregard (1689: 118): 'ne se dit plus guéres aujourd'huy. Ce mot néanmoins peut avoir sa place dans la Poësie, & sur tout dans le Burlesque.'	Twenty-two examples, the last of which dates from 1655; it is significant that the last two examples appear in comic texts by Scarron (1650) and Cyrano de Bergerac (1655).
	Cited by N and C without comment. R defines the term, and then the poetic figurative usage ('onde chenuë'), to which he assigns '+*'. F considers it archaic, but A defines it without comment about its currency, adding examples of the poetic figurative usage.	
9. Maint	Andry de Boisregard (1689: 290): 'On ne se sert de ce terme qu'en Poësie, & encore n'est-ce que dans le Satyrique & le Burlesque.'	Although there are examples of *maint* throughout the century, 409 of the 527 date from before 1660. It is significant that of the remaining 118, eighty-five are by La Fontaine (see below).
	In N and C without comment. R marks it '+' and adds 'vieux mot burlesque'; F agrees that it is really only current in burlesque, while A says it may be used only in some poetry.	
10. Malencontreux	Andry de Boisregard (1689: 293): 'ne se dit que dans le stile burlesque ou satirique'.	Of the thirty-five examples of this term, thirty-one are from the first half of the century. The four remaining examples are by d'Assoucy (1650), Brébeuf (1656), Molière (1663) and Regnard (1698).
	Not in N or O. In C and F without comment. R assigns it '+' and A comments 'il est bas & vieillit'.	

---

* In all cases alternative spellings are included; here, *avanture*, *aventure*, *advanture* and *adventure* were searched for.

Table 3.6 *Words attributed to low-class usage by the* remarqueurs

Word/expression	Comment by remarqueur	Comments in the dictionaries	Usage in FRANTEXT
1. Sans point de faute	Vaugelas (1647: 161–2): 'c'est vne façon de parler de la lie du peuple'.	Not in N, C, O or A; occurs once in a definition in F. R follows Vaugelas in his comments: 'Cette façon de parler est de la lie du peuple de Paris & ne vaut rien.'	No occurrences.
2. Banquet	Vaugelas (1647: 466): 'Ce mot est vieux, & n'est plus guere en vsage que parmy le peuple. Il se conserue neantmoins dans les choses sacrées.'	In N and C without comment. R only allows the sacred usage and cites Vaugelas; F considers it archaic except in the sacred sense; A comments that it is hardly used, although it is more acceptable in the sacred context.	One hundred of the 150 examples date from 1601 to 1643; however, of the remaining fifty examples, there is a slight predominance of usages in a non-sacred context (twenty-eight occurrences).
3. A nuit	Buffet (1668: 51): 'cette façon de parler est ridicule & introduite par le petit peuple'.	Not discussed in any of the dictionaries.	No examples in FRANTEXT.
4. Il est venu à la maison	Bouhours (1675: 258): 'Les honnestes gens disent, *il est venu au logis; il a dîné au logis* [. . .] Il n'y a que le petit peuple qui dise, *il est venu à la maison.*' Andry de Boisregard (1689: 286) repeats the observation.	Not discussed in the dictionaries.	No examples in FRANTEXT (compared with nine occurrences of *venir au logis*).
5. Jours ouvrables	Bouhours (1693: 77): 'il n'y a que le peuple qui dise *jours ouvrables*'.*	Not in N, C, O or R. F comments 'On appelle jours ouvriers, autrement jours ouvrables'; it is also included in A.	No examples.

	Andry de Boisregard	Dictionaries	FRANTEXT
6. Achalander	Andry de Boisregard (1689: 21): 'Il n'y a guéres que le peuple qui parle de la sorte; on dit *accrediter*.'	In N, C, R, F and A. R defines it as 'donner des chalans à quelque marchand' and F as 'mettre une boutique, une maison en reputation d'avoir de bonne marchandise, & à bon prix'; there is no comment as to its acceptability in any of the dictionaries.	There are three examples of this verb in FRANTEXT from Du Lorens, *Premières Satires* (1624), La Fontaine, *Fables* (1678) and Mme de Sévigné's correspondence (1683).
7. Carolus	Andry de Boisregard (1689: 103): 'Le peuple dit un *Carolus*, pour dire dix derniers, mais cette maniere de parler ne vaut rien; au moins ce n'est point ainsi que les honnestes gens parlent. Ce mot ne se dit que par les Crocheteurs & les Harangeres.'	Given in N, C and R without comment. F and A point out that it refers to a coin which is no longer in use.	There are five examples of this word (1603–53): the last two examples are by d'Assoucy.
8. Sauf correction	Andry de Boisregard (1689: 138): 'Cette manière de parler n'est que du menu peuple.'	Not in N, C, O. R cites the example of it from Molière's *L'Avare*. F considers it a proverbial usage in his entry on *sauf*, but A gives it without comment on its acceptability.	Two examples in FRANTEXT: one by Sorel (1627) and one by the valet La Flèche in Molière's *L'Avare* (1669).
9. Mesmement	Andry de Boisregard (1689: 298–9): 'Ce mot n'est plus que du petit peuple'; admits Voiture sometimes uses it, but says he is not to be copied in this.	In N and C without comment. R cites Vaugelas, F says it is less in use than *mesme*, and A considers it archaic.	Chronology confirmed by FRANTEXT: the seventy-two examples date from 1601–56.
10. Petit à petit	Andry de Boisregard (1689: 405): 'c'est un terme qui a cours parmy le petit peuple, il faut dire, *peu à peu*'.	Not discussed in the dictionaries.	Of the ninety-two examples (1603–99), seventy-six occur before 1650, and about one third of the examples are by Sorel.

* It is possible that the association with the lower classes here is partly related to the sense of the expression.

of the metalinguistic comment, and subsequent usage seems to reflect that comment.

Finally Bouhours provides evidence that proverbs were only thought to be acceptable in low-register usage. In an observation entitled *Manieres de parler basses*, he lists expressions such as *tordre le nez* (1693: 149) and *mettre la puce à l'oreille* (1693: 150). The former is included by C and appears as an example in R's entry on *tordre* without comment, but the latter is not cited in any of the dictionaries. In each case, there is only one example in FRANTEXT: *tordre le nez* occurs in Claude d'Esternod's *L'Espadon satyrique* (1619) and *mettre la puce à l'oreille* is found in Racan's *Les Bergeries* (1632).

In Table 3.5, which considers words and expressions labelled *burlesque* by the *remarqueurs*, there again seems to be a high degree of correlation between the metalinguistic comments and textual usage, but what is perhaps most striking is the link between archaisms and burlesque which obtains in eight of our ten examples. In four cases (*n'en pouvoir mais, alambiquer, chenu* and *malencontreux*), the majority of examples date from the first half of the century and the later examples derive almost entirely from burlesque and other comic genres. In two further cases (*gent, maint*), there is a similar concentration of examples in the early part of the century and the majority of later examples come from La Fontaine's fables, in which the author plays with different registers of language and favours archaisms (see Stefenelli 1987). The balance of examples in comic genres is less clear in the case of *par avanture*, although it was clearly beginning to appear old-fashioned by the time of Buffet and Andry. Finally, in the case of *d'avanture* and *accoustrement* there are no textual examples for the last three decades of the century, by which time the predilection for burlesque texts had passed and attitudes towards acceptable lexical usage had become yet more rigid (see Ayres-Bennett 1987: 123).

Of the two remaining examples, *chanceux* does indeed seem to be favoured in comic or informal usages. The only case where there is no association between the word and usage in a particular genre is that of *seriosité*. It was presumably attributed to comedy, satire and burlesque by Vaugelas as the only acceptable genres for such a neologism; however, there is no evidence that this word, created by Guez de Balzac, ever established itself in usage.

The examples of words attributed to low-class usage by the *remarqueurs* in Table 3.6 are much more difficult to evaluate, since the absence of a form from a primarily literary corpus does not of course prove that it *was* used by the lower classes; this is the case for four of our examples (*sans point de faute, à nuit, il est venu à la maison, jours ouvrables*). In another case (*mesmement*) we have evidence that the word fell out of usage in the second half of the century, but again we cannot tell whether it survived in lower-class usage. In three cases the examples of the form, or at least the later attestations, tend to cluster in comic and informal genres (*achalander, Carolus, sauf correction*); here there is only weak evidence that the form was associated with social variation in that it is

Molière's servant La Flèche who employs *sauf correction*. Finally, there are two cases in which the textual evidence seems to be at odds with the comment in the observations. *Banquet* appears to have continued to be used in the later part of the century, with a slight preference for its attestation in non-sacred contexts. While the high proportion of occurrences of *petit à petit* in Sorel is perhaps significant, there is also evidence of its survival in a range of text types in the second half of our period. In short, not only are there fewer data in the metalinguistic texts on SES compared to register or genre (see Table 3.2), it is also much more difficult to find confirmation in the texts of the metalinguistic comments about the usage of the lower classes.

Given these difficulties, I decided to examine the use of vocabulary in my corpus of Mazarinades to see whether these texts, and especially those representing usage of the lower classes, are valuable as sources of popular usages. Once again I compared usage in the Mazarinades with the lexicographers' comments and usage in FRANTEXT (Tables 3.7–3.10). In selecting the feature to discuss I paid particular attention to the traits commonly associated with popular language, including archaisms, proverbs and neologisms (cf. Carrier 1996).

In Table 3.7, the comments by the lexicographers underscore the close relationship in this period between on the one hand forms deemed *bas* and the burlesque genre, especially in Richelet (e.g. *engin, faire le veau*),[29] and on the other hand between low-register usage and the lower classes (e.g. *renasquer, tignon*). The evidence from FRANTEXT also supports the idea that these words were not acceptable in most genres: in two cases the word is not attested at all, while in all the others virtually all the examples are from comedy, satire or burlesque.

Table 3.8 shows that archaisms occur particularly in the burlesque texts in our corpus of Mazarinades, but the pamphlets in patois also tend to be archaizing. It is perhaps worth restating that this, of course, does not necessarily give us information about lower-class usage, since the authors of burlesque texts are generally educated people who are satirizing popular language for comic effect. However, words dying out of standard French often did continue to be used in popular language, perhaps because the lower classes were slower to adapt and less affected by the pressures of the norm. For example, the old French word, *anuy, d'annuy* (or *à nuit*) in the sense of 'today' occurs in the *Agréables Conférences* (pp. 63, 66), which, as we saw in Table 3.6, Buffet associated with low-class speakers. The absence of many of these terms from FRANTEXT underlines the importance of texts such as the Mazarinades and the dictionaries in conveying information about non-standard usages.

In Table 3.9, which considers proverbs and popular expressions, note how the lexicographers include as proverbial expressions both what we would call proverbs (e.g. examples 4, 6) and those that reflect a broader interpretation

---

[29] Note that *chanceux* is also used in a negative sense in the *Agréables Conférences* (p. 146). See Table 3.5.

Table 3.7 *Mots bas/expressions basses**

Source text	Word/expression	Comments in dictionaries	Usage in FRANTEXT
1. (a) *Dialogue de Jodelet et de Lorviatan*	engin (p. 4)	O: 'l'engin, i. le membre viril'; not in this sense in N, C, F or A. R has in his *Remarques sur le dictionnaire* '+engin [. . .] Mot libre & burlesque qui ne se dit qu'en parlant un peu trop crument dans la conversation, ou dans le stile comique, & satirique.'	Three examples with this sense, all from satirical texts (two by Claude d'Esternod (1619), one by Jacques Du Lorens (1646)).
2. (a) *Dialogue de Jodelet et de Lorviatan*	[Viole] a fait le veau (p. 8)	Cited by O, R, F and A. R: '+* veau. Ce mot entre dans quelques façons de parler basses & burlesques. Faire le veau.'	R's comments confirmed by FRANTEXT; two of the three examples are from satirical texts and the third is from La Fontaine's *Fables*.
3. (c) *La Sottise des deux paris*	Non vous auez raison vostre asne pete (p. 10)	Only in O: 'Vous avez raison vostre asne pette, "le vulgaire se sert de cette façon de parler pour desapprouver ce qu'un autre dit".'	There is one example of this expression by Béroalde de Verville (1610); d'Assoucy uses 'l'asne pette' (1650).
4. (d) *La Lettre d'vn secretaire de S. Innocent*	barboüilleur de papier (p. 1)	Noted by C, F, R and A. A considers the usage figurative, while R assigns it both '+' and '*'.	The one example of *barboüilleur de papier* is from Molière's *Les Femmes savantes* where it is used by Trissotin as an insult.
5. (f) *Agreable recit de ce qui s'est passé aux dernieres barricades de Paris*	renasquer (p. 10)	Considered by F a 'terme populaire' and by A as 'bas'.	One example of the infinitive in FRANTEXT, by Brébeuf (1656).
6. (g) *Agréables Conférences*	tignon (p. 65)	In O in the expression 'il se carre comme un poüil sur un tignon'. Not in N or A. C includes it without comment, but R marks it '+' and adds that it is a 'mot du petit peuple de Paris', and F labels it a 'terme populaire'.	No examples in FRANTEXT.
7. (g) *Agréables Conférences*	debleyé (déblayé) (p. 40)	The verb occurs in N, C, and F without comment on its usage. It is not in R. A notes 'il est bas'.	No examples in FRANTEXT.
8. (g) *Agréables Conférences*	Esboby (ébobi) (p. 146)	In O 'étonné, vulg.'. Not in any of the other dictionaries.	One example by the peasant, Pierrot, in Molière's *Dom Juan*, Act 2 scene 1.

* There is, of course, a difficulty in identifying those terms which should be considered *bas*, especially since the evaluation of them may differ between metalinguistic sources. To try and minimize the problem of circularity, I have selected terms which are considered low register or crude by at least one of the lexicographers, which are marked '+' by R, or which occur exclusively in O.

Table 3.8 *Archaisms*

Source text	Archaism	Comments in dictionaries	Usage in FRANTEXT
1. (b) *Les Contens et mescontens*	bouter: 'vous vous boutez en escume' (p. 7)	In N and C. F considers it archaic and adds 'qui ne se dit plus que par le bas peuple & les paysans'; A agrees that it is 'bas' and no longer used.	Twenty-eight examples in FRANTEXT, fourteen of which are pre-1624. There are ten occurrences from Molière (1667–73) and four from Boursault's *Fables*.
2. (f) *Agreable recit de ce qui s'est passé aux dernieres barricades de Paris*	vezardes (p. 3)	Rabelais's usage cited by C, absent from all the other dictionaries.	No examples.
3. (f) *Agreable recit de ce qui s'est passé aux dernieres barricades de Paris*	consulte (noun) (p. 8)	Only C has it as a noun as an equivalent to 'consultation'.	No examples.
4. (f) *Agreable recit de ce qui s'est passé aux dernieres barricades de Paris*	poitrinal (weapon) (p. 14)	Not included as a headword in any of the dictionaries; F uses it in one of his examples.	No examples.
5. (g) *Agréables Conférences*	indagre (adj., indague) (p. 98)	Not in N, O, R or A. C includes it without comment, but F considers it archaic.	No examples.
6. (g) *Agréables Conférences*	treluire (p. 70)	Not in O, R or A. N and C include it without comment, but F notes that the verb is archaic (under *trelu*).	No examples.

of the term as an informal fixed expression (example 2). Whereas in the Renaissance and the early part of the seventeenth century proverbs were associated with culture and valued for reflecting the *génie* of French, as the century progressed they became increasingly associated with the 'people'.[30] This is perhaps also suggested by the relative paucity of examples of them

[30] Bouhours's comments (1675: 503–4) reflect this change: 'Les proverbes estoient autrefois en usage parmi nous, & faisoient méme une partie des richesses de nostre Langue [...] Cela estoit bon pour le temps passé. On seroit ridicule d'user aujourdh'uy de ces sortes de proverbes dans un discours serieux, & dans des compositions relevées.' Sophie Marnette has pointed out (personal communication) that in Old French proverbs are associated with the 'vilains' (peasants), as exemplified in Chrétien's romances.

Table 3.9 Proverbs and popular expressions

Source text	Proverb	Dictionary comments	Usage in FRANTEXT
1. (a) Dialogue de Jodelet et de Lorviatan	de facquin à facquin n'y a que la main (p. 4)*	Only in F and A. A: 'On dit prov. Qu'il n'y a que la main, quand on parle de deux personnes qui font de mesme profession. De Marchand à Marchand il n'y a que la main. de larron à larron il n'y a que la main.'	There are two examples of 'il n'y a que la main', one from Regnard's comedy La Sérénade (1695) and one from Marie-Catherine d'Aulnoy's fairy-tale L'Oiseau bleu (1698).
2. (b) Les Contens et mescontens	& met encor tous les iours au berniquet (p. 4)	Cited only by F and A. F: 'Berniquet, s.m. qui ne se dit qu'en ces phrases proverbiales Envoyer quelqu'un au berniquet. Il est allé au berniquet, pour dire, qu'il est ruiné, qu'il a mal fait ses affaires.'	Berniquet is not attested in FRANTEXT.
3. (b) Les Contens et mescontens	c'est par mon ame pain benist (p. 5)	Cited by O, R, F and A. O: 'c'est pain benit i. "c'est bien employé, il meritoit bien d'estre traité de la sorte"'.	No examples of this usage.
4. (c) La Sottise des deux partis	oignez le vilain il vous poindra, poignez le vilain il vous oindra (p. 9)	Cited by C, O, F and A. F: 'On dit proverbialement, Oignez vilain il vous poindra; poignez vilain, il vous oindra, pour dire, que la Paysans & les petites gens sont ingrates & timides.'	One example by O. de Serres (1603).
5. (c) La Sottise des deux partis	& leur en passoit quinze pour quatorze (p. 9)	Variant of the proverb cited by O, R and F; e.g. F: 'Quinze se dit proverbialement en ces phrases [...] qu'on luy fasse passer quinze pour douze.'	Du Lorens's Satires (1646) includes the following example: 'qu'il en faut passer quinze parmy quatorze'.

6. (d) *La Lettre d'vn secretaire de S. Innocent*	& comme l'appetit vient en mangeant (p. 5)	Given as a proverb by C, F and A. O comments: 'metaph. "cela se dit des larrons qui font facilement une habitude en desrobant"'.	Not attested.
7. (d) *La Lettre d'vn secretaire de S. Innocent*	A trompeur, trompeur & demy, Seigneur Iules (p. 8)	N cites the expression and C, F and A record it as a proverb.	There is one example of a variant of this from P. Corneille's comedy *La Veuve* (1634): 'Un trompeur en moi trouve un trompeur et demi.'
8. (e) *Lettre de Guillaume Sans-Peur*	Vous pensez prendre la Lune avec les dents (p. 4)	Widely cited by C, O, R, F and A. O: 'vouloir prendre la lune avec les dents, i. "vouloir faire une chose impossible"'.	Three examples: one in Du Lorens's *Premières satires* (1624), one in Voiture's letters (1648) and one in Mme de Sévigné's correspondence (1675).
9. (f) *Agreable recit de ce qui s'est passé aux dernieres barricades de Paris*	faire la figue (p. 14)	In R, F and A. F and A term it a proverb, while R gives it '*+*' and adds 'Ces mots signifient se moquer. Ce moquer de quelqu'un en lui faisant quelque grimace.'	Seven examples: three from satirical works by Esternod and Du Lorens, three from Maynard's poetry and one from La Fontaine's fables.
10. (f) *Agreable recit de ce qui s'est passé aux dernieres barricades de Paris*	prendre un rat (p. 18)	In R, F and A. R: 'Il a pris un rat, façon de parler proverbiale dont on se sert à Paris quand on veut se moquer d'une personne qui a manqué son coup.'	One example by Cyrano de Bergerac (1655).

* Note also the omission of the impersonal *il*.

Table 3.10 *Neologisms*

Source text	Neologism	Comments in dictionaries	Usage in FRANTEXT
1. (a) *Dialogue de Jodelet et de Lorviatan*	facquiner (p. 3)	Not in any of the dictionaries.	No attestations.
2. (a) *Dialogue de Jodelet et de Lorviatan*	l'incague (p. 5)	Attested only as a verb in C, F and A.	No examples of usage of the noun.
3. (d) *La Lettre d'vn secretaire de S. Innocent*	Badaudois (adjective) (p. 7)	Not in any of the dictionaries.	One example in Béroalde de Verville (1610).
4. (d) *La Lettre d'vn secretaire de S. Innocent*	bienner (verb)	Not in any of the dictionaries.	No attestations.
5. (g) *Agréables Conférences*	herinté (éreinté) (p. 113)	Not in any of the dictionaries.	One example from Regnard's comedy *Le Distrait* (1698).

in FRANTEXT and by the kinds of texts, notably comedy and satire, in which they do occur (cf. Bouhours 1675: 503). As Carrier notes (1996: 555), they feature regularly in those Mazarinades which present the dialogue of low-class speakers, perhaps suggesting a preference for them in spoken language.[31] In some texts the effect is increased by the accumulation of such proverbs and other informal expressions in close succession as in the following example (text (e), p. 5):

Il y a long-temps que la clemence du Parlement vous attend à resipiscence, si vous vous obstinez dans vos fautes, quand vous voudrez vous reconnoistre peut-estre serez-vous courts d'vn point,[32] & vous fera-on faire le saut de la carpe, & garder sans bonnet de nuit les moutons à la Lune,[33] & puis garre ceux qui craignent le serein à present, ainsi que vous dites, vous morguez les bons & fidels Seruiteurs du Roy auec les yeux roullant en teste, ainsi qu'vn chat qui tombe de quelque gouttiere, mais gardez que vous ne soyez contraints de les morguer vn de ces matins auec des yeux tout clos, ne touchant pas des pieds en terre que de trois ou quatre aulnes de hauteur [. . .]

Turning to neologisms (Table 3.10), it is interesting that the language of the people is portrayed as being at once conservative in retaining archaisms

---

[31] Note the accumulation of proverbs in the speech of the kitchen maid Martine in Molière's *Les Femmes savantes* (Act 5 scene 3, ll. 1641–4).
[32] O: 'il est trop court d'un point, i. "il luy manque quelque chose pour oser entreprendre ou pour parvenir à son dessein"'; F also cites it as a proverb.
[33] O: 'garder les moutons à la lune, i. "estre pendu"'.

and innovative in accepting neologisms. The association of neologisms with lower-class usage in a period when new words and expressions were often criticized is consistent with the evidence of modern studies, which suggests that the upper classes tend to use more standard language and introduce conscious prestige changes (Labov's 'change from above'), whereas the lower classes introduce covert, non-prestige change ('change from below').[34] Here many of the creations are derivations which simply generate a new part of speech from an already existing stem. None of the forms in Table 3.10 is attested in any of the dictionaries.

Finally it is interesting to note that the patois texts use the same limited range of forms – especially exclamations, insults and swear words which entail the deformation of *diable* – to characterize their low-class speakers. These include: *aga* (text (g) p. 88: 'aga tu te boute en eceume'; text (h), p. 4);[35] *guiebe* (text (g) p. 88 'd'où guiebe venas tu don?') or *guieble* (text (i), p. 4); *morgué* (text (g), p. 98), *morguienne* (text (g), p. 106); *parguieu* (text (h), p. 3), *parguié* (text (g), p. 44), *parguienne* (text (g), p. 92).

3.3.3   Pronunciation: [wɛ], [ɛ] and [wa]

Table 3.2 (p. 71) makes it clear that very few observations record variation in pronunciation associated with differences of register (nine out a total of 220 observations devoted to this parameter of variation). There are significantly more comments relating to class differences (twenty-four out of a total of seventy-seven observations), largely because of the important number of comments made by Ménage (1675, 1676). It should be noted, however, that the vast majority of these observations deal with the pronunciation of individual words (e.g *aoust*, Vaugelas 1647: 322; *ormoire/omoire*, Ménage 1675: 80; *j'ay u / j'ay éü*, Ménage 1675: 88–90). It is much rarer for a more wide-ranging question to be raised, such as the pronunciation of 'r', whether at the end of infinitives (Vaugelas 1647: 437), in the final syllable *-eur* (Bouhours 1675: 75), or in general terms (Andry de Boisregard 1689: 466–7).

In this section I shall focus on a question which preoccupied grammarians throughout the century, namely whether 'oi' should be pronounced [wɛ], [ɛ] or [wa]. It is notable for the number and range of texts – observations and grammars in our main corpus, and works on pronunciation, spelling and poetics in my extended corpus (see Appendix, II: F, G, H) – in which this topic is discussed, as Table 3.11 illustrates. It is important to remember that we are dealing here with

---

[34] The conscious creation of new words and expressions, paraphrases and 'fashionable' and striking expressions by the *Précieuses* to distinguish their usage from the ordinary and to avoid naming common or vulgar aspects of everyday life will be discussed in Chapter 4 (see sections 4.5.3 and 4.6.7).

[35] Mentioned by Maupas (1618: 180r) as being frequently used by common folk.

Table 3.11 *Seventeenth-century metalinguistic texts in the corpus which discuss the pronunciation of 'oi'*

Observations	Vaugelas (1647), Dupleix (1651), Buffet (1668), Ménage (1675), Bérain (1675),* Alemand (1688), Andry de Boisregard (1689, 1693), Tallemant (1698); it also appears in the commentaries on Vaugelas's observation by Patru, Corneille and the Academy (see Streicher 1936)**
Grammars	Maupas (1618), Oudin (1632), Irson (1662)
Works on pronunciation	Hindret (1687), Dangeau (1694)
Works on spelling[†]	Dobert (1650), L'Esclache (1668), Lartigaut (1669), Soule (1689)
Works on poetics	Deimier (1610), Mourgues (1724)

* Bérain (1675) follows Ménage in many respects, but he is innovative in suggesting that the spelling 'ai' should be used when the vowel is pronounced [ɛ]. The spelling was not adopted until the 1835 edition of the Academy's dictionary.
** The topic is not discussed by Bouhours in his observations, although it is mentioned briefly in the *Entretiens* (1671).
[†] Poisson (1609) does not discuss the question as such, but many of the words in which there was variation are included in his list, e.g. *aboi, non abbay.*

two separate, albeit interrelated, questions: the replacement in certain words and contexts of [wɛ] by [ɛ], and the replacement of [wɛ] by [wa].

Changing explanations for the use of [ɛ] in place of [wɛ] are offered over the course of the seventeenth century as its sociolinguistic value modifies (see Thurot 1881–3: I, 352–414). While for many words usage of [wɛ] was fixed early on in the century ('oi' is uncontroversially recommended in approximately two thirds of the total of over 150 words and word classes discussed in the metalinguistic texts),[36] in others variation between [wɛ] and [ɛ] remained for very many years (see below). In these cases, from being identified with usage at the royal court, [ɛ] becomes associated with conversation and then prose; conversely 'oi' comes to be considered appropriate for public discourse and declamation, and later in the century is said to find a home in poetry. Use of [ɛ] in certain words by those at the royal court is criticized by writers such as Pasquier and Henri Estienne in the second half of the sixteenth century. Maupas (1618: 16r–16v) confirms this chronology, asserting that this 'mistake' in the pronunciation of certain words, and notably in the imperfect and conditional endings of verbs, by royal courtiers who love novelty, has occurred 'depuis quelques

[36] Some writers attempt to draw generalizations about, for instance, words ending in *-oir, -oire, -oise,* or *-oie,* while others tend rather to list individual examples. The largest number of cases is dealt with by Ménage (1675: 582–91).

annees en ça'.[37] While Oudin (1632: 35–6) still speaks of this as a 'vsage cor-
rompu', Irson (1662) associates the pronunciation [wɛ] with 'les Anciens'. As
for reasons for the change, Maupas (1618: 16v) suggests that courtiers may have
been influenced by the pronunciation of foreigners, and that this has not been
adopted by the 'les Doctes & bien-disans, és Cours de Parlement, & ailleurs'.
Paradoxically, in the case of *avoine* and *aveine*, Vaugelas associates the former
with the court and the latter with the town (1647: 100). Dobert (1650: 222)
asserts that the use of [ɛ] used to be a 'mignardize' of the court, but that it has
now spread so that people are required to follow it, 'sur pęne de rusticité'.

   In the second half of the century, then, use of [ɛ] is no longer associated with
the royal court; rather for Buffet (1668), Ménage (1675), Soule (1689), Andry
(1689) and Patru (Streicher 1936), there is variation in words such as *froid,
estroit, droit* (adj.), *adroit, doit* and *croire* between usage in *discours familier*
or conversation where [ɛ] is preferred and in *discours public* for which [wɛ]
is recommended. Patru and Buffet also include in this adjectives referring to
certain nations, such as *anglais, français* and *hollandais*, one of the categories
most discussed in the period. The same point is made by Alemand with regard
to *avoine/aveine* (1688: 187), and *aboyer/abeyer* (1688: 17), for which he also
makes a distinction between figurative and concrete usages.[38] Finally, Tallemant
(1698) and Mourgues (1724) consider the opposition to be associated rather with
the difference between usage in prose ([ɛ]) and poetry ([wɛ]).

   The second question concerns how the vowel spelt 'oi' should be pronounced,
that is whether [wɛ] or [wa] is recommended. While there are examples of 'oa'
[wa] being attested as early as 1292 (Wüest 1985), it did not enter good usage
and become accepted as the norm until the late eighteenth century. It is of
interest as a very rare example of a popular pronunciation in French eventually
becoming the norm. In the second half of the sixteenth century, it is generally associated with the usage of the people of Paris (for example by Henri
Estienne, Bèze and Tabourot), although Henri Estienne does also seem to associate it with courtiers (Thurot 1881–3: I, 356), perhaps because of his general
dislike of the fashions of the royal court. Despite the occasional reference to
[wa] in grammars for foreigners (Thurot 1881–3: I, 357), seventeenth-century
grammarians all recommend [wɛ], notated as 'oe' with 'e ouvert', 'oai' or even
'oei'; see, for example, Maupas (1618: 16r), Oudin (1632: 35), Dobert (1650:
219) and Dangeau (1694: 20). The few references made to [wa] are critical;
Hindret (1687: aᵛ–aijʳ) comments:

---

[37] Thurot (1881–3: I, 376) quotes Erondell, who in 1605 also talks of this having been happening
     for a few years.
[38] Sometimes homographs are differentiated; for example *soit*, when it is the third person present
     subjunctive of *être*, is said to be pronounced [sɛ], but as [swɛ] when it means 'or' or 'so be it'
     (e.g. Vaugelas 1647; Ménage 1675). Likewise *droit* is to be pronounced with [ɛ] for the adjective
     'right', but the noun referring to the law is to be pronounced with [wɛ].

Combien en voyons nous par exemple à la Cour aussi bien qu'à Paris, qui disent *du boüas, des noüas, troüas, moüas, des poüas, voüar,* pour dire *du bois, des noix, trois, mois, des pois, voir,* dont la prononciation ne nous est pas plus difficile que celle de *fois, Rois, voix, choix, crois, loix, des droits, pouvoir, devoir,* & d'autres mots ou la diphtongue *oi* se prononce comme *oüai.*

Similarly La Touche (1696: 37) describes this pronunciation as 'très mauvaise'. It is not until the eighteenth century therefore that one finds greater tolerance, and finally acceptance, of this variant.

Given the paucity of comments about [wa] in the metalinguistic texts and the impossibility of knowing which pronunciation is represented by the traditional orthography, it is important to look for evidence of the pronunciation of 'oi' in other types of texts. While non-standard lexical items occur in all types of the Mazarinades in our corpus, the different genres of pamphlets are not equally useful in providing evidence of variation in pronunciation. For example, the dialogues between representatives of the lower classes use traditional orthography throughout (i.e. 'oi'), whatever the part of speech, as do the pamphlets written in *style bas*, with the sole exception of *adrettement* ('adroitement', text (d)). The burlesque text is typical of its genre in that the characterization is principally achieved through lexical means, and to a much lesser extent syntactically (see Bar 1960, Richardson 1930). Here again the spelling 'oi' is used almost exclusively.[39] It is thus only the texts in Parisian patois, and principally in the *Agréables Conférences* (g), that we find clear evidence for the variation. The verse texts ((h)–(j)) use 'oi' in the vast majority of words (respectively twenty-six, sixty-two and seventy-two examples), and there are only occasional examples of non-standard forms in each to add colouring to the text (e.g. *tra* ('trois'), *auar* ('avoir'), *dret* ('droit') in text (h); *poas* ('poix'), *paraistre* in text (i) and *estretes* ('estroites' in text (j)). This is comparable to another text written in Parisian patois, *La Nopce de village* (Brécourt 1681); whilst there are sixty-five occurrences of 'oi' in a range of words, there are only very occasional non-standard spellings (*j'acoutoes, pourquas, parqué* and *vela*). Similarly the representation of the peasants' speech in Molière's *Le Médecin malgré lui* almost always uses the traditional 'oi/oy' (*moi, pourroit, croy, touchoit,* etc.), the sole exceptions being *drait* and *ous sayez* (for 'vous soyez', although 'soit' is also attested.[40]

The *Agréables Conférences* are interesting in that they do not simply provide evidence of hesitation between 'oi' [wɛ] and [ɛ] in certain words, which was probably common to the literate and the lower classes alike, as is widely attested in the metalinguistic texts. In addition, in their representation of the popular speech of Paris and its suburbs, the *Conférences* indicate not only the frequency

[39] Note, however, the line 'Des boëtes de boudre d'Iris'.
[40] The edition used here is Paris, D. Thierry and C. Barbin, 1674.

of the popular variant [wa], but also of the reduced variant [a], not discussed in any of the grammars or volumes of observations.

The pronunciation [wɛ] is usually represented in the *Agréables Conférences* by 'ouai'/'ouay', but also occasionally by 'oe' and 'ouée': *un' fouay, deu fouay, mouay, le Rouay, avoer, nouée* ('noix'). The pronunciation [ɛ] is transcribed by 'et' in the case of the third person singular endings of verbs in the imperfect tense (*avet, vandet, fezet*), and by 'ai'/ay' in most other cases: *tay mesme, counais* ('connais'), *je cray*. It is clear that the forms in [ɛ] were more frequent in Paris then than they are today. For example, the metalinguistic texts, including Vaugelas, Ménage and Hindret, all recommend 'ai' [ɛ] for the present subjunctive of *être* (*soit*), and this is the dominant form in the *Conférences* (four examples compared with one of *sas* [a]); the same is true of the adjective *froid* (*fret*). Finally, [wa] is generally represented by 'oua', and more rarely by 'oa' as in *foua, doua, vouar, voatuze* and *couroas* ('croix'). The same word may occur in two different forms; for example, while 'moi', 'toi', etc. generally occur as *mouay, touay* we also find *may, tay*. On a number of occasions the author uses the traditional orthography 'oi'.

Tables 3.12–3.15 set out examples of the occurrences of the different pronunciations and their graphies in the *Agréables Conférences* and the recommendations of the *remarqueurs* and grammarians. In the case of the imperfect and conditional endings there is clear evidence of the establishment of [ɛ] as the dominant pronunciation (166/229 occurrences: 72.5%), particularly for the third person singular forms. However, the popular variant [a] is also well attested (54/229 occurrences: 23.6%), and indeed predominates for the first and second persons singular of the imperfect tense (Table 3.12).[41] As regards the stressed personal pronouns, *moi, toi*, we again find the grammarians' recommendations followed in that the dominant pronunciation is [wɛ], but [ɛ] is also attested in the Parisian patois (Table 3.13). The metalinguistic texts recommend that infinitives ending in -*oir* should be pronounced 'oi'; in our text this is the spelling given for *savoir*. For the verb *choir* all five examples are spelt *chouar* [wa]. However, in the case of the infinitives (*r)avoir* and *voir* the *Agréables Conférences* suggest greater variation than the metalinguistic texts (Table 3.14).[42] In the case of other types of infinitives, [ɛ] is apparently established early on in *connaître* (recommended by Maupas, Oudin, Vaugelas, etc.); in the *Conférences* eight of the nine examples confirm this as the dominant usage, although there is also one occurrence of *connas* [a]. On the other hand, the pronunciation of *croire*

---

[41] It is not clear why there appears to be a difference between the imperfect and the conditional – although the figures for the conditional are low overall – which, to my knowledge, has not been observed by other modern commentators. Seventeenth-century authors of metalinguistic texts discuss the imperfect forms much more frequently than the conditional ones.

[42] This is also true of the conjugated forms in the present tense of *voir*, for which there are similarly examples of [wa], [wɛ] and [a].

Table 3.12

Verb endings	[ɛ] e(t)	ai(s/t)	[a] a/as	'oi'	Total occurrences	Comments in the metalinguistic texts
Imperfect 1st person sing.		9	34	1	44	Maupas still prefers [wɛ], but Vaugelas recommends [ɛ]; most successors agree, but traces of the earlier pronunciation persist for a long time (e.g. Alemand 1688: 5).
Imperfect 2nd person sing.		3	14		17	
Imperfect 3rd person sing.	106	19	2	8	135	
Conditional 1st person sing.		10	3		13	
Conditional 2nd person sing.		2	1		3	
Conditional 3rd person sing.	6	11			17	

Table 3.13

Stressed pronouns, *moi, toi*	[ɛ] ay, ai	[wɛ] ouay, ouai	'oi'/'oy'	Total occurrences	Comments in the metalinguistic texts
	9	31	3	43	Vaugelas, Dupleix, Ménage, Soule, etc. all recommend 'oi'

Table 3.14

Verb form	[wa] oua	oa	[wɛ] oe	[a] a	'oi'	Total occurrences
Avoir, ravoir	2	2	1	9	3	17
Voir	5		0	17	0	22

was variable for much longer; Oudin, Vaugelas and Hindret, *inter alios*, recommend [ɛ], and this seems to have been the pronunciation associated with informal usage, but Patru and Andry de Boisregard consider 'oi' preferable in 'public' discourse, while Tallemant and Mourgues advise this for poetry. Here, in the informal *Conférences*, the anticipated form with [ɛ] (*craize*) occurs.

Table 3.15

Noun	[wa] oua(s)	oa	[wɛ] ouay, ouai	[ɛ] ay, ai	Total occurrences	Comments in the metalinguistic texts
Doigt	3	1	1	3	8	'oi' recommended by Ménage, Bérain
Fois	12	2	3		18 (one example of 'oi')	Ménage recommends 'oi'
Roy	2		34		37 (one example of 'oi')	Generally 'oi', e.g. Oudin, Ménage, Lartigaut

As regards nouns, where the metalinguistic texts recommend 'oi' [wɛ], the *Conférences* tend to have [wa] as the only form; thus we have *joie* (*joua, joas*), *bois* (*boua*), *croix* (*croas, couroas*)[43] and *mois* (*moua(s)*). Occasionally there is a single attestation of a noun with a spelling indicating clearly [wɛ] as in *nouée* (noix) and *touaille* (*toile*). In the case of *fois* and *roi* there is variation between [wɛ] and [wa], while in the case of *doigt* the pronunciation [ɛ] is also attested (Table 3.15). While there are no examples of [a] here, it is attested as the only pronunciation for all thirteen examples of *trois* (spelt either *tra* or *tras*). The transcription -*a*/-*as* is also employed for all ten examples of *bourgeois*.

As we might expect, the majority of transcriptions of the Dauphin's speech suggest he used [wɛ] and [ɛ] (Ernst 1985: 37–40). The pronunciation [wɛ] is occasionally transcribed as 'oe' (as in *boete* or *machouere*), but more usually as the conventional spelling 'oi'/'oy'/'oj'. In most examples, only one of the variants occurs; for example *français*, *boîte* and *droit* are represented only with the pronunciation [wɛ], while *nettoyer* is attested only with the pronunciation [ɛ].[44] However, in a few cases both pronunciations seem to be indicated: *anglé/angloi(s)*; *este, esté, estet, estét/j'estoi, estoit*; *sé(t), set/ soi(t), soï*. The fact that there is also the occasional spelling (*noa*, 'noir'; *troa, toa*, 'trois') which suggests the popular pronunciation [wa], criticized in the metalinguistic texts, implies that it was perhaps already more widespread than the commentators admit.

3.3.4   Syntax: 'Constructions louches'

In the case of syntax, there are very few observations which discuss variation associated with class differences (five out a total of seventy-seven observations,

---

[43] There is one example of the traditional orthography.

[44] In Anne-Marguerite le Mercier's *Livre de raison*, we also find *anetaier* ('à nettoyer'). The pronunciation [wɛ] is indicated by forms such as *entouaille* ('en toile') and *mirouer* ('miroir') (Ernst and Wolf 2001–2).

see Table 3.2); these include the popular usage of *promener* where *se promener* is required (Ménage 1675: 366), the choice of *à* rather than *de* to mark possession (Andry de Boisregard 1689: 1–2), a feature still common in contemporary French, and uncertainty as to whether to use the indicative or subjunctive after *croire* used interrogatively (André de Boisregard 1689: 143).

Although there are more indications of syntactic differences associated with register differences (seventeen out of a total of 220), these comments still represent less than 10% of the total number. Examples include constructions which are considered somehow elliptical – for instance, Alemand (1688: 429) considers that 'il sçait le Latin & le Grec' is only suitable 'pour le discours ordinaire, & pour un stile simple & bas' and that in higher registers 'la langue' must be inserted – and inversions which are only appropriate for 'le stile plaisant' (Andry de Boisregard 1689: 62). Non-standard examples of syntax also illustrate well the difficulty of separating out differences of register from differences of class or medium, since the same non-standard construction may be characterized as typical of speech by one writer, but as low register or as typical of the lower classes by another. For instance, *estre* with *pour* as in 'ils estoient pour auoir encore pis' is deemed *bas* by Vaugelas (1647: 342), but Thomas Corneille associates it with 'les gens tout à fait grossiers'. In each case it is important to consider whether the conflicting judgments arise as a result of a lack of care on the part of the writers of the metalinguistic texts or whether the non-standard usage is typical of both low-register and spoken or lower-class usages. For instance, the periphrastic use of *après (de)* + infinitive, discussed in Chapter 2, is labelled *bas* by Vaugelas (1647: 332–3), but the comparative data suggest that its usage was quite widespread in seventeenth-century speech.

We have seen that many of the literary texts that are supposed to represent low-register or low-class speech nevertheless display a largely standardized syntax. Rosset (1911) has claimed that even the syntax of the *Agréables Conférences* contains nothing original. I therefore decided to examine the corpus of Mazarinades to see whether there is any evidence of the deliberate selection of constructions typical of low-register or lower-class usage.

In a number of texts, and especially in dialogues between representatives of the lower classes (Type 1) and those texts which use low-register vocabulary (Type 2), there are constructions which are of a type the *remarqueurs*, and particularly Vaugelas, might censure for their ambiguity and lack of clarity. For instance, Vaugelas is highly critical of what he terms 'constructions louches' ('cross-eyed constructions') on the grounds that they appear to offer one syntactic interpretation, at least on an initial reading, but actually require a different interpretation, or to use Vaugelas's terms one which 'semble regarder d'vn costé, & [. . .] regarde de l'autre' (1647: 113). He cites the example of 'Germanicus a egalé sa vertu, & son bonheur n'a jamais eu de pareil'. This construction is ambiguous in his opinion, because one might interpret 'sa vertu, &

son bonheur' as coordinated direct objects of the verb 'a egalé' (he ignores the comma), and therefore be, albeit temporarily, misled. This observation illustrates all too well the severity of the constraints placed on classical prose. Bouhours and the Academy are also critical of such constructions; although the Academy does not agree with Vaugelas's judgment about the particular example he cites on the grounds that the verb phrase immediately follows the second coordinated noun, which means that the reader has no time to be misled. A number of examples in the Mazarinades seem to display potential ambiguity:

(i) Les Grands seroient tels s'ils le vouloient estre, si lascheté leur plaist à leur dam (= Les Grands seroient tels s'ils le vouloient estre; si lascheté leur plaist, à leur dam! (text (a), p. 4)). Here the role of the second 'si' clause is not immediately clear and the phrase 'à leur dam' might be taken as dependent on 'plaist'.

(ii) Le peuple est aux extremes de la necessité vient le desespoir, du desespoir la confusion, & le mal-heur aux Autheurs de ces maux (= 'Le peuple est aux extremes; de la necessité vient le desespoir', etc. – text (a), p. 5). Here an initial interpretation might read 'de la necessité' as depending on 'aux extremes'.

A related example is furnished by sentences which contain a vocative or form of address. Vaugelas (1647: 547) criticizes the construction 'ie ne veux pas acheter Madame, si peu de chose à si haut pris; on the grounds that 'Madame' could be taken as the object of the infinitive 'acheter'. The same would be true of the following example from one of the Mazarinades:

(iii) Receuez donc mon cher Camarade, la lettre que ie vous écris (text (d), p. 1).

Another group of constructions criticized by Vaugelas for their lack of clarity are those which include some kind of ellipsis or asymmetrical coordination. For instance, Vaugelas (1647: 358) censures 'il s'est bruslé, & tous ceux qui estoient aupres de luy' on the grounds that a different verb form needs to be understood in the second clause. He also considers 'il a fait tant & de si belles actions' to be archaic and 'rude' (1647: 348). Corneille agrees that it is dated but might still appear in 'un discours qu'on prononceroit', while the Academy disagrees with Vaugelas's description of the construction and argues instead that it may be used in 'le stile soustenu' and in conversation (Streicher 1936). The following constructions from the Mazarinades all involve ellipsis or the coordination of dissimilar elements:

(i) Son pere vendit des drogues, sa mere caracteres & pucelages contrefaits: ses soeurs furent enfilés, & luy prostitué (text (a), p. 4).

(ii) Mais sans pousser l'affaire à bout
Nostradamus & Dieu sur tout (text (f), p. 24).

(iii) Pourquoy le souffre-t'on & autres choses (text (a), p. 4).

(iv) Vous pensez prendre la Lune auec les dents, mais vous vous y trouuerez courts, & ne vous seruira de rien de faire les cheuaux échappez (text (e), pp. 4–5).

It is perhaps noteworthy that these examples occur particularly in our first two types of Mazarinades. However, care must be exercised in interpreting the status of such constructions. First, it is important to note that none of these constructions is explicitly associated with popular or low-register usage by the *remarqueurs*; they are rather condemned for their lack of clarity. Their appearance may be explained by the fact that such constructions were associated with usage of the previous century, and, as archaisms, were considered characteristic of popular and burlesque usage (see section 3.3.2). Alternatively, they may represent one of the ways in which the spoken nature of certain texts is conveyed, particularly our first type of Mazarinades; the spontaneity of dialogue allows less time for the considered removal of potential ambiguity and encourages brevity. Perhaps most significant, however, is the fact that seventeenth-century commentators themselves acknowledge the difficulty of attaining complete clarity and lack of ambiguity; a number of Vaugelas's successors, for example, remark on the severity of the demands imposed on writers and speakers. Moreover, many of the greatest writers of the century, including Boileau, Racine and Pascal, were criticized by seventeenth-century commentators for including potentially ambiguous constructions (Brunot 1905–53: IV, 1102–3). It is noteworthy too how frequently the Academy, analysing Vaugelas's syntactic usage in his translation of Quintus Curtius Rufus' *Life of Alexander*, points out constructions which are not clear (Ayres-Bennett and Caron 1996). All this suggests that the 'errors' noted in the metalinguistic texts were not confined to low-register or popular writing. We therefore have to conclude that it is very difficult to find clear textual evidence of popular syntax in our corpus.

3.4   Conclusion

In both the metalinguistic texts and the literary representations of low-register language, stylistic variation is characterized primarily in lexical terms. As regards social variation, vocabulary and pronunciation are the main ways in which popular language is portrayed. By contrast, relatively little information is provided about syntactic variation; while many lexical features occur frequently in certain types of literary text, it is much more difficult to find representations of low-register or popular syntax. The ambiguous and elliptical constructions which occur in the Mazarinades are criticized only in general terms by the *remarqueurs* as violating considerations of clarity, and do not appear to be confined to popular texts.

In the observations and dictionaries alike it is often difficult to disentangle social and stylistic variation. This is partly because for some writers, once an item has been deemed substandard, the particular reason for its exclusion from good usage is of minor importance. However, it is also due to the fact that social and stylistic variation are seen as intrinsically linked; many of the writers of observations make explicit connections between low-register usage, low-class speakers and a lack of education. This is evident, for instance, in Furetière's definition of *bas* or Richelet's explanation of *proverbe*. While, then, it is impossible to carry out the kind of quantitative research favoured by Labov for seventeenth-century French, our qualitative study suggests patterning between the social and stylistic continuums. There is equally evidence of the relationship between social variation and change; in a period which attempted to fix the language in its classical purity, archaisms and neologisms found a home in popular language.

While many of the low-register and popular terms are found in burlesque texts, these are problematic as sources since they deliberately and artificially juxtapose different registers of language. For the writers of observations, words and expressions considered substandard may appear only in comedy, satire and burlesque, that is, where they are consciously intended to generate laughter. In seventeenth-century polite society one of the greatest pitfalls was to appear ridiculous through inadvertently using an inappropriately pitched term. Burlesque texts, then, may best be used in conjunction with other sources, and particularly to test the validity of pronouncements by *remarqueurs* and lexicographers about the scope of usage of a term. However, as we saw in Table 3.4, here too it is necessary to try and distinguish the extent to which the writers of observations were reflecting or dictating usage.

If in some cases (for example, words considered *bas* or *burlesque*) there is a good correlation between the pronouncements in the metalinguistic texts and usage in FRANTEXT, greater problems of interpretation arise when a form is absent from this corpus. For example, the absence from FRANTEXT of a term associated in an observation with usage by ordinary people does not of course provide any indication of which class of people, if any, actually employed the word or expression. In such cases, as in the case of the popular pronunciation [wa], certain types of Mazarinades provide a valuable source of data, although here too we must be cautious, since some of their authors may themselves have turned to metalinguistic texts as sources of information about low-register and popular usages.[45] As regards [wa], however, the relative lack of comment about this pronunciation in grammars and other works on the French language, together with its attestation in the Dauphin's speech, seems to indicate a degree

---

[45] Note that this study also confirms the findings of previous work on the French of Paris. Seventeenth-century Paris was a place of intersecting and multilayered linguistic varieties. While, as Vaugelas notes, the usage of the Parisian elite was similar to that of the court, the popular usage of Les Halles and the language of the Parisian suburbs and surrounding countryside clearly had much in common.

of authenticity. Moreover, the *Agréables Conférences* furnish evidence of an even more marked variant, [a] for [wa].

Throughout this chapter we have seen once again the need to interpret sources with care and to take account, for example, of who they were written by, and their intended purpose and audience. Providing we keep these considerations in mind, convergence of evidence from different sources can help us construct a better picture of social and stylistic variation in seventeenth-century France.

4   Women's language

4.1   Introduction

Paradoxical attitudes are expressed towards women's language in seventeenth-
century France, at times even within the writings of a single author.[1] On the one
hand, following what Coates (1986: 15) terms the Androcentric Rule whereby
'men will be seen to behave linguistically in a way that fits the writer's view of
what is desirable and admirable; women on the other hand will be blamed for any
linguistic state or development which is regarded as negative or reprehensible',
there is evidence that women's language is perceived as weaker than men's,
as incorrect and full of errors. As we shall see, women are condemned for
their poor spelling, for their creation of new words and expressions, for their
incorrect pronunciation and for their tendency to make grammatical errors.
According to this view (sometimes termed the 'female deficit' approach: see,
for example, Henley and Kramarae 1994: 384) women's language is inferior as
measured against a male norm; this linguistic inferiority reflects women's lower
social status and their lack of education. Sorel in *Du nouveau langage françois*
suggests that women are also much more subject to the whims of fashion than
their male counterparts: 'Les dames se persuadent de bien parler quand elles
disent des paroles qui sont fort à la mode. La pluspart se servent de toute sorte
de mots sans en considérer la signification' (Brunot 1905–53: III, 67).

However, alongside this negative perception, there is a stronger, more interesting current which runs through the discourse about the use of French by
women in the seventeenth century. In this account emphasis is placed on the
'civilizing' role of women, notably in polite society. Women are viewed not
only as arbiters of good taste but also as models of good behaviour, and notably
of good linguistic usage: it is women who are to be consulted on doubtful usage
and it is from women that conversational skills may be acquired. The emphasis
in this account is particularly on oral skills and on the 'natural' use of language
by women, their judgment about the acceptability of terms and expressions.

---

[1] Baron (1986: 1–2, 55–6) notes similar paradoxical attitudes in his discussion of attitudes towards
women's language in England. Labrosse (1996: 11) oversimplifies the situation in seventeenth-
century France by focusing exclusively on 'la muettisation des femmes' in this period.

Not corrupted by the influence of Greek or Latin grammar, they represent an authentic voice and offer untainted opinions on the vernacular.

If in the first account women are presented as uneducated, weak and easily influenced by fashion, in this second account women are assigned status and influence. The most telling, and the most extreme, example of women asserting themselves linguistically in the seventeenth century is in the movement known as *Préciosité*. According to Yaguello (1979: 39), this represents 'l'une des premières tentatives faites par des femmes pour prendre la parole, pour s'attribuer un pouvoir sur la langue, pour se faire une place dans la société patriarcale (dans les limites de la classe dominante bien entendu), pour avoir enfin leur mot à dire.' Here then is an example where women seem not to accept their inferior status,[2] but to use linguistic differentiation as a way of showing solidarity with each other and difference from others. In Milroy's terms, this represents a chance to enter closer social networks within a linguistic community. Yet the whole movement of *Préciosité* is highly problematic, as we shall see, even to the point that its very existence has been questioned. Moreover, as the citation from Yaguello makes clear, it is essentially associated with the higher strata of French society; thus much of what is loosely termed 'women's usage' in the century is that of a particular social grouping.

While there are undoubtedly feminist aspects to the discussion of women's language in this period and especially within the *Précieuses'* movement,[3] it is important not to overstate this. Women are generally viewed as paradigms of good linguistic behaviour not because of any inherent superiority but rather because of their lack of education. While there is praise for some women of distinction such as Anne Dacier, Anna Maria van Schurman and Angélique Arnauld, particularly in the catalogues or lives of famous women,[4] in much of the literature of the period, the term *femme savante* is pejorative, denoting a woman worthy of derision. The best-known example of this attitude is found in Molière's comedy *Les Femmes savantes*, first performed in 1672 (lines 218–26). Clitardre criticizes women who are pedantic or who make ostentatious displays of erudition or false learning:

> Je consens qu'une femme ait des clartés de tout:
> Mais je ne lui veux point la passion choquante
> De se rendre savante afin d'être savante;

---

[2] Cf. Coates (1986: 8): 'In the past, women seemed to accept their inferior status.'

[3] For example, as regards their attitude towards marriage and childbirth. While the definition of *Préciosité* clearly cannot simply be reduced to questions of *Précieuses'* use of language, this will be the exclusive focus of this chapter.

[4] For example, Jean de la Forge's *Le Cercle des femmes sçavantes* (Paris, 1663) or Jacquette Guillaume's *Les Dames illustres* (Paris, 1665). Adrien Baillet (1685) in his four-volume *Jugemens des sçavans sur les principaux ouvrages des auteurs* includes twelve women, including Marie de Gournay and Mme Dacier.

Et j'aime que souvent, aux questions qu'on fait,
Elle sache ignorer les choses qu'elle sait:
De son étude enfin je veux qu'elle se cache,
Et qu'elle ait du savoir sans vouloir qu'on le sache,
Sans citer des auteurs, sans dire de grands mots,
Et clouer de l'esprit à ses moindres propos.

A woman is thus enjoined to hide her knowledge and to avoid giving the impression of superiority; significantly, this stance is also advocated by women such as Madeleine de Scudéry, who recommends that a woman 'sçait cent choses dont elle ne se vante pas' and should avoid 'qu'on puisse dire d'elle, c'est vne Femme sçavante' (Mlle de Scudéry, *Grand Cyrus* X, 401–2, cited in Timmermans 1993: 332).

A further paradox emerges when we consider discussions of women's language in seventeenth-century France: women are presented as models of good linguistic usage and yet there is a relative paucity of information about what constitute the precise features of women's usage. Moreover, the number of women grammarians or women writing on language is relatively small. Why is women's language considered a model? Are women models because they possess highly valued qualities such as *naïveté* and *netteté* to a higher degree than men, or are there specific features of women's language which are praiseworthy? Is there a tension between praise for women's language in general terms and criticism of individual features? In this chapter we will attempt to discover the extent to which concrete examples of differences can be identified and substantiated. In other words, I shall address two principal questions in the case studies: What is the sum of the features of women's language which can be learnt from the metalinguistic texts of the period? To what extent are the observations of the metalinguistic texts borne out in the writings of women of the period?

To evaluate the extent to which women's usage is shaped by or reflects their position in society, we shall first consider the sociocultural context, the position of women in seventeenth-century French society and attitudes towards them (section 4.2). Section 4.3 will look at women's conversation and their role in the salons, while in section 4.4. I shall outline the general characteristics attributed to women's speech. Section 4.5 will examine the *Précieuses*' view and usage of the French language, and data on the specific features of women's usage will be presented in section 4.6.

4.2   The position of women in seventeenth-century French society

4.2.1   Introduction

Contradictory features also typify women's social position in the seventeenth century. Alongside more traditional functions, new and evolving roles for certain women emerged in a number of different domains: for some this meant an active political role during the Fronde, for others a 'civilizing' role in the salons, influencing the ideals of good behaviour and taste, and acting as arbiters of language and literature (cf. Lathuillère 1966: 652). We shall begin by considering the polemic about women's status (section 4.2.2), and then examine the reality of their education and the scope of their knowledge (section 4.2.3), and the opportunities open to them to acquire *la culture mondaine* (section 4.2.4).

4.2.2   *The* Querelle des femmes

The status of women, and in particular their perceived standing in relation to men, continued to be a subject of debate in the seventeenth-century *Querelle des femmes*. According to King (1991: 187), between 1595 and 1655 at least twenty-one works were written in defence of, or against, women. In the first quarter of the century misogynous invectives predominate in which women are presented as weak and inferior (Timmermans 1993: 240); typical is Jacques Olivier's vehemently anti-feminist work *L'Alphabet de l'imperfection et malice des femmes* (1617), which in turn triggered a number of works defending women. This negative attitude towards women may permeate linguistic descriptions. For example, Dobert's explanation of the difference between vowels and consonants (1650: 7) presents women in a negative light:

Qui voudroit resserrer ces reflexions aux seules Creatures raisonnables, & les leur appliquer: il semble d'abord que l'on pourroit dire, que les Femmes qui ont beaucoup plus de babil que non pas les hommes, sont des Voyeles, & les Hommes qui ont plus d'effect que de bruit des Consonantes: mais parce que dans l'ordre des lettres les Voyeles sont fort nobles, ie surseois à cette similitude, puis qu'elle releue les Femmes sous couleur de les raualer, & rauale les hommes en les voulant releuer.

Works in defence of women may argue either for the equality of men and women (a position generally favoured by the women polemicists, Angenot 1977: 4–5), or for female superiority, as in the following passage by Gilbert (1650: 4–5): 'Ie me suis proposé de luy faire voir que les femmes sont plus parfaites que les hommes, & qu'elles ont droit de demander la preference [. . .] ie ne feray pas seulement voir qu'elles surpassent les hommes dans les perfections du corps, mais aussi qu'elles sont plus excellentes dans les avantages de l'esprit.' As the century progressed the qualities deemed ideal for a woman also evolved, being represented, for example, in the 1630s by the *honnête femme* (see below), but by the *femme forte* and *femme généreuse* in the following two decades (Timmermans 1993: 321). The last feminist treatises of major importance in our period are the three by Poullain de la Barre (1679 [^{1}1673], 1674, 1675); in his *De l'égalité des deux sexes* he argues for the superiority of women over men in terms of their linguistic skills and enumerates the qualities of their language (see below).

It is not my intention to elaborate on the details of the quarrel, since these have been well documented elsewhere (see, for example, Timmermans 1993; Angenot 1977). However, the work of two women writing in defence of their sex is of particular interest to us since they also wrote on the French language; indeed these are the only two 'women grammarians' in seventeenth-century France.

The first, Marie Le Jars de Gournay (1565–1645), is best known as Montaigne's 'fille d'alliance' (adopted daughter) and as the posthumous editor of his *Essais*. On her arrival in Paris in 1596 she quickly became involved in the controversy which dominated the first half of the seventeenth century regarding the nature of poetic language. Her complete works – entitled *L'Ombre de la damoiselle de Gournay* (1626) in the first edition and later renamed *Les Advis, ou les presens de la demoiselle de Gournay* (1634, 1641) – set side by side essays on the French language ('Du langage françois', 'Sur la version des Poëtes antiques, ou des Métaphores', 'Des Rymes', 'Des Diminutifs françois') and feminist essays ('Egalité des hommes et des femmes', 'Grief des dames').

While Marie de Gournay, like Malherbe, frequented the salon of Mme des Loges to whom she dedicated her 'Deffence de la Poësie', she vigorously defended the poetic style and linguistic usage of Ronsard and the Pléiade poets, and bitterly criticized the new school led by Malherbe and its aim to control and regulate the use of French and to strip it of words and expressions considered too new, too archaic or too low in register. She aims rather to preserve the richness of the French language, perpetuating sixteenth-century concerns for elaboration of function: 'Les Docteurs en l'art de parler [. . .] luy denient [à la Langue françoise] [. . .] le droict d'emprunt, de translation et de propagation, ainsi qu'ils feroient à quelque Langue morte' (Uildriks 1962: 55). Her dislike of Malherbe's purism is such that she is led to adopt what might appear to us today contradictory positions. In the 'Egalité des hommes et des femmes' and 'Grief des dames' she maintains that there are no fundamental psychological differences between men and women, and that the differences between them would disappear if they were educated in the same way. Moreover, in her 'Apologie pour celle qui écrit' (Dezon-Jones 1988: 158), she defends educated women. Yet she is totally against the role attributed to women as arbiters of good usage by the new school 'parce qu'ils les veulent cajoler [. . .] affin de les tirer à leur party' (Uildriks 1962: 101): 'J'ay peur que ceux qui furent inventeurs de cette regle de si grand credit en la nouvelle Escolle, de ne rien dire que les Dames n'entendissent; n'entendoient rien qui ne leur fust commun avec elles' (Uildriks 1962: 115). Although a salon-goer herself, she was critical of the *Précieuses* and those she termed 'prescheurs de paroles miellees' (Uildriks 1962: 134).

Marguerite Buffet, author of *Nouvelles Observations* (1668), is much less well known, but combines the same interest in feminist and linguistic thought. However, Buffet adopts the position typical of most seventeenth-century *remarqueurs* in defending the usage of the court and polite society of which Marie de Gournay was so critical, and praising 'la clarté & netteté du discours, sa brieveté ou justesse, sa vray-semblance ou probabilité; enfin sa facilité ou son agrément' (1668: 169). While Marguerite Buffet and Marie de Gournay represent opposing views on the French language, they share a belief in the equality of the sexes; indeed Marguerite Buffet asserts that women have 'un plus grand partage des dons du Ciel & de la nature que les hommes' (1668: 230), making them superior in certain respects. Women have therefore been able to play an important role in history and religion:

Que les hommes se vantent donc tant qu'ils voudront, & qu'ils fassent gloire de la grandeur de leur corps & de la grosseur de leurs testes, cela leur est commun avec de tres-stupides animaux, & de tres-grosses & lourdes bestes; il est donc certain, generalement parlant, que les femmes ont plus de vivacité d'esprit que les hommes, ce qui se manifeste dans toutes les rencontres de la vie ou elles sont employees. (Buffet 1668: 228–9)

The biological, religious and philosophical arguments offered by Buffet to assert female superiority are complemented by portraits of individual women.

4.2.3   *Education*

Since women's lack of education, especially in the classical languages, is a principal reason cited by some writers for considering them the best judges of good French usage, it is important to consider the educational opportunities afforded to women in the period. Whereas boys received their education largely through *collèges* and universities, girls' education depended to a large extent on their family and social situation. Brunot (1905–53: V, 41) cites a *Reglement pour les écoles dominicales* dated 1673 which laments the lack of female schooling: 'C'est un grand mal que l'on envoye rarement les filles à l'école, et que celles que les parens y envoyent, n'y restent pas un temps suffisant pour apprendre parfaictement a lire.' Dulong (1984: 31) notes that while most theoreticians argued that educating women would induce the sin of pride in them, others such as Fénelon recognized that ignorance might equally lead to sin, an awareness which led, for example, to the establishment of Saint-Cyr by Mme de Maintenon in 1686.

Three main types of education were open to women in France in the seventeenth century: domestic, formal and informal (Gibson 1989: 20–1). In the first case the girl's education, consisting essentially in housewifery and morals, was supervised by her mother in the home. Frequently the girl would be entrusted to a governess who might give the child some basic religious and social instruction. Later a private tutor might be employed to teach rudimentary general knowledge, but especially skills valued in polite society such as music, singing, dancing and modern languages.

Outside the home, formal instruction for girls was essentially at primary level and could be acquired in charity schools run by either individuals or religious bodies, in *petites écoles* or in convents (Gibson 1989: 25). A convent education was dominated by religious instruction, with reading, writing, spelling and arithmetic taking very definitely second place (Gibson 1989: 27). The Counter-Reformation led to some improvements in women's education in the desire to spread the 'true faith': congregations with women's education as their vocation such as the Ursulines, the Daughters of the Cross and the Visitation Order were established. These mostly attracted girls of high social status, but it was not yet a widely established habit among noble families to send their daughters to board in convents. The *Règlements* of the Ursulines and of the Congrégation de Notre-Dame mention a morning and evening hour of reading, the first of Latin books, the second of French (Gibson 1989: 266), but the emphasis of the education was on repetition and memorizing. In the second half of the century secular congregations, where lower-class girls were received, were founded. Fagniez (1929: 48) concludes that the aim was to produce home-makers rather than educated women. Girls therefore tended to be educated in the basics, while boys received a more thorough grounding in Latin and rhetoric. The lack of women's education in Latin meant not only that they were excluded from knowledge of Latin literature and civilization, but also that access to many other subjects written about mostly or exclusively in Latin, such as law, rhetoric, theology, philosophy, history and science, was also denied.

Clearly a woman's education depended on her class. The figures on illiteracy for the period are revealing. While there were differences according to geographical location and between towns and rural areas, there was a constant difference in the literacy rate of men and women of the order of 20% (Grande 1999a: 210). Marriage contracts for the period 1686–90 suggest a national average of about 14% of women capable of signing (Timmermans 1993: 57; Muchembled 1990: 140). Since education encouraged reading rather than writing, it is likely that the number of women readers was higher, yet even in the big towns barely 40% of French women were capable of signing, though this in itself is of course no clear indication of an ability to write freely.

Given the lack of formal educational opportunities for women, many women acquired their culture informally as adults in the 'Monde': in salons. It is to discussion of this milieu that we now turn.

4.2.4   *Salons and* la culture mondaine

One of the most important arenas for the development of *la culture féminine* in the seventeenth century was the salons, at least for women of the upper echelons of society. Viala identifies two broad phases in their development (Timmermans 1993: 95). From around 1610 to 1650, salon culture was dominated by the aristocratic salon of Mme de Rambouillet, 'la divine Arthénice'. Born and raised in Italy, Mme de Rambouillet is said to have withdrawn to her *hôtel* because of her dislike of the coarseness of the court of Henri IV, receiving her visitors lying in her famous 'chambre bleue'. Here discussion of literature and the French language, social behaviour and taste took place, and conversation was all-important.[5] A similar role was played, for example, by the salon of Mme des Loges at its height in the 1620s. From 1630 to the time of the Fronde, the number of salons increased. Naturalness and lack of pedantry were highly valued. Madame d'Auchy, for example, was criticized for her 'assemblées académiques' (Timmermans 1993: 80–2). Salon activity was somewhat abruptly ended by the Fronde; its failure put an end, however, to the political role some women had carved for themselves during this period and women withdrew into salon and court culture, adopting a different role as social and literary authorities.

In the second period, from 1650 to around 1665, the number of salons multiplied dramatically. While the majority of the salons were Parisian and aristocratic, this period also witnesses an increasing role for bourgeois women in salon culture. Foremost among these is Madeleine de Scudéry's ('Sapho's') 'Samedis', Saturday meetings at her salon from 1651 onwards and especially from 1652–3. Madeleine de Scudéry's salon took up the literary role played earlier by Mme de Rambouillet's, welcoming writers such as Conrart, Pellisson, Ménage, Chapelain and d'Aubignac, while being less aristocratic in nature (Mongrédien 1939: 9). She nevertheless continued to stress the social value and civilizing role of salon culture: 'la politesse ne s'acquiert que dans le monde' (Pekacz 1999: 27). Her published conversations perhaps give us some idea of the typical conversations of the salon; it is moreover likely that novels circulated and were discussed there before being published.

If Madeleine de Scudéry has been termed 'la reine incontestée du mouvement précieux' (Maignien 1991:15), Mme du Plessis-Guénegaud, Mme Foucquet and Mme du Plessis-Bellière 'tiennent les salons les plus brillants de l'époque précieuse' (Lathuillère 1966: 655). Lougee (1976: 53) argues that the 'salons played a central role in the process of social assimilation because within the

---

[5] There has been much debate as to whether Mme de Rambouillet should be associated with *Préciosité*. Certainly, Angélique-Clarice d'Angennes, one of Mme de Rambouillet's daughters, is named as one of the leading *Précieuses* (see section 4.5.2).

salons ladies taught the social graces which covered the new rich with the "*parfum de l'aristocratie*"'. Having analysed the background of the women on Somaize's list of *Précieuses* (see below), she notes (Lougee 1976: 122) that about 40% of the titles held by the families of these women were first-generation titles and nearly one-fifth of the total number of titleholders were new nobles. After about 1665 the centre of gravity moved away from the salons of the town back to the court of Louis XIV and salon life became less important.

The anonymous author of a manuscript entitled 'De la conuersation des femmes' notes that while certain things have to be learnt in books, others must be acquired in polite society 'qui nous enseigne quelque fois mieux que toutes les estudes'. The writer adds, 'Je scay bien encores qu'on apprend deux fois plus dans le cabinet, Mais on apprend la maniere de s'en seruir dans le monde' (BN Nouv. Acq. 124: 180v). As Grande notes (1999a: 227), salon culture 'permit aux quelques femmes nobles . . . de pallier le handicap intellectuel de leur quasi-absence de formation scolaire'. This was a 'culture résolument moderne et non savante' which abandoned the pre-eminence of Latin (Grande 1999a: 226). Instead modern foreign languages, novels, poetry, theatre, music, dance, and classical and foreign literature in translation were the main areas of conversation and debate. In short the salons became 'lieux éminemment pédagogiques' (Dulong 1984: 126).

Grande (1999a: 210; 1999b) cites some telling examples of the educational experiences of women novelists; none of those she studies were convent educated, and they were of course excluded from *collège* and university education. Most were involved in salon life, especially in Mme de Rambouillet's, and there they acquired a familiarity with literature. Mme de Lafayette, for example, was taken there early on by her mother, and there she met Gilles Ménage, who became her mentor. Mlle de Montpensier grew up at the court, where she was exposed to theatre, ballet, painting, music and conversation; she too benefited from the attention of a male mentor, Segrais. Mlle de Scudéry (Grande 1999a: 211), herself later the host of a successful salon, was the only one to enjoy a solid education, tutored by her uncle; the correct spelling of her letters is not typical of female writers of the period.

In short, if women were denied access to formal education, other channels were open to them, notably the *culture mondaine* of the salon milieu. Moreover, salons were also a place where women could form social networks and develop a sense of group consciousness. Presided over and dominated by women, the salons constituted a place where women could function outside the traditional domestic sphere.

Ideas on education and learning evolved as the century progressed. From Malherbe on, there was at court a strong movement against pedantry. This may be seen in changing attitudes towards the so-called 'ignorance' of women, no longer viewed as a reason for censure (section 4.2.5); in the elaboration of the ideals of the *honnête homme* and *honnête femme*, notions intimately linked to salon ideals; and in the 'civilizing' role attributed to women (section 4.2.6).

4.2.5   Women's 'ignorance'

The 'ignorance' of women, or their lack of a formal education, is a constant theme throughout the century. We may point, for instance, to a number of examples of writers and authors who consciously adapt their works for a female audience.[6] This may be a question of the appropriate choice of language, typically the vernacular rather than Latin; Descartes, for example, is said to have decided to write his *Discours de la méthode* (1637) in French so that 'les femmes même pussent entendre quelque chose' (Gibson 1989: 30). Alternatively, the adaptation may be a question of style, tone and format. In presenting specialist knowledge to a broader, female audience, it was considered important to avoid the possibility of boredom, by presenting the material in a clear but brief way, and shunning a pedantic tone and technical terminology. Guez de Balzac (1634: 248) in a letter to Boisrobert dated 25 February 1624 comments: 'Ie tasche tant qu'il m'est possible de rendre tous mes secrets populaires & d'estre intelligible aux femmes et aux enfans, quand mesmes ie parle des choses qui ne sont pas de leur cognoissance.'

The presentation and content of a number of works on the French language were similarly adapted to make them suitable for a female readership. The best-known instance is Vaugelas's *Remarques* (1647) which deliberately avoids both an alphabetical and a part of speech format and favours instead a series of randomly ordered short observations on points of doubtful usage, 'conceuës d'vne sorte, que les femmes & tous ceux qui n'ont nulle teinture de la langue Latine en peuuent tirer du profit. C'est pourquoy i'y ay meslé moins d'erudition que la matiere n'en eust pû souffrir' (Preface XII, 1). Marguerite Buffet adopts a similar presentation, simplifying and abbreviating her material as far as possible to avoid boring her female readers (1668: 7, 119). Conversation manuals could also be aimed at a female audience, as in the case of Bary's *L'Esprit de cour, ou les conversations galantes* (1662), written for women and provincials.

---

[6] Reference to women in the title of a work may occasionally be incidental. Leven de Templery changed the title of his work from *La Rhétorique françoise, très-propre aux gens qui veulent apprendre à parler et écrire avec politesse* (Paris, 1698) to *L'Éloquence du tems enseignée à une dame de qualité, très-propre aux gens qui veulent apprendre à parler et à écrire avec politesse* [. . .] (Paris, 1699) without making any change to the content. Conversely, René Bary's *La fine philosophie, accommodée à l'intelligence des Dames* (Paris 1660) was later published as *Logique où il est donné l'usage de la logique mesme* (1669, 1672), again unchanged.

While for some, women's lack of knowledge is a matter for censure, throughout the century both male and female writers emphasize that affectation of knowledge, for example when it is not properly assimilated (Du Bosc 1633: 78), and above all pedantry from women, are far more unacceptable. For instance, Balzac in a letter to Jean Chapelain maintains, 'Il y a long temps que je me suis déclaré contre cette pedanterie de l'autre sexe, et que j'ay dit, que je souffrirois plus volontiers une femme qui a de la barbe, qu'une femme qui fait la sçavante' (Balzac 1661: 138–9; cf. Andry de Boisregard 1689: 376–7). Similarly, Andry de Boisregard argues that it is worse if women adopt a 'stile Pédantesque', 'parce qu'on sçait bien que leur mérite n'est pas la science' (1689: 375). While some theorists argue that women should be educated, and indeed that knowledge of music, history and philosophy is of great value to them, and may enrich their conversation (Du Bosc 1633: 257, 263),[7] others consider that a women is likely to become a figure of fun if she displays knowledge inappropriate for her sex (Callières 1693: 124–5). Madame de Maintenon is said to have told the nuns at Saint-Cyr to avoid paying overscrupulous attention to correctness in writing and spelling since 'cela sentait trop la pédanterie dans une personne de notre sexe, et l'envie de faire la savante' (Gibson 1989: 273). In short, a balance must be maintained between a woman having the appropriate social skills, such as how to express herself clearly and politely, or how to dance (Callières 1693: 124), and not appearing overtly 'sçavante'. Affectation of ignorance is also condemned: Callières (1693: 126–7) cites the example of a woman using the word *voyelles* in the Queen Mother's circle; all the other women denied that they knew its meaning and only Madame de Montausier was prepared to admit to knowing its sense.

4.2.6   Theories of honnêteté *and the civilizing role of women*

Works on *honnêteté* played an important part in enhancing the status of women, since they devoted considerable space to discussing the civilizing role of women in society. The notion of the *honnête homme* is developed in France primarily by Faret in his work of 1630, subtitled *L'Art de plaire à la court*. In describing the behaviour expected of courtiers or the way to succeed for the *arriviste*, Faret necessarily discusses the role of *honnêtes femmes* and particularly of women's conversation. For Faret, women's conversation is 'l'un des plus doux et des plus

---

[7] In addition to the portraits of *femmes savantes*, certain *Précieuses* were praised for their knowledge; for instance, Clorinde (Queen Christina of Sweden) was said to demonstrate that 'la science est aussi bien naturelle à leur sexe qu'au nostre' (Somaize 1661a: 65). Alemand (1688: 223–4) likewise concludes that 'on ne peut plus refuser aux Dames l'entrée dans les Universitez, & dans les autres Compagnies, où la capacité fait entrer, sur tout, si elles continuent à se rendre si habiles'.

honnestes amusements de la vie' (Faret 1925: 15); moreover, 'comme elle est
la plus douce et la plus agreable, elle est aussi la plus difficile et la plus delicate
de toutes les autres' (Faret 1925: 89).

As the century progressed, works devoted to *honnêtes femmes* began to
appear which presented new ideals of women (e.g. Du Bosc 1633, 1634, 1636;
Grenaille 1639–40), and the notion of *honnêteté* was constantly redefined (see
Timmermans 1993). It is, however, constantly associated with moderation, order
and regularity, and excess is criticized. Conversation with women is considered
an essential element of *honnêteté* and a prerequisite for becoming an *honnête
homme*: 'Le commerce des honnêtes-gens est à rechercher: mais les entretiens
des Dames, dont les graces font penser aux bienséances, sont encore plus nec-
essaires pour s'achever dans l'honnêteté' (Méré 1930: III, 75; cf. Grenaille
1639–40: I, 2). This belief is expressed not only in general, theoretical terms,
but also in relation to individual women; for example, Balzac (1933–4: II, 99)
in a letter to Vaugelas of 25 December 1625 describes Mme des Loges as
'une femme [. . .] qui vaut plus que tous nos livres, & dans la conversation de
laquelle il y a dequoy se rendre honneste homme sans l'ayde des Grecs, ny des
Romains'.

The theme of the civilizing role of women recurs in many different works
throughout the century. Typical is Jacques de Callières's *La Fortune des gens de
qualité et des gentilshommes particuliers* (1661), which links women's positive
role with their 'ignorance':

Le plus grand secret pour purger un gentilhomme de cette ordure est de le produire de
bonne heure dans le monde, de luy prescrire des conversations choisies [. . .] luy ordonner
la conversation des dames, et luy souffrir quelque intrigue avec elles. En vérité, parmy
l'ignorance de ce sexe, les plus sçavans prennent souvent de très utiles leçons. (cited
from Lathuillère 1966: 589)

Certain dictionary definitions of the period underline the role of female conversation in shaping young people and educating them in the ways of polite society.
F's definitions of *façonner* and *polir* are representative: 'La conversation des
Dames *façonne* bien un jeune homme'; 'la conversation des Dames *polit* bien
un jeune homme, le rend propre, galand & delicat'.

In short, numerous texts stress the fundamental role of women in educating
men in the ways of polite society. Men who do not mix with women tend to be
unsociable and coarse (Gilbert 1650: 31). Female influence may be felt on men's
behaviour in general: 'Les femmes qui sont naturellement plus douces, plus
complaisantes, plus gracieuses que les hommes, ont aussi plus de politesse; &
c'est principalement dans le commerce qu'on a avec elles, que l'on apprend
à être civil, & poli, par l'envie qu'on a de leur plaire' (Morvan de Bellegarde
1700: 4–5). Alternatively it may be explicitly associated with the acquisition
of good linguistic skills:

L'art de parler juste & à propos, de ne point mêler une langue avec une autre, pour en
faire un langage barbare, savoir loüer ce qu'un autre desapprouve, & desapprouver ce
qu'un autre loüe, sans paroître entesté ou contredisant; le discernement du Pédantisme
d'avec la science des honnêtes gens, tout cela s'apprend mieux dans la Conversation des
femmes spirituelles, que par le secours des Livres [. . .] C'est avec elles qu'on apprend
à se taire & à parler. (Morvan de Bellegarde 1698: 297–8, 305)[8]

4.3   Women's conversation

4.3.1   Women's conversation and the salons

As we have seen, women were valued for their possible 'civilizing' influence on
men, particularly with respect to the positive effect of conversation with women
at court or in the salons. Gaining access to the spoken language of women is,
of course, problematic; letters, which are sometimes considered a reflection of
spoken language, or conversations in novels, must be approached with great
care since these may be literary artefacts (section 4.3.2). However, a number
of comments in the metalinguistic texts do refer explicitly to women's speech.
Often this aspect of women's linguistic usage is praised, whilst their written
usage, or at least their orthography, is criticized (see below).

   The same concerns and values – the search for elegance, distinction in manners, habits, style and language – but taken to an extreme form, may be seen
in the attention to language and the concern for purity of usage shown by the
Précieuses (section 4.5).

4.3.2   Theories of conversation

The sense of the term 'conversation' itself evolved in the Early Modern period.
In the seventeenth century, its older meaning of 'commerce, fréquentation'
is still attested, but this sense is moribund and R's definiton (1680) of it as
'Entretien familier avec une ou plusieurs personnes' is typical of modern usage.
A number of theoretical works on conversation were produced, notably by
Antoine Gombaud, chevalier de Méré, and literary conversations or 'entretiens'
were published either as self-standing works (e.g. Bouhours 1962 [[1]1671]) or
as part of novels (most famously by Madeleine de Scudéry).

   Certain qualities of conversation are constantly praised by commentators.
Above all speakers should try to please their interlocutor, since, as Méré notes
(1930: I, 171), this has wider social consequences: 'Aussi je conseille aux

---

[8] In the manuscript 'De la conversation', women are said to be responsible for teaching both positive
   qualities such as 'la politesse, la ciuilité, et mesme la finesse' (182v), and negative features such
   as cunning, malice and slander (187r).

Dames de bon air, de songer plus à plaire qu'à faire rire, parce que beaucoup de choses font rire, qu'on n'aime point, mais tout ce qui plaît, se fait aimer.' This is of particular importance in a monarchy, and one might add in an absolute monarchy, since, as Madeleine de Scudéry notes, one is dependent on the good will of the king:

> Il est vrai, reprit Théonor, que la source de la politesse étant le désir de plaire par quelque motif que ce puisse être, soit d'ambition ou d'amour; ce désir doit être plus vif dans un état monarchique que dans une république, parce que les grâces dépendant d'un seul, le désir de lui plaire rend capable de plaire à tous. (Denis 1998a: 137)

Buffet (1668: 120) similarly emphasizes the power and influence which are acquired by women who speak well: 'Ces illustres sont receuës par tout où elles veulent se trouver, avec des deferences duës aux Reines, dans les cercles, dans les ruelles, & dans les conversations les plus celebres.'

The principal way to please is through linguistic conformity, to express one's thoughts and ideas in precisely the same way as one's listener would have chosen: 'car pour estre écouté avecque plaisir, il faut dire des choses que l'on soit bien-aise d'entendre, et les dire agréablement' (Méré 1930: I, 63, see also II, 106). Other positive qualities include a natural and accurate use of language (Méré 1930: I, 14–15).[9] Discretion and modesty are praiseworthy, as is the ability to know when to avoid talking too much and when to keep silent (Du Bosc 1633: 53; Jeanne de Schomberg 1997: 177). Above all, conversation should be immediately and unambiguously comprehensible, as Madeleine de Scudéry emphasizes: 'quiconque parle est obligé de se faire entendre' (Denis 1997: 334). It is therefore important to take account of who is speaking, to whom one is speaking and the subject matter (Buffet 1668: 163). Bouhours (1671: 78–9) observes that while it is necessary to refer to books to learn grammatical accuracy, 'ce n'est gueres que dans les belles conversations qu'on apprend à parler noblement, & naturellement tout ensemble'. This did not prevent the publication of a number of works which included rules on how to behave in conversation; for example, Irson's grammar includes (1662: 203) a section entitled 'Regles generales que l'on doit pratiquer dans les Conuersations', and Renaud (1697: 141ff.) has a chapter 'Du Style Mediocre ou de Conversation' which elaborates on the importance of conversation and cites examples from Mlle de Scudéry, Méré and Bouhours.

Both Méré and Madeleine de Scudéry emphasize that the best conversations are mixed, with a large role assigned to women who are superior to men as conversationalists. Thus in *Clélie* Madeleine de Scudéry observes: 'Pour

---

[9] 'Natural' is used in the sense of a 'naive' or unaffected use of language. For a critique of the different versions of linguistic naturalism from Plato onwards, see Joseph 2000.

l'agrément du langage, la conversation toute seule le peut donner, encore faut-il que ce soit une conversation de gens du monde, dont les femmes fassent la plus grande partie' (Denis 1998a: 95).[10] Méré (1930: III, 168) argues that exclusively female conversations are problematic: 'Il faut mêler des hommes avec les femmes, car lors qu'elles sont seules, rien ne les anime, et les plus habiles m'en ont assuré'. If men excel in the public domain, women's eloquence in the private domain of conversation is of no less importance:

l'auoüe bien que les filles ne remplissent pas les chaises, & qu'elles ne se font point entendre au barreau, mais elles remplissent les cercles, & font tous [sic] l'agrément des plus belles compagnies [. . .] Outre qu'à bien prendre les choses, l'eloquence ne regne pas moins dans les entretiens familiers, que dans les assemblées publiques. (Grenaille 1639–40: III, 206).

A number of critics have commented on the close relationship between letter-writing and conversation in the seventeenth century (see Buffet 1668: 160–1). Goldsmith (1988: 113), for instance, points to a seventeenth-century definition of the letter as a 'conversation des absents' and Fumaroli (1992: 14) describes it as a 'genre littéraire *oral*'. On the other hand, Fumaroli's definition rightly makes it clear that letter-writing constituted an important literary genre, and was therefore limited in its spontaneity: 'De Balzac à Voiture, la correspondance devient en France un genre littéraire majeur, quoique ou parce que dans une dépendance étroite de la conversation orale' (Fumaroli 1992: 26). The same provisos must be made about the conversations published in the seventeenth century. As Fumaroli notes in the preface to an anthology of conversations edited by Hellegouarc'h (1997: II), 'cette suite de traités de "règles du jeu de la conversation" établit d'abord le haut degré de conscience proprement littéraire que la "forme conversation" a connu pendant quatre règnes successifs en France'. Madeleine de Scudéry's conversations were originally conceived as part of her novels, in particular, *Artamène ou le Grand Cyrus* (1649–53; vols. IX and X), and *Clélie, histoire romaine* (1654–60; vols. IV and VIII). From 1680 on, they were published separately, with varying degrees of modification, as ten volumes of conversations alongside newly published ones.[11] As Denis (1998a: 63) concludes, 'la conversation est [. . .] comprise comme l'un des lieux d'articulation privilégiés entre politesse et littérature, entre réalité mondaine et fiction galante'.

---

[10] In a later addition to the published conversations she seems to adopt a contrary position (Hellegouarc'h 1997: 105–6): 'mais je dis, à la honte de notre sexe, que les hommes ont un grand avantage sur nous pour la conversation'.

[11] I follow Denis in citing the text of the original version; the 1680s version may be found in Wolfe 1977.

4.4   General features of women's language

4.4.1   Positive attitudes towards women's language: women as authorities

For authors writing on women's usage of French a key factor is their ignorance of Greek and Latin. Poullain de la Barre (1679: 47) claims that women's dislike of Latin is so great that they cannot even bear their children to speak Latin in their presence. This lack of knowledge of the classical languages is generally presented as a positive advantage and as a reason for considering women as authorities for good usage.

In his famous definition of good usage as that of 'la plus saine partie de la Cour', Vaugelas explicitly includes women (1647: Préface II, 3). Later in the work (1647: 503–5) he goes further, arguing that on points of doubtful usage, it is women, and those who have not studied, who should be consulted, since they are likely to give you a more natural and more authentic response.[12] In this he claims to be following Cicero.[13] When speaking of women as authorities he refers principally to the elite at court and not to 'la lie du peuple, quoy qu'en certaines rencontres il se pourroit faire qu'il ne le faudroit pas exclurre'. This principle of consulting women on questions of doubtful usage is clearly followed by Vaugelas at times in his *Remarques*. For instance, in the observation entitled 'Deux ou plusieurs pluriels suiuis d'vn singulier auec la conionction ET deuant le verbe, comment ils regissent le verbe?' (1647: 378–80) he recommends a singular agreement, maintaining: 'l'Vsage le fait ainsi dire presque à tout le monde, & les femmes que j'ay consultées là dessus, à l'imitation de Ciceron, sont toutes de cet auis'.

Subsequent writers of observations on the French language frequently comment on the validity of this principle. Its most outspoken critic is Dupleix (1651: 10), who considers it absurd, evidencing an 'excez de complaisance ou de flaterie envers les Courtisans & envers le sexe feminin'. In his view authorities on French must know the rules of grammar and rhetoric, Latin and even Greek,

---

[12] One less flattering comment by Vaugelas about women is made in the Arsenal manuscript (69v), and was only published posthumously in his *Nouvelles Remarques* (1690: 29): 'Certes quand on escrit aux femmes, il faut apporter une attention toute particuliere pour cela, et auoir un soing extraordinaire d'esloigner de ces esprits folastres tout ce qui leur peut donner des mauuaises pensées.'

[13] Farrell (2001: 52–83) points out that ancient sources generally regard women as poor speakers, and that, for example, Crassus in Cicero's *De oratore* states that a 'voice that is soft or womanly' is to be avoided. Moreover, when Cicero praises his mother-in-law's speech as retaining older manners since it is less corrupted by conversation with many people, he expresses the praise in terms of recalling the speech of men: 'the very sound of her voice is so straight and simple that it seems to involve no ostentation or imitation. And from this I infer that her father and ancestors spoke this way; not harshly [. . .], not sprawlingly, rudely, or gaspingly, but compactly and evenly and gently.'

and he doubts the possibility of finding a woman with such knowledge. In addition, he questions how one would decide if men and women offered conflicting judgments. He points to inconsistencies in the *Remarques*, noting that there are occasions where Vaugelas himself criticizes women's usage, undermining his definition of good usage (Dupleix 1651: 24–6). Commenting on Vaugelas's consultation of women over the question of agreement cited above, Dupleix argues there are more than enough men worthy of being consulted and concludes: 'Ie suis lassé de tant Grammatizer, & mesmes contre des hommes qui mesprisent ordinairement les preceptes de la Grammaire, & contre les femmes de leur conseil, lesquelles les ignorent' (Dupleix 1651: 268). Other critics of the principle include La Mothe Le Vayer, who, alluding to their fickle nature, maintains that if women are asked the same question seven or eight days later they are likely to have changed their minds (Streicher 1936: 653). Baillet (1685: I, 76–7) notes the widespread belief that women are 'les veritables dépositaires de l'usage',[14] 'qui fait que souvent les ruelles des Dames sont les tribunaux où se jugent les Livres écrits en nôtre Langue, & que ce sont des Ecoles où ceux de nos Ecrivains d'aujourd'hui qui se piquent de politesse, vont puiser leurs lumieres'; he is, however, rather sceptical about their right to act as judges of language and style. Discussing spelling reform, B. de Soule (1689: 16–17) argues against one of the reasons given for basing spelling on pronunciation, namely that this would be advantageous to women, who find it impossible to adhere to current spelling rules; women should not dictate usage to men – this has never happened for any language – and men are criticized if they adopt 'une prononciation feminine, ou plûtôt effeminée'.[15]

Other writers on the French language are much more favourable towards Vaugelas's position and it is endorsed, for example, by the French Academy in their observations on his *Remarques* (1704). Bouhours (1962: 37), alluding to the *Précieuses*, is critical of the jargon of certain women, but he is generally full of praise for the naturalness and spontaneity of women's use of French:

Mais d'où vient, pensez-vous, dit Eugene, que les femmes en France parlent si bien? N'est-ce pas parce qu'elles parlent naturellement & sans nulle étude. – Il est vray, reprit Ariste, qu'il n'y a rien de plus juste, de plus propre, & de plus naturel, que le langage de la pluspart des femmes Françoises. Les mots dont elles se servent, semblent tout neufs, & faits exprés pour ce qu'elles disent, quoy-qu'ils soient communs: & si la nature elle mesme vouloit parler, je croy qu'elle emprunteroit leur langue pour parler naïvement. (Bouhours 1962: 39)

[14] This belief may be related to the fact that it is women's conversational or oral skills which are particularly valued. As we saw in Chapter 2 (section 2.3), Vaugelas stresses the primacy of speech.
[15] Compare Meigret (1550: fo 7r), who is critical of the usage of the 'effeminez miñons' who, in contrast to courtiers, confuse, for example, the pronunciation of open and closed 'e'.

Alemand (1688: 6) also maintains that women usually speak very well, and reports that he asked his own wife about the gender of 'couple' since this was in doubt (451–2). For Renaud (1697: 521–2) one of four ways of making up for deficiencies in language usage is to 'consulter dans les doutes sur la Langue, les Doctes, les Gens de Qualité, & sur tout parmi les Personnes du Sexe, celles qui passent pour les plus polies & les plus intelligentes de l'Usage'.

On the whole, the positive view of women's usage prevails and their 'natural' judgment and good taste allow them to be arbiters (especially in the salons) not only of good usage, but also of literary texts. The praise of writers, courtiers, rhetoricians and grammarians alike for women's speech habits is reflected in the dedication of a number of works such as l'Estang's treatise on translation (1660) dedicated to Madame de Sablé:

Je sais que les maîtres de notre langue vous consultent dans leurs doutes, vous font arbitre de leurs différents et se soumettent à vos décisions. En effet, vous êtes, Madame, la personne du monde qui savez le mieux toutes les lois et toutes les règles du discours; qui savez le mieux exprimer avec grâce et netteté vos sentiments et vos pensées; qui savez le mieux employer ces belles façons de parler si ingénieuses, si charmantes et si naturellement françaises; enfin qui savez le mieux toutes ces délicatesses et tous ces mystères du style dont parle M. de Vaugelas. (François 1959: I, 250)

4.4.2   Negative attitudes towards women's language: women making errors

Occasionally reference is made to the faulty nature of women's language, and especially their written usage. This may be a question of grammatical errors, as when Mme de Maintenon claims that women when writing make 'mille fautes contre la grammaire' (Gibson 1989: 36), or of spelling mistakes (see also below) as in the case of Callières (1693: 127–8), who argues that women should be educated in 'tout ce qu'il faut sçavoir pour s'expliquer correctement, & pour bien parler & bien écrire en nôtre Langue, & qu'on ne fût plus obligé de déviner la plus grande partie de ce qu'elles écrivent, à cause de leur mauvaise Ortographe'. Criticism of women's spelling is also found in Mézeray's *Cahiers de remarques sur l'orthographe françoise* (1673) drawn up as part of the preparatory work on the Academy's dictionary (Marty-Laveaux 1863: ix): 'La Compagnie declare qu'elle desire suiure l'ancienne orthographe qui distingue les gents de lettres dauec les ignorants et les simples femmes, et qu'il faut la maintenir par tout hormis dans les mots ou un long et constant usage en aura introduit une contraire.'[16]

---

[16] According to Beaulieux (1951: 131), Segrais wanted this expressed even more strongly, commenting 'rayer simples'. However, Mézeray's formulation was criticized by Régnier and Pellisson, and it was reworked to remove the reference to women (Marty-Laveaux 1863: 2). Later, in the eighteenth and nineteenth centuries the Academy in fact adopted some of the reformed spellings associated with women's usage (see below). The Abbé de Villiers tolerated

Buffet's principal motivation for writing a volume of observations intended especially for women is that she is conscious of the daily errors many of them commit, which leads her to believe that they haven't read the works on the French language, or, if they have, have not been able to profit from them. She adds (1668: 176) that there are women who appear 'fort habiles', yet who have difficulty writing a letter.

Other writings present a rather stereotypical view of women as typically speaking too much; for instance, Montfleury, in his comedy *La Femme juge et partie* (first performed in 1669), gives the following lines to Julie:

> Qu'importe? Est-ce un défaut qu'on doive condamner?
> Elle parloit beaucoup, faut-il s'en étonner?
> C'est dedans une femme une chose ordinaire,
> Et je n'en ai jamais connu qui sût se taire.[17]
>
> (Montfleury 1739: 67)

The manuscript treatise 'De la conuersation des femmes' begins by outlining the positive features of women's language and then becomes more negative, seeing concern for language as dangerous for morality (BN Nouv. Acq. 124: 195v) since more attention is paid to language than to sincerity. Irson's (1662: 208) discussion of women's use of direct speech suggests that their linguistic inadequacies reflect a more general weakness of their temperament:

> Ce vice est commun aux Ieunes-gens, & encore plus aux Femmes (j'en excepte les Illustres) lesquelles s'amusent à toutes les moindres circonstances qui ne servent de rien à l'histoire; au lieu de s'arrêter au principal, & d'effleurer seulement les circonstances, à moins qu'elles ne soient tres-necessaires.

4.4.3 *Positive qualities of women's language*

Despite these criticisms of their language, women are generally presented as inherently good speakers: 'J'auance encore que le bien parler n'est pas tant vn ornement conuenable aux filles, comme vne propriété attachée à leur nature' (Grenaille 1639–40: III, 207; cf. 'De la conuersation', 189r). Praise of women's language is often expressed in terms of the general qualities of their language, rather than in terms of specific examples of different usages. Poullain de la Barre (1679: 49) summarizes his discussion of the differences between the language of educated men and of women in the following terms:

---

errors in women's spelling because of their lack of education: 'les négligences et les fautes d'orthographe, ne gâtent point les lettres d'une femme, mais elles choquent dans celles d'un homme' (Timmermans 1993: 199).

[17] See also Montfleury, *Le Procez de la femme juge et partie* (scene 2, 1739: 104): 'Hé, nous verrons bien-tôt que malgré la pudeur, / Puisque l'on se plaît tant à ces pointes infames, / Il faudra des gros mots pour contenter les Dames.'

Elles s'énoncent avec grace. Elles ont l'art de trouver les plus beaux termes de l'usage, et de faire plus comprendre en un mot, que les hommes avec plusieurs: & si l'on s'entretient des Langues en general, elles ont là-dessus des pensées qui ne se trouvent que dans les plus habiles Grammairiens. Enfin on remarque qu'elles tirent plus de l'usage seul pour le langage, que la pluspart des hommes ne font de l'usage joint à l'étude.

What are the qualities most frequently associated with female speech? Women are generally seen as possessing the positive qualities of conversation to a higher degree. Not surprisingly, one of the most commonly mentioned is its 'naïveté' or naturalness, as can be seen in the Bouhours citation above. Balzac, in a letter to Madame des Loges dated 20 September 1628, says of her use of language: 'Ny au ton de la voix, ny en la maniere de s'exprimer, on ne remarque rien en vous que de naturel et de françois', and Georges de Scudéry makes a similar comment: 'la facilité de bien parler vous est naturel, au lieu qu'elle nous est acquise' (Timmermans 1993: 83, 149). The following example must stand as representative of numerous others:

L'eloquence est un talent qui leur [women] est si naturel & si particulier, qu'on ne peut le leur disputer. (Poullain de la Barre 1679: 49–50)

Poullain de la Barre makes it clear that this is not merely a question of spoken language, since he goes on to praise women's letters, especially those which treat 'les passions':

Elles les touchent d'une maniere si délicate: & les expriment si naïvement, qu'on est obligé d'avoüer qu'on ne les sent pas autrement, & que toutes les Rhetoriques du monde ne peuvent donner aux hommes ce qui ne coûte rien aux femmes. (Poullain de la Barre 1679: 50)

Other valued qualities of women's speech are those which are highly prized by the *remarqueurs*, as elaborated by Vaugelas (1647: 593):[18]

A la pureté, & à la netteté du stile, il y a encore d'autres parties à ajouster, la proprieté des mots & des phrases, l'elegance, la douceur, la majesté, la force, & ce qui resulte de tout cela, l'air & la grace, qu'on appelle le ie ne sçay quoy, où le nombre, la briefueté, & la naïfueté de l'expression, ont encore beaucoup de part.

Again, one or two examples of women's language being lauded for its clarity or *netteté* must stand for numerous others:

La politesse et la netteté sont encore deux propriétés naturelles aux Dames. (Gilbert 1650: 15–16, cited from Pekacz 1999: 76)

Elles s'expliquent avec plus de netteté et [. . .] elles donnent un tour plus agréable aux choses qu'elles disent. (La Rochefoucauld 1967: 257)

---

[18] The ones which are not mentioned as typical of women's language are perhaps considered the more 'masculine' qualities such as *la majesté* and *la force*.

This, of course, implies a dislike of ambiguity:

On n'entend point sortir de leur bouche des paroles à double entendre. Les moindres équivoques blessent leurs oreilles, & elles ne peuvent souffrir la veuë de tout ce qui choque la pudeur. (Poullain de la Barre 1679: 39)

If *netteté* is concerned with syntactic clarity, women are also praised for the *proprieté* or *justesse* of their language, that is the ability to chose the appropriate word or expression for each concept:

Ce que les femmes ont éminemment par dessus les hommes, est le talent de s'énoncer avec justesse, & de choisir les termes propres pour faire concevoir ce qu'elles veulent dire. (Morvan de Bellegarde, *Lettres curieuses*, cited from Timmermans 1993: 147)

For Poullain de la Barre, the choice of the correct term implies avoidance of technical or overspecialized vocabulary which may hinder comprehension:

elles ne pointillent point vainement sur les mots, & ne se servent point de ces termes scientifiques & mysterieux, si propres à couvrir l'ignorance, & tout ce qu'elles disent est intelligible & sensible. (Poullain de la Barre 1679: 41–2)

Alongside these features which are desirable for all language usage, a number of particularly feminine qualities such as *délicatesse*, *grace*, *agrément* are also mentioned:

Leur imagination est trop delicate pour auoir de grossieres expressions, & ie ne croy pas qu'on les puisse blamer que mal à propos de ce qu'elles parlent bien. En vn mot la force du raisonnement est pour les hommes, mais la grace du langage est pour les femmes. (Grenaille 1639–40: III, 75)

L'ignorance agréable & enjoüée des femmes vaut mieux que la sombre & enuïeuse érudition des savans; Elles parlent avec plus d'ordre & plus d'agrément, & ne se tarissent point, pourvû que la conversation roule sur des matieres qui leur conviennent. (Morvan de Bellegarde, *Lettres curieuses*, 241–2, cited from Timmermans 1993: 147)

Une des choses, reprit *Ariste*, qui me toucheroit le plus dans le commerce des femmes sprirituelles, c'est la politesse de leur langage; elles expriment les moindres bagatelles avec des tours qui y donnent un grand agrément. (Morvan de Bellegarde 1698: 299)

It is interesting to note that precisely the same descriptions are used to characterize the positive features of the use of language of individual women. Particularly striking in this respect is the way Madame de Sévigné's language is described by her contemporaries (Duchêne 1988: 7–11):

Sa conversation est aisée, divertissante et naturelle, affirme [. . .] Mlle de Scudéry. Elle parle juste, elle parle bien, elle a même quelquefois certaines expressions naïves et spirituelles qui plaisent infiniment [. . .] Qui voudroit ramasser toutes les choses que Marie de Rabutin a dites en sa vie d'un tour fin et agréable, naturellement et sans affecter de les dire, écrira son cousin Bussy vers 1685, il n'aurait jamais fait.

As regards women's pronunciation, Bernier, in a letter to Balzac dated 13 January 1661 (Timmermans 1993: 144–5), suggests physical reasons for the 'sweetness' of their pronunciation. He inquires about the way women are treated in India, in particular whether they receive visitors from outside the household:

car cela sert fort à rendre les langues polies, à cause qu'on leur veut plaire, et à cause que, dans la communication avec elles, les hommes apprennent à adoucir la rudesse de leur prononciation, que la mollesse naturelle des organes des femmes ammolit et facilite insensiblement.

The *douceur* of their voices is mentioned by a number of commentators, including Grenaille (1639–40: III, 209) who claims that 'La douceur de leur voix est conforme à celle de leur langage.' Women naturally avoid swearing and a coarse use of language, and favour *politesse*:

Un autre avantage, dit *Arsene*, que l'on retire du commerce des femmes respectables par leur rang ou par leur merite, c'est qu'on n'ose se licentier devant elles à tenir des discours trop libres, qui sentent l'ordure ou le libertinage, ni prononcer de ces paroles qui blessent l'honnêteté, & que la licence du siécle n'a rendu que trop communes parmi les hommes, quand ils ne sont pas devant des personnes qui leur imposent du respect par leur présence. (Morvan de Bellegarde 1698: 293–4)

Not only does female company encourage men to temper their language; model female speakers also exercise moderation in not speaking too much (Grenaille 1639–40: III, 210).

Is the difference between women's and men's language simply a case of general tendencies and qualities? The extent to which we can identify specific linguistic features of women's usage, which perhaps correlate with these general qualities, will be discussed in section 4.6. Many of the works commenting on women's language certainly concentrate on general features, and comments of the type expressed by Madeleine de Scudéry in her conversation entitled 'De parler trop ou trop peu et comment il faut parler', which suggest that there are indeed certain expressions which are peculiar to women, are far less frequent:

il ne faut pas qu'une honnête femme, parle toujours comme un honnête homme et il y a certaines expressions, dont les uns se peuvent servir à propos, et qui seraient de mauvaise grâce aux autres. En effet, reprit Plotine, il y a certaines choses qui sont tout à fait bizarres en la bouche d'une femme, qui ne surprennent pas en celle d'un homme. Car par exemple, si j'allais jurer par le feu sacré, ou par Jupiter, j'épouvanterais ceux à qui je parlerais. Si j'allais juger définitivement de quelque question difficile, je passerais pour ridicule; si j'affirmais ce que je dis d'un ton de voix trop ferme et trop fier, on douteroit si je mériterais le nom de *fille*. (Denis 1998a: 93–4)

Before we consider the evidence for specific linguistic features associated with female usage, we will examine a particular manifestation of women's peculiar use of language in the shape of *Préciosité*.

4.5   *Préciosité* and language

4.5.1   Introduction

From the earliest explicit reference to the existence of the *Précieuses*, the much-quoted letter written by the Chevalier de Sévigné on 3 April 1654 to Christine de France, an association is made between them and their use of a particular 'jargon': 'Il y a une nature de filles et de femmes à Paris que l'on nomme "Précieuses", qui ont un jargon et des mines, avec un déhanchement merveilleux: l'on a fait une carte pour naviguer en leur pays' (Maître 1999: 59).

Subsequent seventeenth-century definitions, whatever their attitude towards the *Précieuses*, continue to refer to their use of language as one of their intrinsic characteristics.[19] Somaize (1661a: I, 5), who in listing the *Précieuses* of his age seems to include nearly all those women who were members of Parisian polite society,[20] nevertheless denies that all *femmes d'esprit* are *Précieuses*, and asserts 'que ce sont seulement celles qui se meslent d'écrire, ou de corriger ce que les autres escriuent, celles qui font leur principal de la lecture des Romans, & sur tout celles qui inuentent des façons de parler bizarres pour leur nouueauté, extraordinaires dans leurs significations'. In the last two decades of the century, the three major monolingual dictionaries, R, F and A, all continue to make the same association. R's definition (1680) is typical in this respect:

Prétieuse, s.f. Ce mot, à moins que d'être accompagné d'une favorable épitete se prend toujours en mauvaise part & lorsqu'il est acompagné d'une épitete favorable il veut dire celle qui rafine sur le langage, qui fait quelque chose & qui se pique d'esprit, mais comme dans ce sens le mot de *prétieuse* est assez rare, lorsqu'on se sert de ce mot sans épitete, ou avec une épitete fâcheuse il signifie celle qui par ses manieres d'agir & de parler mérite d'être raillée [. . .]

+* *Prétieux, prétieuse, adj.* Ce mot se dit des *mots* & du *langage*, & veut dire qui tient du langage des prétieuses, qui a de l'air des prétieuses.

[Façon de parler un peu prétieuse. Mot prétieux.]

4.5.2   Difficulties of definition and of sources

When considering the *Précieuses*'s linguistic usage, the same series of inter-connected problems arises as with all discussions of the movement.[21] First, the very existence of the *Précieuses* has been questioned. It is generally agreed

---

[19] Cf. Scarron, *Epistre chagrine à Monseigneur le mareschal d'Albret*, cited in Lathuillère 1966: 32: '[. . .] de qui tout le bon / Est seulement un langage ou jargon, / Un parler gras, plusieurs sottes manières, / Et qui ne sont enfin que façonnières'.

[20] This broad definition is explicitly adopted by Lougee (1976). Note also Grande's assertion (1999a: 279) that almost all the women novelists she studies 'ont participé à la vogue précieuse'.

[21] See Raynard (2002) for a resumé of some of the main issues.

that seventeenth-century portrayals of *Préciosité* contain a mixture of historical fact and fiction, of reality and caricature, and that the crux of the problem lies in identifying the proportion and identity of each. For Pelous, 'la "préciosité" est d'abord une fable' (1980: 398); Timmermans (1993: 93), on the other hand, contends that the caricature of the *Précieuse* only makes sense if based on a reality, or at least some sort of ideal of which the caricature is a distortion. Maclean (1987) is confident that one can establish some basic facts: that there was a distinct group of girls and women between 1654 and 1660 called *Précieuses*; that they had their own gestures and jargon; that they held new ideas on love and marriage; and that they were found in the *ruelles*, where they discussed not only love and marriage, but also language and literature. As this list suggests, many of the features considered typical of seventeenth-century polite society seem to form a natural basis for *Préciosité*: the rise of the bourgeoisie, the ideal of the *honnête homme*, the refinement of society and concern for taste and good manners, the role of the salons and of *mondain* culture, the rejection of humanist learning and pedantry, and above all the civilizing role attributed to women (cf. Lathuillère 1966: 14, 675), although many of these features were accentuated to the point of excess and the movement also clearly had its own distinguishing features. A related question is the relationship – discussed, for example by Duchêne, Viala and Denis (see Denis 2003) – between *Préciosité* and the 'esthétique galante'. Maître (1999: 431, 650) maintains, however, that *Préciosité* is specifically a feminine movement and has particular attitudes towards love.

A second difficulty concerns the dating of the movement. Some scholars, such as Adam, Pelous and Maclean, argue for a brief chronological span, taking as its starting point the Chevalier de Sévigné's letter of 1654 and pointing to the decline of the movement around 1660/1661, even if some women (such as Madame de Sévigné) remained true to it after this date. Others favour an earlier starting date, Lathuillère preferring 1650 and Sellier 1643 (Raynard 2002: 29–32). Dulong (1984: 151) asserts that already in his *Honneste Fille* (1639–40) Grenaille makes ironic comments about women who want to 'régner dans les compagnies' and even to hold sway over authors, while Timmermans (1993: 92) notes how Sorel, in *Le Rôle des Présentations faictes du Grand Jour de l'éloquence françoise* (c. 1634), a satire directed against the French Academy, refers to women interested in questions of language, foreshadowing the *Précieuses*.[22] The longest periods are given by Brunot (1905–53: III, 69–70), who dates the inception of what he terms this 'petite épisode, artificiellement mise en lumière, de l'histoire littéraire et linguistique' back to

[22] Part of the problem derives from the extent to which the literary antecedents of the movement are taken into account. Lathuillère (1966) details how a number of linguistic features associated with the *Précieuses*, such as their preference for abstract nouns (particularly in the plural), may be found in Balzac, Voiture and Corneille, but he concludes that this influence is not sufficient to define the movement and that the social causes are also vitally important.

the end of the sixteenth century and notes that Bouhours was still discussing *Précieuses*' expressions in the 1670s, and by Sellier, who extends it to 1715 or beyond (Maître 1999: 15). As we shall see, many of the metalinguistic texts in our corpus discuss so-called *Précieuses*' terms throughout the second half of the century.

A third question concerns the difficulty of defining *Préciosité*. As R's definition cited above indicates, the term *précieux/se* was used with both positive and negative values. Before 1654 the adjective tends to have a positive value, whereas after 1654 it is more usual to find it with a negative meaning, although it may still be employed positively, especially when it is applied to a particular individual. In its positive sense, the term *Précieuses* refers to a group of women concerned with civility and politeness, who promoted a pure use of language and displayed considerable interest in literary questions. Foreshadowing future developments of the term, Voiture uses the term *précieuse* in a letter to Julie d'Angennes dated 25 November 1638: 'Je reconnois que vous estes la plus précieuse chose du monde, & je trouve par experience que toutes les delices de la terre sont ameres et desagreables sans vous' (Voiture 1687: 210).[23] Negative values – and especially the connotation of excess – for the adjective are found notably in satirical texts. At the end of the century Morvan de Bellegarde (1700: 9–10) criticizes the affectation of the *Précieuses*, which is contrary to 'le naturel':

Il y a une grande difference entre la veritable politesse, & les petites façons que les Precieuses affectent pour se donner un air de distinction. Leurs grimaces étudiées, leurs minauderies, cette fausse délicatesse, dont elles se parent, font rire les personnes raisonnables.

Perhaps because of the positive and negative connotations associated with the adjective *précieux/se*, a recurrent opposition in many seventeenth-century texts is that between true *Précieuses* and those deemed *fausses* or *ridicules*. All studies of *Préciosité* have been obliged to address the validity of this distinction. In the *Escole des filles. En dialogues* (1657) reference is already made to 'fausses Pretieuses' (Timmermans 1993: 117); Molière also makes this opposition in the Preface to the *Précieuses ridicules*, where he establishes a distinction between the Parisian *Précieuses* and those of the provinces, of whom he is making fun. Somaize (1660) defines the two types differently in his dictionary:

> Vne vieille Fille & qui a de l'esprit. *Vne Pretieuse veritable.*
> Vne Fille Coquette & qui veut passer pour vn bel Esprit. *Vne Pretieuse Ridicule.*

Likewise, within the Abbé de Pure's novel there are different groups of *Précieuses*; some (especially Eulalie and her circle) are represented fairly

---

[23] Note that the term is still used adjectivally here.

sympathetically, whilst others (Didascalie and her companions, Aurélie) are clearly ridiculous (Pure 1938–9). Lathuillère (1966: 39) contends that 'préciosité ridicule' is a pure literary fiction which presents a gross caricature of the facts, even if much of our knowledge of the movement relies on such sources (see below). For some, *Préciosité* became ridiculous when it was extended to the bourgeoisie; for others it is associated with later manifestations of the phenomenon.

So far we have been considering literary portrayals of the *Précieuses*, which aim to represent both the positive and the negative aspects of their desire to be distinctive. When we consider the question in historical terms (see especially Timmermans 1993, Maître 1999), the problem is perhaps even more acute, since no one, except perhaps Mme Deshoulières, described herself as a *Précieuse*, probably for fear of the ridicule this might incur. According to Sellier (1987: 98), there were different networks of *Précieuses*:

• The circle of Mme de Rambouillet and two of her daughters, Julie d'Angennes and Angélique-Clarice de Rambouillet;
• The circle of Mlle de Montpensier;
• The circle of Mme de Lafayette;
• The circle of Mlle de Scudéry.

Maître (1999) adds a fifth important salon, the circle of Anne of Austria, which naturally had links with the court. Fukui (1964) and Duchêne (1995, 2001), on the other hand, provide much more restricted lists of women specifically named as *Précieuses*. Pelous (1980: 378) maintains that three names constantly recur in discussion of *Précieuse* women: Mlle de Rambouillet, Mlle d'Haucourt (the future Maréchale de Schomberg) and Mlle d'Aumale, all of whom regularly attended Mme de Rambouillet's circle. As he asserts (Pelous 1980: 313), we seem to be dealing with 'une secte ridicule composée d'individualités parfaitement estimables'.

A fourth, and for our study perhaps the most acute, difficulty is the question of sources. As Jaouën (1997: 106) notes: 'No text, no author of the period is a self-confessed *précieux*; they are described as such by their enemies.' Those sources that refer specifically to the *Précieuses* (especially those dated 1654–61) tend to be written by their critics. Other texts by women, which appear to share linguistic features with those attributed to the *Précieuses* (see below), are not labelled as such.

Three principal writers are consistently cited as sources of *Précieuses*' language. First, there is the Abbé de Pure's four-volume novel *La Prétieuse* (1656–8, Pure 1938–9), which claims to portray a true account of the meeting of various *Précieuses*.[24] As Maclean (1987: 54) comments, analysis of this work

---

[24] Although no key is provided, commentators have been able to identify the people behind some of the pseudonyms: Eulalie (Henriette de Coligny, Comtesse de la Suze), Parthénoïde (Chapelain), Géname (Ménage), Nidhelie (Hédelin, abbé d'Aubignac).

is dogged by uncertainty about the tone employed – whether it is mocking, parodical, indignant, ironic, satirical or, indeed, neutral – yet Lathuillère (1966: 102)
considers it to be the best source. Secondly there are Somaize's two dictionaries.
The first, *Le Grand Dictionnaire des Pretieuses ou la clef de la langue des ruelles*
(April 1660), claims to be a complete and authentic glossary of all *Précieuses*
terms and expressions; its popularity is suggested by the appearance of a second
edition in 1660. The second, *Le Grand Dictionnaire des Pretieuses, historique,
poetique, geographique, cosmographique, cronologique, & armoirique*, was
published in June 1661, the key to it following shortly after. It furnishes an
alphabetical list of portraits, citing over 600 names. While Somaize identifies
four sorts of women in his preface, including 'pretieuses galantes' and 'veritables pretieuses', his text lists so many women that it would suggest that all
the women in society are more or less *Précieuses*, making it difficult to define
the type. Here again *Précieuses'* words and expressions are defined, and some
are attributed to specific individuals, including Guez de Balzac, although there
are clearly errors of dating and attribution. Of the 159 expressions mentioned,
109 are attributed to a person (Lathuillère 1966: 180), eighty-one (74%) to men
and twenty-eight (26%) to women. Of the forty-four people mentioned as cre-
ators of new expressions, twenty-six are men (59%) and eighteen are women
(41%). Somaize produced a number of other works in close succession, including *Les Veritables Pretieuses, comédie* (1660), *Les Pretieuses Ridicules. Comedie* (1660), and *Le Procez des Pretieuses en vers burlesques, comédie* (1660).
A third source of *Précieuses'* language is Molière's *Précieuses ridicules*, first
performed on 18 November 1659. Molière himself is said to have spread the
rumour that the *Précieuses* depicted in his play were from outside the capital
in order to allow his play to be staged in Paris, and even at some of the major
hôtels. Clearly Somaize had this text before him in composing his dictionary.[25]

The difficulties of using these satirical texts as sources of linguistic data
are obvious. Nevertheless, Denis (1997) identifies some of the same features as
being typical of the usage of Madeleine de Scudéry (see below), described in the
Gazette galante as 'la souveraine des Précieuses' (Sellier 1999: 314). Cuénin
(1973: lix–lx) also suggests that there is continuity between the features of
Précieuses' language and those of women writers more generally: 'Le courant
précieux se signale par des tendances qui vont affleurer dans la langue, sous
des formes bien déterminées, et que des femmes distinguées, comme Mme de
Sévigné, vont contribuer plus tard à répandre'. While Somaize and Molière push

---

[25] These three sources may be supplemented by certain other texts associated with *Préciosité*, none
of which is unproblematic. See, for example, Cuénin (1973: 174–6), Mongrédien (1939), Sellier
(1999: 315) and Lathuillère (1966: 39). Moreover, since much of the influence of the *Précieuses*
relates to conversation, we are faced with the well-known difficulties of obtaining historical
oral data. The conversations in Pure and Mlle de Scudéry are not spontaneous examples of oral
usage, but are carefully crafted.

the tendencies to the point of excess particularly through the accumulation of typical features, there is nevertheless indication of some of the typical features of *Précieuses*' language and style:

L'intérêt de l'oeuvre de Somaize est donc essentiellement méthodologique. Ses laborieuses trouvailles mettent en évidence les procédés linguistiques parce qu'elles les décomposent en leurs facteurs premiers, et, tandis qu'elles les poussent jusqu'à leurs ultimes & absurdes effets, elles en révèlent parfois l'orientation: c'est la vertu des caricatures. (Cuénin 1973: lxv)

4.5.3   The language of Préciosité

In this section I shall examine the general comments made about the *Précieuses*' use of French as attested in Somaize, Pure and Molière and notably in Somaize's *Dictionnaire* (1660), considering the extent to which these satirical texts may be used as sources of information of their language. In section 4.6, I shall analyse the references to use of French by the *Précieuses* in my corpus of metalinguistic texts and examine these findings in the light of actual usage as attested in FRANTEXT. These data will in turn be compared with those found in the satirical texts.

The Abbé de Pure and Somaize follow tradition in asserting that interest in language is the primary concern of the *Précieuses*:

L'objet principal, et qui occupe tous leurs soins, c'est la recherche des bons mots et des expressions extraordinaires; c'est à iuger des beaux discours, et des beaux ouurages, pour conseruer dans l'Empire des Conuersations vn iuste temperament entre le stile rampant et le pompeux. Elles se donnent encor charitablement la peine de censurer les mauuais Vers, et de corriger les passables [. . .] (Pure 1938–9: I, 71; cf. Somaize 1661a: I, 146–7)

As in the case of women in general, their conversation is said to have a civilizing influence:

Vne de leurs conuersations est plus vtile que la lecture des meilleurs Liures, et remplit plus l'esprit que la conference des Docteurs. Outre qu'on n'apprend pas seulement la substance des choses, mais de plus on y forme de belles notions, et la maniere de les débiter. (Pure 1938–9: I, 10)

Their interest in language is further reflected in their passion for novels, poetry – especially *poésie galante* – theatre and literary criticism; Mme de Lafayette's correspondence, for instance, displays a constant concern with reading and evaluating works. In their salon conversations there is a fusion of the literary, the aesthetic and the social (cf. Pelous 1980: 307).

When we come to examine the main features of *Précieuses*' attitudes to language, there are two contradictory thrusts. On the one hand, they share many of the preoccupations of the Purists and of *remarqueurs* such as Vaugelas, favouring use of the *mot juste*, the avoidance of words considered too old, too low in register or too 'realistic', so that, in Somaize's words (1661a: I, 93), 'elles font vne Guerre continuelle contre le vieux langage, l'ancien stile, les mots barbares, les esprits pedants, & les modes passées'. In short, they aim to 'bannir de la société l'impurité des mots aussi bien que des choses' (Pure 1938–9: I, 380). The focus is firmly on contemporary rather than past norms: 'La sixiéme morale qu'elles suiuent, est de faire tousiours plus d'estat du present que du passé, ny que de l'auenir, & principalement en ce qui est du langage & des modes' (Somaize 1661a: II, 9). Very strong constraints are placed on the choice of which words and expressions are deemed acceptable. The value of *chasteté*, at times verging on prudishness, was preached in the salons – as witnessed, for example, in the refusal to allow use of the word *poitrine*, a term which it was thought might offend and which had already been considered inappropriate for usage in poetry by Malherbe. Vaugelas repeats this same criticism in his *Remarques* (1647: 60): he concedes that the reason for its demise – that it is a term shared by humans and animals as in *poitrine de veau* – is ridiculous, but nevertheless concludes that it has disappeared from good usage and therefore must be avoided. In a well-known passage, Tallemant des Réaux claims that Angélique d'Angennes 's'évanouissait quand elle entendait un méchant mot' (Magendie 1925: 131). According to Pelous (1980: 341–2) this prudishness extended even to the phonetic level, requiring the removal of what were deemed to be 'syllabes sales'. In a satirical extension of this tendency to its extreme position, Sorel was said to have decreed the suppression of the masculine gender. We may sum up this trend in *Précieuses*' thinking about language in Magendie's terms (1925: 591): 'En un mot, elles ont appliqué l'esprit de politesse et d'élégance à la conversation, et l'ont dressé comme une barrière contre l'envahissement du style par l'à peu près, la vulgarité, la grossièreté.' This desire for purity of language is not, however, without its dangers. In the satirical texts, the excess is carried to such an extreme that it is difficult to see how the language could function (for example, see below Somaize's satirical play on words where he comments on how they even intended to ban '&'). For Maître (1999: 617) it derives from a confusion of words and things.

If in this first respect the *Précieuses* mirror the concerns of the Purists, this is decidedly not the case as regards their second major preoccupation: the desire for new words and expressions, for paraphrases, 'fashionable' and striking expressions, lively metaphors, etc. (see section 4.6 below). By contrast Vaugelas maintains that nobody, not even the King, has the right to create new words.[26]

[26] In practice Vaugelas is occasionally more tolerant, and significantly accepts Mme de Rambouillet's creation, *debrutaliser* (Vaugelas 1647: 492).

It is this use of new and fashionable expressions that leads to the impression that the *Précieuses* had their own jargon. According to Sauval (1724: III, 83), a declared enemy of *Préciosité*, the origins of this interest were the lotteries held in Mlle de Scudéry's circle. The desire for innovation seems to derive from a desire to distinguish themselves from others, especially from the ordinary, to assert their group identity, and to employ a 'style orné':

Elles sont encore fortement persuadées qu'vne pensée ne vaut rien lors qu'elle est entenduë de tout le monde, & c'est vne de leur[s] maximes, de dire qu'il faut nec-essairement qu'vne Pretieuse parle autrement que le peuple, afin que ses pensées ne soient entenduës que de ceux qui ont des clartez au dessus du vulgaire, & c'est à ce dessein qu'elles font tous leurs efforts, pour détuire le vieux langage, & qu'elles en ont fait vn, non seulement qui est nouueau, mais encore qui leur est particulier. (Somaize 1661a: II, 10 (Maxime VIII))

In the repeated use of certain 'fashionable' words, such as *raisonnable, furieux, furieusement* and *la mine*, they identify themselves as belonging to a certain milieu.

This same desire to 'se distinguer du commun' (Bouhours 1962: 64) may result in excesses. Morvan de Bellegarde (1695: 60–2) comments as follows in his chapter on 'fausses précieuses':

Il y a autant de difference entre le bon langage, & le langage précieux, qu'entre les belles personnes, & les personnes fardées, qui n'ont que de faux agrémens, & qui empruntent tout leur éclat des couleurs artificielles, à quoy elles ont recours pour éblouïr le monde. Le génie françois, qui est naturel & sincere ne peut souffrir tout ce qui a l'air de l'affectation; ceux qui ont un veritable goût de nôtre langue, n'ont pas moins d'aversion pour les expressions qu'on nomme précieuses, qu'on en a dans le commerce du monde, pour certaines gens, qui n'ont rien de naturel, & qui semblent n'agir que par ressorts.

When the fashionable terms and expressions, paraphrases and metaphors (see below) are overused, particularly if they are not properly understood, affectation is likely to be the outcome. Whereas women's language in general is praised for being *naturel* and *agréable*, that of the 'fausses précieuses' is characterized as being 'artificiel' and possessing 'de faux agrémens'.

It will be clear that we are constantly obliged to return to the question of the veracity of our sources. Dulong (1991: 414) rightly maintains:

plus personne aujourd'hui n'est en droit de penser que les Précieuses aient communément parlé comme les satiriques les font parler [. . .] Mais il est vrai que les Précieuses ont fait la chasse aux mots grivois, ou [. . .] *obscènes*. Elles ont condamné toutes les expressions qui évoquaient de grossières réalités physiologiques: *crotter, lavement, être en couches*; elles ont refusé d'appliquer le verbe *aimer* à la fois aux choses matérielles et aux spirituelles: on *aime* sa maîtresse, on *goûte* le melon.

The difficulty lies in assessing the proportion of truth and of exaggeration. As we shall see, much of the effect of Somaize's satire derives from the fact that expressions are taken out of context and presented as if they were definitions. Similarly, many of the features of Molière's language in the *Précieuses ridicules* are common to other writers of the period; it is the accumulation of *Précieuse* features in high concentration which creates the comedy. Mlle de Scudéry, 'incarnation de la préciosité en littérature, n'a jamais appelé les yeux des "miroirs de l'âme", les pieds "des chers souffrants", les seins "des coussinets d'amour", un miroir "le conseiller des grâces", les sièges, "des commodités de la conversation"' (Dulong 1991: 414); however, as we will see below, she does exhibit some of the most pronounced features of *Précieuses*' style, such as the preference for abstract nouns.

4.5.4   Spelling

Another major preoccupation for the *Précieuses*, spelling reform, is associated by Cerquiglini (1996: 125) with their feminist stance, since traditional spelling is considered resolutely masculine:

Latinisante dans son principe, [l'orthographe traditionnelle] exclut les femmes, auxquelles on enseigne quelquefois la lecture, rarement l'écriture, jamais le latin. Cléricale, voire catholique, elle s'adresse aux hommes de l'écrit, professionnels qui disposent seuls du savoir et du Livre [. . .] L'orthographe française est une affaire de mâles latinistes, dont la virilité se mesure au nombre de consonnes superflues.

In his account, women play a role in bringing about spelling reform in three stages. Sixteenth-century reforms are aimed at women, as a way of making reading accessible to more social groups and in particular of widening access to scripture. At the second stage, women's usage becomes the model for a reformed spelling. Praise of women's spelling is already expressed by Meigret in the sixteenth century, and recurs in the seventeenth century, notably in the work of L'Esclache (1668: 36): 'Comme les fames prononsent ordinairement nôtre Langue, plus agréablement que les hommes, qui pâsent leur vie dans leur cabinet, à lire des livres Grecs, et Latins, il leur ét trés-facile de savoir l'Ortôgrafe Françéze; puîque nous devons écrire comme nous parlons.' L'Esclache was criticized a year later by an anonymous author for associating with the *Précieuses*.

The final stage is when women themselves take control of spelling reform, as in Somaize's 'fiction transparente'. According to Somaize (1661a: II, 57–68), M. Le Clerc (Claristène) and three women, Mme Le Roy (Roxalie), Mlle de Saint Maurice (Silenie), and Mme de la Durandière (Didamie), agreed on the desirability of creating a new spelling system, 'afin que les femmes peussent écrire aussi asseurément, & aussi correctement, que les hommes'. The rationale of the system – to base it on pronunciation – was determined, and Mme Le Roy and Mlle de Saint Maurice set about deciding which letters needed to be added or removed to make spelling easier and more accessible. In practice the decision was taken to simplify words by removing all superfluous letters. Somaize then lists some 130 proposed changes, the principal features of which may be categorized as follows:

- Removing silent consonants (*autheur* → *auteur; nopces* → *nôces; indomptable* → *indontable*), especially silent 's' (*teste* → *téte; hostel* → *hôtel; supresme* → *supréme*), and simplifying double consonants (*effarez* → *éfarez; souffert* → *soûfert*). In a number of cases this also involves the addition of an accent, especially an e acute or a circumflex, to mark the quality of the vowel.
- Simplifying the representation of other consonants to give a clearer one-to-one relationship between sound and symbol (*qualité* → *calité; triomphans* → *triomfans*).
- Simplifying the spelling of vowels which were formally pronounced as diphthongs (*raisonne* → *résonne; treize* → *tréze; paroistre* → *parétre*).
- Removing unpronounced internal vowels (*seureté* → *seûrté; extraordinaire* → *extr'ordinaire*).
- Introducing a difference between 'i' vowel and 'j' consonant (*tousiours* → *toûjours*).

Scepticism about the veracity of this account has been expressed, notably by Brunot (1905–53: IV, 97) who considers it to be too much of a coincidence that the discussion resulted in detailing broadly those spellings which were later favoured by L'Esclache (1668) and Lartigaut (1669), and adopted by R.[27] For example, while F and A adopt the traditional spellings *teste, hostel, extraordinaire, treize*, R favours *tête, hôtel, extrodinaire* and *tréze*. It may well be that the general account of the *Précieuses'* discussion of spelling is accurate but that the detail was supplied by Somaize, perhaps based on recently published works on spelling. It is certainly true that a modified spelling was used in polite society. In his samples of seventeenth-century spelling, Brunot (1905–53: IV, 150–67) separates out examples of men's and women's spelling 'pour qu'on puisse juger si la supériorité des uns était telle qu'elle justifiât leur dédain, si souvent affiché, pour l'orthographe des femmes, qui, faute d'avoir appris le latin, étaient déclarées incapables d'apprendre à écrire, "sauf par routine"'. It is evident from his examples that there are differences between the spelling of the 'dames de la Cour' and that of 'femmes de lettres': the former use minimal punctuation, and there is a tendency in some cases, although not all, towards

---

[27] Dumonceaux (in Godard de Donville and Duchêne 1985) indeed calls this 'l'orthographe [. . .] "des dames"'. An anonymous text of 1669 challenges L'Esclache's position, arguing that women should be kept in their place in society.

a more phonetically oriented spelling. For example, Mme de Montmorency uses *souete* (*souhaite*), *nesesere*, *crere* (*croire*), although Mme de Beauvilliers favours more traditional forms such as *jadiouste* (*j'ajoute*), *nepueux* (*neveux*). In the case of the female authors, there is often no perceptible difference from many male authors of the period (see, for example, Mme Dacier's usage), although the absence of punctuation in Mme de Lafayette's manuscript is particularly striking. The Marquise de Rambouillet uses *respecq, auecq, faict*; similarly Mme de la Sablière's spellings are generally conservative (*controollemens, devotte, guerejáy*).

4.6   Specific features of women's language

4.6.1   Methodology

In order to test whether the general qualities of women's language constantly referred to in the literature of the period could be associated with specific linguistic features, I examined my corpus of metalinguistic texts for all occasions when a usage was identified as being associated either with women or with the *Précieuses* (see Table 4.1 for the number of occurrences of references to female usage in each case).[28] As is clear from the table, there is considerable variation in the amount of data provided on women's usage by the different types of metalinguistic text. In the case of dictionaries, there is no special mention of features of women's language in N, C or O, but R, F and A all devote some space in their definitions to this question. R is the principal lexicographical source on women's usage.[29] There is evidence of Richelet himself consulting women about correct usage (e.g. *gorgerette*), but equally he is not afraid to criticize their language. On a number of occasions – for example in the case of flower names – he contrasts the name for something used by women with its technical term (see section 4.6.4). In F, as in A, some entries simply define words used by women for women's things. A number of their entries, however, couple mention of gender differences with a comment on SES (e.g. *les femmes de basse condition, de qualité, du peuple* (F)); notable here are those definitions which refer to expressions and insults used by lower-class women.

---

[28] Note that these figures include comments of a general nature, about women for example, on their civilizing role in polite society, or their status as authorities on good usage. Many of these have been cited in earlier sections. There are also comments on individual women. For instance, both Alemand (1688: 223) and Renaud (1697: 522) praise Mme Deshoulières's verse. In Buffet's 'Traitté sur le Eloges des Illustres Sçavantes, Anciennes & Modernes' (1668) some women are praised for their linguistic abilities, others for their learning. It is interesting to note that, even in a work with a feminist viewpoint, Buffet admires the masculine qualities of Mlle Descartes's writing: 'Elle écrit fort bien en prose, & en vers, mais d'une façon qui n'a rien de feminin. Son style est élegant & pompeux, & remply de doctrine' (Buffet 1668: 279).

[29] R also cites examples from Molière's *Précieuses ridicules* on forty-seven occasions.

Table 4.1 *References to female usage in the metalinguistic texts*

References to usage of:	*femmes/dames*	*Précieux/euse(s)*
(a) *Remarqueurs*		
Vaugelas (1647)	16	0
Dupleix (1651)	13	0
Buffet (1668)	7	1
Bouhours (1674, 1675, 1693)	10	3
Ménage (1675, 1676)	10	4
Bérain (1675)	0	0
Alemand (1688)	10	1
Andry de Boisregard (1689, 1693)	1	7
Tallemant (1698)	0	1
Subtotal	*67*	*17*
(b) Dictionaries		
N (1606)	0	0
C (1611)	0	0
O (1640)	0	0
R (1680)	24	3
F (1690)	11	1
A (1694)	6	0
Subtotal	*41*	*4*
(c) Grammars		
Maupas (1618)	0	0
Oudin (1632)	0	0
Irson (1662)	1	1
Subtotal	*1*	*1*
(d) Commentaires on Vaugelas: Le Vayer, Corneille, Patru, Académie Française (from Streicher 1936)	19	0
Subtotal	*19*	*0*
Total	**128**	**22**

As regards the *remarqueurs*, Vaugelas (1647) offers the largest number of observations that discuss differences between the usage of men and women. Indeed many of the subsequent comments by *remarqueurs* are made in response to an earlier observation by Vaugelas, notably in the case of Dupleix who strongly disagrees with Vaugelas's generally positive stance towards women's usage (see section 4.4.2). In the various commentaries on Vaugelas's text (Streicher 1936), the Academy approves of Vaugelas's methodology, but on two occasions considers the usage of women to be faulty, and the same is true of seven of the twelve comments by Corneille on women's language. Patru, on the other hand, tends to adopt a neutral position.

As for the other *remarqueurs*, Buffet makes very few specific references to the usage of women, but the figures here are misleading since, as we have seen, her work is addressed to women and focuses on their usage. Not surprisingly, she adopts a generally positive stance towards their language. Ménage shows no particular bias in his approach: he supports women's usage on a number of occasions (e.g. *urselines*, *velous*, *busque*), but is also willing to criticize their faults (e.g. *je suis allée à la messe*, see below, section 4.6.6 (b)), and notes that there are many words they do not understand. He criticizes Bouhours for being a *Précieux*, using the term as an insult, and there is a substantial chapter in his second volume of observations (1676: 204–17) in which he discusses those observations where Bouhours comments on women's usage. Bouhours tends to follow Vaugelas; however, in the *Suite* (1693: *Avertissement*) he becomes critical of the 'jargon des Precieuses', in all likelihood stung by Ménage's criticism. Of the three remaining *remarqueurs*, Alemand favours consulting women and is generally tolerant of their usage; Andry de Boisregard has relatively little to say on the question, although he too is critical of the *Précieuses*' use of affected fashionable terms and expressions (1689: Preface); and Tallemant makes very little comment at all on variation.

By contrast with the collections of observations, formal grammars of French make very little reference to differences of usage according to gender, and there is only one comment on the *Précieuses*' modernized spelling in Irson (1662: 139). Of our secondary texts (Appendix, II), Callières (1693) is of the greatest interest, since his second conversation contains a long passage on various usages of women at court. Given the debate over the dating of *Préciosité*, it is perhaps significant that most of the references to the usage of the *Précieuses* occur in the 1670s–1690s; however, the vast majority of these comments are critical of their usage, and F is unusual in commenting on it in neutral terms.

Once I had identified the features associated with women in the metalinguistic texts, I tested the validity of their claims by examining the usage of these features in the 418 texts from the period 1600–99 available in F R A N T E X T at the time of the investigation. Of the 418 seventeenth-century texts in F R A N T E X T, eleven (2.6%) are by women, as listed in Table 4.2. In this way I hoped to be able better to consider whether Grande's assessment of seventeenth-century women's literary writing (1999a: 18) is borne out in their use of language. She argues that at this period '"l'écriture feminine" ne se distingue pas par nature de l'écriture masculine. Certes il y a certains thèmes privilégiés et une façon d'insister sur ces thèmes, mais c'est là question de degré et non de nature.'

As is clear from the F R A N T E X T corpus, women writers seem to favour certain genres. As Grande (1999a) notes, novels are particularly well represented (she identifies thirty-one novels by nine different women which were published between 1654 and 1678, representing 15% of the novels published in that period). Other favoured genres include *poésie mondaine*, *mémoires* and, above all, letters. For this reason I decided to supplement the F R A N T E X T corpus with two additional sets of letters, particularly with a view to gaining access

Table 4.2 *Texts by women in the* FRANTEXT *corpus (1600–1699)*

Marie de Gournay, *Préface sur les Essais de Michel, seigneur de Montaigne* (1635)	[prose, traité ou essai]
Madeleine de Scudéry, *Les Jeux servant de préface* (1667)	[prose, roman]
Madeleine de Scudéry, *Mathilde* (1667)	[prose, roman]
Mme de Sévigné, *Correspondance I: 1646–75* (1675)	[prose, correspondance]
Mme de Villedieu, *Les Désordres de l'amour* (1675)	[prose, roman]
Mme de Lafayette, *La Princesse de Clèves* (1678)	[prose, roman]
Mme de Sévigné, *Correspondance II: 1675–80* (1680)	[prose, correspondance]
Mme de Lafayette, *Vie de la Princesse d'Angleterre* (1693)	[prose, roman]
Mme Deshoulières, *Épîtres* (1694)	[vers, poésie]
Mme Deshoulières, *Idylles* (1694)	[vers, poésie]
Mme de Sévigné, *Correspondance III: 1680–96* (1696)	[prose, correspondance]

Table 4.3 *Women's letters*

(a) Letters of Mme de La Fayette (Beaunier 1942). Our corpus comprises a selection of sixty-eight letters (thirty-five to Ménage, ten to Huet, nine to Mme de Sablé, fourteen to Mme de Sévigné) [the punctuation is modernized, the spelling made uniform, and grammatical 'errors' have been corrected]

(b) Letters of Mme de Scudéry, wife of Georges and sister-in-law of Madeleine de Scudéry (1670–91), from *Lettres de Mesdames de Scudéry, de Salvan de Saliez, et de Mademoiselle Descartes* (Collin 1806) [no details are given of the degree of editorial intervention, although it appears that the spelling has been modernized]

to more informal usage (see Table 4.3). A number of scholars have recently considered the extent to which it is appropriate to consider letter-writing as 'un genre féminin' (Planté 1998). Two main styles of letter-writing may be observed in the seventeenth century: learned ones, 'le genre épistolaire', essentially a masculine genre, and 'mondain' ones, many of which were by women, although they were not necessarily published (cf. Altman 1995). Duchêne (1998: 27) observes that only about 2% of the letters listed in Cioranescu are by women; moreover, it was Balzac, Voiture and Bussy-Rabutin who were held up as model letter-writers in the period 1630–1750. Nevertheless, there is the much-quoted praise of women as letter-writers by La Bruyère in *Les Caractères* (1689) (Planté 1998: 11):

Je ne sais si l'on pourra mettre dans des lettres plus d'esprit, plus de tour, plus d'agrément et plus de style que l'on en voit dans celles de Balzac et de Voiture; elles sont vides de sentiments qui n'ont régné que depuis leur temps, et qui doivent aux femmes leur naissance. Ce sexe va plus loin que le nôtre dans ce genre d'écrire. Elles trouvent sous leur plume des tours et des expressions qui souvent en nous ne sont l'effet que d'un long travail et d'une pénible recherche; elles sont heureuses dans le choix des termes qu'elles placent si juste, que tous connus qu'ils sont, ils ont le charme de la nouveauté, et semblent être faits seulement pour l'usage où elles le mettent; il n'appartient qu'à elles de faire lire dans un seul mot tout un sentiment, et de rendre délicatement une pensée qui est délicate; elles ont un enchaînement de discours inimitable qui se suit naturellement, et qui n'est lié que par le sens. Si les femmes étaient toujours correctes, j'oserois dire que les lettres de quelques-unes d'entr'elles seraient peut-être ce que nous avons dans notre langue de mieux écrit.

Timmermans (1993: 195) also records appreciation of the letters of Mme des Loges, Julie d'Angennes, Mme de Rambouillet and Mme de Sablé, all of whom were famous salon women. The qualites valued include their natural disposition, their lack of 'art', and their *délicatesse, pureté* and *politesse de langage*.

Care needs to be taken in interpreting these letters as examples of informal or spontaneous usage; in particular the question of authenticity, whether these are real letters or simply composed for publication or as models, is delicate. Duchêne (1998: 28–9) points to the extreme example of Du Boscq's *Nouveau Recueil des lettres des Dames de ce temps, Avec leurs réponses* (1635) which is a manual of model letters he himself composed. Duchêne (1998: 27) consequently speaks of 'une pratique de la lettre', that is, the reworking of letters for publication. Examples are Mme de Brégny's *Lettres et poésies* (1666) and Mme de Villedieu's *Recueil de quelques lettres ou relation galante* (1668), which in his view are a mixture of spontaneity and reworking, influenced by literary tradition (Duchêne 1998: 42). According to Duchêne (1998: 46), the ideal was reached by Mme de Sévigné, considered a model author of 'lettres familières'. Another famous example is the letters in Madeleine de Scudéry's *Clélie* (Maître 1998).

4.6.2   Case studies

In this chapter I shall focus on three principal areas: vocabulary, gender and agreement. I shall then review briefly the other areas of language discussed in the metalinguistic texts (section 4.6.6) before looking at the discussion of the *Précieuses*' use of French (section 4.6.7). Except in those cases where the orthography is under examination or is vital to the discussion, the form will be given as it is attested in the source text, on the understanding that this form stands for all the possible orthographic variants found in the corpora.

4.6.3   Vocabulary

Approximately two-fifths of all the comments made about women's language are concerned with lexical issues, suggesting that this aspect of women's language was particularly salient for the *remarqueurs* and lexicographers.[30]

---

[30] In Vaugelas's *Remarques* the largest proportion of observations, amounting to approximately one-third of the total, is devoted to syntactic questions (Ayres-Bennett 1987: 66, 90).

Comments on three main types of lexical questions occur in the metalinguistic texts.

(a)   Terms used exclusively or differently by women

Thirty-seven cases of words or expressions used exclusively or differently by women are found in the corpus of metalinguistic texts.[31] Just under half of the terms recorded in the metalinguistic texts as forms or usages favoured by women do not occur at all in the FRANTEXT corpus.[32] In some cases this absence may be explained by the fact that the context of appropriate usage specified is unlikely to feature in the type of texts found in FRANTEXT. For example, usage may be attributed to lower-class or spoken language (*gorgette* (R, *Remarques sur le dictionnaire*), *lapine* (R)), or to usage in a restricted context, whether specialized (*leau* said to be used only by dairywomen (R), *inventaire* used in the feminine by basket makers and women street sellers (R)), or humorous (*cardinaux* under *ordinaires* (R)). Alternatively, the usage may be described as not yet established (*géanne* rather than *géante* (R)). In three other cases (*faisanne* (R), *méridienne* (R), *bransles de la haye* (F)) no conclusion can be drawn since neither this term nor its supposed alternative(s) occurs; this compares with just one case where the form said to be favoured by women – *bouquet de plumes* (R) – is not attested, whereas there are nineteen examples of its alternative, *panache*, in the sense of 'plume'. There are seven other examples for which there are no attestations either of the word or expression itself, or of the term in the particular sense specified: *Mes coeffes* (F), *Jansenistes* (F), *Prenez/portez ma robe* (A), *Garniture de teste* (A), *Mouchoir à moucher* (Ménage 1675: 278–9, also not attested in R, F or A), *L'entretien provincial* (Buffet 1668: 43), *Pavie* (feminine vs *pavi*, R).

In a second group of examples, the word is well attested in FRANTEXT. This is unsurprising in the case of common words such as *juppe* (F) or *manteau* (A). In some cases virtually all the examples are by male authors. For example, *carogne*, 'terme injurieux, qui se dit entre les femmes de basse condition, pour se reprocher leur mauvaise vie, leurs ordures, leur puanteur' (F), occurs twenty-one times in FRANTEXT, but always spoken by male characters in plays (eighteen from Molière). *Barbon*, 'un mot dont les jeunes gens & les femmes se servent pour railler les vieillards, soit qu'ils portent la barbe longue, ou non' (A), features forty-eight times in FRANTEXT, of which only one example is by a

---

[31] Three of these are not discussed here since the volume of examples in FRANTEXT makes it impossible to analyse them systematically: *dérober* (in the specialized usage by women and ordinary people who sell peas and beans, R; there are 1211 occurrences of the verb in the seventeenth century in FRANTEXT); *quart* (for 'navet' as used by women who sell from baskets in the Parisian streets, R; 594 occurrences); *une fois* (1660 occurrences). A further example is attested in Callières (1693: 149): the use of *Païs estranges* for *Païs étrangers* by women at court.

[32] References to FRANTEXT throughout this chapter refer, of course, to the texts dated 1600–99.

female writer (Mme de Sévigné). Similarly, *toutou*, 'terme populaire & enfantin. C'est un nom que les femmes & les Nourrices donnent à de petits chiens' (F), is attested ten times in FRANTEXT, but only once in a female author (Mme Deshoulières). In the case of *Vertu de ma vie* (R), the examples are few, but again they are all spoken by male characters in Molière plays.

The next two categories are the most interesting from our point of view. First, there are seven cases where women authors seem to feature prominently (c. 18.9%):

(i) *Notre quartier*: According to Bouhours (1675: 186–7) the 'Bourgeoises, & toutes les personnes de basse condition' use *nostre quartier*, whereas the 'Dames de qualité' use *mon quartier*. Ménage argues (1676: 214) that both expressions are used without restriction. However, in FRANTEXT the seven examples of *notre quartier* are all found in the correspondence of Mme de Sévigné. Of the ten examples of *mon quartier*, one is by Mme de Sévigné,[33] and there is an additional example of *mon quartier* in Mme de Scudéry's letters (26 June 1671).

(ii) *Ma petite*: 'A la verité les femmes se traittent quelquefois entre elles, de *ma petite*, quelques grandes qu'elles soient; mais c'est un jargon d'amitié, qui ne merite pas d'estre compté entre les expressions de la langue, & qui n'entre point dans les discours' (Bouhours 1675: 231).[34] In the context where *petite* is used substantively as 'ma petite', there are thirty-one examples in FRANTEXT, thirty of which are by Mme de Sévigné.

(iii) *Demander excuse*: 'C'est grand pitié que cette sotte phrase ait tant de cours dans le petit peuple, & qu'elle se soit communiqué par contagion à quelques femmes du monde, qui d'ailleurs ont de la politesse & du sens. Les honnestes gens de la Cour, & toutes les personnes sçavantes en la Langue ne la peuvent du tout souffrir' (Bouhours 1675: 42). Three of the eight examples in the FRANTEXT corpus are by Mme de Sévigné (e.g. 'Ma chère enfant, je vous demande excuse à la mode du pays'). Two of the others are from Bouhours's *Entretiens*.

(iv) *Plaisant mignon, joli mignon*: 'on ne donne ce nom qu'aux enfans, quand on les caresse, ou si on le donne à d'autre, c'est en soûriant, & un peu en colere, *vous estes un joli mignon*. Les femmes disent cela plûtost que les hommes; & j'ay veû dans une Lettre qu'une dame de grand mérite écrivoit à un homme de qualité son parent & son ami: *Je vous trouve un plaisant mignon, de ne m'avoir pas écrit depuis deux mois*' (Bouhours 1675: 306). In FRANTEXT this example by Mme de Sévigné is cited

---

[33] It is perhaps significant that the other nine are all from Bussy-Rabutin's *Mémoires*, since he enjoyed a prolific correspondence with his cousin Mme de Sévigné. He also co-authored the *Carte de la Braquerie* (1654), a parody of the *Carte de Tendre* and of Preciosity.

[34] Ménage (1676: 214) considers the expression to be elliptical with a word like 'mignonne' understood.

along with Bussy-Rabutin's reply in which he quotes this expression back to her. Of the two examples of *joli mignon*, one comes from a letter by Bussy-Rabutin.

(v) *Il faut voir, il faut savoir*: 'Cela a été quelque tems dans la bouche de tout le monde, surtout dans celle des femmes. Elles ne disoient rien sans, *il faut voir, il faut sçavoir*; & toutes les conversations retentissoient de ces mots' (Bouhours 1693: 30). Of the 120 examples of *il faut voir* in the FRANTEXT corpus, there are twenty-three (c.19%) by women (one by Marie de Gournay, twenty-two by Madame de Sévigné). Of the 157 examples of *il faut s(ç)avoir* one is by Mme de Villedieu, and six are by Mme de Sévigné (4.5%). Note, in addition, that two others are cited from *Les Précieueses ridicules* and fourteen are from Bussy-Rabutin's *Mémoires*.

(vi) *Il est vray*: 'se disoit auparavant de la même sorte [. . .] Ce sont de ces locutions passageres qui ne durent point & qui passent commes les modes: il faut les souffrir quand elles dominent; mais il faut bien se donner de garde d'y prendre plaisir' (Bouhours 1693: 31). Of the 1503 examples of *il est vrai que* in FRANTEXT 208 are by Mme de Sévigné and five by Mlle de Scudéry, making a total of 14% by women. Callières (1693: 151) also points to the overuse of this expression at the beginning of accounts by most women at court. It is perhaps significant that in the satirical letter by Mme de Lafayette 'composée de phrases où il n'y a guère de sens, que bien des gens de la cour mettent dans leurs discours', and in which *il est vray que* occurs at the beginning of six sentences, the other expressions used include *furieusement aimable* and *le dernier desplaisir* (see the discussion of *Précieuses*' language below).

(vii) *Mijaurée*: 'Terme populaire & injurieux, que les femmes disent à Paris, quand elles se querellent. Vous estes une belle, une plaisante *mijaurée*, pour dire une laide, une sotte' (F). There are three examples of this in FRANTEXT, two of which are by Mme de Sévigné (note that she is reporting speech: 'ah! Dit la Bonnelle, voilà une mijaurée qui a eu pour plus de cent mille écus de nos hardes'). The other is spoken by Covielle in Molière's *Le Bourgeois gentilhomme*.

Second, there are two examples from texts where the form under discussion is spoken by a female character:

(viii) *Jour de Dieu*: 'est aussi un serment que font les femmes du peuple' (F); all four examples in FRANTEXT are spoken by female characters in Molière plays (Mme de Sotenville in *Georges Dandin* and Mme Pernelle in *Le Tartuffe*).

(ix) *Mercy de ma vie*: '*Merce* Dieu, *Merci* de ma vie, est une maniere de jurer dont se servent les femmes de la lie du peuple' (F; also in A). There are no examples of *Merce Dieu* or *Merci Dieu*, but *Merci de ma vie* is attested three times in FRANTEXT, and is each time attributed to a female speaker. It is also attested in the *Caquets de l'accouchée* (Fournier 1855) and by a fish-wife in the Mazarinade *Les Contens et mescontens sur le suiet du temps* (1649; see Chapter 3).

There are two remaining examples which are worthy of comment. In the first of these, the source of the examples is perhaps significant:

(x) *Jolies choses*: 'Ce mot [joli] est plus usité que jamais: il se met à tout, & les femmes l'ont presque toûjours à la bouche; elles ne trouvent rien à leur gré, qui ne soit pour elles ou *enchanté*, ou *ioli*: Nous disons particuliérement *jolies choses*' (Bouhours 1675: 144–5). Of the thirty-six occurrences of *jolies choses* in FRANTEXT, ten derive from Pure's *La Prétieuse*, perhaps suggesting usage amongst the *Précieuses* (see below).

Finally there is the special case of *Vostre servante, vostre tres-humble servante*:

(xi) *Vostre servante, vostre tres-humble servante*: 'Parmi les femmes, *Vostre servante, vostre tres-humble servante*, Sont des termes de compliment dont elles se servent dans le discours, & dans la souscription des lettres. *Vostre trés-humble & trés-obeïssante servante*' (A); there are twenty-three examples of *vo(s)tre servante* and one example of *vostre tres-humble servante* in FRANTEXT, although none of these is exactly in the usage mentioned. However, examples of this are common in the corpus of letters: there are four occurrences in those of Mme de Scudéry and six in Mme de Lafayette's letters, e.g. 'je suis tout à fait vostre servante très humble' (3 September [1655]).

If we take together these last three categories, they account for eleven (c. 29.7%) of our examples, suggesting that the comments of the grammarians and lexicographers do reflect usage in the texts to some extent. In a number of cases the types of texts found in FRANTEXT preclude the possibility of finding examples of the usages, notably spoken and lower-register usages, identified in the metalinguistic texts. The high incidence of examples from Mme de Sévigné's letters in those cases where women writers feature strongly is striking and raises a number of questions. Are Mme de Sévigné's letters representative of women's usage in general? Were her letters considered as typical of women's usage by writers of observations and dictionaries, and therefore used as their primary source for making such a judgment? Note that all of these comments are by Bouhours and Furetière, and there is clear evidence that Bouhours knew Mme de Sévigné's letters (cf. Ménage 1676: 204–19).

In no case is a specific link made between the general characteristics of women's language and the eleven examples discussed above. Various allusions do, nevertheless, seem to be significant. First, there are indications of women being linked with conversation and using certain discourse markers (*il faut voir, il faut savoir, il est vray*). Second, there are words and expressions which seem to suggest female affection, friendship and solidarity (*plaisant mignon, joli mignon, notre quartier, ma petite*) and a link with *Préciosité* (*jolies choses*). Third, there are expressions associated with politeness (*vostre* (*tres-humble*) *servante*). A different group is comprised of words, and especially insults, associated with lower-class women.

(b)   New words and expressions

In the majority of these cases (six out of seven), the role of women as the arbiters of new words is invoked. Generally, the newness of the words is suggested by the chronology of the examples which occur in FRANTEXT, but only in the case of *pour que* and perhaps *parapluie* is there any indication that women are associated with usage of the word or expression.

In the case of *sagacité* Bouhours (1675: 136–7) regrets that women do not understand and therefore do not accept the neologism, unless they know Latin. Ménage (1676: 210) refutes this: 'Sa Préciosité peut avoir dit ce mot à quelque Bourgeoise, & à quelque Soubrette, qui ne l'ont pas entendu: mais je lui soutiens que toutes les femmes du grand monde l'entendent fort bien'; he adds that it has been in use at least since the time of Nicot. However, R confirms that it is especially used by those who know Latin. There are twenty-two examples in FRANTEXT dating from 1631 onwards; it is perhaps significant that more than two-thirds of these occur in *traités* or *essais* of a political or philosophical character.

In a number of other cases, the *remarqueur* or lexicographer predicts that the term will become established on the grounds that it is already being used, especially in speech, by certain women. Examples of this are *desagrément* (R;[35] the four examples in FRANTEXT date from 1671 onwards, but none is by a woman), *parapluie* (R; only one example in FRANTEXT, perhaps confirming its primarily oral nature, from Mme de Sévigné's letters and she takes care to gloss the term ('ces deux petits parasols ou parapluies')), and *respect*, 'sorte de petit tabouret', (R).[36] In the case of *Bassa*, a specific link is made with *douceur* and *politesse* of pronunciation: '*Bassa* s'est habillé à la Françoise, ce qui l'a fait recevoir parmy les Dames & parmy ceux qui en les imitant preferent la prononciation douce & polie qui se trouve dans *Bassa* [rather than *bacha*]' (Alemand 1688: 231). There are eight examples of this in FRANTEXT, all by men, dating from 1637 onwards (and only two of *bacha*). This confirms R's view that *bassa* is the correct form. In the case of *securité*, there is considerable debate among the *remarqueurs* about its acceptability, but they all – with the sole exception of Dupleix – examine whether the form is

---

[35] Bouhours (1675: 47) recommends that its general use should be postponed until it is more generally established, since some consider it 'un peu prétieuse'.

[36] I have not traced the use of *respect* in this sense in FRANTEXT, since it occurs 2917 times.

employed by women or not. Vaugelas (1647: 43–4) predicts it will become common usage and that he has heard it used 'mesme à des femmes de la Cour'. Bouhours (1675: 521) notes that the word is used by several good authors, but argues that it is hardly used by women since they do not understand it. Ménage (1676: 211) agrees and then lists a number of other words not understood by women, including *épopée, dramatique, épisode* and 'les termes des Sciences, des Arts, du Palais, de la Guerre, de la Marine, de la Monnoie, de la Pesche, de la Chasse, de la Fauconnerie'. Indeed he suggests that there are more French words not understood by women than those that are. Of the eleven examples in FRANTEXT, one dates from 1615, but all the rest are later (1671 on); none is by a woman.

Finally, the usage of *pour que* is associated with conversation, particularly that of women (Bouhours 1675: 518). A agrees that its usage is almost entirely spoken. However, there are 116 examples of it in FRANTEXT dating from 1610 onwards; fifteen are from Mme de Sévigné's correspondence.

(c)   Acceptability of words/expressions
In six other cases in the metalinguistic texts, women are cited as arbiters of good lexical usage,[37] but there is, on the whole, little evidence to suggest that their opinion had a long-term effect on usage. Vaugelas notes a female aversion for the terms *poitrine* and *face*. Dupleix (1651: 452), however, makes light of it, attributing the dislike of *poitrine* to 'quelque femme grosse, qui avoit en horreur la poitrine de veau'. Both R and A record *poitrine* without comment, while F asserts that the reason cited for its avoidance is 'impertinent'. There is no evidence to suggest non-use of these words in the FRANTEXT corpus (*poitrine* 342 occurrences, (*la*) *face* 367 occurrences). Likewise Vaugelas (1647: 369–70) asserts that *expedition* in the sense of 'vn voyage de guerre' is best avoided in works intended for the court and for women since it is not understood:

j'ay bien pris garde, que des Dames d'excellent esprit lisant vn liure, où ce mot estoit employé au sens dont nous parlons, s'estoient arrestées tout court au milieu d'vn des plus beaux endroits du livre, perdant ou du moins interrompant par l'obscurité d'vn seul mot le plaisir qu'elles prenoient en cette lecture.

Somewhat paradoxically, he advises the addition of the adjective *militaire* to clarify the sense, although he concedes that women do not understand this word either. Dupleix (1651: 275) criticizes Vaugelas for taking heed of women and warns that if such a path were to be followed, two-thirds of French words would disappear since they derive from Latin. *Expedition* is cited in the three

---

[37] Four of them – *Poitrine, face*; *Vomir des injures*; *Mettre* (in the expression *ne mettez gueres*, 'do not be/stay long'); *Expedition* – are first discussed in Vaugelas (1647); the other two – *Queuë*; *Ramasser* – are in R.

monolingual dictionaries in the military sense without comment, and it is well attested in FRANTEXT in this sense with and without the modifier *militaire* (29/70), including by Sorel in *Le Berger extravagant* (1627). It is also used by Mme de Scudéry in a letter dated 15 April 1678.

In the case of *ramasser*, R reports that, contrary to the opinion expressed by the author of the *Observations sur la langue Françoise*, all the women he consulted at court and in the town recommended *ramassez mes gans* and not *amassez mes gans*. As for *queue*, the conflicting opinions of different groups of women are cited and adjudicated upon by R: 'Ce mot se dit en parlant d'habit long, & veut dire la partie de derriere qui traine. Quelques Dames font scrupule de dire ce mot en ce sens, mais d'autres trouvent ce scrupule mal fondé & on pense qu'elles ont raison.'

Only in the case of *Vomir des injures* does there appear to be a correlation between the comments in the metalinguistic texts and usage in FRANTEXT, but even this is only on a relatively short-term basis. Vaugelas (1647: 127–8) notes that while the expression is considered elegant by writers, it is not well received at court, especially by women; since such expressions are 'incompatibles auec la delicatesse & la propreté de leur sexe', they should be avoided when speaking to women so as not to cause displeasure. This comment, in which a clear link is made with women's desire for *politesse* and *agrément* in their use of language, is repeated in R. The majority of commentators, however, do not seem to support Vaugelas's position. Dupleix's (1651) reaction reflects his general view that only effeminate men react in this way, Corneille considers the phrase too expressive for women to want to ban it, and the Academy notes that the expression has become established, citing it in its dictionary without comment (Streicher 1936: 258). Perhaps the most telling observation is by Marguerite Buffet (1668: 78–9) who claims: 'ces mots sont bien receues, bien qu'ils ne semblent pas fort agreables'. There are five examples in FRANTEXT, but, significantly, they all date from the first half of the seventeenth century; it is not until the second half of the eighteenth century that the expression appears to regain currency.

4.6.4   Gender

A number of the *remarqueurs* make general comments about gender. Vaugelas (1647: 299, 390) asserts that French has a preference for the feminine gender, although somewhat paradoxically he also claims that the masculine gender is 'more noble' (1647: 381). Buffet (1668: 192–3) observes how in mixed company 'le masculin a toûjours l'avantage', even if more women than men are present. Alemand (1688: 202) repeats Vaugelas's belief that the French language prefers the feminine gender and suggests the following reason for this:

C'est peut-être parce qu'il est plus doux & plus agreable que le masculin, peut-être aussi que les Dames parlant ordinairement fort bien, & affectant comme elles font, le feminin; l'usage dont elles font la partie la plus considerable, se détermine fort souvent à ce genre, outre que la complaisance entraîne toûjours de leur côté la plus grande partie des hommes, aprés cela doit-on être surpris si nôtre langue a une fois autant de mots feminins que de masculins, c'est une remarque que j'ay faite & que je donne pour veritable. (Alemand 1688: 6)

Here again we see the key terms, *doux* and *agreable*, associated with women's language. Attitudes towards gender may also perhaps be seen as reflecting differing attitudes towards women, since linguistic gender is said to reflect difference of sex in the world (see, for example, the comments of the Port-Royal grammar on the origins of grammatical gender: Arnauld and Lancelot 1660: 39).

Note also that there is the occasional discussion of what the correct feminine form for a particular noun is. For example, Alemand (1688: 43) discusses *accusatrice*, used by Racine in *Phèdre*, arguing that it is gradually becoming established (there are three other instances of it in FRANTEXT, the earliest being from Balzac's *Dissertations critiques* of 1654). On the other hand, Bouhours (1693: 112–13) warns against the use of *courtisanne, coureuse, abandonée*, which, unlike their masculine counterparts, should be avoided.[38]

When we come to consider specific questions of the choice of gender for nouns, Alemand's assertion that women prefer the feminine gender seems to be echoed in the metalinguistic comments on individual words. For convenience I have tabulated my findings (Table 4.4).[39] In more than half of the cases discussed in the table, the 'correct' form recommended by the *remarqueurs* and used by male authors is the masculine, but women are said systematically to prefer the feminine. A contrast is at times made between the gender favoured in technical or specialist usage (*iris, rénoncule, pivoine*) and that chosen by women, who represent the non-specialist. However, except in the case of *estude* and perhaps *couple*, there is little evidence that in practice women chose the feminine gender for these words in written texts. In some cases the observations record a change of usage (e.g. *poison*) or what appears to be a passing fashion (e.g. *ouvrage*). Of the eleven words discussed, four today are feminine, and a fifth (*couple*) can be used in the masculine or feminine according to its meaning.

[38] For recent French government recommendations on the feminization of professional titles, see http://www.culture.gouv.fr/culture/dglf/cogeter/feminisation/accueil-feminisation.html, and Baudino 2001. The question has also received attention in other francophone areas, including Switzerland, Belgium and Quebec; see, for example, Bouchard *et al.* (1999).

[39] Note that, in order to make the statistics manageable, only the singular forms of the words have been analysed. In the case of *amour* the very large number of occurrences (20,357 in the singular alone) made it impractial to treat the word systematically. According to Vaugelas (1647: 390) *amour* may be used in either gender when it refers to 'human love'; many of the best writers make it masculine, but the majority, and especially women, make it feminine (cf. Alemand 1688: 124–5).

Table 4.4 *Comments on gender*

Word	Metalinguistic comment	Masculine occurrences in FRANTEXT (counting only those occurrences where the gender is clear from the context)	Feminine occurrences in FRANTEXT (counting only those occurrences where the gender is clear from the context)	Comment on the choice of gender in the examples
Epithete	Corneille records Chapelain's view (Streicher 1936: 46) that it is masculine since it is not understood by women, who make all Greek and Latin words they use feminine (e.g. *épigramme*	14	6	There is variation in the gender of the word throughout the century, and indeed within the work of one author (Naudé 1669); the three examples of the word being used in Mme de Sévigné's correspondence are all masculine
Ouvrage	Vaugelas states the word is masculine in all senses, but then adds 'Mais les femmes parlant de leur ouurage, le font tousjours feminin [. . .] Il semble qu'il leur doit estre permis de nommer comme elles veulent ce qui n'est que de leur vsage; je ne crois pas pourtant, qu'il nous fust permis de l'escrire ainsi' (1647: 445). Dupleix (1651: 384) criticizes Vaugelas for taking account of women's usage, and significantly Buffet (1668: 193) says the word is always masculine. Corneille maintains that most women make it feminine along with other words such as *orage* and *gages* (cf. Alemand 1688: 5–8),	un ouvrage 227; cet/cest ouvrage 260 (includes one example by Mme de Sévigné)	une ouvrage 1; cette ouvrage 0	It seems that the feminine gender was not employed in writing to any significant degree in the seventeenth century. The one example of the feminine comes from N. de Peiresc's *Lettres* (1637)

(cont.)

although not those who speak well, and the Academy also considers the feminine a fault (Streicher 1936: 754)

Word		Masculine	Feminine	Comment
Poison	Corneille (Streicher 1936: 891) asserts that most women still say *amer comme de la poison*, but that it is now always used in the masculine	327 examples (le poison 198; un poison 86; ce poison 43)	11 examples (la poison 9; une poison 2; cette poison 0)	Date rather than sex seems to be the significant factor here since all the examples in the feminine are from 1627 or earlier; they are all by men
Caramel	'Quelques Dames font le mot de *caramel* féminin, mais les gens du monde qui parlent bien & que j'ai consultez le croient masculin' (R)	0	0	No examples in FRANTEXT
Iris	'Ce mot signifiant une sorte de fleur est fait *masculin* par les Fleuristes [. . .] neanmoins les gens habiles dans la langue, & les Dames qui parlent bien font le mot d'*iris féminin*, & c'est le plus seur' (R)	Referring to the flower, 'iris' 0	Referring to the flower, 'iris' 0	The majority of the 232 examples refer to the goddess Iris. A assigns it feminine gender as does F who nevertheless adds that philosophers use it in the masculine with the meaning 'rainbow'
Rénoncule	'*Morin* [. . .] fait *rénoncule*, masculin, mais les autres fleuristes [. . .] croient *rénoncule*, féminin. Les Dames de qualité à qui j'ai demandé ce qu'elles en pensoient n'ont point hésité à faire *rénoncule* féminin, & ainsi c'est une faute que de le faire de l'autre genre' (R)	0	0	No examples in FRANTEXT

Table 4.4 (*cont.*)

Word	Metalinguistic comment	Masculine occurrences in FRANTEXT (counting only those occurrences where the gender is clear from the context)	Feminine occurrences in FRANTEXT (counting only those occurrences where the gender is clear from the context)	Comment on the choice of gender in the examples
Pivoine	In the body of the dictionary R claims that it is feminine, following the opinion of bird-sellers. In the 'remarques sur le dictionnaire' he retracts this, noting that there is variation as to its gender: 'les hommes savans dans la langue [. . .] sont indifférens pour l'un ou pour l'autre genre, mais quelques Dames qui se piquent de bien parler disent toutes la pivoine est jolie, une pivoine mâle, & une pivoine femelle'	0	0	No examples in FRANTEXT
Aage	Alemand (1688: 5–8) claims 'la pluspart des femmes [. . .] font communément ce mot feminin', as they do many words with the same ending such as *ouvrage, orage, gages, étages*. However, a distinction is made between written and spoken usage: it is only feminin in 'le discours ordinaire'; even women make it masculine 'dans un livre'. In	un aage 145; cet aage 90	une aage 2 (1624, 1637); cette aage 1 (1636)	Very little evidence of feminine in writing and nothing after the 1630s in FRANTEXT

Couple	support of this he cites Mme la Comtesse de la Suze, Madeleine de Scudéry, Mme de la Fayette, Mme de Ville-Dieu, Mme des Houillières (sic) Alemand (1688: 452) consulted his wife on the gender of *couple*: most women make it feminine, and it is masculine only in the expression *un couple de chiens*	99	26	There is variation within the usage of the same author. Mme de Sévigné uses it once in the masculine and once in the feminine. It is used in the feminine in La Pure's *La Prétieuse*. R considers it feminine when it refers to two things, but favours the masculine when it refers to two people; this tendency seems to be borne out in the FRANTEXT examples
Estude	'Ie sçay bien qu'aujourd'huy la complaisance est si grande à la Cour & à Paris envers le sexe feminin, qu'elle passe iusques là que de faire feminins plusieurs mots extraits du Latin & mesmes du Grec [. . .] Cet vsage est encore assez ordinaire dans les provinces pour ce mot *estude*' (Dupleix 1651: 259)	un estude 6	une estude 51	Clear preference for the feminine in FRANTEXT: five of the examples are from *La Prétieuse* and one from Mme de Sévigné's correspondence
Bronze	Alemand (1688: 271) maintains that few people make it feminine, but that he would not condemn its use in this gender since women usually say 'de la bronze'	9	3	Preference for the masculine in FRANTEXT, but none of the examples is by a woman

4.6.5   Agreement

The observations concerning questions of agreement are particularly interesting, and notably the discussion of *la* for *le*, since it is very extensively discussed by different *remarqueurs*. Vaugelas (1647: 27–9) is the first to comment on the usage whereby a woman following a statement by a man about being ill along the lines 'quand ie suis malade, j'aime à voir compagnie', responds using the feminine pronoun to refer to herself, '& moy quand je la suis'. Vaugelas considers this to be a fault typical of almost all women whether in Paris or at the court, pointing out that the plural pronoun *les* would never be used in a similar context (cf. Bérain 1675: 85–6); nevertheless, he suggests that the usage may become established since it is favoured by 'toutes les femmes où l'on parle bien'. Dupleix (1651: 305–6) agrees that it is an error, but not that it will become established. Buffet (1668: 59) confirms it is a common fault, but gives no hint of tolerating it. Corneille notes that most women continue to use the feminine pronoun in these circumstances, and the Academy's comments seem to confirm that the usage is still prevalent since it recommends opposing women who use *la* for *le* (Streicher 1936: 52). A rare dissenting voice is found in a comment by Bouhours (Streicher 1936: 51), who claims that Patru was not always in favour of the use of *le* here, but himself recommends that Vaugelas should be followed until Patru's reasons are known. An anecdote on this topic is also recorded in the *Menagiana* (Ménage 1693: 31) in which Ménage recalls a conversation with Mme de Sévigné; as Duchêne (1998: 46) notes, this may not be authentic, but it is of symbolic value:

Mad. de Sevigny s'informant de ma santé, je lui dis: Madame, je suis enrhumé. Elle me dit: Je la suis aussi. Je lui dis: Il me semble, Madame, que selon les regles de nôtre langue il faudroit dire: Je le suis. Vous direz comme il vous plaira, répondit-elle, mais pour moi je ne dirai jamais autrement que je n'aye de la barbe.

The metalinguistic comments appear to be confirmed by the findings from FRANTEXT: of the eight examples where the expression *je la suis* is used in the pertinent context and there is no obvious feminine antecedent, five are from Mme de Sévigné (e.g. 'n'êtes-vous point effrayé de cette douleur? Pour moi, je la suis beaucoup, je vous l'avoue'); the other three are by d'Urfé (1627), Discret (1637), and Georges de Scudéry (1644). Fournier (1998: 46–7) suggests that the two types of agreement are found throughout the century, with *le* becoming more common as the century progresses. Her evidence is somewhat different from that of FRANTEXT: her four examples of *la* are all by male authors (Corneille 1644, 1664; Molière 1670; Saint-Simon 1697), while four of the five examples of *le* she cites are by female authors (Lafayette 1678, Sévigné 1676; two examples from Maintenon 1678).

Finally, Buffet (1668: 195) argues that women should say *je me fais forte de cela* and *je suis demeurée courte*, with the adjective showing feminine agreement. *Faire forte* occurs three times in FRANTEXT and *demeurer courte* once; all the examples are by male authors.[40]

4.6.6   Other areas

There is relatively little evidence of women being associated with specific morphological or syntactic usages in the metalinguistic texts, suggesting that women are particularly associated with different lexical usage and pronunciation. As ever, phonetic differences are especially difficult to trace in a written corpus.

(a)   Morphology

There are only five cases of different morphological usages being attributed to women in the metalinguistic texts. Moreover, where alternatives are mentioned, the usage of women is often considered incorrect. In three cases, there is little or no evidence of the alternative form being attested in FRANTEXT. According to Corneille (Streicher 1936: 26), many people incorrectly use *recouvrit* rather than the correct form *recouvra*, because women do not like the sound of 'recouvra sa santé'. In FRANTEXT there is only one example of *recouvrit* from Faret's *L'Honneste Homme*, but eighteen of *recouvra* (including one by Mlle de Scudéry). Similarly Corneille maintains (Streicher 1936: 135) that, while only 'le bas peuple' say *vieigne* for *vienne*, many women still say *preigne* for *prenne*. He cites Chapelain's opinion that this is a 'faute barbare'. It is therefore not surprising to find no examples of this form in the corpus (vs 503 of *prenne*, including thirty-six by Mme de Sévigné and two by Mlle de Scudéry). Thirdly, according to Vaugelas (1647: 487), Amyot used *descouuerture* '& ie l'ay aussi ouÿ dire à des femmes de la Cour & de Paris'. In FRANTEXT there are six examples of this noun in the singular, all dating from the first half of the century, compared to eighty-eight of the noun *descouverte*, including one by Mme de Sévigné. In all these cases it is possible that the register or medium of the texts in FRANTEXT precludes us finding examples of the usage. In the case of *lairray* for *laisseray* (Callières 1693: 136) the corpus suggests that date rather than sex is the crucial factor: there are nineteen examples of the former (including one by Marie de Gournay), the last of which dates from 1659. Of the 155 examples of *laisseray*, twenty-one are by women.

In only one case – usage of *milles* in the plural when referring to the number as in 'je vous ay mille(s) obligations' – is there a possibility that the association

---

[40] Note also the discussion of *je suis plus vaillant(e) que vous, je suis plus beau/belle que vous* (Vaugelas 1647: 461–2); although this observation concerns the choice of the appropriate gender, Vaugelas does not associate any of the alternative constructions with women's usage. See also Dupleix (1651: 129), Alemand (1688: 54–7) and Bouhours (1693: 407).

made by the *remarqueurs* between the usage and women reflects common practice. This usage is termed an error by Corneille (Streicher 1936), Ménage (1675: 479) and Bouhours (1693: 416) alike; Bouhours associates it with *le discours familier*. In the FRANTEXT corpus there are eighteen examples of this usage: while only one is by Mme de Sévigné ('qu'il s'est emporté contre son ordinaire et luy a fait milles reproches'), it is perhaps significant that two others come from *La Prétieuse*.

(b)   Syntax

Leaving aside discussion of agreement, there are eight cases of syntactic features of women's usage mentioned in the corpus of metalinguistic texts. Two of these predictably do not appear in FRANTEXT since they refer either to a very crude error ('je le l'ay' for 'je l'ay', Callières 1693: 136) or belong to a style not used in the majority of the texts; Ménage (1675: 395) considers the misplacement of the forms of address *Monsieur, Madame* to be a fault typical of women's usage. Two others proved impossible to investigate using the search facilities of FRANTEXT: the first, the non-use of the subjunctive after *il faut que*, is merely alluded to by Callières (1693: 136). The second, the use of *ils* for *elles*, is of greater interest, since it is still said to be a feature of informal usage today. This is considered a solecism by Vaugelas (1647: 574):

Aux *pronoms*, de mesme, comme quand toutes les femmes & de la Cour & de la ville disent à Paris, en parlant de femmes, *ils y ont esté, ils y sont*, au lieu de dire *elles y ont esté, elles y sont*, & *i'iray auec eux*, au lieu de dire *auec elles*.

Buffet (1668: 196) makes the same point, while Bérain (1675: 29–30) criticizes this usage, arguing that it must be avoided in writing, without attributing it to women.

Of the four remaining cases, there is no evidence in the corpus of what Vaugelas (1647: *459–*460) terms 'Abus du Pronom demonstratif, *celuy*', that is beginning a sentence with the relative pronoun *celui*, etc. when it is used to refer to 'choses morales ou intellectuelles', which he associates with the written usage of courtiers and women. Nor is it possible to trace examples of a usage of *aller* which is considered faulty: 'Quelques femmes, tant de la Cour que de la Ville, font aureste une grande faute sur le mot *aller*. Elles disent, *je suis allée à la Messe*, pour dire, *l'ay esté à la Messe*' (Ménage 1675: 186).

This leaves two other cases. Bouhours (1675: 535) comments as follows on the choice of auxiliary with *sortir*:

Toutes les femmes disent presque, *il y a huit jours que je n'ay sorti; je n'ay sorti qu'une fois cette semaine*, pour dire *il y a huit jours que je n'ay fait de visites, que je n'ay été me promener*, &c. Cependant celles qui parlent de la sorte, si on leur demande, *un tel, qui demeure avec vous, est-il au logis?* elles répondent, *il est sorti* [. . .]

In FRANTEXT there are eleven examples of the *passé composé* of *sortir* being conjugated with *avoir*, one of which is from Mme de Sévigné's correspondence. Fournier (1998: 260) asserts that the *remarqueurs* tried to establish a difference between the two usages: Ménage (1675: 511–12) claims that there is a difference in meaning between *il est sorti* (= il n'est plus là) and *il a sorti* (= il est revenu).

Finally, Dupleix (1651: 190) defends *cela dit* against Vaugelas, who considered it a fault found especially in novels (1647: 519). On this occasion Dupleix expresses the wish that Vaugelas had followed the advice of women who read contemporary novels. In FRANTEXT there are twenty-seven examples of *cela dit*, two of which come from *La Prétieuse*.

(c)   Pronunciation
A number of pronunciations are attributed to female speakers by the *remarqueurs*; many are, however, difficult to trace in a written corpus (e.g. the incorrect pronunciation of the final 'er' of infinitives (Vaugelas 1647: 438), or the faulty pronunciation of (*j'ay*) *e-u* as two syllables rather than as one (*j'ai*) *eu* (Callières 1693: 136)).[41] In a large number of cases, there is no evidence in FRANTEXT of the pronunciation attributed to women (as far as the orthography allows us to determine), and no conclusion can be drawn about the reliability of the metalinguistic comment. These include *le meilleu* for *le milieu* and *au lieur de* for *au lieu de* (Corneille in Streicher 1936: 97); *Urselines* for *Ursulines* (the former being more used 'parmy le peuple & parmy les Dames', Ménage 1675: 31); and *player* or *pléer* for *plier* (Ménage 1675: 68, Corneille in Streicher 1936: 715).[42] As regards *automates* and *autographes*, women and those who do not know Greek are said to pronounce them as they are written, and not to use the learned pronunciations *aftomates* and *aftographes*, favoured, for example, by Hellenists (Alemand 1688: 199). In two further cases for which there are no attested examples in FRANTEXT – *Bernabé*, *Bernabites* for *Barnabé*, *Barnabites* (Alemand 1688: 219) and *Berthelemy* for *Barthelemy* (Alemand 1688: 227–8) – the pronunciation with 'a' is considered 'plus mâle & plus soûtenue', whereas 'les plus délicats' are said to prefer to follow women and pronounce the words with an 'e'. Here, and in examples (i) and (iv) below, we perhaps gain an insight as to how the qualities of *douceur* and *politesse* are interpreted. Since the pronunciation of 'ar' requires a greater opening of the mouth than 'er' it was considered

---

[41] Alemand (1688: 75) notes that the pronunciation *aneau* for *agneau* is not suitable for 'discours public'; rather it should be reserved for 'conversation ordinaire & familiere', and is therefore particularly suitable for women.

[42] See also *l'on za*, *l'on zest* for *l'on a*, *l'on est* (Callières 1693: 136). There are no examples of any of the variant forms discussed in 'S'il faut prononcer Chio, Kio, Scio ou Cio' (Alemand 1688: 358). Alemand claims: 'Il n'y a au reste, que quelques delicats & la pluspart des femmes qui favorisent *Kio* par un *k*, ou *Scio* par un *c* ou par une *s* si nous en exceptions M. Hedelin Abbé d'Aubignac qui écrit *Cio*.'

more vulgar and perhaps therefore more associated with male speakers than the 'politer' forms with 'er'.[43]

In the case of *velours* rather than *velous*, it is the former usage, attributed to the women of the town and court who speak well (Ménage 1675: 42), which is the only one attested in our FRANTEXT corpus (114 occcurences). Equally there are four examples of *busque* recommended by Ménage (1675: 200–1) on the grounds that this is the form favoured by those women at court and in the town who speak the best, but none of *buste* with this sense, which is deemed unacceptable although 'tres-usité parmy les Bourgeoisies'.

In the next three cases, both forms are attested in FRANTEXT (the figures in parentheses indicate the number of occurrences of each form; in each case only the singular noun or infinitive is counted):

(i) *Damoiselle* (197), *madamoiselle* (74)/*demoiselle* (135), *mademoiselle* (1387): Dupleix criticizes Vaugelas for favouring *demoiselle* and *mademoiselle*, the newer forms, and argues that the pronunciations with 'e' which are 'dans la coqueterie des femmes & de ceux qui les cajolent' constitute 'vne preuve du relaschement de la generosité & vigueur masle des François' (1651: 114). In his view they have been adopted in novels and other types of writing to please women. In FRANTEXT there is variation within the writing of one author: for example, Mme de Sévigné and Pure both very occasionally use *damoiselle* and *madamoiselle* (repectively one and two examples), although they favour *demoiselle* and *mademoiselle* (twenty-three and twelve examples respectively).

(ii) *Norrir* (2)/*nourrir* (474): According to Corneille (Streicher 1936: 430) most women use the former pronunciation which he considers 'vicieuse' and 'trop delicate'. R notes the pronunciation but considers the alternative preferable. The two examples of *norrir* are by N. de Peiresc (1625, 1631).[44]

(iii) *Chypre*/*Cypre*: According to Ménage (1675: 376–7) most women pronounce *de la poudre de Chypre*, but prefer *l'Isle de Cypre*; he also tolerates *l'Isle de Chypre*. In FRANTEXT there is one example each of *poudre de Chypre* (Balzac letters) and *poudre de cypre* (d'Urfé). However, examples of *isle*/*île de Chypre* predominate (forty-six versus five).

Both forms are also attested in the case of the next example, but in this case Vaugelas is said by Patru (Streicher 1936) to have relied on the authority of a particular influential woman:

(iv) *Guerir* (962)/*guarir* (69); *serge* (34)/*sarge* (2): Patru argues that one should use *serge* and not *sarge*, which used to be current. He claims that 'La

---

[43] As we saw in Chapter 3, 'ar' for 'er' typically occurs in the representations of peasant patois. Tory already notes the tendency for Parisian women to substitute 'e' for 'a' in 1529.

[44] Note that Anne-Marguerite le Mercier uses *noriture*, *norise* in her *livre de raison* (Ernst and Wolf 2001–2).

Grande Artenice [lui] a dit elle mesme qu'elle est la cause de la remarque de Vaugelas car l'auteur qui est pour *sarge* voyant que ses trois consultans dont il parle dans sa preface estoient pour *serge* il en parla à cette dame qui alors estoit pour *sarge* et qui maintenant a changé d'avis.' Change, rather than sex of speaker, does indeed seem to be the principal factor in the variation here, since the two examples of *sarge* in FRANTEXT date from 1609 and 1624, and the only example by a woman is *serge* used by Mme de Sévigné. Although *guarir* is much better attested, the last example dates from 1650. Mme de Scudéry and Mme de Lafayette also use forms of *guerir* rather than *guarir*.

(d) *Spelling*

As we saw in section 4.4, a number of general comments are made in the seventeenth century about the severe difficulties that women often experience with spelling correctly. However, very few comments indeed appear in the metalinguistic texts on women's spelling. Vaugelas (1647: 196) associates an incorrect spelling which mirrors the spoken form with women: 'On prononce *en affaire*, tout de mesme que si l'on escriuoit *en naffaire*, comme beaucoup de femmes ont accoustumé d'orthografier.' Not surprisingly this spelling is not attested in the corpus. Buffet (1668: 130–1) also associates a phonetically based spelling with female writers: 'Je voy tres-souvent manquer à cette prononciation qui est celle de dire segond, segondement: il y a mesme des Femmes qui l'ont si fort en usage qu'elles ne l'écrivent point autrement, il faut dire second, secondement, & seconder.'[45] There is a single example of *segond* in FRANTEXT, by d'Aubigné (1630). There is also Ménage's amusing anecdote in the *Menagiana* (1693: 126) about a woman's spelling being so poor that it leads to confusion: 'Mad de Longueil mandoit d'Angers à Paris, qu'on luy envoyast deux bonnets piquez qu'elle ortographioit ainsi *bonnes piques*. On attacha avec deux cordes deux piques derriere le coche.'

4.6.7 Précieuses' *language: evidence from the satirical texts*

Given the lack of 'authentic' *Précieuses*' texts, I shall consider the evidence for *Précieuses*' language provided by the satirical texts of Somaize, and to a lesser extent, Molière and the Abbé de Pure, and set this beside the metalinguistic comments and the usage of authors in FRANTEXT. In the next section I shall consider the evidence furnished by the metalinguistic texts. Once again there is

---

[45] Ménage (1675: 468) supports this spelling and it is used on the title-page of his two volumes of observations.

a contrast between the numerous comments of a general nature and the relative paucity of detailed examples.

A number of previous studies of *Précieuses'* language (Lathuillère 1966, 1987, Denis 1998b etc.) have identified the major traits of their usage and these are confirmed by my analysis of Somaize's dictionaries, and especially the 1660 volume. Examples have been placed under one particular category, although many of them illustrate more than one tendency. Lathuillère (1987) substantiates his analysis of the language of the *Précieuses* with similar examples cited by Scarron, Cotin, L'Abbé d'Aubignac, La Forge and Sauval. As we saw in section 4.5.2, features identified as typical of the *Précieuses* are also found in the writings of Madeleine de Scudéry (reference to examples of such usages will be cited where appropriate) and other women such as Mme de Sévigné. Denis (1998b: 54) asserts that Sorel is a precursor of many of the words and expressions later attributed to the *Précieuses* (including the predilection for adverbs in -*ment* and the extension of the use of *dernier*).[46] All this raises the important question, to which we will return below, of the extent to which the features discussed in this section are typical of the *Précieuses*, of women in general, or of 'la langue mondaine' (cf. Denis 1997: 307–8).

While Somaize and Molière provide an extreme portrait of *Précieuses'* language and style, through accumulation and excess, their texts nevertheless give some indication of its typical features: 'Tel détail isolé, conforme à la réalité, se trouve faussé par le contexte, dénaturé par la mise en oeuvre d'ensemble [. . .] Pour l'historien de la langue, il convient de retrouver, en dépit du grossissement et de l'exagération, la juste proportion de la vérité' (Lathuillère 1966: 155). The authenticity of the accounts, in part at least, is suggested by the fact that some of the features mentioned survived.[47] For reasons of space, only two examples of each case will be cited from Somaize (1660); these are representative of numerous others, many of which have been extensively discussed in the literature.

(a)   Creation of new words
As we have seen, the *Précieuses* favoured the creation of new words, especially those formed with the suffixes -*ment* and -*erie*:
  (i) *Que ie serois heureux sans vostre quitterie* [for *esloignement*] (Somaize 1660: 24). *Quitterie* does not occur in R, F or A. It does not appear in *Le Robert* (Rey 1985), while the *Trésor de la langue française* (henceforth

---

[46] Cf. Béchade's characterization (1981: 148–51) of Clorinie's language in *Polyandre* (1648).
[47] As Denis (1998b: 54) observes, Somaize also took some of his examples from contemporary authors, including Corneille, Quinault, Mlle de Scudéry, Balzac and Sorel.

TLF) considers it 'vieux', citing an example from Daudet (1884). According to Sellier (1999) it was first used by Mme de Sablé in the sense of 'end of a liaison'. There are no occurrences in FRANTEXT, but there is an example in Mme de Scudéry's letter to Bussy-Rabutin, 15 April 1671: 'Je suis aussi opiniâtre que vous sur le jugement des quitteries [. . .] Avez-vous oublié qu'elles sont toujours suivies et accompagnées de mépris et d'outrages, et que les quitteurs et les quitteuses ne laissent point leur amitié à la place de leur amour, ce qui seroit toujours quelque consolation?' The forms *quitteurs* and *quitteuses* in this citation illustrate a tendency favoured by Mlle de Scudéry to create new nouns using the suffix *-eur* (e.g. *faiseurs* [*de galimatias*], *diseurs* [*de douceurs*], *allégueurs* [*de proverbes*], Denis 1998a: 88, 54, 109).[48]

(ii) *Deslabirinther* [for *desmesler*] *les cheueux* (Somaize 1660: 19). R, F and A cite only the noun *labyrinthe*. There are no examples of this verb in FRANTEXT. *Le Robert* (Rey 1985) gives 1897 as the date for its first attestation.

(b)   Change of grammatical category
This particularly concerns the creation of nouns from adjectives, considered by Denis (1997: 303) as amongst 'les procédés favoris de la langue mondaine':
(i) *J'ay vn furieux Tendre* (*pour les gens d'esprit*) [for *J'ayme beaucoup*] (Somaize 1660: 2). This example, using *tendre* as a noun, appears to be based on Molière's *Précieuses ridicules*, in which Cathos says 'Pour moi, j'ai un furieux tendre pour les hommes d'épée' (scene 11). A gives *tendre* only as an adjective, but R cites the example from Molière under *tendre* (adjective) and F also notes the substantival usage. The only example of *tendre* as a substantive in FRANTEXT is this one from the *Précieuses ridicules*. Both *Le Robert* (Rey 1985) and the *TLF* consider the usage 'précieux'. In particular, *Le Robert* cites 'Le pays, le royaume du Tendre conçu par Mlle de Scudéry'.

(ii) *Nous ne sçaurions donner de nostre serieux dans le doux de vostre flatterie* [for *Nous ne sçaurions respondre à la douceur de vostre Compliment*] (Somaize 1660: 9). This is again based on Molière's *Précieuses ridicules*, in which Madelon says 'et nous n'avons garde, ma cousine et moi, de donner de notre sérieux dans le doux de votre flatterie' (scene 9). *Doux* is cited in the monolingual dictionaries only as an adjective or adverb. This example has been much discussed since it illustrates well how the satirical texts caricature a tendency by using two adjectives substantivally in close proximity *(le serieux, le doux)* and then combining them with the fashionable expression

---

[48] It is also common in authors such as Guez de Balzac and Corneille, as well as in Pure.

'donner dans' (A: 'Donner dans le sens de quelqu'un, C'est se rencontrer de son sentiment, ou s'y conformer'). There are only three examples of 'le doux de' in FRANTEXT, one of which is the Molière example; conversely there are 284 examples of 'donner dans'.

(c)   Extending the meaning or usage of existing words
The meaning of common words was changed or extended by the *Précieuses*, often by placing them in unusual collocations:

(i) *Il a pour vous vne amitié induë* [for *L'Amitié qu'il a pour vous commance trop tard*]. Somaize comments: 'Ce mot a encore vne autre signification, & l'on dit aussi auoir de l'amitié pour des gens qui ne le meritent pas. *Auoir vne amitié induë*' (Somaize 1660: 4). The monolingual dictionaries all note that the adjective *indu* can only be used in very restricted contexts, typically in the expressions 'à heure induë' and 'une induë vexation'. All nine examples in FRANTEXT use the adjective with the noun *heure*, including one by Mme de Sévigné.

(ii) *Ie vous ay la derniere obligation* [for *vne Grande obligation*]. Somaize comments: 'Il faut prendre garde que dans la langue Pretieuse, le mot de derniere a plusieurs significations [. . .] Il signifie tantost grande [. . .] Tantost il signifie tout à fait, comme l'on peut voir dans cet exemple. *Cela est du dernier Galand* [. . .] Et enfin il signifie premiere, c'est pourquoy l'on doit remarquer que les Pretieuses disent, *la derniere Beauté*, pour signifier la premiere' (Somaize 1660: 32–3). Shaw (1986: 48) notes that, according to Livet, there are examples of *dernier* meaning 'extreme(ly)' in Pascal, Boileau and Bossuet.

Examples of the extended use of existing terms by Madeleine de Scudéry (Denis 1997: 312) include 'cét Amy *évaporé*' and '[il ne faut pas en conversation] *se captiver* eternellement'.

(d)   Preference for nominalization
This is one of the most marked traits of *Précieuses*' language and contributes to its so-called abstract nature:

Les substantifs abstraits sont également massivement préférés à l'adjectif qualificatif correspondant [. . .] Nombreux sont donc les substantifs abstraits, évoquant une qualité, presque toujours préférés à l'adjectif. Ce trait proprement précieux de la langue de Madeleine de Scudéry conduit souvent à des formulations complexes, proches de la périphrase. (Denis 1997: 305–6)

Especially favoured is the structure noun + nominal complement, termed by Lathuillère 'le complement de caractérisation (e.g. 'une indolence de cœur'; 'des vers de qualité'; 'des argumentations de plaisir & d'amour').

(i) *I'ay esté iusques icy dans vn ieûne effroyable de diuertissement* [for *Ie ne me suis point diuertie iusques icy*] (Somaize 1660: 20)

(ii) *Il faut le surcroist d'vn fauteüil* [for *Il faut encore vn fauteüil*] (Somaize 1660: 22). Here the meaning of *surcroist* as 'augmentation' is extended by the use of an unusual nominal complement. F R A N T E X T includes a similar example from Molière's *Précieuses ridicules*: 'quelque surcroît de compagnie' (scene 11).

(e)   Avoidance of 'realistic', vulgar or shameful terms etc.

According to Maître (1999: 619) another aspect of the abstract quality of *Précieuses*' usage derives from the attempt to avoid naming directly unpleasant, common or vulgar aspects of everyday life. It suggests confusion between the name and the thing itself:

(i) *L'instrument de la Propreté* [for *Le Balet à Balayer*] (Somaize 1660: 7)

(ii) *Vostre chien s'ouure furieusement* [for *Vostre Chien fait son ordure*] (Somaize 1660: 13)

(f)   Hyperbolic expressions: especially the use of intensifiers and superlatives

This tendency manifests itself particularly in the use of the adverbs *furieuse-ment, espouuantablement* and *terriblement* rather than 'tout à fait'. *Furieuse-ment*, according to Somaize one of the oldest *Précieuses*' expressions, is extremely common: 'Il n'est point de Pretieuse qui ne le dise plus de cent fois par iour, & [. . .] ceux qui affectent le langage des Pretieuses l'ont con-tinuellement à la bouche' (1660: 74–5). All the monolingual dictionaries note the extended usage of this adverb, and Shaw records (1986: 48) that Racine uses the phrase 'je crains furieusement le chagrin' in a letter of 1660 and that Scarron, one of the strongest critics of *Préciosité*, also employs the adverb in its extended sense. This extended usage is confirmed by F R A N T E X T, where there are examples from Sorel, d'Urfé, Coëffeteau, Pure, Pascal, Molière, Tristan l'Hermite and Mme de Sévigné. A citation from Balzac confirms the associa-tion of the usage with female speakers (Lathuillère 1966: 197). There are far fewer examples in F R A N T E X T of *épouvantablement* in its extended usage, although significantly one is by Mme de Sévigné. As for *terriblement*, exam-ples of the extended usage are by Molière or Mme de Sévigné (e.g. 'qui a été terriblement ému pendant le voyage'). Somaize gives the example 'l'amour a terriblement deffriché mon cœur' (1660: 2) which he glosses as 'l'amour a bien attendry mon cœur'; here again the effect is heightened through the combina-tion of the adverb with an extended use of the verb *défricher*, defined in F as follows: 'Mettre une terre en estat d'être cultivé [. . .] se dit figurément des affaires, des sciences qui sont embrouillées & auxquelles on donne quelque éclaircissement, quelque methode'. Hyberbole is also typical of Madeleine de

Scudéry's usage in the conversations, often achieved through the use of intensi-fying adverbs; for example, 'que de me rencontrer avec ces personnes dont toute la conversation n'est que de longs récits pitoyables, et funestes, qui ennuient terriblement' (Denis 1998a: 70). Other favoured terms such as *dernier* may also be employed to similar effect: 'parce que je ne donne pas mon cœur tout entier; que je ne l'ay pas sensible de la derniere sensibilité' (Denis 1997: 315). The use of exclamations perhaps also adds to this effect: 'Ha Pisistrate, s'écria Cérinthe, vous me faites un plaisir extrême de haïr ces sortes de gens dont vous parlez!' (Denis 1998a: 108).

(g)   Metaphorical and figurative usages
Such usages also often derive from a desire to avoid naming directly the mun-dane and prosaic aspects of life:

(i) *L'ameublement de bouche* [for *Les Dents*] (Somaize 1660: 18)
(ii) *Vn bain interieur* [for *Vn verre d'Eau*] (Somaize 1660: 22)

Personification is sometimes employed, as in the exaggerated example from the *Précieuses ridicules* where Cathos says 'Mais, de grace, monsieur, ne soyez pas inexorable à ce fauteuil qui vous tend les bras il y a un quart d'heure; contentez un peu l'envie qu'il a de vous embrasser' (scene 9). Numerous figurative usages appear in the conversations of Madeleine de Scudéry (Denis 1997: 312), for example, 'un de ces hommes qui sont tousjours *en embuscade* pour estre les premiers à faire des vers sur tous les evenemens extraordinaires'; 'quelques petits chagrins sans raison, qui luy fait *faire treve avec* la joye'. The following example combines the predilection for substantivation with personification: 'cette agreable trompeuse qu'on appelle esperance'.

(h)   Periphrases
These are again symptomatic of the tendency not to name things directly. The periphrasis may relate to aspects of *Précieuses*' society:

(i) *Les sujets de la belle conuersation, ou l'agrement des societez, la politesse du langage, & les diuinitez visibles* [for *Les Femmes*] (Somaize 1660: 28)
(ii) *Vous allez faire pic repic & capot tout ce qu'il y a de plus Galand dans Paris* [for *Vous allez surpasser*] (Somaize 1660: 31); this is again taken from Molière's *Précieuses ridicules*, scene 9. *Pic*, *repic* and *capot* are all terms taken from the card game picquet. The Molière example is the only one cited in FRANTEXT, but the *TLF* cites an earlier example (1656) from Quinault's *L'Amour indiscret*: 'Il me fera vingt fois pic, repic et capot' (I, 4).

Periphrases may offer definitions of *Précieuses*' attitudes towards people or things. An extreme example of this is the satirical comment by Somaize (1660: 84) on the conjunction '&': 'Les Veritables Pretieuses estant pour l'ordinaire

vieilles ne veulent point de conjonction, c'est pourquoy elles ont retranché l'&
de leur Alphabet'.

(i) *Vn inquiet* [for *Vn homme d'Affaire*] (Somaize 1660: 3). *Inquiet* is given
only as an adjective in the monolingual dictionaries and there are no examples of this in FRANTEXT.

(ii) *Les choses que vous dites sont du dernier Bourgeois* [for *Les Choses que
vous dites sont fort communes*] (Somaize 1660: 8) (cf. *Précieuses ridicules*,
scene 4, where Madelon says 'Ah! mon père, ce que vous dites là est du
dernier bourgeois'). A pejorative value for *bourgeois* is already found, for
example in Sorel's *Francion* (1622), where the use of the term is considered
an insult.

They may also make reference to the favourite literary texts of the *Précieuses*.
In the example *Estre vn Amilcar* [for *Estre enjoüé*] the allusion is to a character
in Madeleine de Scudéry's *Clélie* (Somaize 1660: 21).

(i)   Mythological or learned allusions
The periphrases may involve mythological references, and, perhaps more surprisingly given the dislike of pedantry, the occasional learned reference:

(i) *Le vieil Resueur, ou l'Empire de Morphée* [for *Le Lit*] (Somaize 1660: 45)
(ii) *Le troisiéme element tombe* [for *Il pleut*] (Somaize 1660: 59)

(j)   Preference for the plural over the singular
This tendency is once again particularly common in the case of abstract nouns:

La langue mondaine affecte ainsi une prédilection pour l'emploi au pluriel des mots
abstraits: 'il est assez sujet à certaines petites absences de cœur', 'après qu'elle eut
bien grondé, bien crié, & bien dit des extravagances inutiles' [. . .] Ce trait de style est
assez représentatif de la langue précieuse. A ce titre il est une fois encore condamné par
Morvan de Bellegarde: 'Dire des duretez, des pauvretez, ce sont des expressions que les
femmes affectent, mais ces expressions me paroissent bien précieuses.' (Denis 1997:
307)

Somaize cites the following example which seems to illustrate this trait of the
language of the *Précieuses* 's'expliquer dans incertitudes' which is glossed as
's'expliquer sans Heziter' (1660: 37).

These, and other stylistic features such as the use of affective terms and
expressions, exclamations and rhetorical questions, all combine to characterize *Précieuses*' usage, sometimes referred to as 'style enjoué'. Denis notes, for
example, how certain favoured words and expressions are constant in the conversations of Madeleine de Scudéry; these include, for instance, *en mon particulier*,
incommode, raisonnable/raisonnablement, car enfin. A number of expressions
which are termed *précieuse* by contemporaries are found in the conversations.
For example, *avoir la mine de*, made famous by Molière (Denis 1997: 312),

is used on a number of occasions as in 'Un homme qui dit sans qu'il en soit besoin qu'il n'est point amoureux, a bien la mine de l'estre.' Also favoured are *avoir moyen de* (Denis 1997: 313) ('il n'y avoit pas moyen de faire de longs discours en allant si viste'), and *avoir apparence* ('il n'y auroit pas d'aparence d'envoyer cette belle Fille sans une escorte').

4.6.8 Précieuses' *language: evidence from the metalinguistic texts*

We shall now examine what our corpus of metalinguistic texts tells us about specific features of *Précieuses*' usage and consider to what extent these data coincide with what Somaize and the other satirical texts cite as examples of their language. Given the questions about the dating of the movement (section 4.5), it is significant that the metalinguistic texts continue to discuss their use of language in the last decade of the century. Moreover, there is indication of the negative connotations of the word replacing the earlier more positive ones. For example, Tallemant (1698: 104–5) discusses whether it is appropriate to use the expression 'jargon de Precieuse'. On the one hand he considers it inappropriate since 'Les Precieuses cherchent le langage le plus poli'; on the other hand it also refers to 'langage affecté' and then he considers the expression appropriate since 'ce n'est pas la vraye langue que parlent les personnes qu'on appelle Precieuse, ce sont des Phrases recherchées, faites exprés, & quoy qu'elles soient composées de mots choisis & usités, on peut dire que c'est un jargon' (cf. Renaud 1697: 396–7, 'Du Style Afecté').

Of the thirteen features specifically attributed to the *Précieux/ses* in the metalinguistic texts, I have discounted the particular use of *necessaire* noted by F since the very large number of occurrences of the term in FRANTEXT (3129) makes it difficult to analyse systematically.[49] Of the remaining terms, just over half are not attested in FRANTEXT:

  (i) *Une femme fort arrangée*: 'Le P. Bouhours a oui dire *une femme fort arrangée* à quelque Précieuse: & comme il a beaucoup d'estime pour les Précieuses, il a voulu parer sa Préface de cette nouvelle façon de parler' (Ménage 1676: 203–4).

 (ii) *Enchanté*: Buffet (1668: 38) discusses the expression *Resides enchantées*, used to refer to 'des alcauves faites d'une maniere richement embellie', arguing that although it seems somewhat *précieux*, it is well received. Bouhours (1675: 8) considers its usage fashionable but unlikely to last

---

[49] I have included in the statistics the three cases where R specifically defines something as *précieux/se* but have exluded the forty-seven others where the example or definition makes reference to Molière's *Précieuses ridicules*. Sometimes R makes it clear that the word is only found in this text (e.g. *pommader*); at other times examples from other texts are cited, and perhaps notably those by Scarron. The dictionary definitions of *précieux/se* are also excluded from the analysis here.

long; he counsels against using it too much 'de peur de tomber dans l'affectation, & de parler un langage prétieux'. The expressions *Un portrait enchanté, Un habit enchanté* are condemned by Ménage as 'précieuses' (1676: 265, 294).

(iii) *Il est des hommes qui*: 'Cette maniére de parler est un peu précieuse; il faut dire *il y a des hommes*; si ce n'est en Poësie où l'on peut dire, *il y a*. Quand la proposition est négative, on peut dire, *est*, au lieu de *y a*' (Andry de Boisregard 1689: 215).

(iv) *Immisericordieux*: 'Ce mot à [sic] quelque chose d'affecté qui déplaist. Je dis le mesme d'*immortification*, d'*immortifié*, & d'*incharitable*; termes ordinaires parmy les précieuses, mais dont les personnes bien censées ne se servent point' (Andry de Boisregard 1689: 257).[50] Of these only *Immortifié* is attested (see below).

(v) *Bien peuple*: 'Il faut estre bien *peuple* pour croire cela; c'est à dire, il faut avoir l'ame bien basse, & estre bien plein des sentimens du *peuple*. Cette expression plaist à quelques précieuses; mais bien des personnes n'osent encore s'en servir. Je crois pourtant que cette maniére de parler pourra s'establir avec le temps' (Andry de Boisregard 1689: 405–6).

(vi) *Tourneûre d'esprit*: Bouhours (1693: 350) considers this a *Précieux/ses* expression and argues that those who speak well do not use it.

(vii) *Brutaliser*: R defines this as a 'Terme de pretieuse pour dire se divertir amoureusement, prendre des plaisirs sensüels [. . .]'. There are no examples of the verb in FRANTEXT, although there is one example by Cyrano de Bergerac of *débrutaliser* (1655), a term said to have been invented by Mme de Rambouillet (cf. Vaugelas 1647: 492). *Brutaliser* is one of the terms explained by Somaize (1661a: II, 42–3), who claims 'Ce mot a esté mis en vsage au mariage d'vne des plus fameuses Pretieuses de tout leur Empire, & dit par vne des plus celebres & des plus connües.'

Of the five remaining cases, the expression 'le conseiller des graces', defined by R as a 'Phrase burlesque & prétieuese pour dire un miroir' is only attested once in FRANTEXT, in an example from scene 6 of Molière's *Précieuses ridicules*. However, there are four cases for which examples are attested:

(i) *Inclemence*: according to Andry de Boisregard (1689: 260), this is an old word which some people wish to reintroduce. Only the *Précieuses ridicules* use it in prose, but it can be used in poetry. Twelve of the fourteen examples in FRANTEXT occur in verse (including drama), and there are examples from Bertaut (1606) on.

(ii) *Immortifié* (see above): there is one example of this adjective by Fénelon (1697).

---

[50] Ménage (1676: 204–19) considers *incharitable* acceptable for women, but not for a man of Bouhours's profession.

(iii) *Terre*: According to R, 'Ce mot entre en quelques façons de parler plaisantes. [Si vous poursuivez le mérite, ce n'est pas sur nos terres que vous devez chasser. *Moliere, Prétieuses, s.* 9. Cette maniere de parler qui est un peu prétieuse signifie que si on cherche du mérite ce n'est pas nous qu'il faut voir. Billets doux & billet galans sont des *terres inconnuës* pour eux. *Moliere, Prétieuses, s.* 4. C'est à dire, ils ne savent ce que c'est que de billets doux & de billets galants.].' Although there is only the example from Molière of the former expression, the latter occurs in three similar examples in FRANTEXT, two of which are by Mme de Sévigné.

The fourth case is an interesting one, since Ménage (1676: 217) considers the use of *joli* in certain expressions to be favoured by the *Précieuses* (see the discussion of *joli mignon* and *jolies choses* above, pp. 149–52). Finally, there are two observations in Andry de Boisregard (*grief, puis,* 1693: 131–2, 280) where usage of a term is defended against the negative opinion of the *Précieuses*.

4.6.9   The language of Préciosité *and women's language*

To what extent did the *Précieuses* have their own 'jargon'? Pelous (1980) considers the idea that the language of the *Précieuses* is a distinct language, comparable to Italian or Spanish, as 'invraisemblable', and he argues that the language Molière and Somaize present is bizarre, but perfectly comprehensible. He prefers to characterize it as a fiction, comprising a disparate mixture of registers, which no one could conceivably have used: 'un mélange hétéroclite et burlesque de locutions empruntées à des registres très divers' (1980: 345–6). He argues that Livet, who did much to create the modern legend of the *Précieuses*, found no trace of this language outside the parodies of Molière and Somaize. Rather Somaize's technique consisted in isolating a phrase from its context and making it an element of the new language. Pelous cites Pintard's view that 'il suffit de faire subir ce traitement à n'importe quel texte poétique pour en extraire un jargon burlesque et ridicule'. For Pelous then, the language fabricated by Molière and Somaize amplified certain tendencies in the linguistic usage of polite society; he notes (1680: 417), for example, that Bary's recommendations in his *Rhétorique françoise* (1653) of how to make one's style more noble have a number of features in common with this jargon, including the preference for plural over singular forms, and the use of 'grands mots', superlatives and periphrases. One of the examples Bary cites – replacing 'ce que je vous présente est un cercle' with the periphrastic 'la chose dont je vous entretiens est une surface qui est de tous côtés également distante de son centre' – would not be out of place in Somaize's dictionary. In other words, for Pelous the jargon of the *Précieuses* is simply *style enjoué* carried to an extreme.

My analysis has clearly shown that so-called features of *Précieuses*' language are not restricted to the texts of Molière and Somaize; they may be found – albeit much more sparingly – in the works of Corneille and Voiture, in the novels and conversations of Mlle de Scudéry and in the correspondence of Mme de Sévigné. The satire and caricature of Molière and Somaize is achieved through the intensity of the devices used. It is noteworthy that in a number of entries in R, an example of a usage is cited from Molière's *Précieuses ridicules* alongside citations by other authors such as Scarron, who would not be considered *précieux*. Shaw (1986: 48) also notes that a number of the same words and expressions are employed without satire in other plays by Molière.

Brunot (Petit de Julleville 1897: 783–4) points to the positive and negative sides of *Préciosité*:

La préciosité, à côté de ses dangers, a [. . .] eu ses avantages. Mais pour apprécier les uns et les autres, n'oublions pas qu'il faut considérer, outre l'invention des phrases, qui n'est qu'une des formes de la préciosité, la grande action qu'elle a eue sur l'épuration du langage et la constitution de la grammaire mondaine.

If the excesses of the movement inevitably led to its being mocked, certain of the beliefs at the heart of *Précieuses*' attitude to language usage – the emphasis on refinement, the avoidance of terms considered too low in register, 'common' or vulgar – are very much at the heart of seventeenth-century linguistic thought.

Earlier in this chapter, I raised the question how far it is possible to separate out the language of *le monde*, the language of women in general, the language of the *Précieuses*, and the language of certain famous women writers and correspondents. The close relationship between these various social groupings was suggested by Lathuillère (1966: 15) in his characterization of *Préciosité*:

Elle ne se réduit pas, par exemple, au féminisme, à la littérature de salon ou au langage hyperbolique, mais elle n'aurait sans doute pas existé sans eux. Inversement, le féminisme, la littérature de salon et le langage hyperbolique ne sont pas précieux par eux-mêmes; ils le deviennent par les rapports qui s'établissent entre eux et qui se nouent avec les autres composantes de la préciosité.

Note also Denis's assessment of Somaize (1998b: 55): 'Derrière la fiction commode d'une description de la langue à part des précieux, en définitive celle du monde galant dûment caricaturé, il s'agit bien d'une interrogation sur la légitimité de l'usage mondain – et, notoirement, féminin – de la parole.' The same problematic is implied in the debate as to whether Mme de Lafayette, Mme de Sévigné and indeed Mlle de Scudéry should be considered *Précieuses* (see, for example, Raynard 2002: 40–1; François 1987: 45), all of whom had clear links with *Précieuses*. Critics such as Fukui and Duchêne have rightly identified distinctive aspects in these women's writing, particularly in their attitudes towards love and marriage, but we have seen how the works of Mme de Sévigné and Mlle de Scudéry in particular contain many of the linguistic features which are considered typical of *Précieuses* by their contemporaries.

A number of comments in the metalinguistic texts equally suggest that for some seventeenth-century writers the line between the language of the *Précieuses* and that of women in general was not clear-cut. For instance, there is an implicit reference to the *Précieuses* when Bouhours (1962: 37) criticizes 'le jargon de certaines femmes qui se servent à toutes heures d'expressions extraordinaires, & qui dans une conversation disent cent fois un mot qui ne fera que de naistre'. The fusing of the two groups is perhaps even more evident in Ménage's observation entitled 'Remarques sur les endroits des Livres de Langue du P. Bouhours, qui regardent les Dames' (1676: 204), which opens with a criticism of Bouhours for being a *Précieux* 'qui se pique de faire des livres sur nostre Langue à l'usage & en faveur des Dames' and then cites observations where Bouhours refers to the usage of *women*, e.g. *sagacité, sécurité, incharitable, mon quartier, ma petite, un joli mignon* (see the comment on *joli* in section 4.6.3). Similarly in the *Ménagiana* Ménage makes reference to the usage of women, but the example he uses seems to suggest the more restricted usage of the *Précieuses* (1693: 101): 'Des Dames qui étoient dans une Assemblée où la conversation ne leur plaisoit pas, se dirent agréablement l'une à l'autre: Il pleut icy de l'ennuy à verse.'[51] A key question is therefore where to draw the line between features typical of women in general and those said to be typical of *Préciosité*.

4.7   Conclusion

We have seen that women's language is clearly perceived by writers on the French language as being different from that of men. The specificities of women's language may be viewed in a positive or negative light, sometimes within the writing of the same commentator. Baron (1986) identified as one of the paradoxes about the discussion of women's language in England the fact that women were viewed both as conserving the linguistic norms and as innovating upon them. The concept of women's language as conservative (Coates and Cameron 1988: 4–8) is likewise not easy to apply to seventeenth-century France. While women are viewed by many as the arbiters of good usage and as being suspicious of new words which they do not comprehend, the *Précieuses* assert their identity by innovating in their choice of words and expressions.

---

[51] Note that Ménage and Bouhours also make specific reference to Mme de Lafayette and Mme de Sévigné.

Our discussion has shown that the positive or negative opinion of women about the acceptability of a new word or expression had little long-term effect on the evolution of the language. Similarly, women are frequently praised for the naturalness of their use of language and for the authenticity of their judgments about good usage, yet the *Précieuses* – or at least the *fausses Précieuses* – were mocked for their artificiality. The same tensions emerge in the discussion of particular linguistic features, and especially of grammatical gender: while the feminine gender is said to be favoured by French, the masculine is nevertheless described as the more noble gender. Traditional negative stereotypes of differences between the sexes are clearly present at times: for example, the notion that women's views on language cannot be sought since they are fickle, or that for men to adopt women's pronunciation would make them effeminate. Yet the dominant view – itself becoming something of a trope by the end of the century – stresses the positive qualities of female language, and especially its naturalness. This is all the more striking given the long tradition in moral philosophy of viewing women as artificial and duplicitous, overly concerned with external appearance.

It is important to emphasize the difficulty of discussing 'women's language' in general, as if women formed a homogeneous group, since the variable of sex inevitably interacts with other parameters of variation. In the case of seventeenth-century France this is most obviously the case with the socio-economic status of the speaker. While some of the dictionaries make reference to the usage of lower-class women, the *remarqueurs* in particular tend to focus on that of the higher social group, of 'la plus saine partie' of the women at the King's court, or of the salon women whom they frequented. This is also related to the question of education, which, as we have seen, is a key theme in the discussion of women's language. Women became models of the speaker ignorant of Greek and Latin, and of a non-specialist public, but they were not of course the only group to fall into this category as a number of the commentators make clear. The difficulty of separating out the different variables has once more been compounded by the difficulty of identifying reliable sources and the relatively narrow range of texts available to us. It is striking, for example, that although the *remarqueurs* aim to record contemporary usage, their comments on *Préciosité* date from after the period when many modern commentators would end the movement. In addition, as we have seen, it is far from clear whether the *remarqueurs*, when they refer to women's language in general, really describe that of the salon women, or that of certain well-known women writers, notably Mme de Lafayette, Mme de Sévigné and Mlle de Scudéry.

It has been difficult to correlate the general qualities of women's language which are repeatedly praised with the relatively few specific features of their language which are identified in the metalinguistic texts. Women's language is appreciated for qualities which are highly valued by the seventeenth-century *remarqueurs* in general, such as clarity and *proprieté* of word and expression, but it is also attributed more feminine qualities such as *agrément* and *douceur*. The clearest indications of a correlation relate to women's ability to select *termes propres ou justes*, since here there is a predominance of specific comments on lexical issues. Women are seen as paying great care to the choice of the correct term, and as disliking the use of technical vocabulary. Carried to an extreme, this attention to the *mot juste* can result in prudish rejection of words (e.g. *poitrine*) or the excessive creation associated with *Préciosité*. Where the metalinguistic comments are confirmed by the high incidence of examples by female writers in FRANTEXT (and notably by Mme de Sévigné) they seem precisely to refer to expressions associated with salon women, such as *notre quartier, ma petite, demander excuse, plaisant/joli mignon, il faut voir/sçavoir, il est vray*. There is relatively little indication of the usage of *Précieuses'* terms in FRANTEXT – aside from the obvious examples from Molière or the Abbé de Pure – perhaps because *Préciosité* was predominantly an oral phenomenon.

Of the other qualities mentioned, *la délicatesse, la grâce* and *l'agrément* are perhaps associated with women's preference for the feminine gender, which Alemand characterizes as 'plus doux & plus agreable'. The only hint at what might be intended when the *douceur* of their pronunciation is referred to is in the preference of women for 'er' over 'ar' in words such as *Berthelemy, Bernabé, guerir*, since this pronunciation requires less opening of the mouth. It is more difficult to find any correlation in the case of clarity of usage, since there are relatively few comments on syntax, and the discussion of agreement is not formulated in terms of the relative *netteté* of the different constructions. Good usage of French will moreover necessarily require *politesse* as implied by Bouhours's description of the French language as a prude (1962: 45): 'mais une prude agreable, qui toute sage & toute modeste qu'elle est, n'a rien de rude ni de farouche'. Above all the social value of speaking well is stressed; women in society need communicative competence, 'knowledge of when to speak or be silent; how to speak on each occasion' (Milroy 1980: 85).

A number of different explanations to account for the differences between men's and women's language have been offered at least since the 1970s (see, for example, Coates and Cameron 1988, Bauvois 2002). While they have often been seen as competing theories – and they have obvious pitfalls as well as merits – elements of them are pertinent to the discussion of seventeenth-century France. The first of these, associated with Labov and Trudgill in the 1970s (Coates and Cameron 1988: 4–8), relates women's more correct and careful speech to their social role as females: in their view this role involves paying more attention to appearances and superficial aspects of behaviour than is expected of men. A comment by Faret seems to confirm that women can afford to pay more attention to the superficial aspects of language usage since the content of what they say is less weighty; men's language is:

plus vigoureuse et plus libre; et pource qu'elle est ordinairement remplie de matieres plus solides et plus serieuses, ils prennent moins garde aux fautes qui s'y commettent que les femmes, qui ayant l'esprit plus prompt, et ne l'ayant pas chargé de tant de choses qu'eux, s'aperçoivent aussi plutost de ces petits manquements, et sont plus prontes à les relever. (Timmermans 1993: 153)

A similar approach is the 'two cultures view' (Henley and Kramarae 1994: 387), which maintains that women and men have different sociolinguistic subcultures and that the social world of women impacts on their speech. The stereotypical nature of this explanation has rightly been challenged by twentieth-century feminists, as has its treatment of women as if they were a homogeneous group, yet there are aspects of this theory which do seem relevant to our discussion. The cultural, social and educational position of seventeenth-century French women was very different from that of their male counterparts and was seen as a key factor for valuing their judgment as 'naïve' speakers. In the salon culture of the period value was placed on the importance of conversation for the development of the *honnête homme*.

Second, Milroy's concept of social networks seems to be particularly applicable to the salon women of the period. Williams and Giles have argued that 'unlike many minority groups, women are not forced to live closely together in conditions conducive to the collective group consciousness' (Coates 1986: 7), and it has been argued that in many communities women tend to have less close-knit social networks (Coates 1986: 91). Yet the salons were precisely a place where women could form close networks and develop a sense of group consciousness. For the *Précieuses* in particular language was a way of distinguishing themselves from others and showing solidarity with members of the group. Membership of the group and approbation from its members were seen as vital, as is clear from Viala's assessment of the role of the Hôtel de Rambouillet: 'le constat [. . .] est simple: tous les écrivains en renom dans la première moitié du siècle ont, par fréquentation régulière ou par contact plus éloigné, cherché à obtenir de ce groupe une sorte d'attestation de leur mérite littéraire' (cited in Timmermans 1993: 77). Whether conversation was all female or mixed, the establishment of group identity was a key element. The difference for the seventeenth century is the value attached to these close social networks. Whereas for Milroy (1980) tight-knit networks are an important mechanism for the maintenance of vernacular norms, in the case of the *Précieuses* they allowed innovation and the use of jargon.[52]

A third type of explanation, which may be considered to derive from psychological differences between men and women or from social conditioning, maintains that women are more status-conscious and more sensitive to the

[52] The network scores would also have to be calculated on different criteria from the rather male-oriented and work-dominated criteria used by Milroy.

social connotations of speech. In modern discussions this concern is often associated with the insecurity of their social position (Coates and Cameron 1988: 15; Singy 1998); in the case of the seventeenth century we have seen that women of the salon and court milieu were not necessarily deemed inferior to men. There is certainly much evidence to suggest the importance attributed to external behaviour for those wishing to be accepted in polite society. Language was a means of social integration, and given the diverse social origin of some of the salon women this perhaps also explains their preoccupation with acquiring the language which would identify them with polite society.

5   Age, variation and change

5.1   Introduction: attitudes towards change in the seventeenth century

Change presupposes variation. In a century that witnessed the imposition of the ideology of the standard, change was at times regretted since standardization is 'partly aimed at preventing or inhibiting linguistic change' (Milroy and Milroy 1991: 36). The *remarqueurs*, from Vaugelas on, are very much pre-occupied with change, aware of the difference between the language of their sixteenth-century predecessors and that of 'modern authors'. Moreover, they typically considered that the French language had reached a state of perfection which could be jeopardized by any change, or 'corruption' of the language. Of Vaugelas's 549 observations, nearly one-fifth focus on changes in usage, and the evolution of French is also discussed in general terms in his Preface. Likewise, Marguerite Buffet devotes one of the four parts of her work to 'Termes barbares & trop anciens', and the largest number of her observations which explicitly refer to variation are devoted to this parameter. Significant numbers of observations concerned with changing usage are also found in Ménage 1675 (fifty-five observations) and Andry de Boisregard 1689 (sixty observations); Ménage's comments are particularly valuable since his detailed citation of authors provides a much finer calibration of the chronology of the changes he discusses. His chronological horizon also stretches back much further than that of many of his contemporaries.

One of the main functions of later *remarqueurs* was to update the observations of their predecessors, and notably those of Vaugelas; typical in this respect is Bouhours's long observation in his *Remarques nouvelles* entitled 'En quoy il ne faut point suivre les Remarques de M. de Vaugelas' (1675: 516–40).[1] The title of Oudin's grammar (1632) is equally significant in its avowed aim of providing a French grammar 'rapportée au langage du temps', and notably

---

[1] Twenty-three of the topics discussed are ones which explicitly refer to change in usage since Vaugelas's time; these mostly concern the currency of words and expressions, although there are also comments on verb morphology (*cueïllera/cueïllira*) and on pronunciation and spelling (*convent/couvent*).

of updating Maupas's grammar of 1607 (^{2}1618). Andry de Boisregard is perhaps representative of many writers on the French language in the second half of the century. While he is anxious to promote contemporary usage, arguing in his Preface (1689) that, as in the case of dress, it would be ridiculous to adopt old-fashioned ways, he nevertheless favours older, more established terms over new words since they can lend the language 'une force & une noblesse' (1689: 48).

5.2   The analysis of change in seventeenth-century France

5.2.1   The chronology of change

For Vaugelas (1647: Preface X, 1) change occurs over a period of about twenty-five to thirty years. He is, however, at pains to point out that it is the detail of usage which evolves rather than the principles, which in his view are likely to remain constant. Moreover, the majority of usages remain constant in language and change only affects 'la milliesme partie de ce qui demeure'; in addition, syntax changes much less than words and expressions. The stability of the principles guiding French reflects the stability of the court and the monarchy, guardians of *le bon usage*.

Vaugelas's stated chronology for change over a period of twenty-five to thirty years is reflected in the choice of textual examples he makes which fall into three broad chronological tranches. Those writers who flourished in the 1550s–1570s, such as Ronsard and Desportes, are generally cited to represent a past, outdated usage.[2] A second group of writers, comprising Du Perron, Malherbe and Coëffeteau, who flourished in the 1600s–1620s, are also often the subject of criticism, although Vaugelas's attitude towards Coëffeteau in particular is more ambivalent. For example, Coëffeteau is censured for his use of *c'est chose glorieuse* without a determiner (1647: 200) and his usage is at times specifically contrasted with that of Vaugelas's contemporaries (1647: 183–4), but he is praised for the clarity or *netteté* of his syntactic usage (1647: 156). Finally, there are what Vaugelas terms 'nos modernes Escriuains', who are not individually named when they are the object of praise.[3] Writing in the later part of the century, Alemand (1688) broadly adopts Vaugelas's chronology of change but brings it up to date. His own periodization is developed in relation to the stages he perceives in the reform of the French language (Alemand 1688: 1). The first period of the reform of French is associated with Du Perron (1556–1618), Malherbe (1555–1628), Bertaut (1552–1611), Coëffeteau

---

[2] Desportes's secular poetry was published between 1572 and 1583. In his old age Desportes devoted himself to translating the Psalms, a task he finally completed in 1603.

[3] Here, then, the period of productivity (1550s–1570s, 1600s–1620s, 1640s) seems to be more important than the date of birth of the writer (see below).

(1574–1632), Desportes (1546–1606) and Amyot (1513–93), the majority of whom were born in the 1540s or 1550s. The second reform of French is said to be particularly the work of Balzac (1594–1654) and Voiture (1597–1648), along with Vaugelas (1585–1650), Gombaud (1576–1666), Le Vayer (1588–1672) and Sarasin (1614–54). These 'demi-Modernes' constitute the next generation of writers, the majority of whom were born in the 1580s and 1590s. Alemand's third group is, like Vaugelas's, the 'Modernes', authors flourishing presumably in the 1670s and 1680s who are likely therefore to have been born in the early decades of the seventeenth century. Likewise, Bouhours (1671: 66) notes that French has changed since the time of François I (reigned 1515–47) and of Henri IV (reigned 1589–1610); moreover, he identifies a major change in the language in the middle of the reign of Louis XIII, which he associates with Balzac and Vaugelas (1671: 74).

It is interesting that Caron in a recent article (2002) adopts a similar time-span for change. Using the notion of *chronolecte*, he maintains that change occurs over a period of about thirty years and that there is a 'frontier' between two *chronolectes* in the years 1610–20. A text written after 1620 by an adult aged under forty is, in his opinion, likely to exhibit the newer variant rather than the one established in the good usage of 1600–10. Caron cites Matoré (1953: 57–61) who, from a lexicographer's viewpoint, favours the idea of 'generations' for measuring the chronology of change; he suggests that the history of French may be divided into tranches of thirty to thirty-six years, 'moyenne de la vie sociale utile'. Matoré therefore proposes the following pivotal dates for the period which concerns us: 1550, 1585, 1620, 1656, 1688. The case studies (below) illustrate the fallacy of adopting such precise dates for phonetic, morphological and syntactic change, which are gradually adopted by writers according to their particular preferences and the style and genre of the work. It will be seen that, particularly in the case of the position of clitic pronouns, it is difficult to trace a clear linear development.

5.2.2   The reduction of the French language

The evidence of the *remarqueurs* clearly supports the view of the seventeenth century as one of linguistic retrenchment, of a reaction against the *richesse* characteristic of the previous century. Of the nearly 300 observations devoted to changing usages, 137 discuss words and expressions which are going or have gone out of usage, compared to sixty-three which discuss new words or expressions. Emphasis is, moreover, placed on lexical evolution rather than morphological change (twenty-five comments including six devoted to changes of gender, largely from feminine to masculine, e.g. *navire* (Vaugelas 1647: 130), *euesché* (Vaugelas 1647: 368), *aage* (Alemand 1688: 1) or syntactic change (twenty-one comments).

A predominantly negative attitude towards neologisms – at least in theory – is articulated by Vaugelas.[4] In his Preface (IX, 3), he maintains that 'il n'est iamais permis de faire des mots'; he goes on to assert that no one, not even the King, has the right to innovate. However, he quickly moderates this extreme position, and claims that this absolute ban applies only to entire words. As far as derivatives are concerned, they are sometimes tolerated (Preface XI). When we come to look at the individual observations, the theoretical stance is not consistently followed, as is often the case with Vaugelas. Of the thirteen new words discussed in the *Remarques*, eight are accepted wholeheartedly, three are said to have become acceptable although they were initially intolerable, and only two are condemned outright.[5] In the case of words formed using the prefix *de-* (*Deuouloir*, Vaugelas 1647: 490–2), Vaugelas even asserts that *debrutaliser* is likely to succeed because it was created by someone (Mme de Rambouillet) who has the right to create new words 's'il est vray ce que les Philosophes enseignent, qu'il n'appartient qu'aux sages d'eminente sagesse d'auoir ce priuilege'. He is also more openly tolerant of new expressions, providing they are not too close to the original expression (Preface IX, 3), although he equally asserts as a principle that 'vn mot ancien, qui est encore dans la vigueur de l'Vsage est incomparablement meilleur à escrire, qu'vn tout nouueau, qui signifie la mesme chose [. . .] Quand je parle des mots, j'entens aussi parler des phrases' (1647: 334).

Scipion Dupleix, in his eighties when his observations were published, represents the position of a past generation, and is a dissident voice against the prevailing ethos of the period. He very frequently questions Vaugelas's judgment that a particular word or expression is falling out of use (e.g. *c'est chose glorieuse* (1651: 189), *d'abondant* (1651: 225), *souloit* (1651: 578)). Typical is his defence of *longuement* (1651: 317) against the 'retrencheurs de mots' who in his opinion are impoverishing and destroying the language. The debate over the acceptability of new words continues throughout the century. Bouhours is of the opinion that new words should be created sparingly, and only to denote new things (1674: 52–3). In Siouffi's terms (1995: 420), Bouhours invokes the fiction of a 'locuteur collectif' since he suggests that new words must have the support of the people who are to use them. He prefers words which appear rather old to those which are too new, since the former have the advantage of being

---

[4] There are, naturally, other opinions expressed. Although Bouhours generally follows Vaugelas in his dislike of innovations, he also speaks in positive terms about new words and phrases: 'On a beaucoup enrichi la langue Françoise depuis quelques années, soit en faisant des mots nouveaux & de nouvelles phrases: soit en renouvellant quelques termes & quelques phrases, qui n'étoient pas fort en usage' (Bouhours 1962: 52).

[5] Those which are accepted or which Vaugelas hopes will become established are *insideux, securité, intrigue, incendie, conioncture, incognito, deuouloir* and *insulter*. *Feliciter, exactitude* and *transfuge* were initially considered unacceptable but have since become established. Vaugelas is critical of *peur* (for *de peur*) and *gestes*.

'naturels & intelligibles' (1674: 33). Ménage (1676: 161–90) in an observation entitled 'S'il est permis de faire des mots' responds not only that it is permitted, but indeed that it is essential, especially for poets, grammarians, doctors, philosophers, mathematicians and theologians. He, like Andry de Boisregard, often expresses regret that words seem to be falling out of use, and defends older terms. Questions of the currency of words and expressions therefore form a major preoccupation throughout the century.

5.2.3   The interaction of change with other parameters of variation

Writers on the French language are conscious of the interaction between change and other parameters of variation, and notably that of register. For example, Vaugelas notes that innovations such as *comme quoy* are only acceptable in familiar style (1647: 333) and this register is also the last home for many words or expressions which are on the decline (e.g. *d'abondant*: 'ce terme [. . .] a vieilli, & l'on ne s'en sert plus dans le beau stile' (Vaugelas 1647: 230); *à qui mieux mieux*: 'Cette locution est vieille, & basse' (Vaugelas 1647: 224)).

5.3   Stable variation versus change in progress: the case of negation

The potential for change is always inherent in the existence of variants. The simplest way of tracking this change in the case of contemporary language is to analyse the usage of a group of speakers at a given point in time and then to compare this with their usage some years later, that is to track what has been termed 'change in real time'. In the case of historical linguistics tracing change in real time can be highly problematic, since the data available may be imperfect or non-existent. To alleviate this difficulty Labov (1972a: 134) introduces the notion of 'change in apparent time', a notion which has been applied to the study of the contemporary French language, for example, by Ashby (1991). According to this view change in progress is manifested in variation. Ashby maintains that if the older variant has a higher rate of occurrence among older speakers and the newer variant occurs more frequently in the usage of younger speakers, then this age grading or age stratification may indicate that change is in progress. He argues, for example, that the fact that younger speakers exhibit an appreciably higher ratio of *ne* deletion in negative constructions or /l/ effacement in words such as 'il(s)' than older speakers suggests 'in apparent time' that the variation reflects an ongoing change in the structure of French (Ashby 1991).[6]

---

[6] In fact Ashby simplifies Labov's argument (1972a: 134) that the adoption of the new prestige feature will also crucially depend on the speakers' class. In the case of the upper-middle-class speakers the correlation is clearest: the oldest members tend to preserve the older prestige form,

A number of French linguists, notably those working in the Groupe Aixois de Recherche en Syntaxe (GARS), have questioned the validity of the notion of 'change in apparent time' (e.g. Valli 1983; Blanche-Benveniste and Jeanjean 1987). The GARS linguists raise major objections to equating age stratification with change in progress. They argue that, without a diachronic perspective, this notion is meaningless; indeed, evidence often suggests that the same variation is attested in the records of past centuries, that is that we are dealing with 'stable variation'. In other words, synchronic variation that shows age stratification does not necessarily indicate change.

One of the most interesting examples of the difficulty of resolving this debate concerns the non-use of *ne* in negative constructions, which is frequently characterized as a principal feature distinguishing the French of today from that of a century ago (e.g. Pohl 1972).[7] In considering the chronology of the change, it is important first of all to distinguish usage in negative statements and in negative interrogative sentences.[8] In the latter case there are examples of non-use of *ne* dating back at least to the *Roman de la Rose* (e.g. 'Sez tu pas qu'il ne s'ensuit mie . . .', 'Suis je pas bele dame et gente?'). In fact these examples are probably not typical, since usage of *point* rather than *pas* is much more usual in such contexts in the Old and Middle French periods. As regards negative statements, the following example by Marguerite de Navarre is often considered to be the earliest satisfactory example:

Les philosophes du temps passé [. . .] dont la tristesse et la joye est quasi poinct sentye. (Gougenheim 1974: 242)

Given the prevalence of this construction in modern spoken French, it is interesting to note that there are no examples of the non-use of *ne* in negative statements in seventeenth-century model dialogues intended as didactic texts. Of texts in a popular register, the *chronique* of Chavatte, a sayette weaver born c. 1633, has an example of this usage:

et alors le mestier de la saiterie ne vouloit plus rien et on gaignois pas sa vie en travaillant. (Lottin 1979: 130)

---

whereas the younger members adopt the newer prestige form. In the case of the lower-middle-class speakers, however, the reverse situation occurs. In Labov's view, the greater linguistic insecurity of this class leads even middle-aged speakers to follow the newer usage, indeed at a higher rate than younger members of their class, who are less sensitive to social stratification. The working class is said to mirror this pattern, albeit to a lesser extent. Finally, the lower class is said to be largely immune to the tendency to follow the latest prestige norms.

[7] Fuller details of the data may be found in Ayres-Bennett (1994).

[8] Usage also differs in the case of non-finite sentences. Gondret (1998: 57) cites examples of the omission of *ne* with an infinitive from Martin and Wilmet (1980: 34): 'Quel veu? dit l'un – Le veu que vous feistes du partir, dist elle, de *point* coucher avec vostre femme' (*Cent nouvelles nouvelles*). A similar sixteenth-century example by Rabelais is cited by Gougenheim (1974: 242): '*Point* soupper seroit le meilleur'.

There is also an isolated example in one of the *Mazarinades*:

ces nouueaux monstres, ou plustost ses [sic] nouuelles bestes deuorantes, dont on auoit point encore oüy parler dans nos Histoires.[9]

There are, however, no examples in the characterization of peasant or popular speech in Molière's *Dom Juan* or in Cyrano de Bergerac's *Le Pédant joué*. There is a lone example in a letter by La Fontaine to Maucroix dated 1661 (Haase 1898: 265):

Je ne puis te rien dire de ce que tu m'as écrit sur mes affaires, mon cher ami; elles me touchent pas tant que le malheur qui vient d'arriver au surintendant.

An isolated example is also found in a letter by Mme de Châtillon dated 30 December 1678; note how there are two occurrences of *ne* with *pas/point* just before the key clause which uses *pas* alone:

Sy lon na point de vos nouuelles lonne poura pas resister aux offres ci avantaguese que lanvoie de lampereur a faitte [. . .] je nous pouvay pas resister alanvie de vous enfaire part sans que je croye que tout vous est indiferant parce que dieu mercy le roy est audessus de tout et moi passionée. (Haase-Dubosc 1998: 72)

The only metalinguistic text of the century to mention the omission of *ne* is Maupas (1618: 168r–v), whose comments are repeated by Oudin (1632: 290). In both these texts the usage is considered a fault peculiar to foreigners (*i'ay rien fait*), and there is no indication as to whether native speakers also commit this error.

Given the paucity of this evidence it is interesting that it is precisely in the record of the usage of a child, Héroard's journal of the usage of Louis XIII aged between three and a quarter and nine and a quarter, that we find significant numbers of examples of the non-use of *ne* in negative statements. These include examples where it is clearly the predicate that is negated, and examples with both *pas* and *point* as the *forclusif*:

je veu point de cela (15 Jan. 1605)
je vous aime poin (10 Feb. 1607)
je veu pas (11 Jan. 1608)
je sui pa beau (10 Jan. 1609).

Prüssmann-Zemper (1986) found that of 1551 instances of negative constructions (this includes interrogatives), 966, or some 62%, do not include *ne*. Clearly there are linguistic features which help determine the likelihood of the use or

[9] *La Promenade ou les entretiens d'vn Gentil-homme de Normandie avec vn Bourgeois de Paris, sur le mauuais mesnage des Finances de France* (Paris, 1649, Cambridge University Library Ggg.22[15], p. 7). It is perhaps significant here that the *point* could be interpreted as modifying the following adverb, *encore*, rather than the predicate as a whole. The same is true of the examples from La Fontaine below. See Ayres-Bennett 1994: 69–70.

Table 5.1 *Non-use of* ne

Héroard's data for the Dauphin Year/Approximate Age	Percentage of non-use	Pohl's data Age	Percentage of non-use
1605/aged 3¼–4¼	48%		
1606/aged 4¼–5¼	79%		
1607/aged 5¼–6¼	77%	aged 5–6	81.5%
1608/aged 6¼–7¼	62%	aged 6½	75.3%
1609/aged 7¼–8¼	67%		
1610/aged 8¼–9¼	50%		
1611/aged 9¼–10¼	44%		
		aged 12	60.6%

non-use of *ne* (choice of *forclusif*, type of clause, tense employed, pronoun selected, verb type; see Ayres-Bennett 1994: 73), but the most interesting parameter of variation is undoubtedly that of age. Studies of contemporary French indicate that it is a typical feature of children's language to omit negative *ne*. Pohl suggests that the non-use of *ne* is virtually categorical up to the age of three or more (Pohl 1968). He further investigated the acquisition of negative statements by a twin boy and girl from the ages of five and a half to twelve (Pohl 1972), data which in a sense are broadly comparable to that of Héroard. Any similarity in the data might then suggest that we are dealing with a case of stable variation and that for nearly 400 years children have always tended to use the *ne* less than their adult counterparts.

Pohl's data confirm that it took the twins several years to acquire the *ne*, influenced by schooling, parental 'correction' and the influence of the written language. It is instructive to set Pohl's data (1972)[10] on *ne* omission in the usage of the twins beside those of Prüssmann-Zemper's figures (1986: 93) for the Dauphin (see Table 5.1). If we set aside the figures for 1605 and 1609 there is the same steady increase in the use of *ne* by the Dauphin as he matures linguistically, although at a faster rate than with Pohl's children. These data must be interpreted with extreme care, since we are uncertain about the reliability of Héroard's transcription and because we do not have comparable data for the adults in his corpus, whose speech he did not transcribe with the same attention. Of course, these data also do not prove that the age grading found in a number of corpora of contemporary French does not represent change in progress (see Armstrong and Smith 2002); indeed there is considerable evidence to suggest that the change is occurring in the contemporary language, not least that afforded by Ashby's study in 'real time'. However, the evidence from the seventeenth

---

[10] Note that there is some difference in the rate of usage of *ne* by the male and the female twin, but the overall trend for both children is the same.

century should make us wary of a simplistic interpretation of data in apparent time.

Very few of the writers on the French language specifically relate change to differences in the usage of different generations. In our main corpus of *remarqueurs* there are just four observations which make this link. First, Vaugelas (1647: 534) argues that the use of *fuir* followed by *de* is 'ancienne', 'ne l'ayant iamais entendu dire qu'à des gens fort vieux'. Secondly, Alemand (1688: 173) writes of the use of *aucunement* in the sense of *nullement*, that although it is supported by Pellisson 'il n'est pas pour cela sans adversaires, puisqu'il y en a beaucoup qui ne peuvent souffrir ce mot que dans la bouche des sexagenaires, & à la verité ce terme est bien suranné'. Similarly, he attributes the use of *faire des complimens de condoleance* to octogenarian speakers (1688: 403–4). Finally, Andry de Boisregard (1693: 31) says of *bref*: 'Je pardonnerois à un homme de quatre-vingts ans, qui depuis plus de cinquante années n'auroit veu le monde, de s'étonner qu'on luy dît que *bref* n'est plus bon aujourd'huy pour *enfin*; c'est pourtant dequoy s'étonne un de mes Critiques.' Callières (1693: 7–8, 10–11, 101) refers on three occasions to the use of young people in negative terms: the young at court are said to employ a jargon which comprises new words and expressions. It is perhaps significant, however, that one of the examples he cites is *un joly homme* (see section 4.6.3), which he considers 'puerile'. Irson (1662: 208) apparently associates the usage of young people with that of women, for example both groups are said to introduce excessive passages of direct speech into narratives.

In the case studies – and particularly as regards the positioning of clitic pronouns – some attempt has been made to see whether change can be seen to be occurring in the differing usages of the generations. I have also attempted to look at the relationship between 'change in apparent time' and 'change in real time' by comparing the differences in usage between authors of different generations with the changing usage of the same author over his lifetime (see section 5.4.1).

5.4   Case studies

5.4.1   Introduction

The multiplicity of references to changing usage in the seventeenth century makes it difficult to treat this comprehensively in the way we have analysed the references to women's usage in the seventeenth century. This is, of course, particularly true of the lexis. For example, according to the 'Champion Électronique' version of the French Academy's dictionaries (1687–1798), there are at least eleven different formulations for referring to the currency of usage of a particular word or expression, including:

- il n'a guere d'usage
- il n'est en usage qu(')(e)
- il n'a plus guere d'usage
- il n'a d'usage qu(')(e)
- il est aussi en usage
- il n'est guere en usage qu(')(e)
- ce terme n'a d'usage qu(')(e)
- son plus grand usage est
- vieux mot qui n'est plus en usage
- il vieillit
- en ce sens il est vieux

The phrase *guere en usage* occurs 184 times in the 1694 edition and *il vieillit* 109 times. If we were to add to these the formulae used to identify new words and expressions in all our dictionaries, the number and range of references would be vast. For this reason I decided not to examine the lexical examples, but rather to concentrate on three different case studies: the variation between [o]/[u] in pronouncing words such as *chose*; verb morphology; and word order.

5.4.2   Corpus of texts

I decided to focus on usage in three chronological tranches: 1600–19, 1640–59 and 1680–99. The choice of the first period was based on Vaugelas's attitude towards authors writing in the period 1600–20 and belonging to an earlier generation, and on Caron's and Matoré's belief that 1620 somehow constitutes a turning point. The other periods were selected following the *remarqueurs* who argue that change occurs over a period of twenty-five to thirty years and Matoré's division of the history of French into tranches of thirty to thirty-six years. Moreover, Vaugelas clearly considered the usage of writers in the 1640s different from that of our first period, just as Alemand views the usage of his contemporaries in the 1680s as distinct from that of the 'demi-Modernes'.

In each of these three periods, I selected three translations, one by an author aged about thirty, one by an author in his mid-forties and a third by an author aged sixty or over. By looking at the author's date of birth and age at publication of the selected text, I was able to test to some extent the validity of Rickard's assertion that authors born around 1630 inherited a different norm from those born at the end of the sixteenth century:

Thus educated Frenchmen who as children had inherited the language as it was at the end of the sixteenth century, and who acquired their linguistic habits during their formative years, might understandably have some reservations, later in life, about the state of the language in the 1630's; might, indeed actively resist certain changes then in progress. Those born around 1630, on the other hand, inherited a somewhat different norm and, as the language continued to move on, acquired somewhat different linguistic habits and prejudices, but they too, in their turn, might later prove reactionary when faced with new developments. (Rickard 1992: 3)

For the principal corpus I selected translations, for a number of reasons. For many of the leading writers on the French language, translation was viewed as a kind of 'grammaire appliquée'. For example, when asked by his friends to produce a grammar of French, Malherbe referred them to his translation of the thirty-third book of Livy, which he viewed as the model of good French writing. Likewise, Vaugelas's translation of Quintus Curtius Rufus' *Vie d'Alexandre* was considered a model of prose style well into the eighteenth century (see Ayres-Bennett and Caron 1996). Translations are extensively cited by writers on the French language. For instance, Seijido (2001) demonstrates how Andry de Boisregard (1689, 1693) depends heavily on translations in the citations supporting his observations; for example, Perrot d'Ablancourt's translations are cited more than seventy times in the 1689 work, while Vaugelas's *Quinte-Curce* is cited more than fifty times in 1693. In order to examine the link between theory and practice, many of the translations I selected are by authors who also wrote or commented extensively on the French language – Malherbe, Vaugelas, Charpentier and Andry de Boisregard.[11] It should be remembered that in the middle of the century the prevailing ethos of translators was that enunciated by d'Ablancourt in the Preface to his translation of Tacitus' *Annales*:

Le moyen d'arriver à la gloire de son original, n'est pas de le suivre pas à pas, mais de chercher les beautez de la langue, comme il a fait celles de la sienne: En un mot, ne pas tant regarder à ce qu'il a dit, qu'à ce qu'il faut dire, et considerer plus son but que ses paroles. (Zuber 1972: 128–9)

The favour of freedom in their translations earned d'Ablancourt and his followers' translations the soubriquet 'belles infidèles'.

In order to allow broad comparability in the size of each text in the corpus, a section of approximately 7,000 words was selected, the total size of Malherbe's translation of 1615. I therefore selected the passages detailed in Figure 5.1.

5.4.3 *Pronunciation*

There are some thirty comments on changing pronunciation made by the *remarqueurs* compared to just one on spelling.[12] Ménage's observations contain by far the largest number of comments on changes in the pronunciation of French. The discussion of changes in pronunciation illustrates all too well the difficulties

---

[11] Charpentier was the author of a *Deffense de la langue françoise, pour l'Inscription de l'Arc de Triomphe* (1676) and of *De l'excellence de la langue françoise* (1683).

[12] Ménage (1675: 577) notes the change of spelling from *cest* to *cet* which is a better representation of its pronunciation.

Date of publication of text	Author	Year of birth	Text selected	Age at publication (or at death if work published posthumously)
1615	François de Malherbe	1555	*Les Decades qui se trouuent de Tite-Liue en francois [...]*, Book 33, Paris: La Veufue l'Angelier (unpaginated)	60
1615/1621*	Nicolas Coëffeteau	1574	*Histoire romaine [...]*, Paris: S. Cramoisy, chapters 1-15	41/47
1615	Claude Favre de Vaugelas	1585	*Les Sermons de Fonseque [...]*, Paris: R. Thierry & E. Foucault, pp. 1-29	30
1653/1659†	Claude Favre de Vaugelas	1585	1653: *Quinte-Curce, De la vie et des actions d'Alexandre le Grand*, Paris: A Courbé, pp. 505-31; 1659: [...] *Troisiesme Edition. Sur une nouuelle Copie de l'Autheur*, Paris: A Courbé, pp. 501-29	d. 1650 aged 65
1652	Nicolas Perrot d'Ablancourt	1606	*Les Commentaires de Cesar*, Paris: A. Courbé, pp. 155-85	46
1650	François Charpentier	1620	*Les Choses memorables de Socrate [...]*, Paris: A. Courbé, pp. 1-55	30
1686 [¹1685]	Isaac Le Maistre de Sacy	1613	*Le Deuteronome traduit en François [...]*, Paris: G. Desprez, pp. 1-92	d. 1684 aged 71
1699	André Dacier	1651	*Les Œuvres de Platon traduites en françois*, Paris: J. Anisson, pp. 499-532	48
1687	Nicolas Andry de Boisregard	1658	*Panégyrique de l'empereur Théodose [...]*, Paris: J. Langlois, pp. 1-72	29

of separating out the different parameters of variation at this period. Included in the words whose pronunciation is said to be evolving are those containing 'oi' (e.g. *plier/ployer/pléer* (Ménage 1675: 68), *roine/reine* (Ménage 1675: 70), *noyer/neier* (Ménage 1675: 280–1), see above, section 3.3.3) and 'ar'/'er' (e.g. *guarir/guerir* (Vaugelas 1647: 250), *S. Merri/S. Marri* (Ménage 1675: 91), see section 4.6.6 (c)). This reflects both the lack of attention paid by some commentators to the exact nature of the variation – the main factor simply being that the usage is to be avoided – and the close interaction of the different parameters, as I have already suggested above.

As ever, it is often difficult or impossible to find traces of pronunciation habits reflected in the spelling of texts. For example, Vaugelas refers to a number of instances where a consonant which was formerly syncopated has recently begun to be pronounced. His examples include the [l] of *plus* (1647: 230), the medial [s] of *satisfaction* (1647: 157), and the first [r] of *arbre, marbre* (1647: 423); Andry de Boisregard (1689: 235) adds the [r] of *fronde*. In none of these cases is the spelling anything but the standard form in the F R A N T E X T corpus, making it impossible to determine whether the alternative pronunciations were current.

In this section we will focus on one feature of variation of pronunciation which is represented, at least to some degree, in the spelling of texts: the so-called 'ouiste' debate, that is the choice of 'o' [o] or 'u' [u] in tonic or pre-tonic position. According to Thurot (1881–3: I, 240) usage was very divided between 'o' [o] and 'ou' [u] in the sixteenth century in a large number of words (for example *chose/chouse, arroser/arrouser*), and a quarrel developed between those who favoured [u] – termed the *ouistes* – and those promoting [o] – the *non-ouistes*. Many of the sixteenth-century commentators associate the variation with a regional difference. For example, Bovelles (1533) claims that 'ou' is typical of Orléanais, Touraine and Anjou, while 'o' is the northern form, citing *chose, Josse,* and *gros.* Bèze (1584) describes the 'ou' pronunciation as a feature of Bourges or Lyon, while Peletier (1549) maintains that pronunciations such as *troup, noustres, coute, clous* are typical of certain regions 'comme de la

---

Figure 5.1 Corpus of translations

* The translation of Florus's *Histoire romaine* (1615) was later incorporated into Coëffeteau's *Histoire romaine* (1621) without reworking. The work is cited from the 1621 text.

† I have compared the first edition (1653) with the third edition (1659), said to be substantially revised on the basis of a new manuscript and to reflect Vaugelas's latest version before his death in 1650. For the complex history of the translation on which Vaugelas worked for some thirty years of his life, see Ayres-Bennett 1987.

Gaule Narbonnoèse, Lionnoèse é de quélques androèz de l'Aquitéine' (Thurot 1881–3: I, 240–2). Commentators in the second half of the sixteenth century, however, including Henri Estienne (1578) and Tabourot (1587), identify the pronunciation of 'ou' for 'o' in such words as *chouse, j'ouse, repous, grous* as typical of courtiers, and this evaluation is repeated by Palliot in 1608.

In the seventeenth century many of the metalinguistic texts consider the variation between [o] and [u] in terms of changing usage; they note that change has occurred or is occurring and assert that [u] for [o] is no longer acceptable. Thus while in 1604 Du Val simply states that 'o' before 'mm' or 'nn' is pronounced 'ou' in words such as *comme, pomme, homme, somme, bonne* and *personne*, Maupas (1618: 9v–10r) regrets the spread of this pronunciation in contexts where the following consonant is not a nasal:

Le son de cette voyelle ['o'] est assez notoire. Depuis peu en ça on affecte une niaise & vicieuse prononciation en ce mot Chose, & dit-on *Chouse*; autres *Cheuse*, ce que ie n'approuve. Ie sçay que Monsieur de Ronsard en un endroit dit *Chouse*, & en un autre *Compousa*, Mais c'est par une licence Poeticque, avec evidente necessité de la rime [...] Car en mille endroits ailleurs il dit chose, & composer.

Furthermore, while he notes that *homme, comme*, etc. are pronounced as if they were written with a 'u', he excludes from this tendency words which are formed with the prefix *pro-*, words borrowed from Greek, and many words from Latin which retain their learned form (e.g. *homicide, domicile, donation*). By the time of Oudin (1632: 9) not only is *chouse* condemned, he also criticizes *houme, coume*, and *boune*, which he argues are never used by those who speak well.[13]

However, relatively few texts refer to the question in very general terms; for example, the 'ouiste' debate is not alluded to by Simon (1609), L'Esclache (1668) or Lartigaut (1669). It is much more common, especially after Oudin, for the discussion to revolve around the correct pronunciation and spelling of individual words; for instance Hindret (1687) mentions the variation between [o] and [u] only tangentially in his 'Discours sur le sujet de cette Metode', when he lists *un houme* for *un homme* amongst the faulty pronunciations heard at court and in Paris. Likewise Irson (1662: 136–7) includes a number of examples of this variation in his list of words whose pronunciation is doubtful (*arroser, chose, homme, Pentecôte, portrait*) without stating a general principle. Thurot details thirty-six seventeenth-century texts in which words which alternated between [ɛ] and [u] are discussed, including seven grammars published in France (1604–94), six published abroad (1632–96), eight collections of observations (1647–90), four works on orthography (1608–50) and five dictionaries (1606–94) (see Ayres-Bennett 1990: 160–1).

---

[13] Lainé (1655: 22) is also critical of this pronunciation.

Brunot (1905–53: IV, 177) asserts that the pronunciation of *ou* and *u* became more distinct in the course of the century and that the variation was eliminated for the majority of words – about sixty words in the period between the publication of Oudin's grammar (1632) and the second edition of the French Academy dictionary (1718) – if not always consistently (e.g. *porter* but *tourment*). It is striking that in the later part of the century (from Duez's grammar onwards), as one variant came to be accepted as the correct version, the variation is again no longer described in terms of chronology, but other explanations for it are adduced. For example, variants may be attributed to different specialist groups of users (Richelet claims that *cossin* is used by gilders on copper whereas the best speakers use *coussin*), or to be associated with class differences (Richelet claims that the common people use *norriture*, and that *honnêtes gens* favour the forms with [u]). Duez's condemnation (1669: 25–6) is very strong; he asserts that *chouse* is pronounced out of a pure desire for novelty by courtiers, who like pregnant women have unusual cravings, but that the older pronunciation is much better.[14]

A number of words, in which alternative pronunciations with [u] or [o] were used, are discussed by Vaugelas under the headings *Portrait, pourtrait* (1647: 340–1) and *Arroser* (219). He favours *portrait* and *arroser*, although he admits that the majority of people say and write *pourtrait* and *arrouser*. According to him, *o* had for a long time been pronounced as *ou* in words such as *chouse*, *fouβé* and *cousté*, but in the last ten to twelve years these pronunciations, and *chouse* and *fouβé* in particular, had become unacceptable. He argues that poets never rhymed *chose* or *arroser* with *jalouse*.[15] The recent nature of the change is perhaps confirmed by the fact that neither of these observations appears in the Arsenal manuscript, which represents an earlier stage in the genesis of the work.

Vaugelas's observations are much commented on by subsequent writers on the French language (Streicher 1936: 428–31, 581–3). On *portrait/pourtrait* Dupleix recommends *pourtrait* as the form most used, and argues that this is a different question from the pronunciations *chouse, foussé* and *arrouser* which are no longer current forms. Corneille agrees that some people still use *pourtrait*, but that this is not to be recommended, whereas the pronunciations *chouse* and *foussé* have long disappeared from usage.[16] The Academy is in general against the pronunciations with [u], but apparently hesitates as to whether the unacceptable form, *arrouser*, is still sometimes heard. The longest discussion is found in Ménage's first volume of observations (1675: 180–2): he lists twenty-nine

---

[14] 'eine lautere blinde begierde einiger newigkeit etlicher hoffleuten / vnd anderer ihres gleichen / welche / nicht anders als schwangere weiber / offtmals sich wunderliche vnd vngereimte sachen gelüsten lassen'.

[15] On the question of rhymes, see Straka 1985: 90–6.

[16] For his comment on *norrir* for *nourrir*, see section 4.6.6 (c).

words where the correct pronunciation is [o] and twenty-three where the recommended form has [u]. Significantly, however, he includes eleven words where
the pronunciation is still uncertain, suggesting that in the 1670s there was
still some variation. A sample of fourteen of these is considered in Table 5.2:
ten where Ménage considers the established form to have [o] (*arroser, portrait, porfil, froment, profit, alose, chose, fossé, pommade, porcelaine*), two
where [u] is fixed (*fourmi, tourment*) and two which he still considers doubtful
(*Pentecoste/Pentecouste, poteaux/pouteaux*). In each case the changing usage
of these terms is tracked by comparing usage in the various dictionaries and in
the corpus of texts of FRANTEXT.

In the case of the first five examples in Table 5.2 the evidence of the metalinguistic texts and of FRANTEXT for the most part clearly confirms a change
from [u] being favoured to [o] becoming firmly established. In the case of (4)
and (5) examples in the FRANTEXT corpus of the form with [u] are restricted
to the first two decades of the century, while in the case of (1) and (2) there is
an obvious preponderance of examples from the first half of the century. Only
in the case of (3) is the textual evidence less conclusive. In the case of the dictionaries, R frequently records the modern usage, while Cotgrave still includes
the variants.

In the case of examples (6)–(11) the dictionaries almost always simply record
the form with [o]; this is again supported by the evidence from FRANTEXT,
where only in the case of *chouse* are there any examples of forms spelt with
'ou' (1610–36). Example (12) is similar in the clear preponderance of forms
spelt 'o'. The opposite case is illustrated by example (13) where – with the
exception again of Cotgrave – 'ou' is consistently attested. Finally example
(14) illustrates a case where 'ou' becomes established. All the examples of
torment in FRANTEXT date from 1620–30, whereas examples of *tourment*
cover the whole century.

There is very little evidence of the variation between [o] and [u] in the corpus
of translations. For the texts dating from 1600–19 the only form worthy of note is
prouffitable (Vaugelas 1615: 16); otherwise Vaugelas favours the modern forms
nourrice, colombes, soleil etc. In the other two periods, there is no evidence
from the spelling of non-standard pronunciations: for instance, we find *arrosée,
tourner, pourceaux, homme, costau* and *profit* in the texts from 1640–59.

The evidence from Héroard suggests that spelling may to some extent have
masked variant pronunciations. Ernst (1985: 35) records a number of occasions
where today's [o] or [ɔ] are written *ou* or less often *u* as in *doun (donc), boune,
toumbé, roumpu, couchon* and *pou(r)t(r)ai(t)*. The reverse is rare, although
porceau is attested. This would seem to confirm the association of the variation
with court usage, made not only by grammarians (see above), but also by
satirists. The following lines are cited by Rosset (1911: 367) from *Le Satyre de
la Cour* (1624):

Table 5.2 *Variation [o]/[ou]*

	Estienne 1549	Nicot 1606	Cotgrave 1611	Richelet 1680	Furetière 1690	Academy 1694	FRANTEXT
1. arroser/ arrouser	arrouser	arrouser	arrouser (*arroser*, given cross-reference, 'as *arrouser*')	arroser, arrosoir	arroser, arrosoir (but *arrouser* used on five occasions in definitions)	arroser, arrosoir	There are ninety-three examples of *arrouser* in the corpus, compared to thirty of *arroser*. However, eighty-nine of the examples of *arrouser* date from before 1650, and there are only two examples from the 1650s and one from the 1660s. On the other hand, there are examples of *arroser* from 1615 to 1699 with twelve examples dating from the 1690s
2. portrait/ pourtrait	pourtraict	pourtraict	pourtraict	portrait	portrait	portrait	There are 136 examples of *pourtrai(c)t* in FRANTEXT, of which 134 occur before 1650. This compares with 879 examples of *portrai(c)t*, which cover the period 1604 to 1699. (This includes N and V examples)

Table 5.2 (cont.)

	Estienne 1549	Nicot 1606	Cotgrave 1611	Richelet 1680	Furetière 1690	Academy 1694	FRANTEXT
3. porfil/ profil/pourfil	pourfil	pourfil	pourfil (*porfil* as *pourfil*)	profil	profil 'on disoit autrefois *porfil*'	profil	There are four examples of *porfil* (1609–67) with a predominance of satirical and burlesque texts. There are two examples of *profil* from the 1670s and one of *pourfil* (1648) plus an occurrence of both in La Bruyère (1696) where he comments explicitly on changes of usage: 'Profil de pourfil'
4. froment/ froument	froument (*fourment cherchez froument*)	froument as head word, but froment used nineteen times in definitions	froment (*froment see froument*)	froment 'Quelques auteurs du premier ordre ont écrit *froument* pour *froment*, mais l'usage n'est pas pour eux, on dit, & on écrit *froment*'	froment	froment	*Froment* occurs 137 times in the corpus (1601–96) whereas there are only two examples of *froument* (1607, 1610) plus the explicit comment by La Bruyère on changing usage: 'froment de froument'

5. profit/ prouf(f)it	proufit 'Semble qu'on doibt escrire Profict, parce qu'il uient de Profectus' (profict voyez prouffict)	prouffit (On deuroit escrire Profict, par ce qu'il viêt de Profectus'; (profict voyez prouffict, but seventy-two occurrences of profit in the definitions)	profit and prouffit both as headwords, but two occurrences of prouffit versus ninety-one of profit	profit	profit	profit	There are 1022 examples of profit(c)t and forty-nine examples of prouffit(c)t (1601–99). There are four examples of prouffit (1610–25) plus an explicit comment on change by La Bruyère: 'profit de prouffit', and nine examples of prouffit all by François de Sales (1619)
6. alose/ alouse	alose	alose	alose	alose	alose	alose	There are no attestations of either form in FRANTEXT
7. chose/ chouse	chose	chose	chose	chose	chose	chose	There are only ten examples of chouse compared to 17,448 examples of chose; the examples of chouse appear in texts published between 1610 and 1636
8. Pentecoste/ Pentecouste	Pentecoste	Pentecoste	–	Pentecôte	Pentecôte	Pentecoste	Neither of these forms is attested
9. fossé/ foussé	fossé	fossé	fossé	fossé	fossé	fossé	There are no examples of foussé in FRANTEXT; fossé is attested on 233 occasions

(cont.)

Table 5.2 (cont.)

	Estienne 1549	Nicot 1606	Cotgrave 1611	Richelet 1680	Furetière 1690	Academy 1694	FRANTEXT
10. pommade/ poumade	–	–	pommade	pommade	pommade	pommade	*Pommade* is attested twenty-five times (1603–96); there are no examples of *poumade*
11. po(s)teau/ pou(s)teau	posteau	posteau	posteau (*pousteau* as *posteau*)	poteau	posteau	poteau	There are seventeen examples of *po(s)teau* (1620–96); *pou(s)teau* is not attested
12. porcelaine/ pourcelaine	porcelaine (*pourcelaine cherchez porcelaine*)	porcelaine (*pourcelaine cherchez porcelaine*)	pourcelaine (*porcelaine as pourcelaine*)	'porcelaine, pourcelaine. L'un & l'autre se dit, mais le premier est le plus usité'	'*Porcelaine*. Quelques-uns prononcent *Pourcelaine*'	porcelaine (*pourcelaine* occurs twice in the definitions)	There are only three examples of *pourcelaine* in the corpus, all dating from the first half of the century; *porcelaine* is attested fifty-one times (1619–98)
13. formi/ fourmi	fourmi	fourmi	fourmi (*formi* like *fourmi*)	fourmi	fourmi	fourmi	There are seventeen examples of *fourmi* (1615–94); *formi* is not attested
14. torment/ tourment	torment	torment (one of the examples under this heading is *estant en tourmant*)	tourment ('tormant . . . Looke Tourment')	tourment	tourment	tourment	There are sixteen examples of *torment*, all dating from 1620–30; this compares with 808 examples of *tourment* (1601–99).

Il faut, quiconque veut estre mignon de court
Gouverner son langage à la mode qui court.
Qui ne prononce pas *il diset, chouse, vandre,*
Parest, contantemans, fût-il un Alexandre,
S'il hante quelquefois avec un courtisan,
Sans doute qu'on dira que c'est un paysan.

As usage of [u] for [o] declined, this variant seems, however, to have acquired a different sociolinguistic marking. Once the pronunciation of the doubtful words became fixed, the use of the non-standard variable became identified as the province of the illiterate. The *Agréables Conférences* (1649–51) therefore include frequent examples both of 'ou' for 'o' (*counesson* ('connaissons'), *propou* ('propos'), *noute* ('notre')) and of 'o' for 'u' (*cos* ('coups'), *co* ('cou'), *norri* ('nourri')) in order to characterize peasant speech (Wüest 1985, Rosset 1911).

5.4.4 Verb morphology

There are nineteen observations devoted to changing morphology in our corpus of *remarques* of which ten concern verb morphology. Whereas at the beginning of the century the co-existing variants are listed in the grammars, frequently without comment as to their relative currency, as the century progresses there is an increasing tendency to eliminate one or more of the variants and to establish one form as the prestige form. For example, Maupas (1618) generally lists the alternatives without placing them in any hierarchy of acceptability. This is true of seven of the ten questions:
- First person singular present indicative of *aller*: *Ie vay, vais* ou *vois*
- Third person singular present subjunctive of *avoir*: *il ait & il aye*
- Third person plural *passé simple* of *prendre*: *ils prindrent & prirent*
- Third person singular and plural present subjunctive of *dire*: *il dise/die*; *ils disent/dient*
- Past participle of the verb *mordre*: *mors/mordu*
- Infinitive form of *courir*: *courir/courre*
- Present participle of *seoir*: *séant/siésant*.

Of the other three topics, there is no mention as to the correct form of the future of *envoyer* (*enverray/envoyeray*). Only in two cases is a preference expressed over the variants:
- Third person plural *passé simple* of *venir/tenir*: only *ils vindrent* is listed
- Misuse of *recouvrir* for *recouvrer*, especially the past participle *recouvert* for *recouvré*.

The position has already changed by Oudin (1632), where in only three of the nine questions discussed are the co-variants listed without comment (*il ait/aye*; *il dise/die*; *courrir* [sic]/*courre*). Oudin (1632: 157) reports the use of *recouvrir* for *recouvrer*, which he terms an abuse but does not condemn since it is a feature of the usage of even good modern authors. In the case of the other questions a clear preference is expressed, although not always in favour of the form which was to triumph; alternatively, one of the forms may be strongly condemned:

- *Ie vay*: 'Ie *vas* & *vois*, pour la premiere personne ne sont aucunement en vsage parmi ceux qui parlent bien' (Oudin 1632: 153)
- *Prirent* & non *prindrent* (1632: 178)
- *Mordu*: '*mors* pour *mordu* n'est gueres receuable' (1632: 175)
- '*Siesant*, ne se trouue point' (1632: 167)
- '*Tindrent*, & non pas *tinrent*' (1632: 162).

By the time of Irson (1662), who only deals with seven of the topics, grammarians generally come down in favour of the modern form without comment (*ait*, *tinrent/vinrent*, *prirent*, *mordu*, *courir*). Only in the case of *ie vas/ie vais* and *ils disent/ils dient* are variants noted.[17]

I now intend to consider each of these topics in more detail, setting side by side the comments of the *remarqueurs* and usage in the FRANTEXT corpus, the corpus of translations, and the dictionaries where appropriate.[18]

(a)   recouvert *for* recouvré

In contrast with some of the other topics discussed below, the use of *recouvert* for *recouvré* appears to have been a topic of uncertainty for much of the seventeenth century. Vaugelas (1647: 15) suggests that this usage dates from Desportes, who used *recouvert* in order to achieve the correct rhyme. Dupleix (Streicher 1936: 23) typically condemns this as a usage favoured only by those at court who are not well read, while Ménage (1675: 463–5) agrees that it is a recent development, but argues that it did not originate in Desportes's poetry, citing an example from Henri Estienne dated 1579. Ménage argues that this was a usage of the royal court of Estienne's day, just as it is of the contemporary court: 'Ce qui a fait préférer à M. de Vaugelas avec raison, dans une Lettre, ou dans quelque autre petite piéce, *j'ay recouvert* à *j'ay recouvré*.' In his opinion, in a longer work the two forms may be used interchangeably, and he cites examples of usage from the law courts. Patru gives earlier examples of the use of *recouvert* for *recouvré* but denies that the forms may be used interchangeably, as does Corneille. Andry de Boisregard (1689: 539) likewise argues that *recouvré* should be used, while conceding that some people use *recouvert*, citing an example from Bouhours.

---

[17] Schmitt (2002) looks at a corpus of grammars written by foreigners and argues that these works are less normative and therefore a better source of information about linguistic variation than their Parisian counterparts. However, this contention does not seem to be borne out in the case of the ten questions we are discussing.

[18] As Wolf (1991) observes, usage of *recouvert* for *recouvré* and of *je vas* for *je vais* have continued in Canadian French. On the variation between *vas*, *vais* and *m'as* as the first person singular of *aller* used in the compound future in the French of Quebec, see Mougeon 1996.

Indeed Bouhours in his *Suite* (1693: 161ff.) asserts that the form is more used than it was in Vaugelas's day. Tallemant (1698) also concedes that *recouvert* 'a quelque usage', but considers it a fault to be avoided, while the Academy is adamant in its condemnation of this, even in its legal usage (Streicher 1936: 28). Not surprisingly there are no attestations of either *recouvert* or *recouvré* in our corpus of translations. R comments under the heading *recouvrir*: 'j'ai recouvert [. . .] ce mot recouvert signifie aussi recouvré, acquis de nouveau' and refers to Vaugelas's *Remarques*. F, on the other hand, cites only an example from the usage of the law courts of *recouvert* being used with the sense of *recouvrer*. In FRANTEXT there are ninety-five examples of *recouvré* compared with just twelve of *recouvert*; of these twelve examples seven have the sense of *recouvrer*. They date from between 1623 and 1686.

(b)   il aye / il ait
Vaugelas (1647: 90) records a change in usage, arguing that *aye* used to be a third person form, but that it has become an exclusively first person subjunctive. Both Thomas Corneille and the French Academy, commenting on Vaugelas's observation, make it clear that many people continue to use *il aye* despite their condemnation of the form; the Academicians suggest this is perhaps through a false analogy with other third person singular present subjunctive forms which for the most part end in *-e* (Streicher 1936: 177). There are no occurrences of either form in our corpus of translations, but the FRANTEXT corpus confirms the durability of *qu'il aye* as a minor variant as late as 1682. There are forty-eight examples of this dating from 1601–82, forty-two of which date from the first half of the century; this compares with 715 examples of of *qu'il ait (ayt)*, which cover the whole century.

(c)   ils vinrent / ils vindrent; ils tinrent/ ils tindrent
Discussing *vinrent* and *vindrent*, Vaugelas (1647: 97) argues that they are both acceptable, but that *vinrent* is preferable and more used. Whereas Malherbe used *vindrent*, Coëffeteau favoured *vinrent*, and this is the form used by all the court and all modern authors. All subsequent commentators are adamant that *vindrent*, etc. has totally disappeared from usage, and only *vinrent* is current (Ménage 1675: 518; Patru, Corneille, the Academy in Streicher 1936: 194). In our corpus of translations Malherbe does indeed use *vindrent*. Coëffeteau, however, in spite of Vaugelas's claims to the contrary, also employs *vindrent*, *soustindrent*, *deuindrent*. This contrasts with d'Ablancourt's and Le Maistre de Sacy's usage of *deuinrent* and *vinrent*. While there are similar numbers of attestations of *vinrent* (296 occurrences) and *vindrent* (291 occurrences) in the FRANTEXT corpus for the seventeenth century, their chronological distribution is significant. The latest attestation of *vindrent* is 1664 and 266 of the examples of this form date from before 1640; this confirms Ménage's claim that this form

was still current in Vaugelas's day but had completely disappeared by the 1670s. Likewise, there are forty-three occurrences of *tinrent* compared to thirty-six of *tindrent*; the latest example of the latter is 1646.

(d)   ils prinrent / ils prindrent / ils prirent

Vaugelas (1647: 98) maintains that the forms *print*, *prindrent* and *prinrent* are no longer current, although they were used by Malherbe; he claims that only *prit* and *prirent* are used, forms which are 'bien plus doux'. Ménage concurs, although he favours the spelling *prît* in the singular (Streicher 1936: 194).[19] Corneille notes that some people still use the form *aprint* in the provinces, but that it is incorrect, and the Academy agrees that only *prit* and *prirent* are to be employed (Streicher 1936: 194–5). The attestations in our corpus of translations and in F R A N T E X T confirm Vaugelas's chronology for change; of the translators only Malherbe uses *print*, *prindrent*. *Il print* is last attested in F R A N T E X T in 1637 (forty-one occurrences between 1601 and 1637), *ils prindrent* in 1627 (eight occurrences between 1601 and 1627) and there are no examples at all of *ils prinrent*. This contrasts with 452 examples of *il prit* (1601–99) and sixty-six examples of *ils prirent* (1601–99).

(e)   il die/il dise; ils dient/ils disent

This is an interesting example in that it is Dupleix (1651: 236–7), the most conservative of our *remarqueurs*, who records the recent demise of the present subjunctive forms *die*, *dient* in favour of *dise*, *disent*[20] whereas Vaugelas (1647: 349) considers that they may be used interchangeably. While Patru sees the difference between the two forms as one of currency, other commentators on Vaugelas adduce other parameters of variation to explain the distribution of their usage (Streicher 1936: 595–7). For Corneille the difference is one between poetry (*dise*) and prose (*die*), while Andry de Boisregard agrees that *je dise* is more used, but that both are equally good in poetry; in addition he notes that some people consider *je die* 'plus soûtenu' and therefore more suitable for a 'discours public'. By the time of the Academy's commentary on Vaugelas's *Remarques* even the use of *die* in poetry is considered archaic.[21] In the middle of the century d'Ablancourt (1652) uses *interdisent*. Once again the chronology of examples in F R A N T E X T is significant: *qu'il die* occurs twenty-one times, but the last attested example is 1654;[22] *qu'il dise* occurs twenty-four times, but the examples date from 1606 to 1698.

---

[19] Note that this observation is not found in the second edition of 1675.

[20] Le Vayer still prefers *die* to *dise*, although he concedes that 'Messieurs nos Maistres' use *dise*, *disent* (Streicher 1936: 595).

[21] Schmitt's data from grammars produced abroad confirm the change: while Bernard (1607) includes both forms, Wodroephe (1623) already favours *dise* and Mauger (1662) lists only this form.

[22] Straka (1985: 78) gives examples of *die* at the rhyme as late as the 1670s, but notes that Molière, for instance, uses *dise* in the 1660s.

(f)   je vais/je va/je vay/je vas/je vois

It is Bouhours (1675: 519) who, in the long observation devoted to recording changes since Vaugelas's *Remarques*, is the first *remarqueur* to note the evolution in the currency of the different variants for the first person singular present indicative of *aller*. In his opinion *je vais* and *je vas* are the current forms, and *je va* – the form favoured by Vaugelas as the one used at Court despite his recognition that 'tous ceux qui sçauent escrire, & qui ont estudié, disent, *ie vais*, & disent fort bien selon la Grammaire' (1647: 27)[23] – is no longer employed. Only Ménage (1675: 16–17) mentions *je vois* as a very old form used a long time ago; of the other four forms, *je va* and *je vay* are not well supported, but for much of the century both *je vas* and *je vais* are variously endorsed by the *remarqueurs* (see Table 5.3).

The currency of *je vas* as a minor variant in the latter decades of the century is confirmed both by the translations (Le Maistre de Sacy still uses *je vas, je m'en vas*) and by FRANTEXT. In our FRANTEXT corpus there are thirty-four examples of *je vas* compared to 791 examples of *je vais*, but these examples date from 1624 to 1696.[24] On the other hand, there are 349 occurrences of *je vay* (*je vai*); however, 95% of these occur before 1660, which perhaps explains why the form receives relatively little support from the *remarqueurs*.

(g)   mors/mordu; tors/tordu

Ménage (1675: 90) is the only *remarqueur* to discuss this topic. The old past participle *mors* is said to have been replaced by *mordu*; on the other hand, *tors* is current, although some are beginning to use *tordu*. Whereas Furetière only mentions *mordu* as the past participle of *mordre*, he includes both *tordu* and *tors* for *tordre* 'qui se disent en diverses occasions'. The Academy dictionary considers *tordu* to be a participle, and *tors* to be adjectival ('qui est tordu'). Of the grammars considered by Schmitt (2002) only La Faye (1613) mentions both *mordu* and *mors*. There are no examples of *mors* in FRANTEXT (there are eighteen of *mordu*), and one of the earliest translations (Vaugelas 1615) includes *mordu*. On the other hand there are four examples of *tors* as a past participle in FRANTEXT (1624–90) and two of *tordu* (1655, 1667).

(h)   j'enverray/j'envoyeray

The next two examples are cases where Andry de Boisregard (1689) is the first *remarqueur* to mention changing usage. His comment on the future of *envoyer* is very simple: 'Aujourd'hui on dit *j'enverray*, & non pas *j'envoyeray*'.

---

[23] Whereas Maupas (1618: 108r) gives *ie vay, vais* or *vois*, Oudin (1632: 153) lists only *ie vay* and specifically censures *ie vas, ie vois*. Vaugelas adds that there is a preference for each person of the verb to have a different form to avoid any ambiguity.

[24] There is only one example of *je va* (1625).

Table 5.3 *Va, vay, vas, vais*

	Vaugelas 1647	Bouhours 1675	Ménage 1675	Ménage (Streicher: Observations on Malherbe)	Patru	Corneille	Chapelain (recorded by Corneille)	Andry de Boisregard	Academy
va	✓ (court)	X	(Bourgogne)	X		X ('ne se dit plus')			X
vay			X ('anciennement')			(poetry)	✓	(used by Mlle de Scudéry)	
vas		✓	(favoured after *je vais*)	(can tolerate this form)	✓ ('plus usité')			✓	X
vais	(favoured by writers; considered provincial)	✓	✓	✓	(unacceptable in some places)		✓	✓	✓ (only)

The ticks refer to forms which are approved and the crosses to those which are criticized. Glosses on the appropriate uses of these and other forms are given in parentheses.

In FRANTEXT *j'envoyeray* (*j'envoyerai*) is attested 178 times and there are examples throughout the century (1610–92); this compares with forty-seven examples of *j'enverray* (*j'enverrai*), the first of which dates from 1635. There are no examples of either form in our corpus of translations.

(i)   courir/courre

Evaluating the currency of *courre* and *courir*, Andry de Boisregard (1689: 140) comments that the former was judged preferable by Voiture, but that the language has changed somewhat since then, and 'on ne doit pas tenir tout-à-fait à son sentiment'. His examples suggest that *courre* is increasingly becoming restricted to certain set contexts. For Vaugelas (1647: 256) this variation is not related to change. He argues that both are acceptable but that they have different uses. As regards the variants *courre fortune* or *courir fortune*, he asserts that Coëffeteau favoured the former, but Malherbe the latter (in the 1615 translation Malherbe uses *courir*); in his view it is the former construction which is more used. Dupleix unsurprisingly recommends freedom of choice between the variants, while Ménage supports Vaugelas's position. The Academy focuses its comments on particular expressions (Streicher 1936: 490–2). The case of *courre/courir fortune* is perhaps instructive. *Courre fortune* is attested seven times in FRANTEXT between 1620 and 1679; of the lexicographers only R mentions it. *Courir fortune* occurs fifteen times in FRANTEXT with a not dissimilar chronology (1601–78); it is also attested in Cotgrave and in A (under the headword *courir, courre*).

(j)   séant

According to Tallemant (1698: 160) *séant* from *seoir* is archaic and only appears as a noun or adjective (*en son séant, cela n'est pas séant*). This marks a change from the beginning of the century when *seant* is given for example by Du Val (1604: 237) as the only participle of the verb, and by Maupas alongside *siésant*. Tallemant's view of the evolving usage of *séant* is confirmed by usage in our FRANTEXT corpus. Of the seventy-seven examples of the form, only five are as a present participle and these date from 1603–20; in all the other examples it is either substantival or adjectival.[25]

Attitudes towards verb morphology are typical of the age: standardization aims to reduce the number of acceptable forms and limit variation. On the whole, we can see a clear evolution towards the establishment of one variant at the expense of the others. Occasionally there is a transitional period when one of the variants acquires a sociolinguistic marking (for example, *die* is associated with high-register usage as it begins to fall from usage), or the rejected variant

---

[25] It is particularly favoured in the expressions *bien(-)séant* and *mal(-)séant*.

Table 5.4 *Last attested usage of obsolescent verb forms*

Form	Decade of last attested usage in FRANTEXT
Ils prinrent	No examples
Mors	No examples
Ils prindrent	1620s
Je va	1620s (one isolated example for the whole century)
Séant (past participle)	1620s
Il print	1630s
Ils tindrent	1640s
Qu'il die	1650s
Ils vindrent	1660s (but 91% of examples date from before 1640)
Qu'il aye	1680s (but 88% of examples date from before 1650)
Recouvert for *recouvré*	1680s
Je vai/je vay	Still attested in the 1690s (but 95% of examples date from before 1660)
Je vas	Still attested in the 1690s
J'envoyeray/-ai	Still attested in the 1690s
Tors	Still attested in the 1690s

survives in certain restricted contexts (*courre*) or with a different grammatical function (*séant*).

Whilst in terms of the metalinguistic texts the 1630s and 1640s seem to mark a crucial point in the differentiation and thus eventual demise of one of the variants, especially with the work of Oudin and Vaugelas, it is less easy to apply the notion of a threshold between clear *chronolectes* in terms of textual usage. Indeed, the last attested usages in FRANTEXT are spaced throughout the decades of the century (Table 5.4).[26]

5.4.5   Word order: the position of clitic pronouns and negatives

The emphasis on greater syntactic clarity and regularity associated with seventeenth-century writers on the French language has been well documented. This desire to avoid any possible ambiguity requires, for example, the repetition of function markers in co-ordinated structures, the regular use of subject pronouns, and the correct use of syntactic agreement.[27] In this section we will concentrate on questions of word order and particularly on the position of pronouns in the construction Pronoun + Finite Verb + Infinitive (*je le veux faire*)

[26] *Courre* is excluded from this table since it survives in restricted contexts.
[27] Another major preoccupation in the metalinguistic texts is verb government.

versus Finite Verb + Pronoun + Infinitive (*je veux le faire*),[28] and the position of the negative particles (*ne . . . pas, point*, etc.) when used with an infinitive.

Before we turn to our two case studies, it is worth noting that Vaugelas in particular devotes some of his other observations to questions of evolving word order, underlining the importance for him of codifying clear and fixed orders. He comments, for example, on the changing order of accusative and dative pronouns from *je le vous promets* to *je vous le promets* (1647: 53–4). Although both Dupleix and La Mothe le Vayer disagree with this, the change is confirmed by Ménage (1675: 497) and by Andry de Boisregard (1689: 61–2). Similarly, he records the change from *il en y a* (not attested at all in our FRANTEXT corpus) to *il y en a* (1647: 94). He is also concerned with the correct positioning of a nominal subject with the verb *être* (1647: 342); he cites the examples *& fut son auis d'autant mieux receu* and *estant les broüillarts si espais*, which he considers to be 'à la vieille mode'.

(a)   *The position of clitic pronoun with a finite verb + infinitive:*
           the demise of clitic climbing

In a pioneering study, Galet (1971) traces the history of the change in French from Pronoun + Finite Verb + Infinitive, the only construction attested in Old French, to the modern ordering of Finite Verb + Pronoun + Infinitive. The first construction is said to show 'clitic climbing' by generative grammarians such as Kayne (1975): in this analysis the unstressed pronominal complements are basically introduced in post-verb position and are then cliticized by a movement transformation by which they 'climb' to the pre-verbal position. In the sixteenth century the older construction is still predominant: excluding those cases where the word order is influenced by the versification, it is used in 88% of possible constructions by Rabelais in his *Pantagruel* (1532), 100% by Du Bellay in *Les Regrets* (1558), 82% by Montaigne in his *Essais* (1572–87) and 77% by Régnier in his *Satyres* (1603–13) (Galet 1971: 48–54).

This question is different from the others so far discussed in this chapter in that it is the textual evidence which suggests changing usage rather than the meta-linguistic texts. Throughout the century grammarians and *remarqueurs* note the co-existence of the constructions and sometimes express a preference for one or other in relation to particular examples. However, rather than promoting a prescriptive norm, they generally leave the individual speaker or writer to judge which construction sounds better in a given context. For Maupas (1618: 65v–66r) – as for Oudin (1632: 233) after him – there is no difference between the two constructions, and both *ie veux vous l'ottroyer* and *ie vous la veux ottroyer* are equally possible. It is clear, however, that even early on in the century, if the

---

[28] The verbs *laisser, faire, voir, envoyer, entendre* and *sentir* constitute exceptions to the modern rule; they will not be discussed in this section.

infinitive is preceded by a preposition then only the modern order is possible (*Je desire de la vous ottroyer*; *J'ay oublié à les vous enuoyer*; *Je m'appreste à le leur mander*).[29] Vaugelas discusses the construction in three different observations. In the observation entitled *Il se vient iustifier, il vient se iustifier* (1647: 376–7) he argues that both constructions are acceptable but the former is better because it is far more frequently used. He notes that Coëffeteau preferred the modern construction (this is not supported by our data, see below) since it is more regular and less ambiguous, but that the 'transposition' has more grace. The question of ambiguity is picked up in the two other observations which discuss the construction (1647: 142–3, 581–2). In both of these it is made clear that the modern order is to be favoured in coordinated constructions such as *il ne peut se taire ny parler*, since if the clitic is placed before the finite verb this wrongly gives the impression that the pronoun is governed by both of the coordinated infinitives. Both Thomas Corneille and the Academy, commenting on the first observation, agree that both constructions are acceptable and that the ear should be left to decide which sounds better (Streicher 1936: 647–8); they are also in agreement with Vaugelas that any potential ambiguity with co-ordinated infinitives must be avoided. Even in the final decade of the century the same position is repeated by Andry de Boisregard (1693: 172–7); moreover, he still cites Vaugelas approvingly and concludes that 'la maniere la plus naturelle de le [sc. le pronom] placer, c'est de le mettre devant les deux verbes'. In short, as Galet (1971: 57) observes, the grammarians and *remarqueurs* seem to have been embarrassed as to how to account for the changing usage.

Galet aims to trace the evolution of the change by tracking the frequency of usage of the older construction in a corpus of texts of different genres in both prose and verse for the period 1600–1700. The first thing that becomes clear is that, although there is clear overall evidence of a decrease in the use of the older construction, it is impossible to plot a simple straight line of development as the century progresses and that there is variation between the usage of different authors, and indeed within the different works of a single author's oeuvre (see Table 5.5). For example, La Fontaine, typically conservative, still uses both constructions almost equally in the late 1670s, while Molière seems to prefer the modern construction from about 1661 onwards. Bossuet's usage of the older construction is low (29%–36%) in the decade 1661–70, but he uses it in 52% of cases in his *Oraison funèbre* of 1683. Galet considers the work of Pierre Corneille to be particularly significant. This is partly because there is a change in his usage from about 1643; up to then Corneille's use of the older construction tended to exceed 50%; after 1643 he seems to prefer the modern construction until in his last play, *Suréna* (1674), the older ordering is only used

---

[29] Haase (1898: 438) notes that *venir de* constituted an exception to this rule. Scarron, for example, uses the construction 'dont je vous viens de parler' (*Le Roman Comique* (1655 [¹1651])).

Table 5.5 *Percentage usage (based on Galet 1971) of the older construction, Pronoun + Finite Verb + Infinitive. Where there is more than one work by the same writer for a particular year, an average figure is given. Note that the percentages include only those cases where the alternative construction is also possible. Percentages which are 50% or over are shaded*

	Corneille (b. 1606)	La Rochefoucauld (b. 1613)	La Fontaine (b. 1621)*	Molière (b. 1622)	Mme de Sévigné (b. 1626)	Bossuet (b. 1627)	Mme de Lafayette (b. 1634)	Racine (b. 1639)
1629	46%							
1630								
1631								
1632	61%							
1633	66%							
1634	55%							
1635	40%							
1636	56%							
1637								
1638								
1639								
1640	45%							
1641	50%							
1642	44%							
1643	50%							
1644	43%							
1645					57%			
1646	49%							
1647	39%							
1648								
1649								
1650	38%							
1651	36%							
1652								
1653								
1654								
1655				42%		75%		
1656				64%				
1657								
1658						42%		
1659	21%			53%				
1660				62%				
1661	40%			33%				
1662	25%			48%		36%		
1663	40%			41%		33%		41%
1664	42%			42%	47%			
1665		54%		43%				51%

Table 5.5 (*cont.*)

	Corneille (b. 1606)	La Rochefoucauld (b. 1613)	La Fontaine (b. 1621)	Molière (b. 1622)	Mme de Sévigné (b. 1626)	Bossuet (b. 1627)	Mme de Lafayette (b. 1634)	Racine (b. 1639)
1666	31%			38%	51%			
1667	26%			50%				37%
1668			57%	45%				43%
1669				32%		34%		31%
1670	38%			41%	32%	29%		19%
1671				42%	42%			
1672	43%			32%	42%			26%
1673				27%	43%			31%
1674	33%							30%
1675								
1676								
1677								22%
1678			48%				38%	
1679			54%					
1680								
1681								
1682								
1683						52%		
1684								
1685						31%		
1686						32%		
1687						45%		
1688								
1689								18%
1690					32%			
1691								20%
1692								
1693								
1694					36%			
1695								
1696								

* The figures are calculated as follows: books 1–6, edition of 1668; books 7–8, edition of 1678; books 9–11, edition of 1679.

in 33% of possible constructions. What is perhaps more significant is the fact that from 1660 onwards Corneille himself makes revisions to the plays which involve replacing the older order with the newer one, thereby suggesting that the order was now considered archaic (Galet 1971: 334). While different authors naturally remain committed to the older construction for different lengths of time (see Figure 5.2, p. 214), Galet concludes that it is in the second half of the century that the modern construction takes over: 'Quel que soit le genre de l'œuvre, tragédie ou comédie, lettre, oraison funèbre, fable, quel que soit le style propre à l'auteur, la constuction pronom + verbe régent + infinitif régime est archaïque à la fin du siècle' (Galet 1971: 323).

Galet suggests a number of possible reasons for the changing usage. As well as the problem of coordinated infinitives identified by Vaugelas (e.g. 'Alors les soldats ne peurent plus se retenir, ni s'empescher de tesmoigner', Vaugelas 1659: 511), she notes the problem of the choice of auxiliary verb in compound tenses with a pronominal verb: compare 'Mais helas le miserable ne s'est pas sceu conseruer en ceste dignité, il est tombé' (Vaugelas 1615: 15) with 'il n'eust pû s'en garentir' (Charpentier 1650: 4).[30] Alongside these syntactic difficulties, there are some semantic problems with certain verbs when the clitic is in the pre-verbal position. For example, some verbs are potentially ambiguous (especially verbs such as *paraître* or *sembler*, as in *il me semble céder*). Another such possible ambiguity occurs with *il faut*, for instance, *il me faut céder*. Vaugelas (1653: 516) selects the modern ordering in 'ils arrestent de se rendre au point du iour' to avoid ambiguity. Galet argues that these potential problems became more acute in the seventeenth century since there was a tendency no longer to pronounce the final *-r* of infinitives ending in *-ir* or *-er*. This meant that the constructions *il se croit acquitter / il se croit acquitté* and *je les sais bien punir / je les sais bien punis* were henceforth pronounced identically. We may add to this the increased concern for syntactic clarity which preoccupies the *remarqueurs* from Vaugelas onwards.[31]

It is surprising that Fournier (1998: 84) maintains that the two constructions are used side by side throughout the seventeenth and eighteenth centuries 'sans net progrès de la seconde, et sans non plus de spécialisation stylistique', although she is clearly familiar with Galet's work. First, there is evidence that early on in the seventeenth century writers were conscious of the variation. While both constructions are employed by the Dauphin, the older construction dominates. Typical examples for 1605 include *je la veu lavé* (24 September), *je me veu couché* (4 October) on the one hand, and *je veu vou conduire* (22 July), *j'ay pas voulu m'endormi* (18 December), on the other.[32] Ernst (1985: 72) cites the figures for May/June, in which there are fifty-four examples of the older construction with clitic climbing (of which thirty-seven are with *vouloir* and fifteen with *falloir*) compared with six examples of the modern construction. Evidence that Héroard was conscious of the variation is provided by one of

---

[30] Andry de Boisregard (1689: 708) mentions the variation between *il s'est voulu tué* and *il a voulu se tuer*, etc. but does not link this with the question of the place of the clitic pronoun.

[31] The older construction can still be used as a stylistic choice in writing; Haase (1898: 437) notes that it may also be used in *français populaire*.

[32] Note that here the choice may well be determined by the problem of auxiliary selection with a pronominal verb.

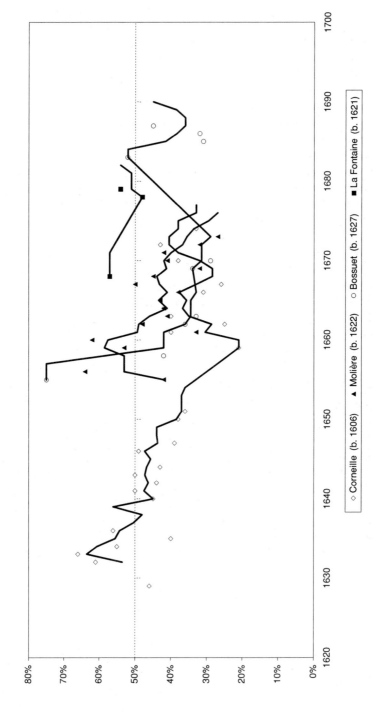

Figure 5.2 Trendlines showing the percentage usage of the older construction (Pronoun + Finite Verb + Infinitive) for Corneille, Molière, Bossuet and La Fontaine

◇ Corneille (b. 1606)   ▲ Molière (b. 1622)   ○ Bossuet (b. 1627)   ■ La Fontaine (b. 1621)

his revisions; he substitutes the construction *je voudré bien me couché* for his original *je me voudré* (26 November 1608).

Secondly, it appears that, again early on in the century, writers were attributing different socio-stylistic values to the variants, as is suggested by the data furnished by Sancier-Château's study (1995: 271–2) of d'Urfé's corrections to the text of *L'Astrée* between 1607 and 1610. What she notes is that, contrary to what we might expect, the modern order used in 1607 is systematically replaced by the older order in 1610. For example:

on doive se contenter (1607) → *on se doive contenter* (1610).

There is also one example of this change between 1619 and 1620:

qu'ils vinssent le trouver (1619) → *qu'ils le vinssent trouver* (1620).

Sancier-Château argues that the new order arose in non-literary language (she argues this establishes the link with the non-pronunciation of final *r* of infinitives ending in *-ir* and *-er*, since H. Estienne considered this a popular pronunciation), and that this therefore led to the characterization of the older order as literary and elegant. However, as the newer ordering became more established in literary usage, judgments about the stylistic value of the older construction were modified until, as we have seen, in the 1660s it came to be considered archaic.

Turning now to our corpus of translations, in each case I calculated the number of occurrences of, and the percentage usage of, the older construction with clitic climbing (see Tables 5.6, 5.7). It is perhaps worth reiterating here that, as with Galet's figures, the percentages are based on the number of actual occurrences of the construction out of the total number of cases where the alternative construction is also possible.[33] In treating the two orders as variables, I am assuming semantic equivalence, which, as we have seen (section 1.2.3), has been a central issue for contemporary sociolinguistic methodology (see also Milroy 1987: 158–61). I analysed the data with a view to identifying:

- The chronology of the shift from Pronoun + Finite Verb + Infinitive as the dominant order to Finite Verb + Pronoun + Infinitive
- Whether the date of birth of the author (rather than the date of publication of the text) was significant
- Whether the usage of the same author modified significantly over time
- Whether the construction occurred particularly with certain finite verbs.

On the first question, it is clear that, even in this relatively small sample, there is a significant shift in usage between our three periods (1600–19: 90%; 1640–59:

---

[33] I am therefore excluding, for example, cases where the infinitive is preceded by a preposition (see above, p. 210). Here again the percentages are intended only to suggest trends.

Table 5.6 *Occurrences in each author of the older order Pronoun + Finite Verb + Infinitive in the corpus of translations (expressed as a proportion of the total number of occurrences where both orders are possible)*

	pouvoir	vouloir	falloir	venir	devoir	aller	savoir	oser	croire	courir	sembler	prétendre	valoir mieux	
Malherbe 1615 (b. 1555)	10/10	7/7	2/2	4/4		2/2								25/25 = 100%
Coëffeteau 1615/1621 (b. 1574)	4/4	1/2				3/5					0/1			8/12 = 67%
Vaugelas 1615 (b. 1585)	5/5	8/9	5/6		1/1		1/1							20/22 = 91%
Vaugelas 1653 (b. 1585)	6/6	2/2		2/2	1/1	1/1		1/1		0/1				13/14 = 93%
Vaugelas 1659 (b. 1585)	6/9	1/1	1/1	2/2	1/1	1/1		1/1		0/1				13/17 = 76%
D'Ablancourt 1652 (b. 1606)	7/8	3/3	2/2	1/1	1/1									14/15 = 93%
Charpentier 1650 (b. 1620)	6/13	2/7	0/2		1/4	0/1	1/2	0/1	0/1			0/1		10/32 = 31%
Le Maistre de Sacy 1685/6 (b. 1613)	1/3	1/2			4/4									6/9 = 67%
Dacier 1699 (b. 1651)	0/2		0/3			0/1	0/1						0/1	0/8 = 0%
Andry de Boisregard 1687 (b. 1658)	1/9	1/8	0/1	0/1	0/1				0/1					2/21 = 10%
TOTAL for the century	46/69	26/41	10/17	9/10	9/13	7/11	2/4	2/3	0/2	0/2	0/1	0/1	0/1	111/175 (63%)

Table 5.7 Occurrences by period of the order Pronoun + Finite verb + Infinitive in the corpus of translations (expressed as a proportion of the total number of occurrences where both orders are possible and as a percentage for the six most commonly occurring verbs)

	pouvoir	vouloir	falloir	venir	devoir	aller	savoir	oser	croire	courir	sembler	prétendre	valoir mieux
TOTAL 1600–19	19/19 (=100%)	16/18 (=89%)	7/8 (=88%)	4/4 (=100%)	1/1 (=100%)	5/7 (=71%)	1/1				0/1		53/59 = 90%
TOTAL 1640–59	25/36 (=69%)	8/13 (=62%)	3/5 (=60%)	5/5 (=100%)	4/7 (=57%)	2/3 (=67%)	1/2	2/3	0/1	0/2		0/1	50/78 = 64%
TOTAL 1680–99	2/14 (=14%)	2/10 (=20%)	0/4 (=0%)	0/1 (=0%)	4/5 (=80%)	0/1 (=0%)	0/1	0/1		0/1			8/38 = 21%

Table 5.8 *Percentage usage of the order Pronoun + Finite*
Verb + Infinitive by the authors of the translations
arranged according to date of birth (here the figures for
Vaugelas 1653 and 1659 are combined)

In order of date of birth	
Malherbe 1615 (b. 1555)	100%
Coëffeteau 1615/1621 (b. 1574)	67%
Vaugelas 1615 (b. 1585)	91%
Vaugelas 1653/1659 (b. 1585)	84%
D'Ablancourt 1652 (b. 1606)	93%
Le Maistre de Sacy 1685/6 (b. 1613)	67%
Charpentier 1650 (b. 1620)	31%
Dacier 1699 (b. 1651)	0%
Andry de Boisregard 1687 (b. 1658)	10%

64%; 1680–99: 21%). It is, however, equally obvious, as in Galet's statistics
(see Table 5.5), that there is considerable variation between the usage of individual authors. In particular, Charpentier (1650) appears to be fairly progressive,
whereas d'Ablancourt (1652) and Le Maistre de Sacy (1685) seem conservative.[34] If we average Galet's figures for the same periods, we find a not
dissimilar pattern (1640–59: 52%; 1680–99: 33%). This suggests then that the
turning point occurs in the 1660s–1670s.[35]

As regards our second question, Table 5.8 gives the percentage usage of
the older construction by the different authors when arranged not according
to date of publication, but by date of birth. Whilst this makes Le Maistre de
Sacy's high usage of the older construction appear a little less anomalous, there
is no clear correlation between a later date of birth and an increased use of
the modern construction. For instance, d'Ablancourt (b. 1606) uses the older
construction as frequently as, or more frequently than, most of the authors born
in the second half of the sixteenth century, and there is a marked difference
in the usage of Le Maistre de Sacy and Charpentier, although they were born
only seven years apart. Nor do these figures suggest that the concept of 'change
in apparent time' could have been usefully applied to our data. In our first
and third chronological tranches, it is the middle-aged author, not the youngest
one, who displays the highest usage of the modern construction, while in our

---

[34] In the case of Le Maistre de Sacy this may well be because we are dealing with a translation of
the Old Testament.
[35] This dating is supported by the figures for the different decades provided by Galet's analysis:
1630s = 56%, 1640s = 47%, 1650s = 51%, 1660s = 42%, 1670s = 36%, 1680s = 36%, 1690s
= 29%.

second period, the middle-aged author has the lowest overall percentage for this order.[36]

On the third question, there is some evidence of a decline in the use of the older construction by Vaugelas by 1659, when usage of the older construction has decreased to 76%; nevertheless, he consistently favours the construction with clitic climbing.

Finally, the choice of verb appears significant in three interesting ways. First, *pouvoir* and *vouloir* account for approximately two-thirds of all the examples, and for some of our verbs (*croire, courir, sembler, prétendre, valoir mieux*) there are no occurrences of the older ordering, although examples of these are attested by Galet. Secondly, as the century progresses and the construction becomes less common, the range of verbs with which clitic climbing is possible diminishes, so that in our final period (1680–99) the construction is found with only three verbs, *pouvoir, vouloir* and *devoir*. Thirdly, towards the end of the century the older construction seems to be more favoured with *devoir* than with either *vouloir* or *pouvoir*.

(b)   The position of negative particles with an infinitive
In Modern French, when an infinitive is negated both particles generally precede the infinitive ((*pour*) *ne pas faire*), whereas in the sixteenth century they were normally placed around the infinitive ((*pour*) *ne faire pas*). The history of this construction has been well documented and illustrated with examples by a number of linguists: see, for example, Hirschbühler and Labelle (1994), Martineau (1994), Gondret (1998).[37] Remnants of the earlier position of the negative particles survive in certain constructions today. Whereas with most verbs the ordering *ne* Infinitive *pas* is archaic and occurs only in literary language, if the infinitive is *avoir* or *être* used as an auxiliary, the negative particles still usually appear before the auxiliary infinitive, especially in speech (*ne pas avoir fait*), but they are quite frequently placed around it, notably in *langue soignée* (*n'avoir pas fait*). This is also true to a lesser extent when *être* is used as a copula and with the construction *avoir à* (Grevisse 1993: 1458–9). Furthermore, in those cases where the infinitive directly governs another infinitive, usually both particles come before the infinitive (*ne pas vouloir faire*), but very occasionally they may be placed around it (*ne vouloir pas faire*).[38] Hirschbühler and Labelle (1994) argue that the change from *ne* Infinitive *pas* to *ne pas* Infinitive occurs

---

[36] Examples of this kind could be multiplied. For example, Furetière (b. 1619) in his *Roman bourgeois* (1666) is more conservative (79% of the older construction) than either Le Maistre de Sacy (b. 1618) or Charpentier (b. 1620). Once again this suggests that other factors, such as the text type or genre, play an important role in the author's choice of construction.

[37] I am excluding from consideration here use of *non* to mark negation, which was still in use in the sixteenth century, with or without a *forclusif*.

[38] Larrivée's (forthcoming) analysis of usage in FRANTEXT for the period 1977–97 seems to confirm these tendencies. Of the 148 occurrences where *pas* follows the infinitive, ninety-three

at different times depending on the nature of the verb: according to their data, lexical verbs undergo the change between 1500 and 1750 (with the modern construction first occurring more than 50% of the time in the period 1650–99),[39] the modal verbs essentially change between 1650 and 1900 (reaching over 50% for modern usage in the period 1800–49), while auxiliaries have been changing at a slow pace since 1650.

It is also important to consider whether the construction includes a clitic pronoun or not. Where this is the case, Brunot (1905–53: IV, 1040) suggests that there was an intermediate stage in the evolution from the older (I) to the modern construction (III): (I) *pour ne le savoir pas* (II) *pour ne le pas savoir* (III) *pour ne pas le savoir*. According to Fournier (1998: 85) and Haase (1898: 446) *ne le savoir pas* and *ne le pas savoir* are in competition in the seventeenth century, but the modern order – *ne pas le savoir* – is rare.[40]

Whether the *forclusif* is *pas* or *point* seems to have little effect on the choice of ordering. However, research has suggested that the evolution with *jamais*, *rien* and *plus* was somewhat different (Hirschbühler and Labelle 1994: 163, 175). *Jamais* occurs in the older construction for longer than *pas* or *point*, and *rien*, *plus* and *jamais* apparently show up in the modern construction more frequently, in the early stages, than *pas* or *point*.

Vaugelas alludes briefly to the position of negative particles with an infinitive in a lengthy observation on negation (1647: 409) in which he states his belief that *pour ne pas* (or *point*) *tomber dans les inconueniens* is much more elegant than *pour ne tomber pas* (*point*) *dans les inconueniens*. Andry de Boisregard (1689: 364) comments that this question is discussed by those concerned with 'politesse'; while many think both positions are equally acceptable, there are others who think that the negatives are better placed around the infinitive. He cites Mlle de Scudéry's example *de ne les suivre pas* and asserts that although her language is sometimes rather affected, there are other more serious authors who favour the same construction.

Ernst's examples of the Dauphin's usage (1985: 88) are interesting since they typically show not only the use of *pas* after the verb, but also that *ne* may be omitted from this construction: for example, *pou n'ete pa moulé* (22 August 1605); *vou m'avé comandé de dire pa car a toa* (20 December 1605); *je li avé comande troa foi d'y regade pa* (17 January 1606); *j'aime mieu y allé pa* (19 August 1607). Sancier-Château (1995: 279–81) looks at the variants in

---

examples are an auxiliary verb (*avoir, être*, modals), twenty-nine are the copula, and twenty-six are lexical verbs of which twenty-two are various uses of *avoir* (e.g. *n'avoir pas de* N, *n'avoir pas la moindre intention de*, etc.).

[39] Martineau's statistics (1994: 68) (51% of the old order in the seventeenth century, 32% in the eighteenth century), while less precise, suggest a similar chronology.

[40] In the sixteenth century it was also common to find *ne* alone with an infinitive (e.g. *ne le faire*). For examples with *point* alone, see note 8 above.

d'Urfé's *L'Astrée*. She notes that the corrections are systematically in favour
of the construction *ne* + Pronoun + Infinitive + *pas/point*, even though this
sometimes involves a change from the modern ordering:

 1607: de ne point les outrepasser   1610: de ne les outrepasser point
 1607: de ne point la lire   1610: de ne la lire point

She adopts the same argument here as with the position of the clitic pronoun
above, asserting that the modern ordering must be considered familiar or popular, and therefore unsuitable for a literary text. If this is true, it is striking
that by the middle of the century Vaugelas considers that the stylistic value
of the modern ordering has become one of elegance. The most frequent order,
however, in the first version is *ne* + Pronoun + *pas/point* + Infinitive which is
usually revised to *ne* + Pronoun + Infinitive + *pas/point*, as in the following
examples:

 1607: de ne te point enquerir de son nom   1610: de ne t'enquerir point
 1607: de ne la luy plus laisser   1610: de ne la luy laisser plus.

In the case of negated infinitives, the number of occurrences in our corpus
of translations is far too small for the percentages to be of any significance (see
Table 5.9).[41] In the texts for the period 1600–19 there are only four instances of
the construction; in three cases there is no pronominal object and the negative
particles are placed around the infinitive (in one case the infinitive is the auxiliary
avoir). In the fourth example, the construction *ne* + Pronoun + Infinitive +
point is employed (*à ne te traiter point*, Vaugelas 1615). In other words, all
the constructions are of the most conservative type. For the period 1640–
59 there is a total of eighteen examples (including both Vaugelas 1653 and
Vaugelas 1659), of which fifteen occur without a pronoun. When there is no
object pronoun, the older construction is used five times out of fifteen (33%),
showing a marked change towards the newer construction. Moreover, there is
variation between the different authors. Despite the recommendations of the
Remarques Vaugelas has one example of the old and one of the new construction in 1653, but in 1659 the example with the newer ordering is reworded
so the negated infinitive disappears. D'Ablancourt's examples are also fairly
evenly balanced between the older (three occurrences) and the newer order
(four occurrences). However, all five of Charpentier's examples are of the
newer order. Of the three examples with a pronominal object, two are the
same construction taken from Vaugelas 1653/1659, in which it is an auxiliary
infinitive which is negated and the ordering *ne* + Pronoun + Infinitive + *pas* is
used (*pour ne luy avoir pas voulu*); in the third example from d'Ablancourt
the ordering *ne* + Pronoun + *pas* + Infinitive is selected (*de ne les pas
traitter*). For the period 1680–99 there is a total of twenty-one examples, of

---

[41] In the table, *pas* is used to refer to any *forclusif*. For discussion of the significance of the choice
of negative particle, see below.

Table 5.9 *Position of the negative particle with an infinitive*

	No pronoun		With pronominal complement		
	Ne + infinitive + *pas*	*Ne pas* + infinitive	*Ne* + pronoun + infinitive + *pas*	*Ne* + pronoun + *pas* + infinitive	*Ne* + *pas* + pronoun + infinitive
Malherbe 1615	1 (infinitive is auxiliary)	0	0	0	0
Coëffeteau 1615/1621	1	0	0	0	0
Vaugelas 1615	1	0	1	0	0
Vaugelas 1653	1	1	1 (infinitive is auxiliary)	0	0
Vaugelas 1659	1	0	1 (infinitive is auxiliary)	0	0
D'Ablancourt 1652	3	4	0	1	0
Charpentier 1650	0	5	0	0	0
Le Maistre de Sacy 1685/6	3	2	2	1	0
Dacier 1699	0	4	0	0	1
Andry de Boisregard 1687	2 (of which 1 is an auxiliary)	2	3	0	1
TOTAL 1600–19	3 (of which 1 is an auxiliary)	0	1	0	0
TOTAL 1640–59	5	10	2 (both cases of infinitive as auxiliary)	1	0
TOTAL 1680–99	5 (of which 1 is an auxiliary)	8	5	1	2

which thirteen occur without a pronoun; now five of the thirteen examples (c. 39%) use the older example, and one of these is with an auxiliary verb. Again there is variation between the different authors, with Dacier using the modern construction all the time. With a pronominal complement there are also signs of development. While there are five examples of the construction *ne* + Pronoun + Infinitive + *pas*, there is one example of the construction *ne* + Pronoun + *pas* + Infinitive and two occurrences of the modern structure *ne* + *pas* + Pronoun + Infinitive, not previously attested in the translation corpus. Nevertheless, the most conservative construction appears to dominate throughout the century. In short, the establishment of the modern position of the negative particles with an infinitive occurred at different periods, depending on whether or not a clitic pronoun was present.

It is difficult to draw conclusions about the influence of the verb type on the choice of ordering, given the small numbers of examples. It is perhaps significant, however, that all the examples where the infinitive is an auxiliary employ the older of the two orderings where there is no clitic pronoun and the oldest of the three orderings where there is. However, the single example of the modal verb *pouvoir* in Andry de Boisregard (1687) uses the oldest ordering (*ne* + Pronoun + Infinitive + *plus*), while the one example with *laisser* in d'Ablancourt (1652) uses the modern ordering. It is equally impossible to say anything about the significance of the choice of *forclusif*, as no clear pattern of usage emerges. For example, in our earliest period all the examples use the oldest ordering, regardless of whether the negative particle is *pas*, *point* or *jamais plus*. Of the examples without a pronoun from our third period, the five examples of the older position include two occurrences of *pas*, two of *jamais* and one of *rien*, but there are equally two uses of *rien* and one of *plus* among the eight examples of the newer construction. This is perhaps unsurprising given the somewhat contradictory evidence about the position of *jamais* cited above.

5.5   Conclusion

Whilst the seventeenth century in France is generally perceived as the principal period of standardization of the language and of the conscious elimination of variation, we have seen that the interplay between the metalinguistic texts and change as recorded in texts is more complicated and subtle than one might imagine. The grammarians and *remarqueurs* have been shown to be particularly slow in responding to changes in the position of the clitic pronoun with a finite verb and infinitive and to that of the negative in infinitival constructions. While the data from the texts support the view that the modern position of the clitic pronoun between the finite verb and the infinitive began to dominate in the 1660s and 1670s, this is not reflected in any of our metalinguistic texts. Particularly striking in this respect is the gap between Andry de Boisregard's theoretical stance and his actual usage. Although he concedes that both constructions are equally possible, he expresses a preference for the older construction with clitic climbing. Yet in his own usage as a translator, in a text published six years before this statement, this construction is selected in only 10% of all possible cases. In the case of the negative, Vaugelas and Andry both permit variation – although each expresses a preference for one construction or the other on stylistic grounds – but again there is no sense of the commentators on the French language driving, or indeed keeping pace with, changing usage.

Conversely, in the case of the variation between [o] and [u], the negative comments of the grammarians are closely matched by the textual usage. For a number of words, the criticized form disappears from usage in the first decades of the century, and in almost all of the examples examined there is very little evidence of the non-standard form after 1650.

A second conclusion which has emerged is that the case studies here do not seem to substantiate the notion of *chronolecte*, which would lead us to expect changes clustering around key dates like isoglosses on a dialect map. This was perhaps most obvious in relation to verb morphology, where the elimination of variation continued throughout the century, but it is also clear in our other two areas. As regards [o]/[u], while the general question ceased to be relevant after the 1630s, debate over individual examples continued well into the second half of the century. In the case of the two word order questions, the position of the negative with the infinitive appears to have been slower in becoming fixed in the modern position than that of the clitic pronoun. Related to this is the question of how to pinpoint the dating of a change. Although where there are two variants, it may be meaningful to see when the modern variant predominates (i.e. where more than 50% of the occurrences are of the modern form or construction), the slow pace of change may mean that the older variant remains as a significant, albeit minor, variant for many years to come.

Thirdly, our analysis, although based on limited data,[42] has cast doubt on the validity and usefulness of the notion of 'change in apparent time', which has been used by linguists working on contemporary language. Rather, our evidence supports the view of the GARS linguists that it is essential to compare data derived from studies of 'change in apparent time' with historical analysis and evidence of 'change in real time'.

Lastly, the relationship between change and sociolinguistic marking has emerged clearly. While [u] for [o] was associated with court usage at the turn of the century, once it was condemned, it became negatively marked. It is therefore one of the traits used to characterize peasant speech in the *Agréables Conférences*. This perhaps explains why the French Academy still felt it necessary to comment on the question, even though the data from the more standardized texts of F R A N T E X T suggest that the question no longer had any real currency. Even in the case of verb morphology, the variant in decline may be associated with a particular style or register.

---

[42] Although our corpus of translations is small, it is interesting to see how well it mirrors, for example, Galet's data for the position of the clitic pronoun.

6   Conclusion

This study has aimed to shed fresh light on the richness and diversity of usage in seventeenth-century France. A second purpose throughout has been to address fundamental methodological questions. While some of these are pertinent to the study of variation in general, others are particularly acute when we are analysing past variation. In this final chapter, I would like to return to some of these general questions and methodological issues.

A major preoccupation throughout has been the question of sources. Traditional histories of French, which focus on the emergence of the standard language – symbolized in the seventeenth century by the birth of the French Academy and the triumph of *le bon usage* – have inevitably relied heavily on literary texts. Literary sources have not been neglected in this book, and the FRANTEXT corpus has proved especially useful in affording access to a large corpus of literary texts that can be used, for example, to provide statistical information about frequency of usage. However, the investigation of variation, of the non-standard, necessarily requires the examination of different types of texts and other kinds of sources, including comparative reconstruction.

The reconstruction of seventeenth-century spoken French using the comparative method is at once highly promising and fraught with potential problems. Although the existence of a feature common to two or more non-metropolitan varieties or creoles which were formed on the basis of spoken French taken abroad by colonizers in that century might suggest that the feature was present in the common ancestor – especially if the varieties are spoken in widely divergent geographical areas – at all times the possibility that these were independent developments has to be borne in mind. In a number of chapters, I have reviewed a range of possible sources and assessed the advantages and disadvantages of each. In some cases a potentially exciting source has proved disappointing. For example, whilst in theory verbatim testimonies in defamation cases or inquisitorial material from witchcraft trials might seem promising sources of authentic spoken language, in practice the role of the legal clerk and the intrusion of legal jargon minimize their usefulness.

An obvious starting point for the investigation of variation was the perception and presentation of the non-standard by seventeenth-century linguists in works on the French language, notably in our principal corpus of observations and remarks. In assessing the comments in the metalinguistic texts, it was essential to compare them with actual usage with a view to determining the extent to which they accurately reflect or attempt to guide contemporary usage. Indeed, wherever possible, I attempted to seek *convergence* between different types of source, to build up a picture of the variety of usages, albeit a fragmented and incomplete one, by comparing the evidence from different types of material.

The search for convergence between the textual sources is perhaps especially important in the case of spoken French. Since we clearly do not have direct access to seventeenth-century speech, we have to seek *traces* of the spoken language in the writing of the past, preferably substantiated by convergence between different types of sources. In Chapter 2, threrefore, I aimed to look at evidence from the metalinguistic texts, from model dialogues in didactic texts, from theatre and from usage in non-metropolitan French. A good example of this is the occurrence of non-inverted interrogatives in our different sources (section 2.5.4). On the other hand, I tried to avoid drawing overambitious conclusions from thin evidence and to accept at times the impossibility of making a firm conclusion. For instance, while, as I noted, usage of *on* for *nous* was clearly possible in seventeenth-century speech, the paucity of examples of the construction together with the instances of *on* used for other pronouns, made me wary of concluding that the modern-day usage was already established in the seventeenth century (section 2.5.2).

In other chapters I used a delimited corpus of texts alongside other types of evidence. In Chapter 3 the corpus of Mazarinades had the advantage of being restricted chronologically, thereby minimizing the possibility of changing usage being a distorting factor. In Chapter 5 the corpus of translations, many of which were written by authors of metalinguistic texts, also enabled me to explore further the complex relationship between theory and practice. In the various chapters I hope to have shown the advantages and disadvantages of, on the one hand, seeking convergence between different sources, and, on the other hand, considering usage in a more coherent and defined corpus.

The question of sources was also acute in the discussion of *Préciosité*, given the satirical nature of many of the principal texts. In setting the data about women's usage from the metalinguistic texts beside that from texts by women in FRANTEXT and from letters, the difficulty of drawing clear demarcation lines between women's usage in general, the usage of certain famous women writers and indeed even that of the *Précieuses* became evident.

Closely related to the question of sources is the problem of separating out the different parameters of variation for discussion. This is, of course, an artificial activity since speakers and texts portray a complex interaction of variables. For instance, certain Mazarinades might equally have been used as sources of spoken language.

A second series of questions concerned the possibility of treating different areas of language with equal ease and rigour. In particular, I have noted how texts, and especially literary texts, frequently portray the non-standard through lexical and phonological means, whereas the morphology and syntax are much more standardized. The same problem is evident to some extent in the metalinguistic texts. For instance, lexical issues figure prominently in the discussion of women's usage in both the volumes of observations and the dictionaries. For this reason, while not neglecting questions of lexis and pronunciation, I devoted more than half of my case studies to morphological or syntactic variation. Discussion of each level of language brings with it its own set of problems. For example, in the case of pronunciation, one must depend heavily on the use of non-standard spellings to identify variation, whilst in the case of lexis it is more difficult to be systematic and exhaustive in the discussion.

In the Introduction I referred to the long-standing debate about the applicability of sociolinguistic methodology to syntactic research (section 1.2.3). My case studies have supported Romaine's contention that, where we are dealing with the simple presence or absence of a term – for example, the *ne* of negation (section 5.3) – the Labovian concept of the linguistic variable is unproblematic. The question is already less straightforward when we consider cases of substitution of one form for another; while there seemed to be no difficulty in establishing semantic equivalence between the forms *quand je le suis* and *quand je la suis* (section 4.6.5), the use of *on* for *nous* (section 2.5.2) was more complex for a number of reasons. First, the use of *on* as a substitute for *nous* does not appear to have privileged status in our period, since the pronoun may be used in place of other personal pronouns, perhaps especially the first person singular. Second, even in context, it is not easy to determine whether *on* is being used in a general or indefinite sense or with a specific reference. Third, comedy in particular deliberately exploited the ambiguity of the pronoun. In other words, in some instances, although probably not in all, the use of *on* for *nous* had a marked stylistic value. All this means that the emphasis has to be placed on the analysis of individual examples and that the generalized use of statistics is highly problematic. The same problems occur when we consider different word orders. Contrary to what I think Romaine implies, in some cases which involve the rearrangement of elements, it does seem possible to speak of 'complementary distribution', that is, to consider the alternatives as semantically equivalent. Examples of this type would be the constructions Pronoun + Finite Verb + Infinitive (*je le veux faire*) and Finite Verb + Pronoun + Infinitive (*je veux le faire*), or the negated infinitival constructions (*ne* Infinitive *pas* and *ne pas* Infinitive, section 5.4.5). On the other hand, the discussion of alternatives to inversion in interrogatives (section 2.5.4) necessarily examined their semantic value. In the case of the use of intonation in total interrogatives, while these were attested in nearly all our sources of spoken French, they were often found to have a particular semantic value, whether seeking confirmation, or expressing surprise or indignation. As regards the use of *est-ce que* in partial interrogatives, the semantic issue was less clear-cut; while some occurrences were echo questions, others appeared simply to request information.

My case studies therefore suggest that it is incorrect to treat all cases of syntactic variation in the same way, or to consider that they all exemplify the same problems. While in some instances questions of semantic equivalence will be difficult or impossible to establish, in others the issue is relatively unproblematic.

This leads us directly to a third issue that I raised at the beginning of this study, namely the applicability of quantitative methodology to sociolinguistic studies of the past. As we have suggested above, where semantic equivalence is unproblematic, it may be appropriate to use quantitative methods to try and establish, for instance, relative frequency of usage, but this is clearly not appropriate in every case. In studies of past variation it is often difficult to use statistical techniques even for analysing phonological variation, since traditional spelling may mask relevant examples of variant pronunciations. Many of the instances I have examined are of rare or infrequent forms or structures, where again quantitative methods are irrelevant. This is not to deny the value of statistics, which have been useful in supporting my conclusions, for example, regarding the question of clitic climbing. I have found reference to FRANTEXT, with its large corpus of seventeenth-century tests, helpful on a number of occasions, particularly in contextualizing information from other sources. Again flexibility of approach seems to be the key issue here. Rather than concluding that quantitative methods are, say, only applicable to phonological studies, I would argue that the range and scope of the data have to be evaluated case by case.

Finally, important questions about the relationship between variation and change have been present throughout the work, and not just in Chapter 5, where I raised serious doubts both about the notion of 'change in apparent time' in relation to discussion of clitic climbing (section 5.4.5), and about the notion of *chronolecte*, which did not seem able to account, for example, for the elimination of non-standard morphological variants during the course of the century. Unsurprisingly, this study has provided additional evidence for the relationship between social stratification and change. Popular and lower-class usage has been shown to be less affected by normative pressures, allowing both innovation and the survival of archaisms. The best-known example of the relationship between social class and language change is, of course, the 'competition' between [wɛ], [ɛ] and [wa] (section 3.3.3). This is a clear case of resistance by certain social groups impeding a change until the Revolution imparted different values to the variables.

Conversely, contrary to previous studies, my study of women's language does not seem to support the contention that 'patterns of sex differentiation deviating from the norm indicate that a linguistic change is taking place' (Trudgill cited in Romaine 1982: 264). It is striking how few of the particular features attributed to women's usage have survived into modern-day usage and how relatively little influence their positive or negative judgment of words or expressions had on the long-term evolution of the language. Despite the prestige attributed to women's language, many of their usages remained confined to the particular social groupings in which they originated. While I have argued that the tight-knit network of the *Précieuses* allowed them, contrary to what one might expect, to innovate and to use their own 'jargon', these close links may have in turn prevented the innovations from spreading beyond that particular social milieu.

Any account of changing usage in seventeenth-century France must necessarily take note of the strength of the drive towards standardization and the elimination of variation. I have tried to emphasize throughout this study of sociolinguistic variation the importance of taking account also of the social structures of seventeenth-century France, and of the linguistic features of the particular genres and styles of literature which were dominant in the period.

Appendix

I PRIMARY CORPUS OF METALINGUISTIC TEXTS

A OBSERVATIONS AND REMARQUES ON THE FRENCH LANGUAGE

Alemand, L.-A. (1688) *Nouvelles Observations, ou Guerre civile des François sur la langue*, Paris: J. B. Langlois.

Andry de Boisregard, N. (1689) *Réflexions sur l'usage présent de la langue françoise, ou Remarques nouvelles et critiques touchant la politesse du langage*, Paris: L. d'Houry.

Andry de Boisregard, N. (1693) *Suite des Réflexions critiques sur l'usage présent de la langue françoise*, Paris: L. d'Houry.

Bérain, N. (1675) *Nouvelles Remarques sur la langue française*, Rouen: E. Viret.

Bouhours, D. (1674) *Doutes sur la langue françoise proposez à Messieurs de l'Académie Françoise par un gentilhomme de province*, Paris: S. Mabre-Cramoisy.

Bouhours, D. (1675) *Remarques nouvelles sur la langue françoise*, Paris: S. Mabre-Cramoisy.

Bouhours, D. (1693) *Suite des Remarques nouvelles sur la langue françoise*, Paris: G. and L. Josse.

Buffet, Marguerite (1668) *Nouvelles Observations sur la langue françoise. Où il est traitté des termes anciens & inusitez, & du bel usage des mots nouveaux. Avec les Eloges des Illustres Sçavantes, tant Anciennes que Modernes*, Paris: Jean Cusson.

Dupleix, S. (1651) *Liberté de la langue françoise dans sa pureté*, Paris: D. Becnet.

Ménage, G. (1675 [¹1672]) *Observations de Monsieur Ménage sur la langue françoise, Segonde édition*, Paris: C. Barbin.

Ménage, G. (1676) *Observations de Monsieur Ménage sur la langue françoise. Segonde partie*, Paris: C. Barbin.

Tallemant, P. (1698) *Remarques et décisions de l'Académie Françoise*, Paris: J. B. Coignard.

Vaugelas, C. Favre de (1647) *Remarques sur la langue françoise utiles à ceux qui veulent bien parler & bien escrire*, Paris: J. Camusat and P. le Petit (facsimile edition by J. Streicher, Paris: Slatkine, 1934).

B DICTIONARIES

Académie Française (1694) *Le Dictionnaire de l'Académie Françoise,* first edition, 2 vols., Paris: La Veuve J. B. Coignard and J. B. Coignard.

Cotgrave, R. (1611) *A Dictionarie of the French and English Tongues*, London: A. Islip.

Furetière, A. (1690) *Dictionaire universel, Contenant generalement tous les mots françois tant vieux que modernes, & les Termes de toutes les sciences et des arts* [. . .], 3 vols., The Hague/Rotterdam: A. and R. Leers.

Nicot, J. (1606) *Thresor de la langue francoyse, tant ancienne que moderne* [. . .], Paris: D. Douceur.

Oudin, A. (1640) *Curiositez françoises, pour supplement aux Dictionnaires. Ou Recueil de plusieurs belles proprietez, avec une infinité de Proverbes & Quolibets, pour l'explication de toutes sortes de Livres*, Paris: A. de Sommaville.

Richelet, P. (1680) *Dictionnaire françois, contenant les mots et les choses, plusieurs remarques nouvelles sur la langue françoise* [. . .], Geneva: J. H. Widerhold.

C GRAMMARS

Irson, C. (1662 [[1]1656]) *Nouvelle Methode pour apprendre facilement les principes et la pureté de la langue françoise Contenant plusieurs Traitez* [. . .], second edition, Paris: P. Baudouin.

Maupas, Ch. (1618 [[1]1607]) *Grammaire et syntaxe françoise, contenant reigles bien exactes & certaines de la prononciation, orthographe, construction & usage de nostre langue, en faveur des estrangiers qui en sont desireux, Seconde Edition. Reveuë, corrigee & augmentee de moitié, & en beaucoup de sortes amendee outre la precedente*, Orleans: O. Boynard and J. Nyon.

Oudin, A. (1632) *Grammaire françoise, rapportée au langage du temps*, Paris: P. Billaine.

D COMMENTARIES

Streicher, J. (ed.) (1936) *Commentaires sur les Remarques de Vaugelas par La Mothe le Vayer, Scipion Dupleix, Ménage, Bouhours, Conrart, Chapelain, Patru, Thomas Corneille, Cassagne, Andry de Boisregard et l'Académie Française*, 2 vols., Paris: Droz.

II SECONDARY CORPUS OF METALINGUISTIC TEXTS

E MODEL DIALOGUES IN DIDACTIC TEXTS

Core

Duez, N. (1669) *Le Vray et parfait guidon de la langue françoise*, Amsterdam: L. and D. Elzevier.

Erondell, P. (1969) *The French Garden 1605*, Menston: Scolar.

La Faye, A. de (1608) *Linguae gallicae, et italicae, Hortulus amoenissimus*, Halle: J. Krusicken.

Others

Oudin, A. (1650) *Dialogues fort recreatifs composez en Espagnol, Et nouvellement mis en Italien, Alleman & François. Avec des observations pour l'accord & la proprieté des quatres langues*, Paris: A. de Sommaville.

Wodroephe, J. (1623) *The Spared Houres of a soldier in his travels. Or the true marrowe of the French tongue, wherein is truely treated (by ordre [sic]) the nine parts of speech* [. . .], Dort: N. Vincentz.

F   WORKS ON FRENCH PRONUNCIATION

Dangeau, L. de Courcillon de (1694) *Essais de grammaire contenus en trois lettres d'un académicien à un autre académicien*, Paris: J. B. Coignard.
Hindret, J. (1687) *L'Art de bien prononcer et de bien parler la langue françoise*, Paris: L. d'Houry.

G   WORKS ON FRENCH ORTHOGRAPHY

Dobert, A. (1650) *Recreations literales et mysterieuses: ou sont curieuesement estalez les Principes & l'importance de la nouvelle Orthographe: Avec un acheminement à la connoissance de la Poësie, & des Anagrames*, Lyon: F. de Masso.
Lartigaut, A. (1669) *Les Progrés de la véritable ortografe ou l'ortografe francêze fondée sur ses principes confirmée par démonstracions*, Paris: L. Ravenau and J. d'Ouri.
L'Esclache, L. de (1668) *Les véritables régles de l'ortografe francéze, ou L'Art d'aprandre an peu de tams à écrire côrectement*, Paris: L'Auteur and L. Rondet.
Mauconduit (1669) *Traité de l'orthographe, Dans lequel on établit, par une methode claire & facile, fondée sur l'usage & sur la raison, les regles certaines d'écrire correctement. Et où lon examine, par occasion, les regles qu'a données M. De Lesclache*, Paris: M. Promé.
Poisson, R. (1609) *Alfabet nouveau de la vrée, & pure ortografe Fransoize, & Modéle sus iselui, en forme de Dixionére*, Paris: J. Planchon.
Simon, E. (1609) *La vraye et ancienne orthographe francoise restaurée. Tellement que desormais l'on aprandra parfetement à lire & à escrire & encor avec tant de facilité & breveté, que ce sera en moins de mois, que l'on ne faisoit, d'années*, Paris: J. Gesselin.
Soule, B. de (1689) *Traité de l'orthographe françoise ou l'orthographe en sa pureté*, Paris: E. Michallet.

H   WORKS ON VERSIFICATION AND PROSODY

Deimier, P. de (1610) *L'Academie de l'art poetique. Où par amples raisons, demonstrations, nouvelles recherches, examinations & authoritez d'exemples, sont vivement esclaircis & deduicts, les moyens par où l'on peut parvenir à la vraye & parfaicte connoissance de la Poësie Françoise*, Paris: J. de Bordeaulx.
Lancelot, C. (1681) *Nouvelle Methode pour apprendre facilement la langue latine* [. . .] *Avec un Traité de la Poësie Latine, & une bréve Instruction sur les Regles de la Poësie Françoise, Huitième édition. Revûë, corrigée & augmentée de nouveau*, Paris: D. Thierry (work on French poetics first included in the second edition, Paris: A. Vitré, 1650).
Mourgues, M. (1724 [[1]1685]) *Traité de la poësie françoise*, Nouvelle édition revûe, corrigée & augmentée, Paris: J. Vincent.

I   MISCELLANEOUS OTHER WORKS INCLUDING CONVERSATIONS,
COMPILATIONS OF OBSERVATIONS, GRAMMARS, WORKS ON STYLE, ETC.

Aisy, J. d' (1685a) *Le Genie de la langue françoise*, Paris: L. d'Houry.

Aisy, J. d' (1685b) *Suite du genie de la langue françoise*, Paris: L. d'Houry.

Bouhours, D. (1962 [¹1671]) *Les Entretiens d'Ariste et d'Eugène*, ed. F. Brunot, Paris: A. Colin.

Callières, F. de (1693) *Du bon, et du mauvais usage, dans les manieres de s'exprimer. Des façons de parler bourgeoises. Et en quoy elles sont differentes de celles de la Cour. Suitte des Mots à la mode*, Paris: C. Barbin.

Du Val, J.-B. (1604) *L'Eschole françoise. Pour apprendre à bien parler & escrire selon l'usage de ce temps & pratique des bons Autheurs*, Paris: E. Foucault.

La Touche, P. de (1696) *L'Art de bien parler françois, qui comprend tout ce qui regarde la Grammaire et les façons de parler douteuses*, 2 vols., Amsterdam: H. Desbordes.

Renaud, A. (1697) *Maniere de parler la langue françoise selon ses differens styles; avec la critique de nos plus celébres Ecrivains, En Prose & en Vers; et un petit traité de l'Orthographe & de la Prononciation Françoise*, Lyon: C. Rey.

Saint-Maurice, A. de (1672) *Remarques sur les principales difficultez que les estrangers ont en la langue françoise*, Paris: E. Loyson.

References

Ablancourt, N. Perrot d' (1652) *Les Commentaires de Cesar*, Paris: A. Courbé.

Académie Française (1694) *Le Dictionnaire de l'Académie Françoise*, first edition, 2 vols., Paris: La Veuve de J. B. Coignard and J. B. Coignard.

Aisy, J. d' (1685a) *Le Genie de la langue françoise*, Paris: L. d'Houry.

Aisy, J. d' (1685b) *Suite du genie de la langue françoise*, Paris: L. d'Houry.

Alemand, L.-A. (1688) *Nouvelles Observations, ou Guerre civile des François sur la langue*, Paris: J. B. Langlois.

Altman, J. G. (1995) 'Women's letters in the public sphere', in E. C. Goldsmith and D. Goodman (eds.), *Going Public: Women and Publishing in Early Modern France*, Ithaca and London: Cornell University Press, pp. 99–115.

Andry de Boisregard, N. (1687) *Panégyrique de l'empereur Théodose, prononcé à Rome par Pacat, En presence de cét Empereur & du Sénat. Traduit de Latin en François*, Paris: J. Langlois.

Andry de Boisregard, N. (1689) *Réflexions sur l'usage présent de la langue françoise, ou Remarques nouvelles et critiques touchant la politesse du langage*, Paris: L. d'Houry.

Andry de Boisregard, N. (1693) *Suite des Réflexions critiques sur l'usage présent de la langue françoise*, Paris: L. d'Houry.

Angenot, M. (1977) *Les Champions des femmes: Examen du discours sur la supériorité des femmes 1400–1800*, Montreal: Les Presses de l'Université du Québec.

Armstrong, N. and Smith, A. (2002) 'The influence of linguistic and social factors on the recent decline of French *ne*', *Journal of French Language Studies* 12: 23–41.

Arnauld, A. and Lancelot, C. (1660) *Grammaire generale et raisonnée* [. . .], Paris: P. Le Petit.

Arnould, J.-C. (1995) 'Canards criminels des XVIe et XVIIe siècles: le fait divers et l'ordre du monde (1570–1630)', in J.-C. Arnould *et al.* (eds.), *Tourments, doutes et ruptures dans l'Europe des XVIe et XVIIe siècles. Actes du Colloque Organisé par l'Université de Nancy II, 25–27 novembre 1993*, Paris: Champion, pp. 149–61.

Ashby, W. J. (1981) 'The loss of the negative particle *ne* in French: a syntactic change in progress', *Language* 57: 674–87.

Ashby, W. J. (1991) 'When does variation indicate linguistic change in progress?', *Journal of French Language Studies* 1: 1–19.

Asselin, C. and McLaughlin, A. (1981) 'Patois ou français? La langue de la Nouvelle-France au 17e siècle', *Langage et Société* 17: 3–57.

Aventin, G. (ed.) (1858) *Œuvres complètes de Tabarin*, Paris: P. Jannet.

Ayres-Bennett, W. (1987) *Vaugelas and the Development of the French Language*, London: MHRA.

Ayres-Bennett, W. (1990) 'Variation and change in the pronunciation of seventeenth-century French', in W. Ayres-Bennett and J. N. Green (eds.), *Variation and Change in French*, London: Routledge, pp. 151–79.

Ayres-Bennett, W. (1991) 'Observations et remarques sur la langue française: histoire d'un genre', *La Licorne* 19: 1–24.

Ayres-Bennett, W. (1994) 'Negative evidence: or another look at the non-use of negative *ne* in seventeenth-century French', *French Studies* 48: 63–85.

Ayres-Bennett, W. (1996a) *A History of the French Language Through Texts*, London: Routledge.

Ayres-Bennett, W. (1996b) '"Tres-estrange & tres-François": l'usage du terme *français* au XVIIe siècle et la tradition de la *latinitas*', in R. Lorenzo (ed.), *Actas do XIX Congreso Internacional de Lingüística e Filoloxia Románicas (Universidade de Santiago de Compostela, 1989)*, Vol. 8, Corunna: Fundación 'Pedro Barrié de la Maza, Conde de Fenosa', pp. 81–90.

Ayres-Bennett, W. (2000) 'Voices from the past. Sources of seventeenth-century spoken French', *Romanische Forschungen* 112: 323–48.

Ayres-Bennett, W. (2002) 'An evolving genre: seventeenth-century *Remarques* and *Observations* on the French language', in R. Sampson and W. Ayres-Bennett (eds.), *Interpreting the History of French*, Amsterdam, New York: Rodopi, pp. 353–68.

Ayres-Bennett, W. (2003) 'Sociolinguistic variation in the work of the French seventeenth-century *remarqueurs*', to appear in G. Hassler (ed.), *History of Linguistics in Texts and Concepts*.

Ayres-Bennett, W. and Caron, P. (eds.) (1996) *Les 'Remarques' de l'Académie française sur le 'Quinte-Curce' de Vaugelas 1719–1720. Contribution à une histoire de la norme grammaticale et rhétorique en France*, Paris: Presses de l'École Normale Supérieure.

Baillet, A. (1685) *Jugemens des sçavans sur les principaux ouvrages des auteurs*, 4 vols., Paris: A. Dezallier.

Balzac, J.-L. Guez de (1634) *Lettres du sieur de Balzac, Reveües & corrigées en cette derniere Edition*, Paris: C. Banqueteau.

Balzac, J.-L. Guez de (1661) *Lettres familieres de M. de Balzac à M. Chapelain*, Amsterdam: L. and D. Elzevier.

Balzac, J.-L. Guez de (1933–4) *Les premières lettres de Guez de Balzac 1618–1627*, ed. H. Bibas and K.-T. Butler, 2 vols., Paris: E. Droz.

Bar, F. (1957) 'Style burlesque et langue populaire', *Cahiers de l'Association Internationale des Etudes Françaises* 9: 221–37.

Bar, F. (1959) 'Le roman réaliste en France au XVIIe siècle: problèmes de style', in P. Böckmann (ed.), *Stil- und Formprobleme in der Literatur. Vorträge des VII. Kongresses der Internationalen Vereinigung für moderne Sprachen und Literaturen in Heidelberg*, Heidelberg: C. Winter, pp. 215–23.

Bar, F. (1960) *Le Genre burlesque en France au XVIIe siècle. Étude de style*, Paris: Éditions d'Artrey.

Bar, F. (1981) 'Aperçu du langage parlé au XVIIe siècle', in J. Jehasse *et al.* (eds.), *Mélanges offerts à Georges Couton*, Lyon: Presses Universitaires de Lyon, pp. 111–20.

Baron, D. (1986) *Grammar and Gender*, New Haven: Yale University Press.

Bary, R. (1662) *L'Esprit de cour, ou les conversations galantes. Divisees en cent dialogues.* Paris: C. de Sercy.

Baudino, C. (2001) *Politique de la langue et différence sexuelle: la politisation du genre des noms de métier*, Paris: L'Harmattan.

Bauvois, C. (2002) *Ni d'Eve ni d'Adam. Étude sociolinguistique de douze variables du français*, Paris: L'Harmattan.

Bayley, P. J. (1980) *French Pulpit Oratory 1598–1650: A Study in Themes and Styles, with a Descriptive Catalogue of Printed Texts*, Cambridge University Press.

Beaulieux, Ch. (1951) *Observations sur l'orthographe de la langue Françoise. Transcriptions, commentaire, et fac-similé du manuscrit de Mézeray, 1673, et des critiques des commissaires de l'Académie*, Paris: É. Champion.

Beaunier, A. (ed.) (1942) *Madame de La Fayette, Correspondance*, 2 vols., Paris: Gallimard.

Béchade, H. D. (1981) *Les Romans comiques de Charles Sorel. Fiction narrative, langue et langages*, Geneva: Droz.

Bellegarde, J.-B. Morvan de (1695) *Réflexions sur l'élégance et la politesse du stile*, Paris: A. Pralard.

Bellegarde, J.-B. Morvan de (1698) *Modeles de conversations pour les personnes polies. Seconde Edition augmentée*. Paris: J. Guignard.

Bellegarde, J.-B. Morvan de (1700) *Reflexions sur la politesse des mœurs, avec des maximes pour la société civile. Suite des Reflexions sur le Ridicule. Seconde édition augmentée*. Paris: J. and M. Guignard.

Bérain, N. (1675) *Nouvelles Remarques sur la langue française*, Rouen: E. Viret.

Berrendonner, A., Le Guern, M. and Puech, G. (1983) *Principes de grammaire polylectale*, Lyon: Presses Universitaires de Lyon.

Bertrand, D. (1997) 'Le voyage en pays burlesque selon Dassoucy: le bruissement des langues', in Y. Giraud (ed.), *Contacts culturels et échanges linguistiques au XVIIe siècle en France. Actes du 3e Colloque du Centre International de Rencontres sur le XVIIe siècle, Université de Fribourg (Suisse) 1996*, Paris, Seattle, Tübingen: Papers on French Seventeenth Century Literature, pp. 147–58.

Beugnot, B. (1971) *L'Entretien au XVIIe siècle. Leçon inaugurale*, Montreal: Presses de l'Université de Montréal.

Biber, D. (1995) *Dimensions of Register Variation. A Cross-Linguistic Comparison*, Cambridge University Press.

Bickerton, D. (1981) *Roots of Language*, Ann Arbor: Karoma.

Bickerton, D. (1984) 'The language bioprogram hypothesis', *The Behavioural and Brain Sciences* 7: 173–221.

Blanche-Benveniste, C. (1995) 'De quelques débats sur le role de la langue parlée dans les évolutions diachroniques', *Langue Française* 107: 25–35.

Blanche-Benveniste, C. (1997) 'La notion de variation syntaxique dans la langue parlée', *Langue Française* 115: 19–29.

Blanche-Benveniste, C. and Jeanjean, C. (1987) *Le Français parlé: Transcription et édition*, Paris: Didier.

Blasco-Couturier, M. (1990) 'Les constructions caractérisées par la réduplication aux XVIIe et XVIIIe siècles', *Recherches sur le Français Parlé* 10: 9–18.

Bollème, G. (1971) *La Bibliothèque bleue: la littérature populaire en France du XVIIe au XIXe siècles*, Paris: Julliard.

Bonnard, H. (1975) 'Les mots indéfinis', in *Grand Larousse de la langue française en sept volumes*, vol. 4, Paris: Larousse, pp. 2623–37.

Bouchard, P. *et al.* (1999) *La Féminisation des noms de métiers, fonctions, grades ou titres: au Québec, en Suisse romande, en France et en Communauté française de Belgique*, Brussels: Duculot.

Bouhours, D. (1674) *Doutes sur la langue françoise proposez à Messieurs de l'Académie Françoise par un gentilhomme de province*, Paris: S. Mabre-Cramoisy.

Bouhours, D. (1675) *Remarques nouvelles sur la langue françoise*, Paris: S. Mabre-Cramoisy.

Bouhours, D. (1693) *Suite des Remarques nouvelles sur la langue françoise*, Paris: G. and L. Josse.

Bouhours, D. (1962 [¹1671]) *Les Entretiens d'Ariste et d'Eugène*, ed. F. Brunot, Paris: A. Colin.

Boutet, J. (1988) 'La concurrence de ON et I en français parlé', *LINX* 18: 47–66.

Branca-Rosoff, S. (1989) 'Vue d'en bas: des écrits "malhabiles" pendant la période révolutionnaire', *Langage et Société* 47: 9–27.

Branca-Rosoff, S. and Schneider, N. (1994) *L'Écriture des citoyens. Une analyse linguistique de l'écriture des peu-lettrés pendant la période révolutionnaire*, Paris: Klincksieck.

Bray, L. (1986) *César-Pierre Richelet (1626–1698). Bibliographie et œuvre lexicographique*, Tübingen: M. Niemeyer.

Bray, L. (1990) 'Les marques d'usage dans le *Dictionnaire françois* (1680) de César-Pierre Richelet', in Glatigny 1990: 43–59.

Brécourt, G. M. de (1681) *La Nopce de Village. Comedie*, Paris: J. Ribou.

Brunot, F. (1891) *La Doctrine de Malherbe d'après son commentaire sur Desportes*, Paris: G. Masson.

Brunot, F. (1905–53) *Histoire de la langue française des origines à 1900*, 13 vols., Paris: A. Colin.

Buffet, M. (1668) *Nouvelles Observations sur la langue françoise. Où il est traitté des termes anciens & inusitez, & du bel usage des mots nouveaux. Avec les Eloges des Illustres Sçavantes, tant Anciennes que Modernes*, Paris: J. Cusson.

Callières, F. de (1693) *Du bon, et du mauvais usage, dans les manieres de s'exprimer. Des façons de parler bourgeoises. Et en quoy elles sont differentes de celles de la Cour. Suitte des Mots à la mode*, Paris: C. Barbin.

Caron, P. (2002) 'Vers la notion de chronolecte? Quelques jalons à propos du français préclassique', in Sampson and Ayres-Bennett 2002: 329–52.

Carrier, H. (ed.) (1982) *La Fronde: Contestation démocratique et misère paysanne. 52 Mazarinades*, 2 vols., Paris: EDHIS.

Carrier, H. (1989) *La Presse de la Fronde (1648–1653): Les Mazarinades. 1. La Conquête de l'opinion*, Geneva: Droz.

Carrier, H. (1991) *La Presse de la Fronde (1648–1653): Les Mazarinades. 2. Les Hommes du livre*, Geneva: Droz.

Carrier, H. (1996) *Les Muses guerrières. Les Mazarinades et la vie littéraire au milieu du XVIIe siècle: courants, genre, culture populaire et savante à l'époque de la Fronde*, Paris: Klincksieck.

Carruthers, J. (1999) 'A problem in sociolinguistic methodology: investigating a rare syntactic form', *Journal of French Language Studies* 9: 1–24.

Cerquiglini, B. (1996) *Le Roman de l'orthographe au paradis des mots, avant la faute, 1150–1694*, Paris: Hatier.

Charpentier, F. (1650) *Les Choses memorables de Socrate, ouvrage de Xenephon Traduit de Grec en François. Avec La Vie de Socrate, Nouvellement composée & recueillie des plus celebres Autheurs de l'Antiquité*, Paris: A. Courbé.

Charpentier, F. (1676) *Deffense de la langue françoise, pour l'Inscription de l'Arc de Triomphe*, Paris: C. Barbin.

Charpentier, F. (1683) *De l'excellence de la langue françoise*, 2 vols., Paris: La veuve Bilaine [sic].

Chaudenson, R. (1973) 'Pour une étude comparée des créoles et parlers français d'outre-mer: survivance et innovation', *Revue de Linguistique Romane* 37: 342–71.

Chaudenson, R. (1979) *Les Créoles français*, [Paris]: F. Nathan.

Chaudenson, R. (1989) *Créoles et enseignement du français*, Paris: L'Harmattan.

Chaudenson, R. (1992) *Des îles, des hommes, des langues. Essai sur la créolisation linguistique et culturelle*, Paris: L'Harmattan.

Chaudenson, R. (1994) 'Français d'Amérique du Nord et créoles français: le français parlé par les immigrants du XVIIe siècle', in Mougeon and Beniak 1994: 167–80.

Chaudenson, R., Mougeon, R. and Beniak, E. (1993) *Vers une approche panlectale de la variation du français*, Paris: Didier.

Chervel, A. (1983) 'La "langue parlée" au XIXe siècle', *Recherches sur le Français Parlé* 5: 163–75.

Cheshire, J. (1996) 'Syntactic variation and the concept of prominence', in J. Klemola, M. Kytö and M. Rissanen (eds.), *Speech past and present: Studies in English Dialectology in Memory of Ossi Ihalainen*, Frankfurt: Lang, pp. 1–17.

Coates, J. (1986) *Women, Men and Language: A Sociolinguistic Account of Sex Differences in Language*, London, New York: Longman.

Coates, J. and Cameron, D. (eds.) (1988) *Women in their Speech Communities: New Perspectives on Language and Sex*, London, New York: Longman.

Coëffeteau, N. (1615) *Histoire romaine de Lucius Annaeus Florus. Continuée depuis la fondation de la Ville de Rome jusques à l'Empire de Tybere. Mise en nostre langue par le commandement du Roy, Et dediée à sa Majesté*, Paris: S. Cramoisy.

Coëffeteau, N. (1621) *Histoire romaine, contenant tout ce qui s'est passé de plus memorable depuis le commencement de l'Empire d'Auguste jusques à celuy de Constantin le Grand [. . .]*, Paris: S. Cramoisy.

Cohen, M. (1946) *Le français en 1700 d'après le témoignage de Giles Vaudelin*, Paris: H. Champion.

Cohen, M. (1954) 'Comment on parlait le français en 1700', in M. Cohen, *Grammaire et style 1400–1950: Cinq cents ans de phrase française*, Paris: Éditions Sociales, pp. 73–9.

Collin, L. (ed.) (1806) *Lettres de Mesdames de Scudéry, de Salvan de Saliez, et de Mademoiselle Descartes*, Paris: L. Collin.

Corneille, T. (1694) *Le Dictionnaire des arts et des sciences*, 2 vols., Paris: Veuve de J. B. Coignard and J. B. Coignard.

Coseriu, E. (1970) *Einführung in die strukturelle Betrachtung des Wortschatzes*, Tübingen: Narr.

Costa, C. (ed.) (1998) *Jacques Jacques, Le faut mourir et les excuses inutiles qu'on apporte à cette nécessité. Le tout en vers burlesques*, Paris: H. Champion.

Cotgrave, R. (1611) *A Dictionarie of the French and English Tongues*, London: A. Islip.

Coveney, A. (1996) *Variability in Spoken French. A Sociolinguistic Study of Interrogation and Negation*, Exeter: Elm Bank Publications.

Coveney, A. (2000) 'Vestiges of *nous* and the 1st person plural verb in informal spoken French', *Language Sciences* 22: 447–81.

Cuénin, M. (1973). *Molière, Les Précieuses ridicules. Documents contemporains. Lexique du vocabulaire précieux*, Geneva: Droz.

Cyrano de Bergerac, S. (1977) *Œuvres complètes*, ed. J. Prévot, Paris: Belin.

Cyrano de Bergerac, S. (1981) *Mazarinades. Préface de René Briand*, Paris: Éditions de l'Opale.

Dacier, A. (1699) *Les Œuvres de Platon traduites en francois, avec des Remarques* [. . .], vol. 1, Paris: J. Anisson.

Dagenais, L. (1991) 'De la phonologie du français vers 1700: les systèmes vocaliques de Hindret (1687, 1696) et de Vaudelin (1713, 1715)', *La Linguistique* 27(2): 75–89.

Dangeau, L. de Courcillon de (1694) *Essais de grammaire contenus en trois lettres d'un académicien à un autre académicien*, Paris: J. B. Coignard.

Dauzat, A. (1927) *Les Patois: évolution, classification, étude*, Paris: Delagrave.

Davis, N. Z. (1988) *Pour sauver sa vie. Les récits de pardon au XVIe siècle*, Paris: Éditions du Seuil (American edition, 1987).

De Gorog, R. (1990) 'Early seventeenth-century French and Héroard's *Journal*', *Romance Philology* 43: 431–42.

Deimier, P. de (1610) *L'Academie de l'art poetique. Où par amples raisons, demonstrations, nouvelles recherches, examinations & authoritez d'exemples, sont vivement esclaircis & deduicts, les moyens par où l'on peut parvenir à la vraye & parfaicte connoissance de la Poësie Françoise*, Paris: J. de Bordeaulx.

Deloffre, F. (ed.) (1961) *Agréables Conférences de deux paysans de Saint-Ouen et de Montmorency sur les affaires du temps (1649–1651)*, Paris: Les Belles Lettres.

Deloffre, F. and M. Menemencioglu (eds.) (1979) *Journal d'un voyage fait aux Indes orientales (1690–1691) par Robert Challe, écrivain du Roi*, Paris: Mercure de France.

Denis, D. (1997) *La Muse galante. Poétique de la conversation dans l'œuvre de Madeleine de Scudéry*, Paris: H. Champion.

Denis, D. (ed.) (1998a) *Madeleine de Scudéry, 'De l'air galant' et autres conversations: pour une étude de l'archive galante*, Paris: H. Champion.

Denis, D. (1998b) 'Ce que parler "prétieux" veut dire: les enseignements d'une fiction linguistique au XVIIe siècle', *L'Information Grammaticale* 78: 53–8.

Denis, D. (2003) 'Préciosité et galanterie: vers une nouvelle cartographie', in D. Wetsel and F. Canovas (eds.), *Les Femmes au Grand Siècle. Le Baroque: musique et littérature. Musique et liturgie. Actes du 33e congrès annuel de la North American Society for Seventeenth-Century French Literature*, vol. 2, Tübingen: Narr, pp. 17–39.

Désirat, C. and Hordé, T. (1976) *La Langue française au 20e siècle*, Paris: Bordas.

Dezon-Jones, E. (ed.) (1988) *Marie de Gournay. Fragments d'un discours féminin*, Paris: J. Corti.

Dobert, A. (1650). *Recreations literales et mysterieuses: ou sont curieusement estalez les Principes & l'importance de la nouvelle Orthographe: Avec un acheminement à la connoissance de la Poësie, & des Anagrames*, Lyon: F. de Masso.

Du Bosc(q), J. (1633 [¹1632]) *L'Honneste Femme. Seconde edition, reveue, corrigée & augmentée par l'Autheur*. Paris: J. Jost.

Du Bosc(q), J. (1634) *L'Honneste Femme. Seconde Partie*, Paris: A. Soubron.

Du Bosc(q), J. (1636) *L'Honneste Femme. Troisiesme et derniere partie*, Paris: A. Courbé.

Duchêne, R. (ed.) (1988) *Madame de Sévigné, Lettres choisies*, Paris: Gallimard.

Duchêne, R. (1995) 'A la recherche d'une espèce rare et mêlée: les Précieuses avant Molière', *Papers on French Seventeenth Century Literature* 22: 331–57.

Duchêne, R. (1998) 'La lettre: genre masculin et pratique féminine?', in Planté 1998: 27–50.

Duchêne, R. (2001) *Les Précieuses ou comment l'esprit vint aux femmes* [. . .], Paris: Fayard.

Duez, N. (1669) *Le Vray et parfait guidon de la langue françoise*, Amsterdam: L. and D. Elzevier.

Dulong, C. (1984) *La Vie quotidienne des femmes du Grand Siècle*, [Paris]: Hachette.

Dulong, C. (1991) 'De la conversation à la création', in N. Z. Davis and A. Farge (eds.), *Histoire des femmes en Occident. Volume 3: XVIe–XVIIIe siècles*, [Paris]: Plon, pp. 403–25.

Dupleix, S. (1651) *Liberté de la langue françoise dans sa pureté*, Paris: D. Becnet.

Durand, Y. (ed.) (1966) *Cahiers de doléances des paroisses du bailliage de Troyes pour les États généraux de 1614*, Paris: Presses Universitaires de France.

Du Val, J.-B. (1604) *L'Eschole françoise. Pour apprendre à bien parler & escrire selon l'usage de ce temps & pratique des bons Autheurs*, Paris: E. Foucault.

Ernst, G. (1980) 'Prolegomena zu einer Geschichte des gesprochenen Französisch', in Stimm 1980: 1–14.

Ernst, G. (1985) *Gesprochenes Französisch zu Beginn des 17. Jahrhunderts. Direkte Rede in Jean Héroards 'Histoire particulière de Louis XIII' (1605–1610)*, Tübingen: Niemeyer.

Ernst, G. (1999) 'Zwischen Alphabetisierung und "français populaire écrit". Zur Graphie privater französischer Texte des 17. und 18. Jahrhunderts', *Sociolinguistica* 13: 91–111.

Ernst, G. and Wolf, B. (2001–2) *Textes français privés des XVIIe et XVIIIe siècles*, 2 CD-ROMs, Beihefte zur Zeitschrift für romanische Philologie 310, Tübingen: M. Niemeyer.

Erondell, P. (1969) *The French Garden 1605*, Menston: Scolar.

Estienne, R. (1549) *Dictionaire Francoislatin, autrement dict Les mots Francois, avec les manieres duser diceulx, tournez en Latin*, Paris: R. Estienne.

Evang, A. (1984) 'Description grammaticale et code parlé: l'emploi du passé simple et du passé composé dans des manuels d'étude parus entre 1600 et 1650', *Travaux de Linguistique et de Littérature* 22(1): 161–77.

Fagniez, G. (1929) *La Femme et la société française dans la première moitié du XVIIe siècle*, Paris: J. Gamber.

Faret, N. (1925) *L'Honneste Homme ou l'art de plaire à la court*, ed. M. Magendie, Paris: Presses Universitaires de France.

Farrell, J. (2001). *Latin Language and Latin Culture from Ancient to Modern Times*, Cambridge University Press.

Fatio, O. (ed.) (1994) *Jacques Flournoy, Journal 1675–1692*, Geneva: Droz.

Fillon, A. (ed.) (1996) *Louis Simon, villageois de l'ancienne France*, Rennes: Éditions Ouest-France.

Finke, A. (1983) *Untersuchungen zu Formen und Funktionen der Satzfrage im Theater des 17. und 18. Jahrhunderts*, Geneva: Droz.

Fleischman, S. (1990) *Tense and Narrativity. From Medieval Performance to Modern Fiction*, London: Routledge.

Fleischman, S. (1996) 'Methodologies and ideologies in historical grammar: a case study from Old French', in R. H. Bloch and S. G. Nichols (eds.), *Medievalism and the Modernist Temper*, Baltimore, London: Johns Hopkins University Press, pp. 402–38.

Foisil, M. (1986) 'L'écriture du for privé', in P. Ariès and G. Duby (eds.), *Histoire de la vie privée*, vol. 3, Paris: Seuil, pp. 331–69.

Fournier, É. (ed.) (1855) *Les Caquets de l'accouchée. Nouvelle édition.* Paris: P. Jannet.

Fournier, É. (ed.) (1855–63) *Variétés historiques et littéraires. Recueil de pièces volantes rares et curieuses en prose et en vers*, 10 vols., Paris: P. Jannet.

Fournier, É. (ed.) (1858) *Chansons de Gaultier Garguille, Nouvelle édition suivie des pièces relatives à ce farceur*, Paris: P. Jannet.

Fournier, N. (1998) *Grammaire du français classique*, Paris: Belin.

Fournier, N. (2001) 'Langage, discours, métadiscours, style dans l'*Histoire comique de Francion*', *Littératures Classiques* 41: 155–66.

Fournier, R. and Wittmann, H. (eds.) (1995) *Le Français des Amériques* (= *Revue Québécoise de Linguistique Théorique et Appliquée* 12), Trois-Rivières: Presses Universitaires de Trois-Rivières.

François, A. (1959) *Histoire de la langue française cultivée des origines à nos jours*, 2 vols., Geneva: A. Jullien.

François, C. (1987) *Précieuses et autres indociles. Aspects du féminisme dans la littérature française du XVIIe siècle*, Birmingham, Alabama: Summa.

Frei, H. (1982 [¹1929]) *La Grammaire des fautes*, Geneva, Paris: Slatkine reprints.

Fukui, Y. (1964) *Raffinement précieux dans la poésie française du XVIIe siècle*, Paris: A. G. Nizet.

Fumaroli, M. (1992) *Le Genre des genres littéraires: la conversation*. The Zaharoff Lecture for 1990–91, Oxford: Clarendon Press.

Furetière, A. (1690) *Dictionaire universel, Contenant generalement tous les mots françois tant vieux que modernes, & les Termes de toutes les sciences et des arts [. . .]*, 3 vols., La Haye/Rotterdam: A. and R. Leers.

Furetière, A. ([1955]) *Le Roman bourgeois*, ed. G. Mongrédien, Paris: Le Club du meilleur livre.

Gadet, F. (1996) 'Une distinction bien fragile: oral/écrit', *Travaux Neuchâtelois de Linguistique*, 25: 13–27.

Gadet, F. (1997a) *La Variation en Syntaxe* = *Langue Française* 115.

Gadet, F. (1997b) 'La variation, plus qu'une écume', *Langue Française* 115: 5–18.

Galet, Y. (1971) *L'Évolution de l'ordre des mots dans la phrase française de 1600 à 1700*, Paris: Presses Universitaires de France.

Garapon, R. (1957) *La Fantaisie verbale et le comique dans le théâtre français du Moyen Age à la fin du XVIIe siècle*, Paris: A. Colin.

GEHLF (1992) *Grammaire des fautes et français non-conventionnels*, Paris: Presses de l'École Normale Supérieure.

Gibson, W. (1989) *Women in Seventeenth-Century France*, Basingstoke: Macmillan.

Gilbert, G. (1650) *Panegyrique des dames*, Paris: A. Courbé.

Glatigny, M. (ed.) (1990a) *Les Marques d'usage dans les dictionnaires (XVIIe–XVIIIe siècles)* = *Lexique* 9.

Glatigny, M. (1990b) 'Présentation: l'importance des marques d'usage', in Glatigny 1990a: 7–16.

Glatigny, M. (1998) *Les Marques d'usage dans les dictionnaires français monolingues du XIXe siècle. Jugements portés sur un échantillon de mots et d'emplois par les principaux lexicographes*, Tübingen: M. Niemeyer.

Godard de Donville, L. and Duchêne, R. (eds.) (1985) *De la mort de Colbert à la Révocation de l'Édit de Nantes: un monde nouveau? XVIe colloque C.M.R.17, janvier 1984*, Marseilles: C.M.R. 17.

Goldsmith, E. C. (1988) *'Exclusive Conversations'. The Art of Interaction in Seventeenth-century France*, Philadelphia: University of Pennsylvania Press.

Gondret, P. (1998) 'La place des éléments négatifs avec l'infinitif, du XVIème siècle au XVIIIème siècle', in J. Baudry and P. Caron (eds.), *Problèmes de cohésion syntaxique de 1550 à 1720*, Limoges: Presses Universitaires de Limoges, pp. 49–75.

Gougenheim, G. (1931) 'L'observation du langage d'un enfant royal au XVIIe siècle d'après le journal d'Héroard', *Revue de Philologie Française* 43: 1–15.

Gougenheim, G. (1971) *Étude sur les périphrases verbales de la langue française*, Paris: A.-G. Nizet.

Gougenheim, G. (1974) *Grammaire de la langue française du seizième siècle*, Paris: A. & J. Picard.

Gournay, M. Le Jars de (1626) *L'Ombre de la damoiselle de Gournay, œuvre composé de meslanges*. Paris: J. Libert [= first edition of collected works].

Gournay, M. Le Jars de (1634, 1641) *Les Advis ou les presens de la demoiselle de Gournay*, Paris: T. du Bray [= second edition of collected works].

Grafström, Å. (1969) '*On* remplaçant *nous* en français', *Revue de Linguistique Romane* 33: 270–98.

Grande, N. (1999a) *Stratégies de romancières. De 'Clélie' à 'La Princesse de Clèves' (1654–1678)*, Paris: H. Champion.

Grande, N. (1999b) 'L'instruction primaire des romancières', in C. Navitel (ed.), *Femmes savantes, savoirs des femmes: Du crépuscule de la Renaissance à l'aube des Lumières*, Geneva: Droz, pp. 51–7.

Greive, A. (1984) 'Remarques sur l'histoire du français parlé', *Cahiers de l'Institut de Linguistique de Louvain* 10: 65–76.

Grenaille, F. de [sieur de Chatounières] (1639–40) *L'Honneste Fille*, 3 vols., Paris: J. Paslé; T. Quinet; A. de Sommaville and T. Quinet.

Grevisse, M. (1993) *Le Bon Usage. Grammaire française refondue par André Goosse*, thirteenth edition, Paris/Louvain-la Neuve: Duculot.

Guillaume, J. (1665) *Les Dames Illustres ou Par bonnes & fortes raisons, il se prouve que le Sexe Feminin surpasse en toute sorte de genres le sexe Masculin*, Paris: T. Jolly.

Guiraud, P. (1958) *La Grammaire*, Paris: Presses Universitaires de France.

Guiraud, P. (1965) *Le Français populaire*, Paris: Presses Universitaires de France.

Haase, A. (1898) *Syntaxe française du XVIIe siècle*, trans. M. Obert, Paris: A. Picard.

Haase-Dubosc, D. (1998) 'Madame de Châtillon. Aperçus d'une correspondance politique 1678–1679', in Planté 1998: 67–82.

Harris, M. B. (1978) *The Evolution of French Syntax: A Comparative Approach*, London: Longman.

Hausmann, F. J. (1975) 'Gesprochenes und geschriebenes Französisch', *Romanistisches Jahrbuch* 26: 19–45.

Hausmann, F. J. (1979) 'Wie alt ist das gesprochene Französisch? Dargestellt speziell am Übergang von *j'allons* zu *on y va*', *Romanische Forschungen* 91: 431–44.

Hausmann, F. J. (1980) 'Zur Rekonstruktion des um 1730 gesprochenen Französisch', in Stimm 1980: 33–46.

Hausmann, F. J. (1992) 'L'âge du français parlé actuel: bilan d'une controverse allemande', in GEHLF 1992: 355–62.

Hazaël-Massieux, G. (1996) *Les Créoles: Problèmes de genèse et de description*, Aix-en-Provence: Publications de l'Université de Provence.

Hazaël-Massieux, M.-C. (1999) *Les Créoles: l'indispensable survie*, Paris: Editions Entente.

Hellegouarc'h, J. (ed.) (1997) *Anthologie. L'Art de la conversation. Préface de M. Fumaroli*, Paris: Garnier.

Henley, N. M. and Kramarae, C. (1994) 'Gender, power and miscommunication', in C. Roman, S. Juhasz and C. Miller (eds.), *The Women and Language Debate: A Sourcebook*, New Brunswick/New Jersey: Rutgers University Press, pp. 383–406.

Hindret, J. (1687) *L'Art de bien prononcer et de bien parler la langue françoise*, Paris: L. d'Houry.

Hirschbühler, P. and Labelle, M. (1994) 'Change in verb position in French negative infinitival clauses', *Language Variation and Change* 6(2): 149–78.

Hudson, R. A. (1980) *Sociolinguistics*, Cambridge University Press.

Hull, A. (1979) 'Affinités entre les variétés du français', in Valdman 1979: 165–80.

Hull, A. (1994) 'Des origines du français dans le Nouveau Monde', in Mougeon and Beniak 1994: 183–98.

Hunnius, K. (1975) 'Archaische Züge des langage populaire', *Zeitschrift für französische Sprache und Literatur* 85: 145–61.

Hunnius, K. (1981) 'Mais des idées, ça, on en a, nous, en France: Bilanz und Perspektiven der Diskussion über das Personalpronomen on im gesprochenen Französisch', *Archiv für das Studium der neueren Sprachen und Literaturen* 218: 76–89.

Irson, C. (1662 [¹1656]) *Nouvelle Methode pour apprendre facilement les principes et la pureté de la langue françoise Contenant plusieurs Traitez* [. . .], second edition, Paris: P. Baudouin.

Jacob, P. L. (ed.) (1859) *Paris ridicule et burlesque au dix-septième siècle par Claude le Petit, Berthod, Scarron, François Colletet, Boileau, etc.*, Paris: A. Delahays.

Jamerey-Duval, V. (1981) *Mémoires: enfance et éducation d'un paysan au XVIIIe siècle*, ed. J.-M. Goulemot, Paris: Éditions le Sycomore.

Jaouën, F. (1997) 'Civility and the novel: De Pure's *La Prétieuse ou le mystère des ruelles*', *Yale French Studies* 92: 105–25.

Joseph, J. E. (2000) *Limiting the Arbitrary. Linguistic Naturalism and its Opposites in Plato's 'Cratylus' and Modern Theories of Language*, Amsterdam, Philadelphia: J. Benjamins.

Juneau, M. (1972) *Contribution à l'histoire de la prononciation française au Québec: étude des graphies des documents d'archives*, Quebec: Les Presses de l'Université de Laval.

Juneau, M. and Poirier, C. (1973) *Le Livre de comptes d'un meunier québécois (fin XVIIe–début XVIIIe siècle). Édition avec étude linguistique*, Quebec: Les Presses de l'Université de Laval.

Kayne, R. S. (1975) *French Syntax: The Transformational Cycle*, Cambridge, MA and London: MIT Press.

King, M. L. (1991) *Women of the Renaissance*, Chicago and London: University of Chicago Press.

Koch, P. (1988) Review of Ernst (1985) and Prussmann-Zemper (1986), *Romanistisches Jahrbuch* 39: 153–62.

Koch, P. and Oesterreicher, W. (1990) *Gesprochene Sprache in der Romania: Französisch, Italienisch, Spanisch*, Tübingen: M. Niemeyer.

Labov, W. (1972a) *Sociolinguistic Patterns*, Philadelphia: University of Pennsylvania Press.

Labov, W. (1972b) 'Some principles of linguistic methodology', *Language in Society* 1: 97–120.

Labov, W. (1994) *Principles of Linguistic Change*. Vol. 1: *Internal Factors*, Cambridge, MA and Oxford: B. Blackwell.

Labrosse, C. (1996) *Pour une grammaire non sexiste*, Montreal: Remue-ménage.

La Faye, A. de (1608) *Linguae gallicae, et italicae, Hortulus amoenissimus*, Halle: J. Krusicken.

La Forge, J. de (1663) *Le Cercle des femmes sçavantes*, Paris: P. Trabouillet.

Lainé, P. (1655) *A Compendious Introduction to the French Tongue* [. . .], London: A. Williamson.

Lancelot, C. (1681) *Nouvelle Methode pour apprendre facilement la langue latine* [. . .] *Avec un Traité de la Poësie Latine, & une bréve Instruction sur les Regles de la Poësie Françoise, Huitième édition. Revûë, corrigée & augmentée de nouveau*, Paris: D. Thierry [work on French poetics first included in the second edition, Paris: A. Vitré, 1650].

La Rochefoucauld, F., duc de (1967) *Maximes*, ed. J. Truchet, Paris: Garnier.

Larrivée, P. (forthcoming) 'Qu'est-ce qu'une donnée linguistique? Le cas des données littéraires', to appear in *Actes du Colloque International Littérature et Linguistique: Diachronie/Synchronie*, University of Savoie, 14–16 November 2002.

Lartigaut, A. (1669) *Les Progrés de la véritable ortografe ou l'ortografe francêze fondée sur ses principes confirmée par démonstracions*, Paris: L. Ravenau and J. d'Ouri.

Lathuillère, R. (1966) *La Préciosité. Étude historique et linguistique. Tome I: Position du problème – Les Origines*, Geneva: Droz.

Lathuillère, R. (1984) 'Pour une étude de la langue populaire à l'époque classique', in *Mélanges de langue et de littérature médiévales offerts à Alice Planche*, Nice: Les Belles Lettres, pp. 279–86.

Lathuillère, R. (1987) 'La langue des Précieux', *Travaux de Linguistique et de Littérature* 25: 243–69.

La Touche, P. de (1696) *L'Art de bien parler françois, qui comprend tout ce qui regarde la Grammaire et les façons de parler douteuses*, 2 vols., Amsterdam: H. Desbordes.

Lavandera, B. (1978) 'Where does the sociolinguistic variable stop?', *Language in Society* 7: 171–83.

Le Brun de la Rochette, C. (1618) *Les Proces civil, et criminel* [. . .], *Reueus, corrigez & augmentez par l'Autheur en ceste derniere Edition*, Lyon: P. Rigaud.

Legendre, G. (ed.) (1979) *Les Annales de l'Hôtel-Dieu de Montréal, 1659–1725. Marie Morin, Histoire simple et véritable*, Montreal: Presses de l'Université de Montréal.

Le Maistre de Sacy, I. (1686 [[1]1685]) *Le Deuteronome traduit en françois, avec l'explication Du sens litteral & du sens spirituel, tirée Des saints Peres & des Auteurs Ecclesiastiques. Seconde edition.* Paris: G. Desprez.

Le Roy Ladurie, E. and Ranum, O. (1985) *Pierre Prion: mémoires d'un écrivain de campagne au XVIIIe siècle*, Paris: Gallimard, Julliard.

L'Esclache, L. de (1668) *Les véritables régles de l'ortografe francéze, ou L'Art d'aprandre an peu de tams à écrire côrectement*, Paris: L'Auteur and L. Rondet.

Lesure, F. (ed.) (1963) *Marin Mersenne, Harmonie Universelle: contenant la théorie et la pratique de la musique (1636)*, Paris: CNRS.

Leven de Templery, J. (1698) *La Rhétorique françoise, très-propre aux gens qui veulent apprendre à parler et écrire avec politessse*, Paris: M. and G. Jouvenal.

Leven de Templery, J. (1699) *L'Éloquence du tems enseignée à une dame de qualité, très-propre aux gens qui veulent apprendre à parler et écrire avec politessse* [. . .], Paris: J. Léonard.

Lindemann, M. (1997–98) 'Le Dictionnaire de l'Académie française de 1694 – les principes et la réalisation', in M. Bierbach *et al.* (eds.), *Mélanges de lexicographie et de linguistique françaises et romanes, dédiés à la mémoire de Manfred Höfler* (= Travaux de Linguistique et de Philologie, two vols. in one, 35–6), Paris: Klincksieck, pp. 281–97.

Lodge, R. A. (1991) 'Molière's peasants and the norms of spoken French', *Neuphilologische Mitteilungen* 42: 485–99.

Lodge, R. A. (1993) *French: From Dialect to Standard*, London: Routledge.

Lodge, R. A. (1996) 'Stereotypes of vernacular pronunciation in seventeenth- and eighteenth-century Paris', *Zeitschrift für romanische Philologie* 112: 205–31.

Lodge, R. A. (1998) 'Vers une histoire du dialecte urbain de Paris', *Revue de Linguistique Romane* 62: 95–128.

Lottin, A. (1979) *Chavatte, ouvrier lillois. Un contemporain de Louis XIV*, Paris: Flammarion.

Lougee, C. C. (1976) *Le Paradis des femmes: Women, Salons and Social Stratification in Seventeenth-Century France*, Princeton University Press.

Lyons, J. (1977) *Semantics*, 2 vols., Cambridge University Press.

Maclean, I. (1987) 'La voix des précieuses et les détours de l'expression', in Richmond and Venesoen 1987: 47–71.

Magendie, M. (1925) *La Politesse mondaine et les théories de l'honnêteté, en France, au XVIIe siècle, de 1610 à 1660*, Paris: Presses Universitaires de France.

Maigne, V. (1992) 'Tallemant des Réaux et les déviances linguistiques. Les remarques sur la langue dans les *Historiettes*', in GEHLF 1992: 105–15.

Maignien, C. (ed.) (1991) *Madeleine de Scudéry, Les Femmes illustres ou les Harangues héroïques 1642*, Paris: Côté-femmes éditions.

Maître, M. (1998) 'Lettres de Sapho, lettres de Madeleine? Les lettres dans la *Clélie* et la correspondance de Mlle de Scudéry', in Planté 1998: 51–66.

Maître, M. (1999) *Les Précieuses. Naissance des femmes de lettres en France au XVIIe siècle*, Paris: H. Champion.

Malherbe, F. de (1615) 'Traduction du troisiesme Livre de la quatriesme Decade de Tite-Live', in *Les Decades qui se trouvent de Tite-Live en francois avec des annotations et figures pour l'intelligence de l'antiquite Romaine. Plus une description particuliere des lieux et une Chronologie generale des principaux potentas de la terre. Par B. de Vigenere*, 2 vols., Paris: La Veufve Abel l'Angelier, vol. 2, unpaginated.

Malherbe, F. de (1666) *Les Poësies de M. de Malherbe; avec les observations de Monsieur Menage*, Paris: T. Jolly.

Marchello-Nizia, C. (1979) *Histoire de la langue française aux XIVe et XVe siècles*, Paris: Bordas.

Marchello-Nizia, C. (1995) *L'Évolution du français: ordre des mots, démonstratifs, accent tonique*, Paris: A. Colin.

Marchello-Nizia, C. (1998) 'Dislocations en diachronie: archéologie d'un phénomène du "français oral"', in M. Bilger, K. Van den Eynde and F. Gadet (eds.), *Analyse linguistique et approches de l'oral. Recueil d'études offert en hommage à Claire Blanche-Benveniste*, Leuven/Paris: Peeters, pp. 327–37.

Martineau, F. (1994) 'Movement of negative adverbs in French infinitival clauses', *Journal of French Language Studies* 4: 55–73.

Martineau, F. and Mougeon, R. (2003) 'A sociolinguistic study of the origins of *ne* deletion in European and Quebec French', *Language* 79 (1): 118–52.

Martinet, A. (1974 [¹1947]) 'La phonologie du français vers 1700', in *Le français sans fard*, Paris: Presses Universitaires de France, pp. 155–67.

Marty-Laveaux, Ch. (ed.) (1863) *Cahiers de remarques sur l'orthographe françoise Pour estre examinez par chacun de Messieurs de l'Académie. Avec des observations de Bossuet, Pellisson, etc.*, Paris: J. Gay.

Matoré, G. (1953) *La Méthode en lexicologie: domaine français*, Paris: M. Didier.

Mauconduit (1669) *Traité de l'orthographe, Dans lequel on établit, par une methode claire & facile, fondée sur l'usage & sur la raison, les regles certaines d'écrire correctement. Et où lon examine, par occasion, les regles qu'a données M. De Lesclache*, Paris: M. Promé.

Maupas, Ch. (1618 [¹1607]) *Grammaire et syntaxe françoise, contenant reigles bien exactes & certaines de la prononciation, orthographe, construction & usage de nostre langue, en faveur des estrangiers qui en sont desireux, Seconde Edition. Reveuë, corrigee & augmentee de moitié, & en beaucoup de sortes amendee outre la precedente*, Orleans: O. Boynard and J. Nyon.

Meigret, L. (1550) *Le Tr̨etté de la gramm̨ere françoęze*, Paris: C. Wechel.

Ménage, G. (1675 [¹1672]) *Observations de Monsieur Ménage sur la langue françoise, Segonde édition*, Paris: C. Barbin.

Ménage, G. (1676) *Observations de Monsieur Ménage sur la langue françoise. Segonde partie*, Paris: C. Barbin.

Ménage, G. (1693) *Ménagiana*, Paris: F. and P. Delaulne.

Méré, A. Gombaud, chevalier de (1930) *Œuvres complètes*, 3 vols., ed. Ch.-H. Boudhors, Paris: F. Roches.

Milliot, V. (1995) *Les Cris de Paris ou le peuple travesti. Les représentations des petits métiers parisiens (XVIe–XVIIIe siècles)*, Paris: Publications de la Sorbonne.

Milroy, J. (1992) *Linguistic Variation and Change. On the Historical Sociolinguistics of English*, Oxford and Cambridge, MA: B. Blackwell.

Milroy, J. and Milroy, L. (1991) *Authority in Language: Investigating Language Prescription and Standardisation*, second edition, London: Routledge.

Milroy, L. (1980) *Language and Social Networks*, Oxford: B. Blackwell.

Milroy, L. (1987) *Observing and Analysing Natural Language: A Critical Account of Sociolinguistic Method*, Oxford: B. Blackwell.

Moignet, G. (1965) *Le Pronom personnel en français*, Paris: Klincksieck.

Molière (J.-B. Poquelin) (1674) *Les Œuvres de Monsieur de Molière*, vol. 4, Paris: D. Thierry and C. Barbin.

Molière (J.-B. Poquelin) (1971) *Œuvres complètes*, ed. G. Couton, 2 vols., [Paris]: Gallimard.

Mongrédien, G. (1939) *Les Précieux et les Précieuses. Textes choisis et présentés avec introduction et notices suivis d'un appendice bibliographique*, Paris: Mercure de France.

Montfleury, A. J. (1739) *Théatre de Messieurs de Montfleury pere et fils. Nouvelle edition. Tome second*. Paris: Compagnie des Libraires.

Mougeon, R. (1996) 'Recherche sur les origines de la variation *vas, m'as, vais* en français québécois', in T. Lavoie (ed.), *Français du Canada, français de France. Actes du quatrième colloque international de Chicoutimi, Québec, du 21 au 24 septembre 1994*, Tübingen: M. Niemeyer, pp. 61–77.

Mougeon, R. and Beniak, E. (eds.) (1994) *Les Origines du français québécois*, Sainte-Foy: Les Presses de l'Université de Laval.

Mourgues, M. (1724 [^{1}1685]) *Traité de la poësie françoise, Nouvelle édition revûe, corrigée & augmentée*, Paris: J. Vincent.

Mousnier, R. (1969) *Les Hiérarchies sociales de 1450 à nos jours*, Paris: Presses Universitaires de France.

Muchembled, R. (1990) *Société et mentalités dans la France moderne XVIe–XVIIIe siècles*, Paris: A. Colin.

Muchembled, R. (1991) *La Sorcière au village XVe–XVIIIe siècle*, second edition, Paris: Gallimard/Julliard.

Müller, B. (1985) *Le français d'aujourd'hui*, trans. A. Elsass, Paris: Klincksieck.

Muller, Ch. (1970) 'Sur les emplois personnels de l'indéfini *on*', *Revue de Linguistique Romane* 34: 48–55.

Nicot, J. (1606) *Thresor de la langue francoyse, tant ancienne que moderne* [. . .], Paris: D. Douceur.

Nisard, Ch. (1980) *De quelques parisianismes populaires et autres locutions non encore ou plus ou moins imparfaitement expliquées des XVIIe, XVIIIe et XIXe siècles*, facsimile of the Paris 1876 edition, Paris: Éditions de la Butte aux Cailles.

Nyrop, K. (1916a) 'Étude syntaxique sur le pronom indéfini "on"', *Bulletin de l'Académie Royale des Sciences et Lettres de Danemark* 2: 169–79.

Nyrop, K. (1916b) 'Nouvelles remarques sur le pronom indéfini "on"', *Bulletin de l'Académie Royale des Sciences et Lettres de Danemark* 4: 321–27.

Oudin, A. (1632) *Grammaire françoise, rapportée au langage du temps*, Paris: P. Billaine.

Oudin, A. (1640) *Curiositez françoises, pour supplement aux Dictionnaires. Ou Recueil de plusieurs belles proprietez, avec une infinité de Proverbes & Quolibets, pour l'explication de toutes sortes de Livres*, Paris: A. de Sommaville.

Oudin, A. (1650) *Dialogues fort recreatifs composez en Espagnol, Et nouvellement mis en Italien, Alleman & François. Avec des obseruations pour l'accord & la proprieté des quatres langues*, Paris: A. de Sommaville.

Pekacz, J. T. (1999) *Conservative Tradition in Pre-Revolutionary France: Parisian Salon Women*, New York: P. Lang.

Pellisson, P. and d'Olivet, P.-J. T. (1858) *Histoire de l'Académie Française par Pellisson & d'Olivet*, ed. Ch.-L. Livet, 2 vols., Paris: Didier.

Pelous, J.-M. (1980) *Amour précieux, amour galant 1654–1675. Essai sur la représentation de l'amour dans la littérature et la société mondaines*, Paris: Klincksieck.

Petit de Julleville, L. (ed.) (1897) *Histoire de la langue et de la littérature française des origines à 1900. Vol. 4: Dix-septième siècle (Première partie: 1601–1660)*, Paris: A. Colin.

Planté, C. (ed.) (1998) *L'Epistolaire, un genre féminin?* Paris: H. Champion.

Pohl, J. (1968) 'Ne dans le français parlé contemporain: les modalités de son abandon', in A. Quilis (ed.), *Actas del XI Congreso Internacional de Lingüística y Filología Románicas*, vol. 3, Madrid: n.pub., pp. 1343–58.

Pohl, J. (1972) 'Ne et les enfants', in *L'homme et le signifiant*, Paris: Nathan; Brussels: Labor, pp. 107–11.

Poisson, R. (1609) *Alfabet nouveau de la vrée, & pure ortografe Fransoize, & Modéle sus iselui, en forme de Dixionére*, Paris: J. Planchon.

Poplack, S. (1989) 'The care and handling of a megacorpus: the Ottawa-Hull French project', in R. Fasold and D. Schiffrin (eds.), *Language Change and Variation*, Amsterdam: Benjamins, pp. 411–51.

Poplack, S. (1992) 'The inherent variability of the French subjunctive', in C. Laeufer and T. A. Morgan (eds.), *Theoretical Analyses in Romance Linguistics: Selected Papers from the Nineteenth Linguistic Symposium on Romance Languages (LSRL XIX)*, Amsterdam, Philadelphia: Benjamins, pp. 235–63.

Posner, R. (1994) 'Historical linguistics, language change and the history of French', *Journal of French Language Studies* 4: 75–97.

Posner, R. (1997) *Linguistic Change in French*, Oxford: Clarendon Press.

Poullain de la Barre, F. (1674) *De l'Éducation des dames pour la conduite de l'esprit dans les sciences et dans les mœurs. Entretiens*, Paris: J. Du Puis.

Poullain de la Barre, F. (1675) *De l'Excellence des hommes contre l'égalité des sexes*, Paris: J. Du Puis.

Poullain de la Barre, F. (1679 [[1]1673]) *De l'égalité des deux sexes, discours physique et moral, Où l'on voit l'importance de se défaire des préjugez, seconde édition*, Paris: A. Dezallier.

Price, G. (1971) *The French Language: Present and Past*, London: E. Arnold.

Prüssmann-Zemper, H. E. F. (1986) *Entwicklungstendenzen und Sprachwandel im Neufranzösischen. Das Zeugnis des Héroard und die Genese des gesprochenen Französisch*, doctoral dissertation, Bonn: Rheinische Friedrich-Wilhelms-Universität Bonn.

Pure, Abbé M. de (1938–9) *La Prétieuse ou Le Mystère des ruelles*, ed. É. Magne, 2 vols., Paris: Droz.

Radtke, E. (1994) *Gesprochenes Französisch und Sprachgeschichte. Zur Rekonstruktion der Gesprächskonstitution in Dialogen französischer Sprachlehrbücher des 17. Jahrhunderts unter besonderer Berücksichtigung der italienischen Adaptionen*, Tübingen: M. Niemeyer.

Ramm, R. (1902) *Beiträge zur Kenntnis der französischen Umgangssprache des 17. Jahrhunderts*, doctoral dissertation, Kiel: Fiencke.

Raynard, S. (2002) *La seconde Préciosité. Floraison des conteuses de 1690 à 1756*, Tübingen: G. Narr.

Renaud, A. (1697) *Maniere de parler la langue françoise selon ses differens styles; avec la critique de nos plus celébres Ecrivains, En Prose & en Vers; et un petit traité de l'Orthographe & de la Prononciation Françoise*, Lyon: C. Rey.

Rey, A. (ed.) (1985) *Le Grand Robert de la langue française. Dictionnaire alphabétique et analogique de la langue française de Paul Robert, Deuxième édition entièrement revue et enrichie*, 9 vols., Paris: Le Robert.

Rey, A. (1990) 'Les marques d'usage et leur mise en place dans les dictionnaires du XVIIe siècle: le cas de Furetière', in Glatigny 1990a: 17–29.

Rey-Debove. J. and Rey, A. (eds.) (1993) *Le Nouveau Petit Robert. Dictionnaire alphabétique et analogique de la langue française, Nouvelle édition remaniée et amplifiée*, Paris: Le Robert.

Richardson, L. T. (1930) *Lexique de la langue des œuvres burlesques de Scarron avec une introduction grammticale*, Aix-en-Provence: Imp. Universitaire de Provence Nicollet.

Richelet, P. (1680) *Dictionnaire françois, contenant les mots et les choses, plusieurs remarques nouvelles sur la langue françoise [. . .]*, Geneva: J. H. Widerhold.

Richmond, I. and Venesoen, C. (eds.) (1987) *Présences féminines. Littérature et société au XVIIe siècle français. Actes de London, Canada (1985)*, Paris, Seattle, Tübingen: Papers on Seventeenth-Century French Literature.

Rickard, P. (1992) *The French Language in the Seventeenth-Century. Contemporary Opinion in France*, Cambridge: D. S. Brewer.

Roche, D. (ed.) (1982) *Journal de ma vie. Jacques-Louis Ménétra compagnon vitrier au 18e siècle*, Paris: Montalba.

Romaine, S. (1981) 'On the problem of syntactic variation: a reply to Beatriz Lavandera and William Labov', *Working Papers in Sociolinguistics* 82: 1–38.

Romaine, S. (1982) *Socio-historical Linguistics: Its Status and Methodology*, Cambridge University Press.

Romaine, S. (1984) 'On the problem of syntactic variation and pragmatic meaning in sociolinguistic theory', *Folia Linguistica. Acta Societatis Linguisticae Europaeae* 18 (3–4): 409–37.

Romaine, S. (1988) 'Historical sociolinguistics: problems and methodology', in U. Ammon, N. Dittmar and K. J. Mattheier (eds.), *Sociolinguistics: An International Handbook of the Sciences of Language and Society*, vol. 2, Berlin, New York: W. de Gruyter, pp. 1452–69.

Rosset, Th. (1911) *Les Origines de la prononciation moderne étudiées au XVIIe siècle d'après les remarques des grammairiens et les textes en patois de la banlieue parisienne*, Paris: A. Colin.

Rosset, Th. (1972 [^{1}1904]) 'E féminin au XVIIe siècle', in *Mélanges de philologie offerts à Ferdinand Brunot*, Geneva: Slatkine reprints, pp. 433–50.

Roy, É. (ed.) (1924–31) *Charles Sorel, Histoire comique de Francion*, 4 vols., Paris: Hachette.

Sainéan, L. (1907) *L'Argot ancien (1455–1850). Ses éléments constitutifs, ses rapports avec les langues secrètes de l'Europe méridionale et l'argot moderne. Avec un appendice sur l'argot jugé par Victor Hugo et Balzac*, Paris: H. Champion.

Saint-Maurice, A. de (1672) *Remarques sur les principales difficultez que les estrangers ont en la langue françoise*, Paris: E. Loyson.

Salazar, P.-J. (1995) *Le Culte de la voix au XVIIe siècle. Formes esthétiques de la parole à l'âge de l'imprimé*, Paris: H. Champion.

Salazar, P.-J. (1999) 'La voix au XVIIe siècle', in M. Fumaroli (ed.), *Histoire de la rhétorique dans l'Europe moderne 1450–1950*, Paris: Presses Universitaires de France, pp. 787–821.

Sampson, R. and Ayres-Bennett, W. (eds.) (2002) *Interpreting the History of French: A Festschrift for Peter Rickard on the Occasion of his Eightieth Birthday*, Amsterdam and New York: Rodopi.

Sancier-Château, A. (1995) *Une esthétique nouvelle: Honoré d'Urfé correcteur de L'Astrée (1607–1625)*, Geneva: Droz.

Sankoff, G. (1973) 'Above and beyond phonology in variable rules', in C. J. Bailey and R. Shuy (eds.), *New Ways of Analysing Variation in English*, Washington DC: Georgetown University Press, pp. 42–62.

Sankoff, G. and Thibault, P. (1977) 'L'alternance entre les auxiliaires *avoir* et *être* en français parlé à Montréal', *Langue Française* 34: 81–108.

Sauval, H. (1724) *Histoire et recherches des antiquités de la ville de Paris*, 3 vols., Paris: C. Moette and J. Chardon.

Scarron, P. (1981) *Le Roman comique*, ed. Y. Giraud, Paris: Garnier-Flammarion.

Scarron, P. (1988) *Le Virgile travesti*, ed. J. Serroy, Paris: Garnier.

Schalk, F. (1957) 'Bemerkungen zum Pron. Indef. in der französischen Sprache des 17. Jahrhunderts', in G. Reichenkron, M. Wandruszka and J. Wilhelm (eds.), *Festschrift für Ernst Gamillscheg zum 70. Geburtstag*, Tübingen: M. Niemeyer, pp. 511–18.

Schapira, C. (1995) 'De la grammaire au texte littéraire: valeurs grammaticales, sémantiques, stylistiques et pragmatiques de *on* en français classique', *Neophilologus* 79(4): 555–71.

Schlieben-Lange, B. (1983) *Traditionen des Sprechens. Elemente einer pragmatischen Sprachgeschichtsschreibung*, Stuttgart: W. Kohlhammer.

Schmitt, C. (2002) 'Aspects historiques de la normalisation du système verbal français: le point de vue extra-hexagonal', in Sampson and Ayres-Bennett 2002: 151–79.

Schneider, E. W. (2002) 'Investigating variation and change in written documents', in J. K. Chambers, P. Trudgill and N. Schilling-Estes (eds.), *The Handbook of Language Variation and Change*, Malden, MA and Oxford: B. Blackwell, pp. 67–96.

Schomberg, J. de (1997) *Règlement donné par une dame de haute qualité à M*** sa petite-fille, pour sa conduite, & pour celle de sa maison: avec un autre règlement que cette dame avoit dressé pour elle-mesme*, ed. Colette H. Winn, Paris: H. Champion.

Schøsler, L. (forthcoming) 'Grammaticalisation et dégrammaticalisation. Étude des constructions progressives en français du type *Pierre va/vient/est chantant*', unpublished manuscript.

Schweickard, W. (1983) 'Zur Diskussion um die Historizität gesprochener Sprache: français parlé und italiano parlato', in G. Holtus and E. Radtke (eds.), *Varietätenlinguistik des Italienischen*, Tübingen: Narr, pp. 211–31.

Seguin, J.-P. (1964) *L'Information en France avant la Périodique: 517 canards imprimés entre 1529 et 1631*, Paris: G.-P. Maisonneuve et Larose.

Seguin, J.-P. (1985) 'Le Journal de ma vie de J.-L. Ménétra: une syntaxe populaire?', in *Mélanges de langue et de littérature françaises offerts à Pierre Larthomas*, Paris: Collection de l'ENS, pp. 437–50.

Seguin, J.-P. (1999) 'La langue française aux XVIIe et XVIIIe siècles', in J. Chaurand (ed.), *Nouvelle histoire de la langue française*, Paris: Seuil, pp. 225–344.

Seijido, M. (2001) 'Étude critique d'un remarqueur de la fin du XVIIe siècle: Nicolas Andry de Boisregard', 2 vols., unpublished doctoral dissertation, Université de Aix-Marseille I.

Sellier, P. (1987) 'La Névrose précieuse: une nouvelle Pléiade?', in Richmond and Venesoen 1987: 95–125.

Sellier, P. (1999) '"Se tirer du commun des femmes": La constellation précieuse', in R. Heyndels and B. Woshinsky (eds.), *L'Autre au XVIIe siècle. Actes du 4e colloque du Centre International de Rencontres sur le XVIIe Siècle*, Tübingen: G. Narr, pp. 313–29.

Shaw, D. (1986) *Molière. Les Précieuses ridicules*, London: Grant and Cutler.

Simon, É. (1609) *La vraye et ancienne orthographe francoise restaurée. Tellement que desormais l'on aprandra parfetement à lire & à escrire & encor avec tant de facilité & breveté, que ce sera en moins de mois, que l'on ne faisoit, d'années*, Paris: J. Gesselin.

Singy, P. (ed.) (1998) *Les femmes et la langue. L'insécurité linguistique en question*, Paris: Delachaux and Niestlé.

Siouffi, G. (1995) 'Le "génie de la langue française" à l'Age classique. Recherches sur les structures imaginaires de la description linguistique de Vaugelas à Bouhours', unpublished doctoral dissertation, Université de Paris IV.

Söll, L. (1969) 'Zur Situierung von ON "nous" im neuen Französisch', *Romanische Forschungen* 81: 535–49.

Söll, L. (1985 [¹1974]) *Gesprochenes und geschriebenes Französisch*, third edition revised by F. J. Hausmann, Berlin: E. Schmidt.

Somaize, A. Baudeau, sieur de (1660) *Le Grand Dictionnaire des Pretieuses ou la clef de la langue des ruelles*, second edition, Paris: E. Loyson.

Somaize, A. Baudeau, sieur de (1661a) *Le Grand Dictionnaire des Pretieuses, historique, poetique, geographique, cosmographique, cronologique, & armoirique* [. . .], 2 vols., Paris: J. Ribou.

Somaize, A. Baudeau, sieur de (1661b) *La Clef du Grand Dictionnaire historique des Pretieuses*, Paris: npub.

Sorel, Ch. (1664) *La Bibliotheque françoise*, Paris: Compagnie des Libraires de Palais.

Soule, B. de (1689) *Traité de l'orthographe françoise ou l'orthographe en sa pureté*, Paris: E. Michallet.

Stéfanini, J. (1994) 'Approches historiques de la langue parlée', in *Histoire de la grammaire*, ed. V. Xatard, Paris: CNRS Éditions, pp. 187–97.

Stefenelli, A. (1987) *Die lexikalischen Archaismen in den Fabeln von La Fontaine*, Passau: Andreas-Haller-Verlag.

Stein, P. (1987) 'Kreolsprachen als Quelle für das gesprochene Französisch des 17. und 18. Jahrhunderts', *Archiv für das Studium der neueren Sprachen und Literaturen* 224: 52–66.

Steinmeyer, G. (1979) *Historische Aspekte des français avancé*, Geneva: Droz.

Stimm, H. (ed.) (1980) *Zur Geschichte des gesprochenen Französisch und zur Sprachlenkung im Gegenwartsfranzösischen. Beiträge des Saarbrückes Romanistentages 1979*, Wiesbaden: Steiner.

Straka, G. (1985) 'Les rimes classiques de la prononciation française de l'époque', *Travaux de Linguistique et de Littérature* 23(1): 61–138.

Streicher, J. (ed.) (1936) *Commentaires sur les Remarques de Vaugelas par La Mothe le Vayer, Scipion Dupleix, Ménage, Bouhours, Conrart, Chapelain, Patru, Thomas Corneille, Cassagne, Andry de Boisregard et l'Académie Française*, 2 vols., Paris: Droz.

Strosetzki, C. (1978) *Konversation. Ein Kapitel gesellschaftlicher und literarischer Pragmatik im Frankreich des 17. Jahrhunderts*, Frankfurt am Main: P. Lang.

Tallemant, P. (1698) *Remarques et décisions de l'Académie Françoise*, Paris: J. B. Coignard.

Thurot, Ch. (1881–3) *De la prononciation française depuis le commencement du XVIe siècle, d'après les témoignages des grammairiens*, 2 vols., Paris: Imprimerie Nationale.

Timmermans, L. (1993) *L'Accès des femmes à la culture (1598–1715): un débat d'idées, de François de Sales à la marquise de Lambert*, Paris: H. Champion.

Tolmer, L. (l'Abbé) (1938) 'Un appendice au discours physique de la parole de Cordemoy (1668). La leçon de phonétique de J.-B. du Hamel (1673)', *Le Français Moderne* 6: 243–51.

Tory, G. (1529) *Champ fleury* [. . .], Paris: G. Tory and G. de Gourmont.

Trésor de la langue française. Dictionnaire de la langue du XIXe et du XXe siècle (1789–1960) (1971–94), 16 vols., Paris: Éditions du CNRS, Gallimard.

Uildriks, A. ([1962]) *Les idées littéraires de Mlle de Gournay*, Groningen: Kleine.

Valdman, A. (1978) *Le Créole: structure, statut et origine*, Paris: Klincksieck.

Valdman, A. (ed.) (1979) *Le Français hors de France*, Paris: H. Champion.

Valdman, A. (1988) *Ann pale kreyòl: An Introductory Course in Haitian Creole*, Bloomington: Creole Institute.

Valli, A. (1983) 'Un exemple d'approche du problème des variantes syntaxiques en linguistique diachronique', *Recherches sur le Français Parlé* 5: 125–46.

Valli, A. (1984) 'Changements de norme, décalages grammaticaux et représentations du français parlé: l'exemple du *Télémaque travesti* de Marivaux', *Recherches sur le Français Parlé* 6: 7–21.

Vaugelas, C. Favre de (1615) *Les Sermons de Fonseque sur tous les Evangiles du Caresme: Avec une Paraphrase perpetuelle sur toutes les parties des Evangiles. Traduits d'Espagnol en François par C.F.D.V. Œuvre remplie de Conceptions nouvelles, doctes, curieuses & devotes, non seulement à l'usage des Predicateurs, & des doctes; mais de toutes personnes pieuses*, Paris: R. Thierry & E. Foucault.

Vaugelas, C. Favre de (1647) *Remarques sur la langue françoise utiles à ceux qui veulent bien parler & bien escrire*, Paris: J. Camusat and P. le Petit (facsimile edition by J. Streicher, Paris: Slatkine, 1934).

Vaugelas, C. Favre de (1653) *Quinte Curce, De la vie et des actions d'Alexandre le Grand, De la Traduction de Monsieur de Vaugelas* [ed. V. Conrart and J. Chapelain], Paris: A. Courbé.

Vaugelas, C. Favre de (1659) *Quinte Curce, De la vie et des actions d'Alexandre le Grand. De la traduction de Monsieur de Vaugelas. Troisiesme Edition, Sur une nouvelle Copie de l'Autheur, qui a esté trouvée depuis la premiere, & la seconde impression* [ed. O. Patru], Paris: A. Courbé.

Vaugelas, C. Favre de (1690) *Nouvelles Remarques de M. de Vaugelas sur la langue françoise. Ouvrage posthume. Avec des Observations de M. ***** Avocat au Parlement*, Paris: G. Desprez.

Vaumorière, P. d'Ortigue de (1688) *L'Art de plaire dans la conversation*, Paris: J. Guignard.

Veÿ, E. (1911) *Le Dialecte de Saint-Étienne au XVIIe siècle*, Paris: Librairie Ancienne.

Viollet, C. (1988) 'Mais qui est *on*?', *LINX* 18: 67–75.

Voiture, V. (1687) *Lettres et autres œuvres de Monsieur de Voiture, Nouvelle édition*, Brussels: L. Marchant.

Wild, F. (2001) *Naissance du genre des ana (1574–1712)*, Paris: H. Champion.

Wittmann, H. (1995) 'Grammaire comparée des variétés coloniales du français populaire de Paris du 17e siècle et origines du français québécois', in Fournier and Wittmann 1995: 281–334.

Wodroephe, J. (1623) *The Spared Houres of a soldier in his travels. Or the true marrowe of the French tongue, wherein is truely treated (by ordre [sic]) the nine parts of speech* [. . .], Dort: N. Vincentz.

Wolf, L. (1984) 'Le Français de Paris dans les remarques de Vaugelas', *Cahiers de l'Institut de Linguistique de Louvain* 10: 357–66.

Wolf, L. (1991) 'Le langage de la Cour et le français canadien. Exemples de morphologie et de syntaxe', in B. Horiot (ed.), *Français du Canada – Français de France. Actes du deuxième colloque international de Cognac du 27 au 30 septembre 1988*, Tübingen: M. Niemeyer, pp. 115–23.

Wolfe, P. J. (ed.) (1977) *Choix de conversations de Mlle de Scudéry*, Ravenna: Longo.

Wooldridge, T. R. (1977) *Les Débuts de la lexicographie française: Estienne, Nicot et le 'Thresor de la langue françoyse'*, Toronto and Buffalo: University of Toronto Press.

Wüest, J. (1985) 'Le "patois de Paris" et l'histoire du français', *Vox Romanica* 44: 234–58.

Yaguello, M. (1979) *Les Mots et les femmes. Essai d'approche socio-linguistique de la condition féminine*, Paris: Payot.

Zoberman, P. (1998) *Les Cérémonies de la parole. L'éloquence d'apparat en France dans le dernier quart du XVIIe siècle*, Paris: H. Champion.

Zuber, R. (ed.) (1972) *Nicolas Perrot d'Ablancourt, 'Lettres et préfaces critiques'*, Paris: M. Didier.

MANUSCRIPTS

BN MSS français Nouv. Acq. 124. De la conuersation des femmes ou il est traité sçauoir s'il est utile aux ieunes gens de les hanter, et de conuerser auec elles, fol 177r–209v.

Mazarinades, Cambridge University Library (Ggg. 19–37, F164.c.4.2–3), and Taylorian Library, Oxford (Vet Fr IB.192–197, 221).

ELECTRONIC RESOURCES

L'Atelier historique de la langue française, CD-ROM, Marsanne: Redon, [2001].

Base textuelle FRANTEXT, CNRS-ATILF (http://atilf.inalf.fr/frantext.htm).

Les Dictionnaires de l'Académie Française (1687–1798), CD-ROM, Paris: Champion Électronique, 2000.

Dictionnaires du XVIIe et XVIIIe siècles, CD-ROM, Paris: Champion Electronique, 1998.

Textes français privés des XVIIe et XVIIIe siècles, 2 CD-ROMs, ed. G. Ernst and B. Wolf, Beihefte zur Zeitschrift für romanische Philologie 310, Tübingen: M. Niemeyer, 2001–2.

Index of concepts

adjective
  mille 161
  superlative 21, 38
age variation 185–9, 190–1, 215–16, 218–19
  age grading, age stratification 185–6, 188
  (*see also* children's language)
agreement 38, 126, 160–1, 178
  non-agreement of past participle 19
  (*see also* pronoun, personal: *la* for *le*)
ana, as sources of spoken French 35–6
article 19
  omission of 77, 182
auxiliary, *see* verb

Bibliothèque bleue 75–6, 83
burlesque 7, 16, 27, 32, 64–5, 67, 68, 74,
    75–7, 78, 81, 82, 83, 84, 85, 88–9, 92,
    102, 108, 109, 198
  archaisms and 76, 88–9, 92, 93
  bas and 76, 93, 94
  comédies burlesques 31
  composite language of 76, 109
  morphology 76–7
  syntax 76, 77
  texts 75–7, 82, 84

ça 12, 19
cahiers de doléances, as sources of spoken
    French 35
Canadian French 33–4, 44–5, 49, 202n
  in Acadia 32, 44
  in Quebec 32, 44–5
  origins of 33–4
  (*see also* French in North America)
canards, as sources of spoken French 35
caricature 30–1, 37, 74, 78, 81, 134, 138,
    166, 167, 175
change, linguistic 9, 100–2, 181–224
  analysis of in the seventeenth century
    182–5
  attitudes towards in the seventeenth century
    181–2

chronolecte 183, 208, 224, 228
  chronology of 182–3
  interaction with register 185, 221, 224
  lexical 183
  morphological 181n, 183, 201–8
  in pronunciation 181n, 191–201
  reduction of the French language 183–5
  syntactic 183, 208–23
  (*see also* variation and change)
children's language 42, 52, 187–8
codification, *see* standardization: codification
comedy, comic forms 30, 31, 54, 57, 68, 74,
    75, 78–9, 81, 85, 86–7, 92, 93, 98, 109,
    141, 227
  (*see also* burlesque; satire; theatre)
comparative reconstruction
  as a source of spoken French 32–5, 37,
    44–5, 48–50, 59, 225
constructions lou(s)ches, see syntax
convergence of evidence, *see* sources
conversation 21, 22, 123–5
  and letter-writing 22, 27, 125
  positive qualities of 123
  published, literary conversations 22, 32,
    37, 118, 123, 125, 171
  theories of 123–5
  use of the term *conversation* 21, 22, 22n,
    23, 123
    conversation familière 24, 66, 74
    conversation ordinaire 24
  women's 123–5, 151, 153
  works on conversational skills 22, 37, 120
  (*see also* model dialogues/conversation
    manuals; salons)
corpus, choice of 7, 8–9
  (*see also* FRANTEXT; sources;
    translations)
courtesy manual 22, 61
creole 32–5, 38, 44, 46, 47, 48–9, 50, 56,
    225
  Americo-Caribbean 32–3, 44, 46, 48–9, 50
  creation of 34

254

literacy 18, 117
literary texts 9, 225, 227
  as sources of popular French 75–9,
    106
  direct speech in, as source of spoken French
    30–2
  romans réalistes 31, 75, 77
  (*see also* burlesque; conversation:
    published, literary conversations;
    FRANTEXT; theatre)
livres de raison, see 'private texts'

marques d'usage, see style labels
Mazarinades 37, 75, 81, 84n, 82–5, 93–9,
    102–5, 106–8, 109, 151, 187, 226
  types of 83–5, 102
  (*see also* Index of names: *Agréables
    Conférences*)
memoirs, *see* 'private texts'
metalinguistic texts, *see* dictionaries;
    grammars; linguistic commentaries;
    model dialogues, conversation
    manuals; observations and remarks on
    the French language; pronunciation:
    works on; spelling: works on; sources;
    style: works on; versification, poetics:
    works on
model dialogues, conversation manuals 9,
    28–30, 36–7, 37n, 39, 43, 46, 47, 50,
    53, 59, 186
  as sources of spoken French 28–30, 43, 46,
    53
  as sources of variation 9
  pragmatic features in 29
morphology 71, 76, 78, 81, 161–2, 227,
    228
  morphological variation 201–8, 228
  of spoken French 38
  women's usage 161–2
morphology, verb 19, 25, 45–6, 181n, 201–8,
    224
  changes in 19, 181n, 201–8, 224
  future tense
    je laisserai/je lairrai 4, 161
    j'enverray/j'envoyeray 201–2, 205, 207,
      208
  imperfect subjunctive 45
  infinitive
    courir/courre 201–2, 207
  je + -ons (j'avons, etc.) 31, 41, 81
  passé simple 25, 38, 45
    ils prinrent/ils prindrent/ils prirent
      201–2, 204, 208
    *ils vinrent/ils vindrent; ils tinrent/ils
      tindrent* 201–2, 203–4, 208

past participle
  mors/mordu; tors/tordu 201–2, 205,
    208
  recouvert for *recouvré* 201–3, 208
present indicative
  je vais/je va/je vay/je vas/je vois 201–2,
    205, 206, 208
present participle
  séant/siésant 201–2, 207, 208
present subjunctive 161
  il aye/il ait 201–2, 203, 208
  il die/il dise; ils dient/ils disent 201–2,
    204, 208

negation 10, 11, 12, 14, 17, 19, 31, 45, 77, 82,
    185–9, 208–9, 219–24, 227
  in Montreal French 10
  non-use of *ne* 12, 14, 19, 31, 185, 186–9,
    220, 227
  position of negative particles with an
    infinitive 208, 219–24, 227
non-metropolitan varieties of French 32–5,
    38, 44–5, 56, 225, 226
  (*see also* Canadian French; French in North
    America)
noun morphology
  simplification of 19

observations and remarks on French
  as sources of variation 7–8, 38, 39, 47, 50,
    85–93, 99–100, 103–5, 106–8, 135,
    177, 194, 202–8, 209–10, 223–4, 226,
    227
  attitude towards variation in 4, 13, 126–8
  commentaries on 9
  format of 8, 120
  influence of 39
  linguistic change in 181–5
  linguistic terminology in 14
  models of variation in 63
  relationship between spoken and written
    French in 25–7
  style labels in 68–72
  women's language in 144–5, 147–65
    (*passim*)
Old French
  dislocation in 20
  use of *on* in 40
  use of *si* in 14
  use of tenses in 6
on, see pronoun, personal

Paris 74, 101, 109n, 194
  Cour/Ville 62, 69–70, 73, 74, 101
  Parisian patois 74, 80–2

satire   32, 75, 82, 85, 86, 87, 91, 92, 93, 94,
    96, 97, 98, 109, 135, 137, 138, 139,
    141, 165–72, 175, 196, 198, 226
si, clause initial   14, 30
social class   27
    and educational level   62, 109
    social structure of seventeenth-century
        France   61, 63–4, 229
social variation,   61–110
    and variation according to sex   143, 152,
        177
    interrelation with change   224, 228
    interrelation with stylistic variation   61–4,
        70, 93–9, 108–9
    style labels, expressions to refer to
        bourgeois, bourgeoisie   63–4, 65n
        (le) peuple, la lie du peuple, le (petit)
        peuple (de Paris), le menu peuple, la
        populace   64, 65, 67, 68, 70, 72, 74
        le vulgaire   66, 70, 72
    usage of
        the bourgeoisie   65, 70, 73, 77–8
        the people   69–70, 73, 85, 90–9
socio-economic status, *see* social class
socio-historical linguistics
    aims of   2–3
    development of   1–3
    methodology for   1–15, 225–8
        anachronistic judgments   14, 20, 59
        choice of linguistic features   9–10
        'conceptual inertia'   14
        differentiating between parameters of
            variation   12–14
        quantitative methodology   11–12, 59,
            74n, 109, 228
        semantic equivalence   10, 227–8
        syntactic variation   10–11, 227–8
        use of statistics in   11–12, 227, 228
        (*see also* sources)
    value of   15–16
        for literary studies   15–16
sociolinguistic studies of contemporary
    French   1
sources   3, 5–9, 16, 73–85, 177, 225
    convergence of   7, 31, 35, 59, 85, 109–10,
        226
    interpreting 110 (*see also* variation:
        separating different parameters)
    literary texts as   9, 225
    metalinguistic texts as   7–10, 28, 63, 73, 85,
        100, 102–5, 109–10, 113, 123, 143–5,
        148–74 (*passim*), 176, 194–6, 223–4,
        225, 226, 227
        dictionaries   8
        formal grammars   8

linguistic commentaries   9
model dialogues, conversation manuals
    9
observations and remarks on the French
    language   7–8
other textual   9
works on French pronunciation   9
works on French spelling   9
works on style or usage   9
works on versification, poetics   9
(*see also* dictionaries; grammars; model
    dialogues; linguistic commentaries;
    observations and remarks on the
    French language; pronunciation: works
    on; spelling: works on; style: works on;
    versification, poetics: works on)
of informal, low-register, substandard or
    semi-literate usages   7, 73–85, 93
of *Précieuses*' language   136–8, 226
    metalinguistic texts   172–4
    satirical texts   137, 138, 139, 140–1,
        165–72, 226
of spoken French   6, 17, 27–37, 59–60
of variation and change   6, 190–3
(*see also ana; cahiers de doléances;*
    canards; comparative reconstruction;
    legal documents; letters; literary texts;
    Mazarinades; *Préciosité;* 'private
    texts': *livres de raison*, journals,
    memoirs, etc.; theatre, dialogue in;
    translations)
spelling   100, 101–3, 127, 141–3, 181n, 191,
    227
    correspondence with pronunciation   127,
        143, 193, 228
    Précieuses' reforms of   141–2
    women's   111, 142–3, 165
    works on   9, 28, 99–100, 194
spoken French   6, 10, 17–60, 73, 98, 123, 178,
    226
    'age' of modern spoken French   1–2, 18,
        18n, 19, 38, 39–45, 52, 186
    innovative or conservative   13, 15, 18–19
    medium versus register   12–13, 17–18, 31,
        36, 38, 62, 106, 108
    range of   17
    relationship between written and spoken
        French   25–7
        in dictionaries   27
        in grammars   25
        in observations and remarks   25–7
    sources of   6, 17, 27–37, 59–60, 226
        comparative reconstruction   32–5, 44–5,
            48–50, 225
        direct speech in narrative texts   31–2

Index of names

Abbadie, Jacques 55–6
Ablancourt, Nicolas Perrot d' 191, 203, 204, 216, 218, 221–2, 223
Académie Française 8, 9n, 13, 21, 23–4, 27, 36, 39, 47, 50, 64, 65n, 65–6, 67, 85–99, 100, 107, 108, 127, 128, 128n, 133, 134, 142, 143–4, 148–9, 150, 151, 153, 154, 157, 160, 166–8, 189–90, 195, 197–200, 203, 204, 205, 206, 207, 210, 224, 225
Adam, Antoine 134
Agréables Conférences 31, 37, 75, 80, 83, 84, 93, 93n, 94, 95, 98, 102–5, 106, 110, 201, 224
Aisy, Jean d' 8n
Alemand, Louis-Augustin 8, 26n, 70, 71, 72, 87, 100, 101, 104, 106, 121n, 128, 143n, 144, 145, 152, 154–5, 155n, 161n, 163, 163n, 178, 182–3, 189
Altman, Janet Gurkin 146
Amyot, Jacques 161, 183
Andry de Boisregard, Nicolas 4, 8, 27, 42, 44, 47, 70, 71, 72, 87, 88–9, 90–1, 92, 99, 100, 101, 104, 106, 121, 144, 145, 173, 174, 181, 182, 185, 189, 191, 193, 202, 204, 205–7, 209, 210, 213n, 216, 218, 220, 223
Angenot, Marc 114, 115
Anne of Austria, Queen of France 1601–66 136
Armstrong, Nigel 188
Arnauld, Angélique 112
Arnauld, Antoine 155
Arnauld d'Andilly, Robert 87
Arnould, Jean-Claude 35
Ashby, William J. 1, 57, 185, 185n, 188
Asselin, Claire 33n
Assoucy, Charles Coypeau d' (Dassoucy, Dassouci) 75, 76, 76n, 78, 86, 89, 91, 94
Aubignac, François Hédelin, abbé d' 118, 136n, 166

Aubigné, (Théodore) Agrippa d' 43n, 165
Auchy, Charlotte des Ursins, vicomtesse d' 118
Aulnoy, Marie-Catherine Le Jumel de Barneville, comtesse d' 96
Aumale, Mlle d' 136
Aventin, Gustave 54
Ayres-Bennett, Wendy 3, 4, 4n, 8, 9n, 14n, 27, 28, 30, 38n, 45, 92, 108, 147n, 186n, 187n, 188, 191, 193, 194

Bacqueville de la Potherie, Claude-Charles Le Roy de 33n
Baillet, Adrien 112n, 127
Balzac, Jean-Louis Guez de 22n, 39, 76, 88, 92, 120, 121, 122, 125, 130, 132, 134n, 137, 146, 155, 164, 166n, 167n, 169, 183
Bar, Francis 37, 74, 76, 77, 79n, 102
Barbaud, Philippe 33
Baron, Dennis 111n, 176
Bary, René 22, 120, 120n, 174
Baudino, Claudie 155n
Bauvois, Cécile 178
Bayley, Peter J. 17
Beaulieux, Charles 128n
Beauvilliers, Mme de 143
Béchade, Hervé 78, 166n
Behnstedt, Peter 57
Bellegarde, Jean-Baptiste Morvan de 22, 122–3, 131, 132, 135, 140
Beniak, Édouard 33, 33n, 41, 45, 49
Benserade, Isaac de 86
Bérain, Nicolas 26n, 38, 70, 71, 100, 105, 160, 162
Bernard, Samuel 204n
Bernier, François 55, 132
Béroalde de Verville, François 94, 98
Berrendonner, Alain 10n
Bertaut, Jean 173, 182
Berthod, sieur (or Bertaut, François) 81, 81n
Bertrand, Dominique 76, 76n